UTAH HISTORIANS

and the

RECONSTRUCTION *of* WESTERN HISTORY

UTAH HISTORIANS *and the* RECONSTRUCTION *of* WESTERN HISTORY

GARY TOPPING

UNIVERSITY OF OKLAHOMA PRESS
Norman

Also by Gary Topping

Ghost Towns of the Old West (New York, 1991)
Gila Monsters and Red-eyed Rattlesnakes: Don Maguire's Arizona Expeditions, 1876–1879 (Salt Lake City, 1997)
Glen Canyon and the San Juan Country (Moscow, Idaho, 1997)
Great Salt Lake: An Anthology (Logan, Utah, 2002)

Publication of this book was made possible in part by generous support from the Charles Redd Center for Western Studies.

Library of Congress Cataloging-in-Publication Data

Topping, Gary, 1941–
Utah historians and the reconstruction of western history / Gary topping.
p. cm.
Includes bibliographical references and index.
ISBN 0-8061-3561-1 (hc: alk. paper)
1. West (U.S.)—Historiography. 2. Historiography—West (U.S.)—History—20th century. 3. Historians—Utah—Biography. 4. Historiography—Utah—History—20th century. I. Title.

F591.T675 2003
979'.007'20792—dc21
2003047396

The paper in this book meets the guidelines for permanence and durability of the Committee on Production Guidelines for Book Longevity of the Council on Library Resources. ♾

1 2 3 4 5 6 7 8 9 10

Dedicated to

Richard W. Etulain
Lee M. Nash
the late Don D. Walker
Robert C. Woodward

Contents

IV. WALLACE STEGNER

V. FAWN McKAY BRODIE

Illustrations

ACKNOWLEDGMENTS

ONE DAY WHILE engaged in the research for this book, I ran into an old friend I had not seen for some years. During the few minutes we spent getting reacquainted, she asked me what I was working on. When I told her it was a critique of western historical writing, she slyly inquired if I were familiar with the etching by M. C. Escher depicting a hand holding a pen drawing an identical hand holding an identical pen, in which the subject and the object cannot be distinguished. It was a good joke, and I had to admit to a risk of self-absorption inherent in the study of historiography. Surely the risk is justified, though, by the advantage of self-criticism in the internal debates by which the discipline of history and other scholarly fields improve themselves. Historical scholarship is thus, paradoxically, one of the most solitary and one of the most communal of endeavors. I should like to thank my colleagues in the archives and history professions who have joined me in this enterprise by providing sources and critical suggestions.

Most of the writers who are the subject of this book found it necessary to leave Utah in pursuit of educational and career opportunities. Happily for me, though, their personal papers for the most part have found their way back home, and I was able to do most of my research very compactly in two repositories, the University of Utah's Marriott Library and the Utah State Historical Society, both located in Salt Lake City. The staffs at those institutions served me cheerfully and effectively, and I offer them my sincere thanks. Two staff members at the Marriott deserve special recognition. Ann Reichman, curator of the immense Wallace Stegner collection, went out of her way to identify materials of interest to me in that collection and to make them available for my perusal even while the collection was still being accessioned and processed. And Walter Jones made microfilm miraculously materialize for me in another part of the library while the Special Collections section was closed for remodeling. During my one research trip outside Utah, Polly Armstrong of the Special Collections in the Green Library of Stanford University enabled me to make the most of my time by cheerfully and punctually producing the papers of Bernard DeVoto.

Bernice Maher Mooney, my predecessor as Archivist of the Catholic Diocese of Salt Lake City made available to me the papers of Archbishop Robert J. Dwyer and shared her memories of him, as did his friend and housekeeper, Tomi Taniguchi of Piedmont, California. Several other friends and scholars have read this manuscript in part or in full, and I am deeply grateful for their criticisms and encouragement. Polly Aird read every chapter and shared her vast knowledge of violence on the Mormon frontier. Richard W. Etulain, Charles S. Peterson, John Drayton, and Charles E. Rankin critiqued the manuscript for the University of Oklahoma Press. The editorial skills of Alice Stanton and Drew Bryan greatly improved the manuscript. Marianna Allred Hopkins assisted in proofreading and continued her often futile efforts to improve my writing.

My interest in historiography was created, nurtured, and shaped under the tutelage of four great scholars who, in the grandest tradition of American higher education, generously transcended their roles as teachers to become my valued friends and mentors. Anything worthwhile that I have achieved in my career I owe in large part to their willingness to take time from their more promising projects to help me with mine. I have used the dedication page to acknowledge a debt that I can never repay.

UTAH HISTORIANS

and the

RECONSTRUCTION *of* WESTERN HISTORY

Introduction

Surveying western historiography at the time of World War II, Earl Pomeroy concluded that the field was, if not moribund, at least in a state of decline. The influence of the imaginative essays and syntheses of Frederick Jackson Turner, Frederic L. Paxson, Herbert E. Bolton, and Walter Prescott Webb that had enlivened the field and energized debate beginning in the 1890s had largely run its course. Turner's ideas in particular, and to a lesser degree those of Bolton and Webb, would continue to be discussed in graduate seminars and in historiographical essays, but the field was in need of new directions and inspiration. Even though western history continued to be written and taught, most new works were factual narratives of limited scope and creativity with little sense of the dramatic or intellectual potential of their material. Further, Pomeroy observed, the nation had lost interest in the West. If most nonwesterners thought of the West at all, they thought of the boring Babbitry of Sinclair Lewis's Midwest or the dreary and deserted Dust Bowl of the Great Plains.[1] In any event (to go beyond Pomeroy), interest in regional matters of any kind was giving way to an international focus as the country mobilized to face the Axis and assume a new role in the postwar world.

Pomeroy charged that postwar western historical writing "was as traditional as if nothing had happened in the field since Turner or [Hubert Howe] Bancroft," and that "Pulitzer prizes went to works in

Western history that were completely conventional in interpretation." But he concluded his essay by noting the emergence of new writers who were producing "sound and well-written histories of discovery and exploration," with an eye for the "dramatic possibilities" of their material. Prominent among them were Bernard DeVoto, Dale Morgan, and Wallace Stegner.[2] Perhaps it is only coincidental that all three of these writers grew up in Utah, though all three left the state and did most of their work elsewhere. But I would add two more Utah-bred scholars—Juanita Brooks and Fawn McKay Brodie—whose historiographical orientation and literary skill paralleled Pomeroy's trio, and I would note that Utah, although it did not produce every western historian of importance during the war years and after, was the seedbed for a remarkable number of them.[3] I argue further that the creative tension with their native culture was the combustible material that ignited and propelled their careers.[4]

Another common element, in addition to their Utah backgrounds, was that none of them had earned so much as an undergraduate degree in history. DeVoto and Morgan held only bachelor's degrees, DeVoto's from Harvard in writing and Morgan's from the University of Utah in art. Brooks and Brodie had master's degrees, Brooks from Columbia and Brodie from the University of Chicago, both in English. Stegner held a doctorate from the University of Iowa, but in English. DeVoto, Stegner, and Brooks all taught in the fields of their professional training and wrote history as something of a sideline, though DeVoto and Brooks are known more for their historical work than anything else. (DeVoto, it is true, is famous—or infamous—for his writings on literary criticism and conservation as well as other cultural matters, but his historical works, most people would agree, constitute the core of his achievement.) Morgan supported himself through various government jobs until landing a position at the Bancroft Library. Brodie actually held an academic appointment in history, at UCLA, though it was because of her fame as a writer of biographies and as a pioneer in psychobiography. From the standpoint of academic historical professionals, these were mostly self-trained amateurs.

Measuring the influence of any individual historian on the profession is difficult. A Frederick Jackson Turner, of course, is easy to place in the first rank of importance by any standard, but assessing lesser scholars' influence is likely to evoke lively debate. A case for each of the writers in this group as influential historians, however, can be made in several ways: the debate over their books within the profession, the widespread circulation of their books among both a popular audience and an academic audience, and the place their works hold on reading lists in western history courses. In each of those areas, their standing seems secure, though Brooks's work has been less influential than the others' outside of Utah and Mormon history.[5]

The historical profession has been aware of the contribution of these writers, for each of them but Morgan has attracted a biographer, and Brodie's *No Man Knows My History* has inspired a published collection of critical essays.[6] When the subject of fur trade historians comes up, Morgan's name is usually the first mentioned, often in tones of hushed reverence, as is the name of Brooks in Mormon history. Stegner's biography of Maj. John Wesley Powell is an acknowledged classic that dominated its subject until Donald Worster's massive and definitive study appeared in 2001, and Stegner's *The Gathering of Zion* is accepted by Mormon and non-Mormon alike as a masterpiece of Mormon Trail literature. DeVoto and Brodie are the *bêtes noires* of the group. DeVoto's trilogy on western exploration and expansion is still in print and widely read, though the first one to appear, *The Year of Decision 1846*, was greeted with howls of objection that still echo within the profession for his use of literary devices, for his overdrawn character portraits, and for his extravagant prose. Brodie's unflattering biography of the Mormon prophet Joseph Smith provoked caustic reviews by Mormon scholars and led to her excommunication from the Mormon Church even as it was being hailed by non-Mormon readers as a well-researched and convincing portrait. Her subsequent development of techniques of "psychobiography" in her studies of Thaddeus Stevens and Sir Richard Burton were well-received, but her biographies of Thomas Jefferson and Richard Nixon elicited mixed reactions from conventional biographers, particularly the Jefferson book, which aroused protests bordering on the intemperate from the Jefferson establishment.[7]

Curiously, though, Earl Pomeroy remains the only student of

western historiography to have seen common features in research, writing, and interpretation in these Utah writers. Even the most recent and thoroughgoing survey of western historical writing, Gerald D. Nash's *Creating the West: Historical Interpretations, 1890–1990*, mentions Stegner's name as a western regional writer and cites his Powell book in the bibliography, and only briefly touches on DeVoto.[8] The present book is thus the first instance in which these writers have been subjected to searching scrutiny as a group, the first book to note that their works possess common historiographical traits.

Like all other historians, these Utah writers did some things well and others not so well. It is my thesis that their strengths were twofold: They were industrious researchers who tirelessly exploited existing sources and discovered and published others in a relentless drive to establish an accurate factual record of the past. Also, they were excellent writers, DeVoto, Stegner, and Morgan among the best the historical profession can boast. On the other hand, they interpreted their findings with remarkable ineptness. That ineptness occurred at two polar extremes: DeVoto, Brodie, and Stegner advanced extravagant interpretations, sometimes nothing short of metaphysical and running far ahead of what their sources could sustain; whereas Morgan and Brooks fell far short of the interpretive potential of their sources—Morgan asserting that the facts would somehow convey their own meaning without any help from him, and Brooks refusing to follow her sources to conclusions that might embarrass her church.

People study history for a variety of reasons, from the simple entertainment of stories of colorful characters and dramatic deeds to a philosophical quest for illumination of the human condition. The governing assumption of this book is that history reaches its highest potential in its interpretive dimension, when it examines the characteristics of human nature through the study of human accomplishments, or the unbroken continuum between past and present, in which an understanding of present conditions can be derived from a study of their evolution out of past circumstances. History thus leads to self-understanding by functioning as the memory of a society, in the same way that individual self-understanding is grounded in individual memory.

Looked at in this way, the historian has a twofold role: to reconstruct the past as fully and accurately as possible through critical study of historical records, and to show how that past experience has shaped the present. In fulfilling these roles, as Joseph J. Ellis points out, the historian stands at a checkpoint between past and present, attempting to regulate a flow of intellectual traffic in both directions by guarding against two fatal errors.[9] One is presentism, in which the present raids the past for support of a current cause. In guarding against presentism, the historian must insist upon the integral otherness of the past—its essential pastness. Thus, for example in Ellis's study of the character and ideas of Thomas Jefferson, instead of judging him for his failure to live up to our modern conceptions of equality and democracy, he attempts to determine what the ideas of equality and democracy meant to Jefferson and where Jefferson stood in the process of evolution of those ideas toward the ways in which we understand them today. The opposite error is what Ellis calls "pastism," in which the otherness of the past is so extreme that it has nothing to say to the present. Whether this pastism is grounded in some postmodern idea of the essential impossibility of reconstructing a reliable version of the past, or simply in a lack of interest on the historian's part in relating the past to the present, the result is a past walled off from present relevance, an exclusive playground of historians. Standing at Ellis's metaphorical checkpoint, then, the historian has the task of blocking presentist traffic while waving traffic in the other direction on through.

Historical interpretation is the most essential and yet the most difficult and perilous of the historian's tasks. This is not to minimize the other difficulties of the historian's job. Locating sources—sometimes even creating them, through interviews or photographs—can require a great deal of energy, persistence, and ingenuity. Critical evaluation of the authenticity and credibility of those sources can demand logical adroitness and perhaps even an expertise—acquired or borrowed—in scientific and technological disciplines. Assembling one's research into a plausible narrative sequence of cause and effect, ideally cast in graceful and vivid prose (for history is traditionally one of the literary arts), requires careful reflection and conceptualization. But interpretation of one's material, which involves the weighing of the relative significance of one fact over another and perhaps relating those facts to theoretical models from other disciplines, is surely the historian's most daunting responsibility. It calls upon the most elusive and hard-won qualities of adult maturity: a sense of balance, judiciousness, appropriateness, and circumspectness, tempered by a willingness to live with a certain quotient of tenuousness, ambiguity, incompleteness, and, perhaps, a degree of contradiction.

The historians who are the collective subject of this book bequeathed an ambiguous legacy to the writing of history. On the one hand, they did a fine job at what one might call the more mechanical aspects of history: the discovery and critical evaluation of sources to establish an accurate factual record. Emerging out of a historiographical environment dominated by church-sponsored orthodoxy grounded in a selective body of facts, they insisted upon rigorous new standards of research, factual accuracy, and absolute honesty in embracing the conclusions toward which those facts led. On the other hand, they generally did an unsatisfactory job of interpreting their material. They either refused to recognize an obligation to explain the past at all, as Morgan did, presenting instead a meticulously constructed factual narrative with no apparent relevance to the present and with little or no attention paid to causative forces. Or, like DeVoto and Stegner, they raided the past for evidence to support their own cultural biases that sometimes took the form of high-flown metaphysical notions they despised in others.

I ascribe these interpretive shortcomings to their reaction against the heavy-handed pro-Mormon interpretations prominent in most Utah histories of their day, and to their lack of academic training in history. To be sure, the historiographical sophistication in the one history department to which they all had immediate access, the University of Utah, which was dominated by the likes of Levi Edgar Young, Andrew Love Neff, and Leland Hargrave Creer, would not have impressed them with the value of such training. Nor were there many other ready mentors. Mormon history was locked in the ironclad orthodoxy of Orson Whitney, Andrew Jenson, and Milton R. Hunter, and popularizers like J. Cecil Alter of the Utah State Historical Society or Hubert Howe Bancroft had little zeal for factual accuracy and no more interpretive sophistication than their colleagues at the university (Bancroft's idea of interpretation, as we shall see, was simply to assemble claims on both sides of a question and let readers muddle their way through to a conclusion as best they could).

One may question the fairness of holding this group of writers, who had little or no formal training in history, to the rigorous standards of the historical profession. Such standards would be obviously unfair if applied to the many amateur historians who happily devote their impressive industry to the study of local or family topics with little higher philosophical or cultural significance, or to popularizers and writers of historical fiction. But the writers we are concerned with here considered themselves to be producing scholarly history, and they compared their work with that of academic professionals, often concluding that theirs was superior. They published their work in respected regional, academic, or commercial outlets, they were reviewed in academic journals, and Brodie even held a chair in a university history department. In short, they themselves embraced the standards to which I hold them, standards universally accepted in the historical profession in their day as in ours.

Of course I have scrupulously tried to avoid holding them to interpretive insights available only through source material discovered since they wrote. The body of primary sources available to historians has expanded exponentially in the decades since the WPA Historical Records Survey, as public monies and energies have strengthened public archives and manuscript repositories and created institutions such as the National Historical Publications and Records Commission and the Association for Documentary Editing. That proliferation of sources has made it possible for younger scholars to bolster, modify, or refute older interpretations. Some of the writers considered here, particularly Brooks and Morgan, were major contributors to the movement to discover and publish sources, and they would certainly have accepted and applauded the new insights those sources have made possible, and did during their lifetimes. Where I could do so economically, I have sketched the outlines of that recent research in my endnotes, but of course I have not held my subjects to account on the basis of facts they did not have. My interest has been in what they made of the facts they did have.

My study begins with a chapter establishing a sense of the state of historical writing, both in general American history and more specifically in Utah history, in about 1940, at about the time most of the subjects were beginning to write. My purpose is to describe the context out of which they came and against which they reacted. Subsequently, there is a chapter on each writer that establishes his or her basic background and intellectual orientation, but which comprehensively examines that writer's major historical works. The most original contributions of this book, however, are the brief critical essays on each historian that follow the comprehensive chapter. These essays examine a specific interpretive problem in that writer's work, generally narrowed to a specific theme or a single book. These critical essays, of widely varying length, occur in no particular order and largely stand alone, so that readers who are already familiar with the work of the writer in question may jump right in and read those first, though the essays do in some cases refer to facts established in the main chapter.

As I venture forth into my own version of what Richard Hofstadter called "parricidal forays," I hope the reader will keep in mind that I do so with humility. I freely acknowledge that while I am dealing with issues of methodology and philosophy, my book is only, in the words of the French medievalist Marc Bloch, "the memorandum of a craftsman who has always liked to reflect over his daily task, the notebook of a journeyman who has long handled the ruler and the level, without imagining himself to be a mathematician." I would add further, in the words of another great French scholar, Etienne Gilson, "that in criticizing great men, as I shall do, I am very far from forgetting what made them truly great."[10] The great men—and great women—whose works I examine here wrote the books from which I first learned western history and to which, through the years, I have returned over and over again. If, in the following pages, I am spare with praise and generous with criticism, it is because their greatness is so well established that I feel free to venture critical judgments without them being considered a protracted exercise in *lèse majeste*.

Criticism can be as sincere a form of flattery as imitation. Life is too short to waste on criticism of inferior books, as it is too precious to debase by imitating them. All the books I discuss here *invite* criticism as much as praise, for they provoke our intellect, they stimulate our imagination, they enlarge our vision. I shall be pleased if the essays in this book have a similar effect. Also, because all these writers operated to one degree or another within a Mormon cultural environment, I would not have been able to probe very deeply without somehow coming to grips with that environment. My readers are free to disagree with my interpretations, but I hope they will see that the problems I am exploring here obligate me to examine and comment on Mormon ideas. But I must ask those readers, whatever their religious affiliation, to accept my assurance that I offer my criticisms purely as an intellectual exercise, with no conscious awareness of ill will toward the Mormon people or the Mormon culture within which I have happily lived and worked for the past thirty years. Finally, I plead thoroughly guilty to the potential charge that I hold my subjects, as I hold myself, to an untarnished standard of perfection. I have certainly fallen short of that goal in the pages that follow, but who would abdicate excellence by aspiring to anything less?

THE TRADITION
Utah Historiography to about 1940

To UNDERSTAND the historiographical significance of the historians who are the subject of this book, we need first to understand the historiographical environment against which they were reacting. While doing so, we must realize that few if any revolutions in history (and I am not claiming to describe one here) are completely revolutionary. Most leave more elements of the past in place than they change. My thesis is that in their re-energizing of western history these historians reacted strongly against the historiographical traditions of their youth, but they also retained in their work important elements of that older tradition.

Although only Juanita Brooks remained a lifelong active Mormon, all members of the group grew up in a Mormon cultural environment and all were thoroughly familiar with the historical literature of Mormonism. So our study begins with that literature.[1] The deliberate, conscious creation and compilation of an official record of the history of the Mormon Church began with Joseph Smith's initiation in 1839 of what became a multivolume documentary compilation called the "History of Joseph Smith." Various hands worked with Smith on the project until 1842, when he appointed Willard Richards as the first official Church Historian. Richards applied a gargantuan energy to the project, both in Nauvoo, Illinois, and later in Salt Lake City, extending his predecessors' work by thousands of handwritten pages in recording events up to roughly a year before Smith's death in 1844. This was eventually edited and published in five volumes by B. H. Roberts.

In assembling the "History of Joseph Smith," Richards's and his predecessors' method was to collect various dictations and writings of Smith and his intimate associates and weave them into a continuous first-person narrative with daily entries that read like a personal diary. Although Smith had ordered in two revelations in 1830 and 1831 that some kind of historical record be kept as an official activity of the church, he never clearly stated his motives for such a record nor what its function was to be. But two powerful motives could well have been behind the project. Smith was well aware that Mormonism was historically remarkable and saw that a detailed historical record of its development would help explain it. Also, Smith was aware of the intemperate attacks that had been mounted against the church, most of which were based on various misperceptions of what Mormonism was, and he no doubt saw the value of a historical record as a factual reference point. Richards's method of compiling a simple, unemotional, nonpolemical daily factual record seemed to serve both of those purposes well.

Whatever its original function was to have been, the "History of Joseph Smith" became a powerful model for subsequent Mormon historical projects, both by Richards's successor, George A. Smith, and especially by the remarkable Andrew Jenson, who, although he never became the official Church Historian, was the most intrepid of all Mormon collectors and compilers of historical material. Among the most notable projects of those early historians was the "History of Brigham Young," a record of Young's life similar to Richards's "History," which was extended somewhat beyond Young's death as the "Documentary History of the Church." Jenson's "Journal History of the Church" was an immense scrapbook compilation consisting of several hundred volumes of various historical records (in its later years mostly newspaper clippings) documenting Mormon history from the beginning of the church until well into the twentieth century. Access to the vast resources of the Journal History was facilitated by its chronological organizational scheme and a running subject index on thousands of index cards.

Thus a major tradition in Mormon historiography has been the collecting and compiling—but not the interpreting—of historical records. At its best, this tradition has produced laudable results, such as the church's strong encouragement of diary keeping by individual members, and of the compilation of family genealogies and scrapbooks of family history materials. This tradition has also led to the magnificent Family History Library, the finest genealogical facility in the world. Among its less laudable results, though, is the perpetuation of the naive assumptions that this collecting and compiling constitutes history, that application of the active intellect of the historian toward interpreting historical materials is unnecessary or undesirable, and that an objective and meaningful historical narrative can be created by simply stringing factual records out in a chronological sequence. The Mormon historical mind has had a hard time coming to grips with the idea that the mere selection of facts is in itself an interpretive act. The only truly unbiased historical records exist at such a low level of intellection—like counting the people present in a Sunday School class or recording the license plate numbers of the cars in the parking lot—that they have no inherent meaning; they have to be placed into some larger context to be historically significant.

Much of Mormon and Utah history has been written on the basis of these great Mormon compilations, though as one would expect, the more reliance one sees on them, the more celebratory and uncritical the history becomes. Obviously, the official Church Historian was not going to include much material critical of the Mormons in the compilations. Another consequence of those compilations was an intellectual laziness on the part of the historians who used them. Given the richness of information and the diverse nature of the compilations, it was all too easy simply to sit down in front of them and extract the material one needed without ever seeking material that offered a different point of view. So, for all the welcome factual detail one finds in the early histories by men such as Edward Tullidge, Orson F. Whitney, and B. H. Roberts, there is a depressing sameness in their pro-Mormon interpretation.

Beginning around the First World War, young Utah historians began seeking graduate degrees, primarily at the University of California, and began to write Utah history according to critical professional standards. They continued to use the Mormon compilations because the Church Historian's Office had no competent archival program to arrange and catalog its manuscript materials in a way that provided effective access to scholars. Until creation of the Historical Department in 1972 at the instigation of Apostles N. Eldon Tanner and Howard W. Hunter with Leonard Arrington as Church Historian, access to the church archives was capricious at best. Arrington, the first professional historian to serve as Church Historian and the most loyal of Mormons, learned this as a young scholar working on his dissertation.[2] Over subsequent years, as the church built its present state-of-the-art, professionally run archives program, scholars have used the great early compilations less and less, preferring instead to go back to the original records.[3]

The first history of Utah written outside the Mormon Church and based on primary sources other than the church compilations was that of Hubert Howe Bancroft.[4] The story of Bancroft, the wealthy bookseller, is well known. His "literary industries" was an assembly line history factory in San Francisco where he and his staff collected, researched, wrote, published, and marketed his multivolume history of the states and territories of the Pacific Slope.[5] Aware of the Mormons' suspicion of outsiders, who had written polemics against the church in the past, but compelled to include a volume on Utah to complete his series, Bancroft approached the First Presidency to ask for access to source material. He assured them he had no axe to grind and would treat Utah and Mormon history as objectively as possible. Mormon leaders at first were wary of entrusting their history to an outsider. Orson Pratt, Church Historian in 1880, offered to provide Bancroft with a Mormon-authored history if he would print it "without mutilation," but that was not Bancroft's method. He replied to Pratt in a lengthy and eloquent letter, asking once again for manuscript material and this time successfully assuring Pratt of his objectivity and his ability to produce a history acceptable to the Mormon people. Mormon President John Taylor, no doubt sensing the impending antipolygamy tempest that would burst forth that decade, and also remembering the vital assistance rendered in past crises by non-Mormons like Thomas

L. Kane, saw the advantage of having the truth about Mormon history presented by an objective outsider. Accordingly, he dispatched Apostle Franklin D. Richards, Assistant Church Historian, to collect the materials Bancroft was requesting and to serve as church liaison for his project.[6]

Bancroft could hardly have hoped for better cooperation and assistance than Richards provided. For one thing, Richards solicited manuscript histories of local Utah communities and autobiographies of their residents. This was the opening that the congenial but calculating Bancroft wanted, and he exploited it with cyclonic energy to build what Charles S. Peterson characterizes as "Mormon-Utah collections that Bancroft himself nurtured with periodic visits, flattery, honest sympathy, and the work of a battery of dictation-taking salesmen."[7] Richards also invited Bancroft to Salt Lake City to examine the records in the Church Historian's Office. Finally, and of particular interest to a modern historian, Richards made sure the story of Mormon women was included (thus indicating that defense of polygamy as an essentially benevolent institution was in the forefront of his and President Taylor's minds), both through solicitation of women's autobiographies and through interviews with Mrs. Richards by Mrs. Bancroft. The Bancroft-Richards collaboration launched two enterprises of fundamental importance to Utah historiography: the writing of Bancroft's *History of Utah*, which was the first objectively motivated and industriously researched history of the Mormons and Utah written by a non-Mormon; and the assembling of the nucleus of the Utah portion of what came to be known as the Bancroft Collection, one of the finest repositories of Mormon Americana outside of Utah.

In the context of its times, Bancroft's Utah history was a considerable success. As a sort of lowest common denominator between Mormon and non-Mormon views of Utah and the Mormons, it pleased virtually everyone and held its place in Utah literature for many years. As late as 1954, Utah historian S. George Ellsworth asserted that "it is still a useful standard narrative and is indispensible as a bibliographical guide for the first forty years of Utah's history of settled occupation."[8] Viewed in the light of the critical standards of modern historiography already emerging in Utah at the time Ellsworth wrote, however,

Bancroft's methods of research and interpretation were both becoming unacceptable.

For one thing, as Charles S. Peterson points out, Bancroft wrote in the romantic mode of the great New England historians Francis Parkman, George Bancroft, and William H. Prescott, a mode that emphasized dramatic scenes and adventures and colorful, heroic characters. Although romance was still acceptable in Bancroft's day if applied to western themes, it was already yielding, in literature and historiography, to a more restrained and scientific realism. In his grand vision of western history's continental significance, Bancroft anticipated Bernard DeVoto's thesis that the growth of American nationalism was a western theme.[9]

Moreover, Bancroft's factual accuracy, particularly on the pre-Mormon period he should have known best through his previous research in western history (the Utah volume appeared late in the series) is deplorable. He indicates, for example, that the Cardenas detachment of the Coronado expedition reached Glen Canyon instead of the Grand Canyon—an error that anyone even casually aware of the vast differences in geographic scale between the two canyons would have been able to correct from Cardenas's description—and thus he mistakenly credits Cardenas with the first European *entrada* into present-day Utah. Perhaps more understandable given the proximity of the two streams, he indicates that the Dominguez-Escalante expedition of 1776 reached Utah Valley via the Provo River rather than Spanish Fork. He asserts that the William Henry Ashley party of fur trappers reached Utah Valley after leaving the Green River in 1825, and that they established a "Fort Ashley" on the site of modern Provo.

Once he reached the Mormon period, Bancroft's factual accuracy improved, in part because he submitted proof sheets of his narrative to the Church Historian's Office for correction. At that point, though, other problems emerge. For one thing, Bancroft's impressive mastery of the secondary literature threatens to overwhelm his basic narrative, as does his extensive quoting of undigested primary sources, which, as Earl Pomeroy slyly observed, often makes copying Bancroft not an act of plagiarism.[10] Footnotes creep farther and farther up the page until they sometimes completely supplant the text, and it seems that Bancroft is writing two separate books—one in the text and one in the footnotes. Furthermore, as one might expect given the sources he was using, the text at times becomes almost fawningly pro-Mormon. Opening the book almost at random, one finds the following account of the succession of leadership of the church from Joseph Smith to Brigham Young: "Thus Brigham Young succeeded Joseph Smith. The work of the latter was done. It was a singular work, to which he was singularly adapted; the work yet to be done is no less remarkable, and a no less remarkable agent is raised up at the right moment." There is little of the fearsome Lion of the Lord in that new "remarkable agent," Brigham Young, but rather the suffering servant of his people. "Soon we shall find him rousing his followers from the lethargy of despair, when their very hearts had died within them, and when all cheeks blanched but his; speaking words of cheer to the men, and with his own sick child in his arms, sharing his scant rations with women and children who held out their hands for bread."[11]

Bancroft was not unaware of the pro-Mormon bias of the text. He was a man of his word, and he had promised to present the story of the Mormons as they presented it to him. But he had also warned them that in the interest of fairness he was going to have to present their opponents' case as well. This he did, at least to some degree, in the footnotes, but one would have to conclude that the Mormon viewpoint got a good deal more space. Most of the immense footnotes were factual and bibliographic elaborations of points made in the text rather than objections to it.

This thesis-antithesis of text and footnotes represented objectivity to Bancroft. In his preface, he indicates a keen awareness of the difficulty of achieving that objectivity out of a literature of violent partisanship and outright falsehood; "never before," he tells us, "has it been my lot to meet with such a mass of mendacity." To deal with that polarized literature, Bancroft found himself presented with three alternatives: "to follow the beaten track of calumny and vituperation," "to espouse the cause of the Mormons as the weaker party, and defend them from the seeming injustice to which from the first they have been subjected," or finally, "in a spirit of equity to present both sides, leaving the reader to draw his own conclusions."[12] It was the third course that he chose, presenting one position in the text and the other in the footnotes.

This method, Bancroft speculated, had little likelihood of pleasing everyone, and would probably please no one. Still, he took comfort in the old bromide that if both sides in a partisan conflict are displeased with an arbitration, then the arbitrator can be confident of having achieved objectivity. "Having abandoned all hope of satisfying others," he concluded, "I fall back on the next most reasonable proposition left—that of satisfying myself."[13]

This may be neutrality—with a vengeance—but is it objectivity?[14] Objectivity entails a willingness to judge fairly between two conflicting positions rather than merely present them as a disinterested bystander, and modern critical historiography places the burden of that judgment squarely upon the historian. Thus, to a critical historian, Bancroft's method is an abdication of the historian's responsibility. Such an objection to Bancroft's method is grounded in purely logical terms, without holding him to professional standards of scholarship that have only recently emerged. Is it reasonable to expect that piling up lies on both sides of a question will produce truth? How can it produce anything more than a multiplication of lies? And why does Bancroft think the reader would be in a better position than the historian to judge between two conflicting positions, when it is the historian who presumably has read and considered all the sources? If two witnesses to the same event present diametrically conflicting accounts, only two conclusions are possible: either one or both are mistaken, in which latter case the truth lies elsewhere, or it falls somewhere in between, and who is going to be better situated to decide which is the case than the historian? One cannot say that Bancroft is morally remiss for rejecting that responsibility, but his timidity significantly diminishes the intellectual potential of his work.

As we shall see, the two philosophical assumptions that lie beneath the official Mormon compilations and the narrative of Hubert Howe Bancroft have exhibited a remarkable durability in Utah historiography. Even in the work of a powerful and critical mind like Dale Morgan, for example, there is unquestioned faith in the ability of the historian to determine with absolute objectivity what historical facts are. Once that has been accomplished and those facts thrown out upon the table, the truth will automatically emerge with no further intellection on the part of the historian.

In 1898, after completion of Bancroft's histories, his research material, including the Utah collection, found its way to the University of California, Berkeley. Augmented periodically since that time—the Utah portion most notably, perhaps, by a large collection of Historical Records Survey materials donated by Utah HRS director Hugh F. O'Neil—the Bancroft Collection (later the Bancroft Library) has been a powerful magnet for western historians for more than a century.

Among the early users of the Bancroft Collection was a succession of aspiring young Mormon historians, beginning around the First World War and continuing until well after the Second. Utah had no history graduate programs until this group finished their degrees and returned home to create them, and they found Berkeley an attractive place to do their graduate work for several reasons.[15] One of Berkeley's attractions in that era of railroads and primitive automobiles was no doubt its relative closeness, geographically, to Utah; some Utahns went to UCLA or USC, but the University of Chicago (which did lure a few) was a good deal farther away. Another Berkeley attraction was a superb graduate faculty in history. Most of the Utahns wrote their dissertations under either Herbert E. Bolton or Lawrence Kinnaird. Lastly, of course, was the Bancroft Collection, the only substantial collection of Mormon Americana at that time in a university collection.

So these new Utah historians had three major bodies of records available to them: the great Mormon compilations, which by this time were becoming overworked; federal government archives, of which few historians, for some reason, made any substantial use; and the Bancroft Collection. Sad to say, the early dissertations and monographs based on the Bancroft Collection fell considerably short of Bancroft's own work. Bancroft was well aware that his collection, provided entirely by the Mormons, was pro-Mormon. Thus he provided at least something of the other side in his footnotes. The young Mormon historians who used the same collection failed to provide any similar corrective effort, and the result was one-sided history endorsed by their academic credentials.

Although no one has yet studied Utah's first academically trained historians in the light of their cultural environment, it seems reasonable to link them to two basic developments in the late nineteenth and early twentieth centuries: the state's first authentic system of public education; and the attempt to develop a new sense of Mormonism's place in the national history after the assault on Mormon institutions that began in earnest in the 1880s. The "Americanization" process that surrounded Utah's attainment of statehood entailed the creation of a new history as well. This new history needed to come not from within the Mormon Church, but from scholars with recognized academic credentials. But it also needed to present a positive image of Mormon history that would show Mormonism as an inherently American phenomenon.

Thus, in Leland H. Creer's introduction to Andrew L. Neff's massive *History of Utah, 1847 to 1869*, he explains that Neff "has given greater emphasis to such every-day activities as farming, colonization, business, industry, transportation, government, and education than to such lurid and sensational themes as the institution and practice of polygamy, the Utah War, the Mountain Meadows Massacre, and the presumed arrogance of the Mormon hierarchy."[16] In other words, Neff sidestepped everything about Mormonism and Mormon history that begged for an explanation and offered instead a history that dealt only with those aspects of the church that could be made to appear conventionally American. None of these new scholars recognized any problems inherent in Mormon thought and values, and therefore treated Mormon colonization as an almost entirely positive event. None regarded the immense tragedy of the Mountain Meadows Massacre as anything but a highly localized aberration perpetrated by a deranged fanatic, John D. Lee. For all of them, Utah history and Mormon history were identical; Indians are portrayed as mere obstacles to progress, and non-Mormon whites are villainous rogues. Finally, all of them were lazy researchers who were content to exploit only those research collections discussed above that lay readily at hand. It is little wonder, given the quality of work produced by that first generation of academic historians, that the group that is the focus of this book found little reason to undertake academic preparation for their work.

Levi Edgar Young (1874–1963), author of *The Founding of Utah* (1923), the first Utah history by an academically trained scholar, was not a Berkeley graduate, nor did he receive a Ph.D.[17] Born in Salt Lake City, Young was a grandson of Joseph Young, one of Brigham's brothers. After graduating from the University of Utah in 1895, he taught English in Salt Lake City, then left in 1898 for study at Harvard, where he hoped to receive a graduate degree, and later in Europe. Young's Harvard diary reveals a person ablaze with youthful enthusiasm for all knowledge and all life-enlarging experience. "At last my dream has been realized, I am off for Harvard," it begins. "Only one of my dreams, though, for there are many that go to make up the ideal of my life."[18] His dream of a Harvard degree, however, never came to pass. When he presented his undergraduate credentials, he was admitted as a "special" student, which meant he would be allowed to enroll only in undergraduate courses until he proved himself, with the provision that he could enter graduate school midyear if his grades were good enough.

He never did. Three history courses in a semester with the likes of Albert Bushnell Hart in American history and Ephraim Emerton in medieval history proved to be more than he could handle. His Mormon background turned out to be particularly poor preparation for wrestling with the great issues of church history like the Arian controversy, which he mentions that he struggled to grasp in Emerton's class. Evidently he lowered his aspirations midyear to simply getting an undergraduate degree, but his advisor, as the year drew to a close, discouraged him from applying even for that, and he left Cambridge with a wealth of experience but no degree.[19] Nor did later study in Europe produce a degree. Finally, in 1910, he took the M.A. at Columbia University with a thesis that would become *The Founding of Utah*.

Despite the book's academic origins, it is not a scholarly work. When it appeared in 1923, the Mormon Church was still struggling to gain acceptance by the nation at large. Many people still had their doubts about the sincerity and degree of Utah's "Americanization," its adoption of a democratic political system, and its abandonment of polygamy. Young's apparent goal was to create a brief, popularly written history of the state, distributed by a national publisher, that would help lay that skepticism to rest. As an engaging writer, a member of one of the first families of Mormondom, and a scholar with solid academic credentials, Young was uniquely suited to the task. "Utah means 'on the heights,'" he points out in the book's last paragraph. "It is the duty of Utah's citizens to live up to the ideals of good citizens, and to be true to the State and Nation."[20] It was the basic theme of the book.

The Founding of Utah has many virtues. Although Young flits from one topic to another like a honeybee in a field of wildflowers, never landing anywhere long enough to drink much nectar, and though he omits any kind of scholarly documentation, his book must have come as an immense relief to non-Utahn readers whose only alternative for an objective history had been Bancroft's ponderous volume with its burdensome scholarly apparatus. Its more than four hundred pages belie the book's accessibility. It is printed in large type on small pages (approximately 5 x 7) in an attractive bright blue binding with gold titles and a golden beehive on the cover. Even teenagers would find it easy reading.

Not the least of the book's virtues is Young's buoyant personality, which comes through in bright hues on every page. Although Young was a controversialist and a missionary as far back as his Harvard days and spent much of his literary energy writing defenses of Mormon teachings, he was the gentlest of men who never lost his innocent love of life and of all the earth's good things. Young's prose and his interpretive perspective may be as antiquated as a pair of button shoes, but his unfeigned love for Utah in all its multifarious aspects bursts forth everywhere.

Finally, it would turn out to be a long time before other professional historians caught up with Young's views on Utah Indians, prehistoric and historic. As a Mormon, Young no doubt accepted the notion of modern Indians as "Lamanites," now-degraded members of a once highly civilized race, and at the points where he has to deal with Mormon-Indian conflicts, he treats the Indians as culturally inferior to the whites in some respects. But what sets Young apart from other professional Utah historians of his generation is that he also treats the Indian cultures as having value in their own right, and he encourages further anthropological and archaeological study. "We are interested in the Indians," he tells us, "not only because they bring us in touch with the manners and customs of primitive peoples of all ages, but because their history is so little known." Later, discussing an Anasazi dwelling near Blanding, he urges preservation of such sites in the interest of science. "Unfortunately travellers [*sic*] going through the country have destroyed some parts of the ruin. It is very important that this site, with the many hundreds of others in Utah, be properly investigated and preserved, since there is every reason to believe that additional light would thereby be thrown on the life and culture of the people who inhabited these ruins."[21] As evidence of his sincere interest in and respect for Indian cultures, Young salts his narrative throughout the early chapters with stories from Indian legends and supposed verses from Indian songs. Such songs and stories seem naive to modern readers, but they indicate Young's view of Indians as real people with valid cultures worthy of serious consideration and study. As we shall see, views like Young's were rare in the historiography that followed.

Unfortunately, the book's shortcomings are as conspicuous as its virtues. For one thing, as one would surmise from the title, the book is primarily the story of the Mormon pioneer period, from 1847 to 1869. The soldiers at Camp Floyd and Ft. Douglas, the Forty-niners and other miners, the non-Mormon merchants, and other minority groups get short shrift if they receive any mention at all. Even though Young could deal with Utah Indians in his romanticized way, he could find no reason, in a concluding chapter called "Utah To-day," to acknowledge the enormous influx of eastern and southern Europeans that had made the mining towns of Carbon County and the Oquirrh Mountains some of the most ethnically diverse communities in America.

Finally, Young's research is extremely shallow and his interpretations the most conservatively Mormon. His account of the Mountain Meadows Massacre, for example, not only exonerates Brigham Young (which later research would support), but virtually the entire Mormon population of southwestern Utah as well. Although Young indicates that "some white settlers" took part in the murders, he names none of them and places the blame completely on the Indians, who were provoked to the deed by the "encroachment" (!) of the emigrant wagon train. "The Mountain Meadows Massacre," he blandly concludes, "was one of those incidents in our history which we all regret, but in this western land in the early days, the Indians often perpetrated deeds which were terrible and which we wish had never happened."[22] As to why the "white settlers" participated, Young is silent.

Other scholars followed the trail blazed by Young, with mixed results. The first Utah Ph.D. at Berkeley under Herbert Eugene Bolton was Andrew Love Neff. Born in rural Salt Lake County in 1878, his baccalaureate degree from Brigham Young University in 1902 was the beginning of his higher education, which included study at Stanford University and the University of Chicago before his doctoral work at Berkeley. After he took his degree in 1918, he returned to his native state as a faculty member at the University of Utah, and served in that capacity until his death in 1936.[23] While Neff completed his graduate work, he served intermittently as principal of three Utah high schools.

"Like Frederick Jackson Turner, whom he admired," Davis Bitton and Leonard Arrington observe, "Neff seemed to be unable to complete works he started."[24] One's eyebrows raise at any analogy between Neff and Turner, one of America's truly original minds, but Neff did have an unfortunate penchant for starting projects he was unable to complete. That said, Neff's shortcomings did not include laziness. His monkish commitment to frugality and hard work is comically evident in the extant letters from his wife that, in an apparent effort to save paper, he interlineated with handwritten notes on Mormon history. As a result, his output, at least in manuscript form, was impressive.

The first of his big projects began immediately after his return to Utah with his doctorate in hand. At the end of World War I, the Utah Council of Defense, a war mobilization agency, had acquired $5,000 in state funds to produce a history of Utah's contribution to the war. The council then turned that money over to the Utah State Historical Society, which contracted with Neff to do the work.[25] It was the society's first big project since its founding in 1897, and it made possible the hiring of its first two paid employees, secretaries who supported Neff's research and began the society's files of news clippings. Neff worked industriously and frugally, producing about three hundred pages of text for just over $660. Unfortunately, though, he found it impossible to complete the history because he could identify no major themes that would unify his research. He proposed to change the project to a series of essays on aspects of the war effort, but the council refused and hired Noble Warrum to write a new history. Neff's manuscript, incomplete and unpublished, remains at the Utah State Historical Society.

Neff's successor at the University of Utah, Leland Hargrave Creer, acquired from Neff's widow the manuscript of Neff's magnum opus, which he also left uncompleted at his untimely death in 1936. It was a projected three-volume history of Utah, of which Neff finished most of only the first volume. Creer prepared it, at her behest, for publication in 1940 as *History of Utah, 1847 to 1869*. Creer's introduction to the book claims that his editorial work consisted of adding the text of Neff's dissertation, "The Mormon Migration to Utah," minus its scholarly documentation, to the beginning of the book, some 150 pages of Creer's own composition interspersed throughout several chapters, and a bibliography that is essentially the bibliography published in Creer's own two books, *Utah and the Nation* and *The Founding of an Empire*.[26] The result was a massive volume of more than nine hundred printed pages. The epitome of Berkeley scholarship on Utah and the Mormons during the interwar period, it merits extensive scrutiny.

If Neff's book is, as the title promises, a "history of Utah," it is a history with tunnel vision. Utah history to Neff was the history of Mormon males and little else. Even women, who would become enshrined in later Mormon historiography as courageous, suffering saints, are almost completely missing from Neff's narrative. He can hardly avoid mentioning women in his chapters on education, but even there the parsimonious place he gives them seems grudging. He brings them on stage to testify against the antipolygamy movement that began in the 1860s, whereupon they vanish once again.[27]

It is Utah Indians, though, who suffer most in Neff's unabashedly racist interpretation. In a narrative of more than nine hundred pages covering the twenty-two years of the Mormon pioneer period, a period during which the dynamics of the complicated relationships between Mormon settlers and Indians was the basic fabric of Utah history, Neff devotes sustained attention to the Indians in just one chapter, a chapter significantly titled "The Indian Problem."[28]

In Neff's view, the Mormon-Indian encounter during Utah's pioneer period was the story of a vastly superior people meeting a degraded remnant of a once noble race. In that encounter, the Mormons attempted to elevate and save the Indians from their degradation, but received for their altruism only ingratitude and violence. Statistically analyzing the native-born Mormons who came to Utah during the pioneer era, Neff notes a preponderance of residents of five states—New York, Illinois, Iowa, Pennsylvania, and Ohio—all of which "represented advanced economic and culture areas. Generalizing from this collective data it would seem that the component human elements constituted a superior society." Contrasting the pioneers to the Indians, it was apparent to Neff that these paragons of virtue were "elements in a rising culture while the decadent stocks were sadly reminiscent of the day when Mayan, Aztec, and Pueblo civilizations were ablaze with light and achievement."[29]

In Neff's view, by the mid-nineteenth century, Indian cultural degradation, as seen in their improvident waste of natural resources, threatened to destroy their economic base, and they would have suffered extinction had the timely arrival of the benevolent Mormons not saved them from that fate. "As a result of the exploitation, in some instances, even the extermination, of the buffalo, beaver, and other wild life during the hunting and trapping regime, the aborigines were being forced to still lower standards of living when the humanitarian [Mormon] colonists arrived to teach ways of augmenting the food supply." In the nick of time, then, the Mormons brought the possibility of redemption. "The timely arrival of Basin colonists heralded the emancipation of the natives from their servile dependence on an obdurate nature, providing of course they would accept the white man's guidance and leadership."[30]

But would they? Although "the Mormon Church projected its program of broad humanitarianism and social welfare work for the savage from the moment of its arrival in the Basin," native obstinacy kept that benevolence from achieving its happy result: the complete embrace of the white man's ways. "The hope of the whites was in weaning the red men from the lower to the higher law, but the native mind assimilated the rudiments of civilization but slowly."[31]

To Neff, central Utah became the Armageddon in which the

Indians' perverse resistance to Mormon benevolence came to a violent denouement. He acknowledges that the bloodshed of the Walker and Black Hawk wars was provoked by Mormon encroachment on Indian lands, through which those lands were rendered useless for the Indians' traditional pursuits of hunting, gathering, and trading. But he blames the Indians for failing to accept that transformation as being in their best interest. They insisted instead upon the validity of their prior claim; the Indians "pushed their priority claim to the land to the limit, imposing and exacting burdensome tribute which was almost unbearable. The excessive demands and militant importunings of these human parasites became at times insufferable to the colonists." Ingratitude thus led to war.

Any reader conversant with the *Book of Mormon* will recognize the origin of Neff's views in Joseph Smith's notion of the American Indians as Lamanites, unfortunate beings in a state of decline whom the Mormons feel obligated to redeem. In most Mormon literature, though (Levi Edgar Young's book is a good example), the idea appears in a considerably softened form that recognizes elements of value in primitive cultures and an inclination to permit retention of those elements within an otherwise Mormon way of life. In Neff's historical explication of the idea, however, one finds the apogee of Mormon ethnocentric intolerance.

On the Mountain Meadows Massacre, the quintessentially controversial issue in Utah history, Neff helped develop what became the standard Mormon interpretation, that the episode was a highly localized aberration having no larger roots in the Mormon doctrine of blood atonement and carried out without the knowledge of Brigham Young and other church authorities in Salt Lake City. The Fancher emigrants were not without blame in provoking the massacre, but it was the lone fanatic John D. Lee who bore the responsibility on the Mormon side and who was justly executed for his role.[32] Neff had advanced beyond the almost complete denial of Mormon participation one finds in Levi Edgar Young, but he was not willing to consider that the massacre might have revealed the violent potential in Mormonism's attitude toward the outside world. It would take another decade before

Juanita Brooks became the first Mormon historian willing to take a glimpse into that abyss.

Neff was not incapable of advancing adventuresome interpretations, however. In fact, he originated one of the most durable conceptions of the Mormon settlement process, the idea that Brigham Young created an "outer cordon" of settlements to serve as a defensive network protecting the inner area of Mormon communities. This outer cordon, which included such far-flung outposts as Forts Limhi, Bridger, and Supply, the Elk Mountain Mission, Las Vegas, and San Bernardino, marked the far boundaries of Mormon country until the invasion of federal troops during the Utah War forced Young to abandon them in favor of protecting the inner cordon in northern and central Utah. Adopted wholesale by Leland Creer, Milton R. Hunter, and later scholars of Mormon settlement, Neff's idea endured for more than three decades in Mormon historiography until Eugene Campbell called it into question. The haphazardness of the outer settlements, Campbell pointed out, defy the notion of a central plan, and most of them had already outlived their usefulness and were being abandoned before the arrival of the army.[33]

Neff's book still ranks as one of the most ambitious histories of Utah written by an academically trained scholar. However impressive in scale the book may have been, though, it did not meet with approval by contemporary reviewers, nor has it proved to have enduring value. Reviewers were inclined to blame some of the book's shortcomings on the difficulties of posthumous collaboration between Neff and Creer, his editor. Nels Anderson, for example, in a letter to Creer, observed that "considering it was another man's book, and apparently a man with a mission, you did a good job. Naturally you could not take liberties with a text already written." Dale Morgan echoed that "Creer himself had a thankless job, of course, having to fill in the lacunas of a dead man's book and not having the right to revise and condense such a work as the author himself would do in preparing it for the press. . . . And had Neff lived to complete it, I am sure it would have been a better book." On the other hand, neither could excuse Creer for the shortcomings that remained after he had done his work, nor for those that his editorial work had introduced. "Frankly," Anderson offered, "the book would have been much more useful to me if you could have reduced the text by 100,000 words and used that many words for reference footnotes." (Anderson, who had not seen the original manuscript, could not have known that Neff had included at least sketchy footnotes that Creer had largely replaced with his own "editor's notes" that had little value as citations.) "In addition to its own disabilities," Morgan added, "it incorporates errors Creer brought into it from his own work."[34]

Both Anderson and Morgan recognized a shallowness in Neff's research, though Anderson found it excusable in view of Neff's purpose and audience. "The book was obviously written," Anderson said, "not for historical purposes as much as to tell a story for folks in Utah, and especially for members of the Church who want the kind of history they want and who have a viewpoint which they expect history to confirm. For that purpose, for a general review of Utah history told in a journalistic style, Neff has done a good work." Morgan was not so forgiving. "[I]t did not make the most even of the Church archives to which he had access, . . . and no such history could be regarded as satisfactory until it had consulted the manuscript archives of the Government itself." The most caustic assessment of Neff's research, however, came from Fr. Robert Joseph Dwyer, whose *The Gentile Comes to Utah* overlapped Neff's treatment of Utah politics in the troubled 1860s. Even though "Neff was a conscientious student, and his work displays a sincere, if ponderous, effort to achieve a balanced view," Dwyer conceded, "[i]t is difficult to understand why a man of his training and caution should have failed to take into account the possibility that the government archives might contain, as they do, rich sources of material that would modify, in important respects, his conclusions." Nor could Dwyer understand, any more than could Anderson, "why the author and editor should have wished to issue the book with citations almost wholly omitted."[35]

Leland Hargrave Creer (1895–1968) was the third of the Berkeley Ph.D.s from Utah, taking his degree under Bolton in 1926. Although Creer served two stints in academic administration (as president of Gila

Junior College in Thatcher, Arizona, from 1920 to 1924 and Weber State College in Ogden, Utah, from 1935 to 1937), his greatest influence came as a history professor at the University of Washington (from 1926 to 1935) and especially at the University of Utah, where he replaced Neff in 1937 and served until his retirement in 1965. Creer also served as a board member (1949–65) and president (1957–61) of the Utah State Historical Society, though his tenure there was notorious for his reluctance to embrace the society's emerging professionalization.[36]

During Creer's day, the University of Utah was well on its way to achieving credibility as an authentic institution of higher learning. Under the presidencies of Dr. John R. Park and Dr. A. Ray Olpin, it had shed the image of its predecessor, the University of Deseret, as a glorified high school, and it had attracted faculty members with earned doctorates, like Neff, and developed its library holdings and curriculum. Creer was a good fit, not only with his Ph.D., but also with his flamboyant teaching style, which made him something of a cult figure among undergraduates. "I can't even count the credits," Philip Sturges remembers one of his fellow Creer disciples saying, "but I've just got to take one more course from Dr. Creer before I graduate." Like his formidable contemporary Jesse D. Jennings in the anthropology department, Creer turned the history department into a personal fiefdom within which he exercised benevolent reign over his awestruck vassals. "Often a timid Freshman would venture into Dr. Creer's office," Sturges continued, "only to meet a great roar and apparent outburst of disapproving outrage. For a moment the hapless student would contemplate flight or other desperate measures. But only for a moment—only for the length of time it took to note the twinkle in the life-loving eyes. And the student knew then that he had found a new friend."[37]

Although Sturges generously credited his mentor with "a long and distinguished list of books and articles," Creer's bibliography was in fact neither long nor distinguished. His scholarly achievement rests on three books: *Utah and the Nation*, his Berkeley dissertation published by the University of Washington Press while he was a faculty member there; his editorial work on Neff's *History of Utah*; and *The Founding of an Empire: The Exploration and Colonization of Utah, 1776–1856*, which appeared in 1947.[38]

For a doctoral dissertation, *Utah and the Nation* was a relatively promising work. It was the first published general history of the Mormon pioneer period in Utah based on the Bancroft Collection since Bancroft's own book, and it also made some use of the Mormon source compilations and of published government records. As such, it was a pioneering work in developing and reaffirming some of the major themes and contours of Utah history. Creer's preface promises much: without specific mention of Frederick Jackson Turner, he asserts that much of Utah history is the history of a frontier experience, but he warns as well that the dominance of Mormon institutions and ideals separated the Utah frontier in important ways from the general American frontier. And he promises to eschew the polemics that have vitiated so much of the literature of Mormonism and stick objectively to the factually verifiable aspects of the Mormon historical experience (though his first chapter, understandably, is a historical sketch of Mormon beginnings and beliefs).

Unfortunately, Creer failed to deliver on his promises. For one thing, his research was barely adequate. Although he did have available to him a few published primary sources that had appeared since Bancroft's work in the 1880s, Creer did not attempt to open up the riches of the National Archives, which, as Morgan and Dwyer observed in their criticism of Neff's book, would have greatly deepened his insights. Instead, he contented himself with published government reports. He also largely abandoned his promise of a comparison of the Mormon frontier with that in other western areas and thus missed his opportunity to critique the Turner thesis from a Mormon perspective—a most worthwhile avenue of investigation. Finally, in a capitulation reminiscent of Bancroft, Creer confused objectivity with a failure to make any critical comments regarding the possible shortcomings of Mormon values and institutions as a basis for settlement of a frontier.

Creer's editorial work on Neff's book has already been partially examined. It is true, as Morgan and Anderson observed, that Creer's felt obligation to preserve the integrity of Neff's work hobbled him in imposing whatever his own ideas might have been. It is also true, as Dwyer and Anderson pointed out, that Creer actually suppressed some of the virtues of Neff's manuscript, for instance footnotes. That omission is particularly unfortunate because instead of compiling a bibliography based on Neff's footnotes, Creer simply reprinted, with a few added citations of recent secondary works, his own bibliography from *Utah and the Nation*. Consequently, we have no idea, without laboriously consulting the original manuscript, what Neff's actual sources were.

The Founding of an Empire, which appeared in 1947, was embarrassingly deficient in scholarship. Although it covered much of the same ground as his dissertation, it added little in research or interpretation and was careless and uncritical in factual detail. Once again, Creer added citations of recent secondary literature, but his list of primary sources in the bibliography is virtually identical to that in his dissertation of twenty years before. This scholarly laziness is nothing short of appalling in view of the immense number of newly available primary sources that had been collected and transcribed by the Historical Records Survey of the Works Progress Administration as well as by industrious individual scholars, many of whom were being published in the *Utah Historical Quarterly*. Dale Morgan, who had been in the forefront of collecting, publishing, and using the newly available sources, bought a copy of Creer's new book on a trip home to Salt Lake City in 1948 and was outraged by what he read. "I regret very much to report," he wrote to Fawn Brodie, "that it is the shoddiest kind of historical workmanship." Creer's avoidance of "the touchy Mormon problems" (such as those raised in Brodie's recent biography of Joseph Smith) was forgivable, Morgan conceded, because Creer was writing a history of Utah Territory, not of the Mormon Church. "But my God, his treatment of the fur trade, for instance, is slipshod in the extreme. Thus he quotes something from [Harrison] Dale's Ashley-Smith Explorations, then follows it with a quotation from a newspaper piece I wrote for the [WPA] Writers' Project which presents later research wholly invalidating the quotation from Dale, then without seeing the slightest conflict between the two, he goes ahead in the old canon, etc. Hell! Worse still, he doesn't have the slightest feeling for primary sources. Anything is grist for his mill."[39]

Another Berkeley Ph.D., Milton R. Hunter, who took his degree under Bolton in 1936, published his dissertation in 1940 under the title *Brigham Young the Colonizer*.[40] Rather than seeking an academic career like Neff and Creer, Hunter went to work in the educational department of the Mormon Church, for which he wrote a long string of books and articles defending and propagating Mormon history and teachings. In those days, when the official Church Historian was not a professionally trained historical scholar, Hunter, a General Authority with a prestigious Berkeley degree, became something of a "house historian" for the church.

Although he was widely admired and read within the church, Hunter's scholarship, like Creer's, was reviled for its shallowness and partisanship by the younger scholars who are the focus of this study. The smugness of Hunter's *ex cathedra* affirmations, from behind the walls of church headquarters, of some of the hoary myths of Mormon history that Morgan and his generation were striving to undermine, was certain to prove galling to them. Dale Morgan, once again, objected to "the amazing misstatements in his *Brigham Young the Colonizer*," to wit, that "when he takes [Richard] Burton's observation that Mormonism is a perfect government for those who set no value on liberty (or something of that sort)—Hunter quoted the first part of the observation, but omitted the qualification!"[41] A younger scholar, Brigham D. Madsen, recalled an incident in 1948 while he was working on his own Ph.D. under Bolton that illustrates the divergence of opinion at the time over Hunter's scholarship. Madsen happened to meet Thomas Stuart Ferguson, who was collaborating with Hunter on a book purporting to offer external evidence corroborating the *Book of Mormon*—a highly dubious enterprise in Madsen's opinion. Madsen countered Ferguson's boasting of Hunter's skill as a historian by passing along Bolton's report that he had found more than four hundred errors in *Brigham Young the Colonizer* and had made Hunter correct every one before he would agree to write the preface that Hunter had requested. Ferguson, who eventually abandoned the *Book of Mormon* corroboration project, was so outraged at the time that he nearly assaulted Madsen.[42] Geographer Wayne Wahlquist, in a review of the literature of Mormon settlement, praised Hunter's book for its handy tabulation of all Mormon colonies before Brigham Young's death in 1877, but scored it for its superficial treatment of the colonization process, on such issues as land titles and distribution and the types of lands settled, and for failing to recognize that the colonization process did not end with Brigham Young.[43]

On the other hand, some of Hunter's work has real merit. *Utah in Her Western Setting* (1943), for example, is a textbook of Utah history for schoolchildren in which Hunter's lively (though antiquated) writing style shows his authentic love for the state, which comes through almost as engagingly as that of Levi Edgar Young. The first and last chapters, for example, are imaginary airplane and bus trips in which students are joined by knowledgeable teachers who answer their questions about Utah geography and natural history. Rather than merely narrating the material, Hunter's device of *showing* it to the children, as best he can through their own eyes, is refreshing. When Hunter reissued essentially the same text as *Utah—The Story of Her People* in 1946 as an unofficial commemoration of the centennial of the arrival of the Mormon pioneers, he removed the pedagogical devices like end-of-chapter review questions as well as the travelogues, and the result is a pedestrian narrative.[44]

These two works exhibit both the prevailing cultural biases of their day and Hunter's own myopic cultural vision. Fully imbued with the patriotism, the chin-up optimism, and the faith in progress held by Mormons and other Americans during the World War II period, the books promote unrestrained industrial development and exploitation of natural resources. But they completely ignore Utah's cultural diversity, a result of immigrants from southern and eastern Europe and Mexico who had come to work in Utah's mines and livestock industry around the turn of the twentieth century, and the laborers in Utah's war industries who were swelling the communities in Tooele and Weber counties even as Hunter wrote.

In the school textbook, Hunter could not avoid dealing with the Indians of Utah, who after all had been there for centuries before any Europeans, but he dealt with them in almost as condescending a manner as Neff had. He echoed Neff's emphasis on Mormon benevolence during the settlement era. "The Utah pioneers believed that if they could teach the Indians how to farm, live in houses and adopt the customs of the white men, the natives would become civilized," Hunter tells us. "Then the two peoples could live side by side in harmony with each other, and the whites could more easily teach the red men Christianity." When the white settlers followed the benevolent policies of the Mormon leadership, violent confrontations were rare. "Most of the troubles that did occur, however, were brought about by disobedient Mormons, unscrupulous Gentile immigrants, or renegade fugitive whites." Even Hunter cannot find a way to blame that gallery of rogues for all the Indians' misfortunes, but where Mormon encroachment was the culprit, the encroachers were good enough to provide farms where the Indians could learn to fit into the new circumstances; at the Spanish Fork Indian farm, "the raising of the crops and the feeding and clothing of the Indians proved to be a great hardship on the whites who had been called to do the job."[45] (One hopes the Indians were grateful.) Hunter's centennial history solves the issues of Utah Indians the same way it deals with the non-Mormon immigrants from Europe and Mexico: it makes no mention of them—in a volume called *Utah—The Story of Her People!*[46]

By the 1940s, most of the creative ideas about Utah and Mormon history and institutions were coming from within the ranks of social scientists rather than historians. Encouraged by the famous economist Richard T. Ely's pioneering look at "Economic Aspects of Mormonism" in 1903, young Mormon social scientists began to realize there was much virgin soil for scholarly cultivation right under their feet.[47] Social psychologist Ephraim Edward Ericksen, for example, published *The Psychological and Ethical Aspects of Mormon Group Life* in 1922, based on his 1918 dissertation at the University of Chicago, while a series of articles in the 1920s and 1930s by sociologist Lowry Nelson contributed in 1952 to his *The Mormon Village: a Pattern and Technique of Land Settlement*.[48] Most influential on the writers who are the subject of this study, however, was sociologist Nels Anderson, whose historical and sociological study of the Mormons, *Desert Saints: The Mormon Frontier in Utah*, appeared in 1942.[49]

Anderson, a footloose Bohemian, left his Michigan home in the early years of the century to wander about from job to job. In 1908, on a journey leading vaguely toward Panama, where he intended to seek work on the new canal, Anderson found himself stranded in southwestern Utah, where he was taken in by the family of Mormon polygamist Lyman L. Woods of Clover Valley. Impressed by the friendliness of the Mormon people and the organized purposefulness of their society, Anderson became a Mormon and lived in their community for ten years, graduating from Dixie Academy in St. George and Brigham Young University before doing his graduate work in sociology at the University of Chicago. His academic career was as unconventional as his personal life. "Because of my background," he explained, "I was drawn into studies of hobos, prisoners, and other fringe elements, until I felt myself a pariah among respectable sociologists, with little hope of finding a professorship." Although he did find employment at Columbia University on a year-to-year contract basis, most of his working career was spent in various government agencies working on actual social problems. A regular academic position in a Canadian university came only after he had reached retirement age.[50]

Based on research done in 1934, largely in the rich collection of historical records in the St. George temple, *Desert Saints* was six years in the making, written as Anderson could afford the time while working a government job. It was a pathbreaking book, though a curious one by modern standards. Assuming, probably correctly, that Mormonism and Mormon history were so unfamiliar to the reading public that a sociological study of life in southern Utah would be about as comprehensible as a treatise on the geography of the moon, Anderson found it necessary first to explain who the Mormons were and where they came from before he could proceed to his real topic, the sociology of "the Mormon frontier in Utah." Accordingly, the first twelve of his sixteen chapters are a straightforward narrative history of the origins and progress of Mormonism through the migration to Utah and the Manifesto of 1890 that abandoned polygamy and led to statehood. They serve, in effect, as an extended introduction to the last four chapters, in which he gets to the real meat of the book, Mormon economic, political, and social practices in southern Utah.

Although the tail does wag the dog to a considerable degree in *Desert Saints*, the last four chapters are well worth waiting for, and the book exerted a profound influence on Dale Morgan and Juanita Brooks, both of whom knew Anderson well. Morgan never spelled out the nature of Anderson's influence on him, but it can be seen in Morgan's view that Mormon history could be explained entirely in sociological terms; once one had delineated the social circumstances out of which Mormonism grew and within which it developed, one had a sufficient explanation for the religion itself. When Bernard DeVoto accused Morgan, during their heated debate over Fawn Brodie's biography of Joseph Smith, of being a "spoiled sociologist," he was pointing unwittingly to the Nels Anderson influence at the core of Morgan's thought.[51]

Anderson was a neighbor of Juanita Brooks while he was doing his research in St. George, often walking in her back door uninvited and unannounced. "He was the most unconventional mortal you ever saw," she reminisced. His influence on her was twofold: he recognized in her an intelligent and literate heir of the Mormon pioneer experience, and he helped her write her first published article, "A Close-up of Mormon Polygamy."[52] In his persistent encouragement and critical shaping of her writing, a role taken over later by Morgan, Anderson was a sort of midwife to the career of one of Utah's greatest historians. Also, it was Anderson who showed Brooks that the history of Mormon pioneering and the rural Mormon experience was a great theme, something to be taken with intellectual seriousness, and worthy of a scholarly career. Anderson's influence with both Morgan and Brooks was no mean achievement.

By the early 1940s, the only book strictly within the discipline of Utah history that was more than marginally competent was *The Gentile Comes To Utah: A Study in Religious and Social Conflict (1862–1890)*, a doctoral dissertation at the Catholic University of America by Fr. Robert Joseph Dwyer, a priest of the Catholic diocese of Salt Lake City, published by Catholic University Press in 1941. Dwyer (1908–76) was a native of Salt Lake City. The only child of John and Mabel Dwyer, he was educated at Judge Memorial Catholic grammar and high schools.[53] After attending seminaries in Pennsylvania and California, Dwyer was ordained in 1932 for the diocese of Salt Lake City, thus becoming the first native Utahn ordained to the Catholic priesthood.

In 1938 he began graduate work in history at the Catholic University, which led to the Ph.D. in 1941 and publication of his dissertation. Dwyer's career as a historian was a sideline to his calling as a priest, and he advanced impressively in the church. He became rector of the Cathedral of the Madeleine and was named Monsignor in 1951. In 1952 he was consecrated Bishop of Reno and in 1966 appointed Archbishop of Portland, Oregon. Ill health forced his retirement to Piedmont, California, on San Francisco's east bay, in 1974, and he died there in 1976.

Despite the ever-increasing demands of his ministry, the energetic Dwyer remained an active historian and served as a member of the governing and editorial boards of the Utah State Historical Society from 1943 to 1952, during which time he was a powerful force in developing the *Utah Historical Quarterly* and promoting scholarly standards in the study of Utah history. In addition to authoring several *Quarterly* articles, Dwyer edited two complete volumes of the journal: the diary of Albert Tracy, a soldier in Albert Sidney Johnston's troops during the Utah War, which appeared in 1943, and the 1946 volume on Brigham Young's brother, the Mormon pioneer Lorenzo Dow Young, which appeared in commemoration of the centennial of the 1847 arrival of the Mormon pioneers in Utah. The latter volume is particularly noteworthy for its quiet testimony to Dwyer's ecumenism long before that became fashionable, as well as to his competence in and enthusiasm for Mormon history.

But *The Gentile Comes to Utah*, a definitive work that has become one of the classics of Utah historiography, was Dwyer's greatest historical contribution. The book's only shortcomings are literary: the sometimes archaic diction of Dwyer's prose and the lengthy block quotations that betray its inception as a dissertation. Those clouds, though, have their silver linings, for the antiquated diction nicely complements Dwyer's dry wit, which is one of the book's great virtues, and the lengthy quotations were taken from primary sources that Dwyer was frequently the only scholar to have examined.

Dwyer was the first Utah historian to maintain a consistent critical objectivity toward his materials. The polemical element, either for or against Mormonism, which had vitiated most of the literature of

Mormon and Utah history before his time, is completely absent from his book. On the other hand, Dwyer was not hesitant to offer informed criticism when it was due—a giant step forward from the false objectivity Bancroft thought he was attaining by simply presenting both sides of a question and disdaining to judge between them. An excellent example of Dwyer's critical deftness is his scoring of Brigham Young for his failure to develop some kind of middle ground on the polygamy issue that might have effected a compromise and avoided the suffering of the antipolygamy crusade that developed after his death. Dwyer does concede that Young had little elbow room in the matter given that Mormons regarded the doctrine to have been transmitted through divine revelation.[54]

Dwyer's objectivity was grounded in his sense of irony, which he was the first scholar to apply to the study of Mormon and Utah history. Irony, an observer's perception of the discrepancy between pretensions and reality, has been an essential element in Catholic thought since the time of St. Augustine. In *The City of God*, he exposed the gap between the claims of Classical thinkers who maintained the possibility of creating a perfect political order on earth and the realities of the fifth-century Mediterranean world they had actually produced.[55] Irony had not appeared as a perspective on Utah and Mormon history before Dwyer's time because irony is essentially alien to Mormon thinking. Mormonism represents an attempt to resurrect (though not in Classical terms) the idea of creating an ideal human order on earth. To Dwyer, the very earnestness with which Mormons go about the task of building Zion blinds them, from a Catholic point of view, to its inherent impossibility.

There is a double irony in *The Gentile Comes to Utah* in the Mormons' attempt to build their unique Zion and in the Gentiles' equally dogged attempts to prevent them from it and to impose instead a secular order defined in broadly American terms. In the end, according to Dwyer, the Gentiles won the struggle, not by the inherent superiority of their cultural ideals but by dint of increasing numbers and superior political, legal, and even military power. Dwyer's narrative gives a far more profound assessment of the basic tensions of Utah history than anything accomplished by his predecessors. Previous historians had sought to avoid explaining those tensions by dealing only with the pioneer period before the Gentile assault or otherwise marginalizing those tensions by marginalizing the non-Mormon population as being in some way morally degraded. Dwyer, by extending Utah history beyond the pioneer period to 1890, exposed the shortsightedness of the Mormon triumphalist view and found on that longer scale that the Gentiles were the ultimate victors. Even though Utah, because of Mormon dominance, will always remain a counterpoint to mainstream America, it was forced by Gentile pressure to comply with a national norm. By the 1890s we see not a Mormonism triumphant but a Mormonism in retreat from its original aspirations, a Mormonism making a transition to a new "American" phase. Dwyer's predecessors had skirted that story. It would be a long time before another Utah historian would match the maturity of Dwyer's analysis.

By the early 1940s, then, Utah historical literature could boast one commendable work produced within an academic setting. Why was it that Dwyer's example did not influence the next generation, which is the focus of this book, to seek academic training? Or at least why did Dwyer not become a mentor to the younger historians? Answers are possible only in individual cases, for there were many reasons why the next generation failed to seek academic training in history. In general, though, Dwyer was not in a situation to exert much influence except through his writings and his work with the Historical Society. In the first place, although he was academically trained, he was not a professor in an academic institution where he could develop a cadre of graduate students to train directly in historical method and interpretation. Also, he was a Catholic priest with a degree from a Catholic institution, and to younger Mormon historians, a Catholic priest would have seemed as suspicious as a voodoo practitioner. Catholic University of America, which was a continent away geographically but a universe away culturally, would not have appealed to them as a place to seek professional training. Finally, Dwyer himself was not the kind of warm and welcoming personality that would have invited informal mentoring. Like most shy people, Dwyer was able to relax and joke only in intimate settings with close friends. To others he seemed abrupt and aloof.

With almost the single exception of Dwyer, then, Utah historiography at the beginning of the 1940s was bleak. Its conspicuous features were a Mormon triumphalism that glorified the Mormon pioneer experience while turning a blind eye to its shortcomings and either denigrating or ignoring the contributions of other groups. That triumphalist interpretation led the younger scholars to a conclusion similar to Bancroft's, that *all* historical interpretation is false and that historiography should simply be the establishment of factual accuracy. Further, there was a laziness of research that failed to explore beyond the church compilations, the Bancroft Collection, and published government documents; a chronological focus that rarely extended outside the pioneer period; a lack of commitment to factual accuracy; and an inability to develop what Bernard DeVoto called, in another context, "the continental mind," that is, a feeling for the larger dramatic and interpretive implications of Utah history beyond Mormon triumphalism. This, then, was the Utah historiographical tradition with which the younger generation who came to intellectual maturity during the 1940s and 1950s had to deal. We shall see that they transcended it magnificently in some ways, but remained its prisoner in others.

Bernard DeVoto

Bernard DeVoto

THE PROPHET

As HE SAT down to work one day in early 1928, Bernard Augustine DeVoto was in an expansive mood. His mood was not always buoyant, for he occasionally suffered from migraine headaches and bipolar mood shifts that had been known to drive him to the brink of suicide. But when he worked, he was always in a manic phase. With DeVoto, it was full throttle or dead stop. In 1928 he had plenty to feel expansive about; with three published novels to his credit and an ever-increasing string of magazine articles, essays, and reviews, his literary career was promising. He had recently declined a promotion and resigned from what he regarded as a dead-end teaching position at Northwestern University. He had moved back to Cambridge, Massachusetts, in the shadow of Harvard University, where he had spent his last three undergraduate years and where he hoped to find a salubrious environment for a freelance writing career among his former professors and current university students. And he had married one of his students at Northwestern, Helen Avis MacVicar—bright, beautiful, fashionable, and liberated in the 1920s manner—who brought him domestic contentment, intellectual stimulation, and an inclination to flaunt social unconventionality that complemented his own. "A vast, yeasty mass of ideas bubbles within me," he wrote to a friend. "I am about to Explain America." As he thought about it further, he raised the stakes even higher: "God has appointed me to Explain America. All other understanders have been ignominiously betrayed."[1]

DeVoto did Explain America, for almost three decades after his proclamation, thundering his affirmations and denunciations like an Old Testament prophet. He did it in some of the wittiest, most colorful prose in our literature, in some of the most sweeping (to the point of extravagant) terms, with the most tireless research and critical examination of his sources, and with a zest for controversy that relished flattening the noses and trampling the toes of his intellectual opponents. Establishing a fact or developing an interpretation was always a pleasure for him, as it is for all historians, but for DeVoto it was never so pleasurable as when it was done nose-to-nose with an opponent and to his embarrassment or discomfiture. Scholarship, for DeVoto, was combat. "One of the abiding satisfactions in life," he wrote to historian Kenneth P. Williams, "is annoying the right people."[2]

And yet combat for DeVoto was always in the ring with the gloves on. Despite his profound contempt for some of his opponents' ideas, he never went after them bare-knuckled in the parking lot to settle a personal grudge. Nowhere does the tenderness beneath his pugnacity show more than in his response to a gracious invitation from Van Wyck Brooks, of whom DeVoto had become a most implacable opponent, to participate in a conference on world peace in 1943. The primary purpose of DeVoto's *Mark Twain's America* (1932) had been to rescue Twain from what he regarded as Brooks's incompetent interpretation in *The Ordeal of Mark Twain*, and his attack on Brooks had not been done with pillows. He was about to skewer again the ideas of Brooks and the other Young Intellectuals of the 1920s in *The Literary Fallacy* (1944), and to boot, he was totally unsympathetic with the stratospheric high-mindedness of the goals of the conference. Brooks himself was the gentlest of men and an authentic truth-seeker who, throughout his career, had demonstrated (in Wallace Stegner's words) "an admirable capacity to learn and grow, a true open-mindedness that steadily enlarged his books and opinions." Brooks had never directly rebutted DeVoto's attack and had in fact tried to learn from it. DeVoto felt he was in a trap, for he knew that if he ever met Brooks personally, he would like him so much that it would defang his dissatisfaction with the man's ideas. Thus his letter declining the invitation is a masterpiece of circumlocution, protecting in his mind the distinction between Brooks the man and Brooks's ideas.[3]

The distinction was vital to maintain, for once one made it inside DeVoto's circle of friends, one was mothered with affection, protection, nurturing, and support of all kinds. He was, as Stegner knew personally, "immensely tender of his friends." Many examples of this are available, but one of the most dramatic is the succor DeVoto offered Clarissa Hagler, sister of DeVoto's college chum Kent Hagler, in his heroic assistance in investigating—from the impossibly disadvantageous location of Ogden, Utah—Hagler's apparent suicide in Paris. Throughout his career DeVoto had about him an ever-changing group of literary stray dogs: down-on-their-luck writers or other unfortunate people who deserved, in DeVoto's mind, a free meal, a loan, or a timely word with a publisher or agent.[4]

At the root of much of DeVoto's complicated and cross-grained relationship with his world was Ogden, Utah, where he was born on January 11, 1897.[5] If not a breech birth, DeVoto's delivery must have been sideways, for never in his life was he any less than ninety degrees at odds with virtually everything Ogden represented, and more often he was at a full one hundred eighty. His very family symbolized the disjunctures of his world. His father, Florian DeVoto, was an apostate Catholic, his mother, Rhoda Dye, a backslidden daughter of Mormon pioneers. Florian DeVoto acceded to his devout sister's wish to have Bernard baptized a Catholic at age four, but Catholicism found stony ground in the boy and eventually withered. Being the only boy in a convent elementary school no doubt impressed upon him his misfit relationship with the church, and DeVoto related a humorous anecdote illustrating his ineptness as an altar assistant to Monsignor Patrick M. Cushnahan, pastor of St. Joseph's in Ogden. "Bernardo," Cushnahan whispered during the liturgy as DeVoto wrestled clumsily with the Latin responses, "for the love of God *et cum spiritu tuo*, hurry up, Bernardo, I'm lapping you!"[6]

As DeVoto began to come of age intellectually in high school, the friction between him and his cultural environment, which was always at the point of combustion, came less from his tepid Catholicism than from his rancorous father. Life had not been kind to Florian DeVoto, a perpetual student, classical scholar, and sometime instructor at Notre Dame who had migrated west in an ultimately futile search for his true calling. "A brilliant, contrary, sometimes lovable, mule-headed eccentric with a paralyzed will," as Stegner characterized him, Florian somehow never found a way out of unchallenging and underpaid jobs where he watched helplessly as "his talents rotted away" and he found "his nature gone sour and murky with self-contempt that emerged as a compulsion to insult everyone he talked to."[7] Bernard seems to have found in his father's mocking cynicism a defense mechanism for his adolescent alienation from the intellectual stultification and the closed social order of predominantly Mormon Ogden. Beneath DeVoto's mockery of his environment was a certain love of combat, the smile on the gladiator's face as the lion bounds toward him, that was probably missing in his father. There was also a genuine resentment that father and son shared, and the mix of those two emotions makes it impossible to map the labyrinth of DeVoto's true feelings toward his birthplace. One could hardly find a greater contrast than the one between DeVoto's attitude toward Ogden and Wallace Stegner's attitude toward his hometown of Salt Lake City, a slightly more cosmopolitan setting a mere thirty-five miles to the south. Stegner, whose peripatetic father led his family on an extended hegira from Iowa through Saskatchewan, Montana, and other places to Utah in search of the elusive end of the rainbow, wrote an essay later in life called "At Home in the Fields of the Lord." In that essay he admits that "while Salt Lake City is foreign to me, as to any non-Mormon," if "I am *forced* to select a hometown, I find myself selecting the City of the Saints, and for what seems to me cause."[8] To DeVoto, on the other hand, Ogden was that "scurvy little Mormon-Gentile dump that created all my neuroses." DeVoto graduated from high school in 1915 and enrolled at the University of Utah, the closest available institution of higher learning. The former University of Deseret, which then and now proudly proclaims its status as the oldest university west of the Mississippi, had only begun to emerge from its long-held reputation as a glorified high school and become a genuine university. But 1915 was a year of crisis. The university's president, Joseph T. Kingsbury, engineered the dismissal of four faculty members for dubious reasons that appeared to be violation of academic freedom, and seventeen unaffected faculty members resigned in protest. The episode attracted national attention when the American Association of University Professors mounted its first investigation of an institution for academic practices.[9] To DeVoto, the incident proved that Salt Lake City was fully as provincial and intellectually dead as Ogden, and that his intellectual interests would be best pursued elsewhere. At the end of the year he applied to Harvard and was accepted.

During his three years at Harvard pursuing a major in writing, his studies were directed by faculty members who, although not writers themselves, were gifted teachers who respected student talent even when it expressed itself in ways unfamiliar to them. It was the type of handling to which DeVoto could respond, and he developed close ties to all his teachers, particularly Byron Hurlbut. Another positive experience at Harvard came from being assigned to a mess with other "outsider" students (those from outside New England), with whom he naturally developed a sense of his unique background. It was his first awareness of what it might mean to be a westerner in a culture dominated and directed by eastern traditions.

World War I interrupted his education as it violently interrupted the culture of which he was a part. At first skeptical of United States involvement, DeVoto eventually enlisted and proudly earned his second lieutenant's bars at Camp Lee, Virginia. Hoping to be sent to France where he could bathe himself in glory in a typical adolescent's romantic vision, he was disappointed to learn that his boyish target practice sessions with a .22 rifle and pistol in the Wasatch Mountains had paid off all too well. He accumulated an excellent marksmanship record and was assigned to domestic service as a musketry instructor. Thus he spent the war stateside, ingloriously by his standards, until he could return to Harvard and graduate belatedly in 1920.

Instead of seeking employment with his new Harvard degree, DeVoto felt the creative energies of his aspiration as a writer and so returned to Ogden to help care for his now widowed father and to see if he could get something into print. Although probably not part of his plan, he also fell in and out of love more than once. That emotional turmoil, together with the difficulties of trying to write well day after day and break into print, led him repeatedly into depression, sometimes nearly to suicide.

Salvation, at least for the moment, came in 1922 when one of his Harvard teachers engineered an appointment for him as a writing instructor at Northwestern University. He taught there until 1927, and although he came to have harsh feelings toward the provincial values of the institution and its environment and resigned haughtily in 1927, throwing the university's offer of promotion to assistant professor back into its face, he should have seen his Northwestern years as an important developmental time in his career. It was there that he met his wife Avis, who became an intellectual and social alter ego that helped him establish his place in the society of Evanston and later Cambridge, as well as his larger role as a culture critic. He also established some undying friendships among fellow faculty members, particularly the historian Garrett Mattingly, who would advise and assist him in later years in vitally important ways as well as provide lively companionship over cocktails. Finally, it was during the Northwestern years that DeVoto broke into professional writing—two novels published and a third completed, as well as an impressive string of popular magazine articles, essays, stories, and reviews that far exceeded the expected output of a typical overworked young university instructor.

The 1920s was a significant period in American history by almost any standard, a confusing time of both conservatism and upheaval, of prosperity and poverty, of progress and pride on the one hand and oppression, intolerance, and disillusionment on the other. DeVoto's confused and inconsistent participation as both a spokesman for the era's skepticism and disillusionment and at the same time one of its bitterest critics, is a telling symbol of the nation's confusion.

One of the conspicuous cultural figures of the 1920s, and one who played a major role in DeVoto's life as he developed his ideas about American culture, was Henry Louis Mencken (1880–1956). H. L. Mencken was a lifelong resident of Baltimore and a newspaper writer, particularly for the *Baltimore Sun*, but his most important role in DeVoto's life—and in the life of the nation—was in his role as editor of the *American Mercury*, a monthly magazine of opinion. The federal census of 1920 had revealed that for the first time more Americans lived in some kind of urban community instead of on a farm, and Mencken became one of the leading proponents of the country's emerging urban sophistication. At the same time, he became a leading critic of what he identified as persistent rural values that inhibited the emergence of that sophistication. A brilliant, if extremely biased, satirical writer, Mencken hilariously hammered away in the pages of the *American Mercury* at what he called the "areas of cornbread and revival." Rural-minded people, in his view, dreamed of an anti-utopia in America of puritanical repression and Victorian prudery, a country of fundamentalist fanaticism, prohibition, censorship, and cultural banality. "They dream it," he wrote in "The Husbandman," his most famous diatribe against the farmer, "on their long journeys down the twelve billion furrows of their seven million farms, up hill and down dale in the heat of the day. They dream it behind the egg-stove on winter nights, their boots off and their socks scorching, Holy Writ in their hands."[10] And so on. Sophomoric but unfailingly entertaining, Mencken's prose kept the heat burning under the cultural wars between urban and rural America, the modern and the traditional, that wracked the country over and over again during the 1920s.

Bernard DeVoto, having only recently escaped from the repressive cultural environment of Ogden, Utah, found much to applaud in Mencken's diagnosis, and he shared Mencken's way with wickedly witty satire. He became a disciple. Although the two men apparently did not meet until the spring of 1928 when DeVoto's stint at the *American Mercury* was almost finished, and then only in a large dinner group, DeVoto was profoundly impressed with Mencken. "He looks like a hardware drummer—but God! how the man can talk," DeVoto reported. "Conversationally, even intellectually, it was the high point of my year. He, too, craves Devotian," he punned.[11]

In his Mencken mode during the late 1920s, DeVoto wrote three articles satirizing his home state and predictably bringing down its wrath. DeVoto had reviewed one of Mencken's books in the local Evanston, Illinois, newspaper while at Northwestern, but the piece that really got Mencken's attention was an article called "Ogden: The Underwriters of Salvation," written at Mencken's recommendation for *The Taming of the Frontier*, an anthology edited by a journalist named

Duncan Aikman. The article was, in Stegner's characterization, "bald scorn and name-calling, with enough fact in it to make it uncomfortable." Aikman submitted it for reprint in the *American Mercury*, and although Mencken found the piece too long for the magazine, he encouraged DeVoto to contribute something else. DeVoto responded with an even more satirical piece called simply "Utah," which ran in the March 1926 issue. To Mencken, who considered Utah one of the "cow states" for its rural provincialism and who surely found Mormon Utah a haven for fanatical fundamentalism, DeVoto's article was a dead center bull's-eye hit. And DeVoto had fired the biggest caliber in his arsenal. "This time," Stegner said, "he was not going to blow up a sentry post, he was going to bring the whole fortification down. . . . DeVoto's first substantial contribution to a national magazine, like his first novel and his first essay, would be an uninhibited attack on his amniotic home."[12]

It was the beginning of a brief but intense and significant publishing relationship. "Mencken was a recurrent jackpot," Stegner observes. "He poured out dimes and quarters every time DeVoto pulled the handle." The vivid metaphor is a bit misleading: DeVoto wrote eight articles for the *American Mercury*. Four of them appeared in that astonishingly productive year of 1926, then only one per year until 1930, when his last contribution was "The Centennial of Mormonism," about Utah's predominant religion if not the state itself. Nor was DeVoto himself entirely forthright about his *American Mercury* appearances. Writing in 1930 to Robert C. Elliott, an editor at the *Salt Lake Telegram* who challenged him about the factual basis for his Utah articles, DeVoto asserted that they had been a labor of love in pure pursuit of the truth, that he had made more than ten times the money writing for the *Saturday Evening Post*, but the *Post* would not print such caustically critical pieces. Actually, DeVoto did not begin hitting the high-paying markets like the *Post*, *Harper's*, and *Redbook* until November of 1927, after he had already pretty much had his say about Utah and Mormonism. More accurately, Mencken's *American Mercury* provided DeVoto with his first exposure in the pages of a major national magazine, an exposure he was glad to have for any amount, and his submissions declined only later, after more lucrative markets opened up for him.[13]

DeVoto's anti-Utah articles represent an important stage in his intellectual development and his establishment of a Menckenesque pole in his interpretation of rural America and the culture of the 1920s (he would establish another pole when he began the book that became *Mark Twain's America*). It is easy to see why the articles outraged Utah Mormons (though they reportedly delighted Msgr. Cushnahan, his old priest). The "Utah" article, as Stegner characterized it, was "a calculated piece of mayhem that out-Menckened Mencken, . . . spit out with vigor and venom that only the twenties or Bernard DeVoto, or the two in combination, could have generated."[14] "Ogden: The Underwriters of Salvation," however, is just as caustic. Ogden, DeVoto says, is "a small backwater American city," festering in the hideous squalor of its run-down buildings, which were outstandingly ugly even in their original condition. A traveler disembarking at Ogden's Union Station would be appalled. "What manner of folk, he wonders, what kind of Digger Indians, can suffer this daily assault upon the credo of Kiwanis?" Mormonism, Ogden's predominant religion, is "the most colorless of American heresies." Introduced to Utah by Brigham Young, "this low-comedy prophet," the religion consists of "equal parts of smugness, ignorance, and superstition." Devoid of any transcendent or aesthetic dimensions, Mormonism is completely materialistic in its culture, "a religion of this earth, a deification of produce and merchandise and high interest."[15]

As for Utah's artistic and cultural life, one could not expect much from a state settled by a "ruddy, illiterate, herd-minded folk[,] . . . a state where the very process of survival demanded a rigorous suppression of individuality, impracticability, scepticism, and all the other qualities of intelligence." The cultural sterility of the place taxed DeVoto's descriptive eloquence: "How am I to suggest the utter mediocrity of life in the new Utah? How can I suggest its poverty in everything that makes for civilization?" Not to force the Mormons alone to bear the brunt of the blame for Utah's artistic impoverishment, the Gentiles have their part as well. "No artist ever lived there ten minutes after he had the railroad fare out. If the presence of one should become known, the Mormons would damn him as a loafer and the Gentiles would lynch him as a profligate." Things in fact are hopeless. "Civilization does not exist in Utah. It never has existed there. It never will exist there."[16]

The reaction back home was predictably violent, though DeVoto with equal predictability exaggerated both its degree and duration. The second article, "Utah," seemed particularly offensive, as DeVoto later recalled. "It hit the local inferiority complex dead center. . . . I not only got the Church's curse in hundreds of columns, practically every paper in the state raised hell with me and went on raising hell for, literally, years."[17] DeVoto was anything but the first hostile critic of Utah and Mormonism, even from within the state and the church, and although his articles did indeed jostle the hornet's nest, Utah journalism found other issues than DeVoto's attacks to discuss during ensuing decades. Nevertheless, he was *persona non grata* whenever his name came up or one of his books was reviewed in Utah, and in time he found it expedient to issue a public apology for at least some of his more extreme characterizations. The reasons for that apology, its nature and extent, and even the degree to which it was an apology will be examined separately, but they need to be seen in the light of the thesis of his first great historical work, *Mark Twain's America*, in which DeVoto established the other pole of his thinking about rural American culture and its prevailing interpretation in the critical literature of the 1920s.

The disillusionment of the 1920s is one of the famous themes of that decade. It is important to realize, though, that disillusionment was largely confined to writers and intellectuals (though agricultural depression kept the farmers disgruntled as well). While mainstream working and middle-class Americans took advantage of the general prosperity of the Harding-Coolidge years to purchase homes, automobiles, radios, and bootlegged liquor, intellectuals lamented the failed promises of the Progressive movement and the popular backlash against its ideals, as well as the dangerously unstable and unjust resolution of World War I. Some disillusioned writers found the America of the Red Scare, the Sacco-Vanzetti case, the Ku Klux Klan, and the Scopes trial so repulsive that they left altogether and became what

Gertrude Stein called the "Lost Generation" in Paris. Those who remained behind, among whom were the Young Intellectuals such as Lewis Mumford, Waldo Frank, Malcolm Cowley, and Van Wyck Brooks, developed an unflattering view of American culture as dominated by puritanism and commercialism and essentially inimical to the life of the imagination.

Bernard DeVoto became the implacable opponent of the Young Intellectuals, of their interpretation of American culture in general and of the West in particular, of their view that a culture is defined by its literature and that literary critics can and should be reformers, and of their deductive method, which began by formulating a theory of culture and then searching the literature for supportive evidence. In his assault on the movement, DeVoto went directly for the taproot, Van Wyck Brooks, the finest mind of the group and its most eloquent and prolific spokesman. Born in 1886 and trained at Harvard, Brooks began his long career as a literary critic before World War I. Brooks supported himself primarily as an editor, first at Doubleday, Page and Co., then at the Century Co. His most lasting achievement is probably a three-volume literary history of nineteenth-century America: *The World of Washington Irving*, *The Flowering of New England*, and *New England: Indian Summer*. The book that most aroused DeVoto's ire, however, was his iconoclastic *The Ordeal of Mark Twain*, which appeared in 1920, the year in which DeVoto graduated from Harvard and embarked upon his literary career. DeVoto's lengthy assault on Brooks's ideas and the school of thought he represented almost became a vendetta. The assault began in 1932 with his *Mark Twain's America*, a thoroughgoing refutation of Brooks's Twain interpretation, and continued through a series of articles, speeches, and reviews, culminating with *The Literary Fallacy* in 1944. In these, DeVoto went after Brooks and the Young Intellectuals root and branch until he had demolished not only their conclusions, but their premises and methods as well.[18] As part of his larger project to Explain America, DeVoto first had to clear away the underbrush that obscured a proper view of the subject.

In Brooks's view, whatever literary power and ambition young Samuel Clemens may have had was emasculated by the culturally sterile frontier environment of Hannibal, Missouri, and its narrowly pragmatic values that allowed no place for the flowering of a genuine literary talent. His cultural "ordeal" began when his mother forced him as a young boy to swear on his father's casket that he would "amount to something" in the world, meaning that he would apply himself toward material success. Although he did achieve some success first as a printer, then as a newspaper writer in Nevada and California, any lofty literary ambitions he may have felt were constantly attenuated by his early oath and by the low level of the frontier audiences he had to reach as a writer. Thus, instead of becoming a Wordsworth or a Shelley, the cultural ceiling under which he operated kept him from becoming anything but an author of low frontier humor. Even after relocating during his mature years to Hartford, which one might assume to be a more salubrious cultural environment, Twain found his most creative impulses inhibited by his bowdlerizing wife and by genteel friends like William Dean Howells and Richard Watson Gilder, who kept cleaning up his writings to make them acceptable to Victorian audiences.

To DeVoto, this was all the sheerest nonsense. In the first place, Brooks was pontificating about something of which he had no knowledge: the rural West. "He had no knowledge of the frontier and considered none essential." Like the "Saturday Club," the group of New England literary pundits among whom Twain tried to find a place, unsuccessfully because they perceived his western manners and humor as barbaric, Brooks was "rich in ignorance of the world outside." Even though books and libraries, literary clubs, and higher education were scarce in the rural West, their lack did not necessarily indicate cultural sterility, any more than their presence would guarantee cultural vitality. "That the villagers were not too enlightened is apparent," DeVoto argued. "[T]hat they were therefore fools or savages or Puritans is a judgment that lacks a probably desirable logic." What Hannibal *did* have was a rich tradition of native western folklore and humor, all of which Brooks ignored, and out of which Twain fashioned, as Emerson had urged in 1837 in *The American Scholar*, an authentically American literature based on indigenous American materials. And, being located on the Mississippi River, the greatest artery of the American continent, Hannibal gave Twain an unparalleled access to humanity. "The vast life of a vast nation existed there," DeVoto pointed out. "And floating downstream came every variant of human experience. . . . When Samuel Clemens grew up and went tirelessly about the world, he found no one, he said, whom he had not met before on the river." Brooks, furthermore, had failed to understand Twain's literary aspirations. "It is not that Mark Twain never became anything but a humorist, realist, and satirist of the frontier; he never desired to be anything else . . . yet it is Mr. Brooks's strange thesis that Clemens really wanted to be Shelley."[19]

At the base of Brooks's misconception of Twain was a misconceived method of doing literary history. The Young Intellectuals, appalled at the stultifying materialism of the age of Harding and Coolidge that had caused the expatriation of some of America's best literary talent, had read their own cultural frustration with the present back into history and assumed that American culture had at all times and in all places been oppressive to literary aspiration. DeVoto properly identified this as a deductive method in which one begins with a theory and then marshals facts that support the theory. Although we shall see that DeVoto himself was no dilettante when it came to grand theorizing, he always presented himself as a man of facts, of hard empiricism, and a skeptic of anything not firmly grounded in reality. "Beautiful thinking," DeVoto called such theorizing, and he warned at the outset of *Mark Twain's America* that he had not "adventured far into literary criticism," for "that department of beautiful thinking is too insulated from reality for my taste." The basic flaw of Brooks's book was that he had presented a theory as a representation of reality, one which could not be consistently sustained by the facts. "A literary theory is a form of metaphysical autobiography. It permits its contriver to reconstruct facts in harmony with his prepossessions. . . . But when a set of notions arranged in the form of a literary system is submitted as objective truth, a description of something, it must accept sterner criteria." Throughout his career, nothing raised DeVoto's blood pressure quicker or higher than "beautiful thinking," or "great thinking," as he sometimes called it—lofty ideas ungrounded in fact. "Although I have not read the complete works of Mr. [Bruce] Bliven, I have read those of Mr. [Lewis] Mumford," he wrote to the historian Crane Brinton, "and as God is my guide, Mumford is the greatest great thinker to think greatly in my time. . . . I bet you that Lewis can think greater from a standing start in one page than Bruce can in twenty."[20]

The Brooks debate aside, *Mark Twain's America* was a serious, major book that earned DeVoto his first real national reputation. "For him or against him," Stegner says, "people did not ignore this one. They paid attention to it as they had paid attention to none of his novels."[21] Even though the book was significant in establishing DeVoto as a bold, reckless controversialist—a characteristic of all his writing—it was much more. In making his arguments, DeVoto established his insistent demand that all theory had to be grounded in fact, indeed had to *originate* in fact. Literary criticism, he maintained (not altogether validly), is a basically unscientific undertaking, the essence of which is theory and opinion. But if one ventures to present those theories and opinions as fact—if one claims to be writing history—then the inductive, empirical method is necessary. Finally, *Mark Twain's America* established DeVoto as a major spokesman for the West—if you will, in Alfred Kazin's sneer, a "professional Westerner."[22]

By the time *Mark Twain's America* appeared, DeVoto was back in Cambridge. His productivity while at Northwestern encouraged him to reject a promotion and to strike out on his own as a freelance writer. Cambridge offered intellectual stimulation and a social life among the Harvard faculty and students, access to the immense resources of the Widener Library, and close proximity to publishing outlets both in Boston and New York City. He was to spend most of the rest of his life there, as a part-time instructor at Harvard (1929–1936) and as an editor, columnist, and cultural commentator as well as a western historian.

At the same time DeVoto was settling down physically in the East, *Mark Twain's America* was pulling him intellectually back to the West. Although he eventually apologized, in at least a left-handed way, for some of the extreme language with which he had denounced his home town and state, DeVoto never abandoned his basic assessment of the backwardness and cultural sterility he observed there. At the same time, his love for the canyons of the Wasatch Mountains kept drawing his heart back. His thrill at the realization, as he studied western history, that his youthful hikes and camping trips had retraced the moccasin prints of the Indians and the mountain men whom he idolized, impressed him with an awareness of the area's central place in the drama of western history. Some of the most heartfelt and poetic passages in his later writings are evocations of the natural beauty and historical significance of his homeland. DeVoto "loved the west but not the westerners," Arthur M. Schlesinger, Jr. observed.[23] In the end, it was Ogden and Utah that gave him the place to stand and the lever with which he moved the world.

In addition, although DeVoto may not have been the kind of mind that needed enemies (though he had plenty of them), he certainly needed a foil. DeVoto was not comfortable making his points on their own merits; he was best when making them *against* someone or something. When he was in Ogden, he implicitly used eastern cultural sophistication as a point of comparison from which he lambasted Utah backwardness. When he moved to Cambridge, he became the homespun wise man from the West who, between bites of locusts and wild honey, explained the rest of the country to the rubes at Harvard. In one scene (the literary term is appropriate, as we shall see) in *Across the Wide Missouri*, DeVoto's great history of the fur trade, he has the Boston merchant Nathaniel Wyeth trying to explain the religion of the Flathead Indians to Jason Lee, the prospective Methodist missionary from Massachusetts. He describes them as Deists, DeVoto says, "which might barely bring them within the understanding of Boston."

Wyeth himself, in Cambridge seeking information about the fur trade before his own departure for the far West, ran up against "a resolute lack of interest in the rude and distant region where it was conducted, which made his study difficult, [and which] has been bequeathed through generations of Cambridge librarians down to today." Wyeth's plan, derived from "the wretched Western material of Cambridge libraries," was to base a business on salmon from Oregon and furs from the Rocky Mountains. It looked foolproof on paper but eventually failed in the face of competition from the shrewd western fur entrepreneurs who had preceded him. "Nat Wyeth lived in Cambridge, and in Cambridge the world has always seemed simpler, more high-minded, and more amenable to reason than it proves to be when one goes out to mingle with the children of darkness."[24]

Most effectively and memorably, DeVoto Explained America in a magnificent trilogy of histories of the exploration, acquisition, and settlement of the American West: *The Year of Decision 1846* (1943); *Across the Wide Missour*i (1947); and *The Course of Empire* (1952). Like James Fenimore Cooper's fictional biography of his frontiersman Natty Bumppo in *The Leatherstocking Tales* (DeVoto would not have cared for the comparison), which tells the story backwards from old age to youth, DeVoto's trilogy of the trans-Mississippi West moves backwards from the completion of the United States's transcontinental empire with the Oregon treaty and the Mexican War in 1846, through the heyday of the Rocky Mountain fur trade in the 1830s, to the earliest Spanish explorations of the mainland of the Gulf of Mexico, the struggles of the French, the British, and the Americans for North America, and the progress of Lewis and Clark to the Pacific Coast of Oregon in 1805. As DeVoto found his sea legs in his transition from novelist to historian, his purview progressively widened, from the microscopic focus of one year (1846), to a decade (the 1830s), and finally to a sprawling epic across several hundred years.

It would be difficult to overestimate the significance of DeVoto's trilogy in western and indeed in American historiography. Its significance is not in originality of research, for although DeVoto exhibited a virtuosity in his mastery of the primary sources (less thorough, of course, as he moved back in time and covered increasing expanses of material), his histories are syntheses whose originality lies in their general thesis and their methods rather than in their presentation of new data. Although disapproved of and even vilified by traditional historians possessing what Wallace Stegner calls "the monographic mentality," DeVoto's works were devoured by general readers and more adventuresome scholars. DeVoto, who had been only a marginally successful novelist, found his true calling in applying to history the fictional techniques he could never completely master for fiction.

While religiously respecting the factual record, DeVoto found that he could "make a fact go a long ways," as his friend Robert Frost said. For one thing, DeVoto could recognize a dramatic, defining moment in history, and when he found a good scene, he would draw it out and milk its dramatic potential to the maximum. "No point in putting a silencer on the gun when you shoot a sheriff," he told Stegner. Similarly, he had an eye for giant-size characters whom he could portray in equally dramatic terms. "Drums should have rolled and trumpets sounded," he wrote at the point in his narrative where Mormon Apostle George A. Smith brought mountain man James Bridger into the main camp to meet Brigham Young, "or the supernatural stage management of this millennial creed should have provided signs from on high, for the Mormons had now met the master of these regions, their final authority."[25] Also, DeVoto brought to the writing of history narrative techniques previously employed only in fiction: simultaneity, in which the seamless fabric of history is simulated by rapidly shifting the narrative flow from one character to another, and synecdoche, in which a part stands for the whole, as the year 1846 or the career of the mountain man James Clyman stand for the disparate forces that promoted and participated in the westward movement. Finally, DeVoto knew how to gather his immense flock of factual details into an easily comprehensible whole. While the myopia of the "monographic mentality" carefully assembled a new factual apparatus but timidly shrank from the risk of attaching too much significance to it, DeVoto boldly rushed in and explained it all in unmistakable terms. His cavalier rounding off of history's rough edges and leapfrogging of inconvenient chasms may have frustrated and even outraged the scholars whose careful research had disclosed unsettling complexities, but DeVoto's histories made sense to the general reader. They *explained* things, and he quickly tapped into a public that was hungry for clear meanings and ready to grasp them while leaving the scholar to pan the gold dust out of history's finer sands.

All three books in DeVoto's trilogy share the same grandiose and controversial thesis, which unites the trilogy despite the diverseness of its chronological span. That thesis is there is an essential geographic unity of the area that became the empire of the United States and that the American people's exploration, occupation, and defense of that territory and its unity against secession and the Civil War was an inevitable necessity. The thesis is vulnerable to challenge at any number of points, beginning with DeVoto's assertion of geographic unity of a vast continental expanse crossed by mountain ranges and drained in every direction by rivers that seem to divide as much as unify. The inevitability of expansion and western settlement appeared deterministic in spite of DeVoto's protestations to the contrary. The idea of Manifest Destiny, which repelled most historians because of its jingoism, appealed to DeVoto. While he did not refer to *God's* will as justification, he saw it nevertheless as the American people's natural and logical expansion into what was clearly theirs. Finally, DeVoto saw the Civil War as inherent in western expansion because it forced the issue of slavery, that totem of the schism between two rival civilizations—the antiquated and increasingly moribund South and the vital, progressive North—a schism that must yield to an American unity if the nation were to survive and realize the potential suggested by its geography.[26]

The first volume of the trilogy, *The Year of Decision 1846*, was quintessential DeVoto, in which all the novelistic devices of his historical writing were evident: synecdoche, simultaneity, vivid characterization and narrative, and grandiose thesis. When the name of Bernard DeVoto comes up, *The Year of Decision* comes most readily to mind. Since this was the first appearance of the characteristic DeVoto approach and it appeared, because of DeVoto's hell-for-leather forwardness in presenting it, to be a frontal assault on conventional historical writing, the book became a lightning rod for criticism as neither of the later books did.

Most of the criticism seemed to focus on the title, which to a casual reading appeared to be a thesis: that the year 1846 possessed a unique significance in American and western history. "*A* year of decision, yes," says Wallace Stegner in summary of DeVoto's critics on that point. "A very important year. But other years just as crucial in our history might have been picked; any year closely scrutinized becomes a year of decision."[27] Or any person, he might have added, pointing out a corresponding peril of biography when a single person is made to stand for an era. Before long, this criticism had found form in a proverbial retort that has echoed through university history departments to this day, that the only thing unique about the year 1846 is that it was the only year that fell between 1845 and 1847. But a closer reading of DeVoto's introduction (or a better introduction) would have defanged that objection, for it should have been clear that DeVoto was not stating a thesis, but rather explaining a literary device: synecdoche. "This book tells the story of some people who went west in 1846," DeVoto says. "But 1846 is chosen rather than other years because 1846 best dramatizes personal experience as national experience. . . . The origins of some of them [the year's events], it is true, can be traced back as far as one may care to go, and a point of the book is that the effects of some are with us still, operating in the arc determined by 1846. Nevertheless, the book may properly be regarded as the chronicle of a turning point in American destiny within the limits of one year." What DeVoto had found, then, was a literary device—an opportunity to *dramatize* the theme of the westward movement by focusing on the events of one year. In retrospect, DeVoto could probably have saved himself some trouble by using the term synecdoche and defining it as he applied it to historical writing. But he did not. In fact, he may not have been aware of the term. It was Wallace Stegner, whose academic training in literature far exceeded DeVoto's, who recognized the device and identified it as synecdoche. Unfortunately, few of DeVoto's readers recognized it either, and their misunderstanding has perpetuated a misconception of his purpose. "The only real mistake in the whole book," said Dale Morgan in Stegner's paraphrase, "was the title, which threw the emphasis on a doubtful generalization and diverted attention from the brilliant re-creation of individual people and events."[28]

"The story of some people who went west in 1846" was DeVoto's tongue-in-cheek understatement of what is actually a dazzling panorama of diverse individuals, groups, motives, and expectations, all recounted in DeVoto's vivid prose and with his eye for telling detail brought forth from his complete mastery of his sources. The Mormons' expulsion from Nauvoo and the beginning of their migration to the Great Basin (DeVoto cannot resist fudging ahead into 1847 to tell the whole story); the onset of the Mexican War (which he again tells in full military and diplomatic detail to 1848); the settlement of the Oregon Question; the Oregon, California, and Santa Fe Trails; the marches of the Mormon Battalion and Alexander Doniphan's Missourians; the California intrigues of John C. Fremont, Robert Stockton, and Stephen Watts Kearny; and the mountain men who served as guides and sources of information to most of the above—all of these, whose stories DeVoto narrates as groups and symbolizes in a series of smaller synecdoches, are the substance of *The Year of Decision*.

DeVoto also mentions people and events outside the West, for his goal was to demonstrate the role of the West in forging a nation. As John L. Thomas points out, *The Year of Decision* was written while America fought for its life during the early years of World War II, and DeVoto wanted to explore the roots of America's nationhood and to defend it. To him, American nationalism was a western story.[29] Accordingly, he brings in the occasional observation from Henry David Thoreau, who was in the midst of his sojourn at Walden Pond, and he recounts the ups and downs of the utopian community at Brook Farm, whose anemic idealism stood in pathetic contrast to its western counterpart, the Mormons, whose muscular millennialism was on its way to build Zion in the mountains. Completing the background is the politics and international relations that created the legislative and diplomatic expressions of what DeVoto regarded as an irresistible folk movement into the continental interior.

DeVoto's perennial nemeses reappear: the Great Thinkers of the eastern literary establishment in the form of their intellectual ancestors, the airy idealists at Brook Farm who "will accept no hybrid of brute and angel; they desire Utopia and will not settle for the human race. They love the people but they hate the mob." They were good people, the Associators at Brook Farm, but naive: "generous, high-minded, self-sacrificing people, literary folk mostly, who felt the world's pain and lacked a sense of reality." The Mormons, DeVoto believed, for all the bogus history of the *Book of Mormon*, the bizarre theology, and labyrinthine bureaucracy, nevertheless had what the Associators lacked: a genuine feeling of community forged by their history and welded by the iron authority of their priesthood. "They were members of one another much more truly than Brook Farm—and may leave our history the moral that Association needs the lowest social denominator."[30]

The Mormons, of course, do not pass through DeVoto's pages unscathed by his corrosive wit. "From the beginning they have had the complete smugness of a people on whom a monopoly of truth and virtue had been conferred by Almighty God," DeVoto rails. Only Brigham Young's despotic authority had forged a sense of community out of the sheep scattered by the death of Joseph Smith, who had left them only "the cheap story of the golden plates and the colonization of the American continent by emigrants from Jerusalem, the mumbo-jumbo of illiterate, semi-Biblical, degraded Masonic rituals, the apocalyptic nonsense of the Mormon metaphysics." When the Boston Brahmin Francis Parkman, descendant of New England ministers in the Puritan tradition, was mistaken for a Mormon out on the Oregon Trail, he "suffered no greater indignity anywhere in the West."[31]

And finally, the "literary men," the intellectual progenitors of Van Wyck Brooks and the Young Intellectuals, are represented by the likes of Parkman, John C. Fremont, and Lansford W. Hastings, the California promoter whose shortcut on the California Trail—the Hastings Cutoff—the Donner party followed to their tragic end. "Realism," DeVoto observes in what could have been an epigraph on a chapter about "literary men" in the West, "is the most painful, most difficult, and slowest of human faculties." Accordingly, Parkman followed part of the Oregon Trail in pursuit of examples of his Rousseauian idealization of American Indians, but for all his close contact with real Indians never really saw them for what they were. Nor could he appreciate the largest *volkwanderung* in modern history in the form of the Mormons and Oregon emigrants, whose unwashed proletarian exteriors offended his genteel senses and sensibilities. Thus Parkman both witnessed and participated "in one of the greatest national experiences" without understanding "the smallest part of it." The "parochialism of his class" blinded him to that movement "and we lost a great book." It was the same book we lost when Van Wyck Brooks failed to understand the ferment of folk culture that produced Mark Twain, and as Don D. Walker observes, it is "too bad he [DeVoto] couldn't also have claimed Van Wyck Brooks as Parkman's great grand nephew."[32]

John C. Fremont was "primarily a literary man . . . who had a literary wife." [DeVoto's ellipses] His fecund literary imagination created, it is important to note, a fanciful image of the West, for his reports "were adventure books, they were charters of Manifest Destiny, they were texts of navigation for the uncharted sea so many dreamed of crossing, they were a pageant of daring, endurance, and high endeavor in the country of peaks and unknown rivers." Moreover, Fremont's literary impulses created John C. Fremont, a figure of Byronic scope whom DeVoto refers to repeatedly as "Childe Harold" or "The Conqueror" among less flattering terms like "popinjay" and "Major Jinks of the Horse Marines." Fremont's self-image, unfortunately, was not confirmed in reality. From the beginning of his third expedition of 1845–46 and especially on his last two less fruitful, even pathetic, ones, Fremont "was to go, always subtly, astray. Nothing came out quite the way it should have done. Lord Byron, who had imagined him, could not make him rhyme."[33]

Hastings, whose popular piece of California promotional literature, *The Emigrants' Guide to Oregon and California*, had proposed the infamous Hastings Cutoff south of the Great Salt Lake and across the salt flats, was "a Fremont in miniature. . . . Whatever was in his mind, he did not have quite enough stuff. Put him down as a smart young man who wrote a book—it is not a unique phenomenon in literature—without knowing what he was talking about."[34] Not only a Fremont in miniature, in other words, but a diminutive Van Wyck Brooks as well.

Rarely, if ever, had an American historian been so *present* in his work. Not only was he present in his antipathies, but in his loves as well. Anticipating the objection that the grisly story of the Donner party is recounted in such detail that it overbalances DeVoto's narrative of the other characters, he forthrightly admits that the pathos of the story exerts a claim for more space. His real reason, though, is that he grew up in the Wasatch Mountains and along the edge of the Great Salt Lake desert that impeded the Donners' progress and sealed their doom, and he could not resist indulging his youthful fascination.[35] The book also contains one of the most beautiful passages DeVoto ever wrote, giving tribute to the deep love his homeland embeds in its residents by its harshness: "It has its hideousness, it has its beauty, nor are they separated in the depths of any mind that has known them. A hard, resistant folk had found a hard, resistant land, and they would grow to fit one another. Remember that the yield of a hard country is a love deeper than a fat and easy land inspires, that throughout the arid West the Americans have found a secret treasure."[36]

To the frustration of the unimaginative professional historian and to the delight of the general reader, DeVoto brought to his dramatization of history all the fictional techniques he had only marginally developed in his novels. Although he had loved to ridicule the Mormons for seeing signs and portents in the heavens confirming the rightness of their cause, DeVoto himself used such phenomena with telling effect to create a mood in his histories. In *Mark Twain's America* he had noted (with prompting from Twain himself) the coincidental appearance of Halley's Comet in Twain's birth and death years as brackets to his life. *The Year of Decision* opens with two such portents early in 1846: a group of Santa Fe traders shocked to see the shape of an eagle silhouetted against the red sun along the horizon after a thundershower, and another comet, Biela's, streaking around the earth and breaking in two. The appearance of the American eagle in the west and the simultaneous shattering in two of a dramatic heavenly body thus introduced the themes of the book: Manifest Destiny and its concomitant, sectional division and civil war.

Simultaneity in DeVoto's narrative was another revolutionary device as applied to history. DeVoto stumbles into it, however, and he warns his readers at the outset that in order to get to the action they must endure a lengthy period of scene-setting. "In getting it [the narrative] under way," he warns, "I have chosen the stern but kinder way of throwing at him a first chapter of grievous weight. If he survives that, he will find things happening from then on." That first chapter, "Build Thee More Stately Mansions," does indeed separate the sheep from the goats, and one wonders how many potential readers have not persevered. Those who have, though, have found DeVoto as good as his word. Things from that point on not only happen, they happen in a realistic manner rare in historical writing, for DeVoto performs an amazing feat of juggling a half-dozen or more stories at the same time. Realizing that what he was doing was unprecedented, DeVoto asked the reader for active participation. "It is required of you only to bear in mind that while one group is spotlighted the others are not isolated from it in significance." DeVoto asked readers to exert a literary form of persistence of vision, the ocular phenomenon that makes a series of still images appear to move continuously in a motion picture. And the device works with dazzling success in DeVoto's hands. Witness the culmination of the book, when David Wilmot, representative from Pennsylvania, introduces the Wilmot Proviso, a rider to the appropriations bill for the Mexican War requiring that slavery be banned from any territory acquired as a result of the war. As Wilmot rises to speak, DeVoto makes in one page a dramatic gallop all the way around his herd of characters, reminding his readers exactly where all the characters are and what their role has been in creating the American empire that must deal with the fateful issue Wilmot is about to address. Riding back into camp, DeVoto reports that "slavery was out of the closet, and it was going to stay out. . . . David Wilmot . . . had made A. Lincoln President of the United States."[37]

Across the Wide Missouri, the second volume in the trilogy and the one sometimes regarded as DeVoto's masterpiece, is a book he almost missed writing. Wallace Stegner has told the story of the tangled negotiations among two (perhaps three, depending on how one counts) publishers and three difficult people, including DeVoto himself, and the tale merits only the briefest of summaries here.[38] In 1935, Mrs. Mae Reed Porter, a wealthy art collector in St. Louis, purchased from the Peale Museum in Baltimore approximately one hundred watercolors by Baltimore artist Alfred Jacob Miller, which he had painted in 1837 during a trip to the Rocky Mountains as part of the entourage of Scottish baron William Drummond Stewart. At least vaguely aware that the paintings had some historical significance, Mrs. Porter fell under the influence of one Emery Reves, a Hungarian emigre, literary agent, and proprietor of a defunct publishing firm called Hyperion Press. He persuaded her to allow him to approach Houghton Mifflin as her agent with a proposal to publish some of the paintings as a collaborative project with Hyperion, with a historical introduction by her. During the negotiations, the name of Bernard DeVoto came up as a qualified western historian who might be engaged to write some twenty thousand words of captions for the paintings.

DeVoto's examination of the paintings led him to the conclusion that they were a priceless historical record of the Rocky Mountain fur trade during its climax, and that a mere twenty thousand words of captions would not begin to do justice to their significance. What was needed, he urged, was nothing less than a major book, a comprehensive history of the fur trade in which exhaustive research in the primary sources would be added to the record of Miller's paintings and brought to bear upon their interpretation. Several significant obstacles needed to be overcome, however, in order to amplify the Porter-Reves proposal to DeVoto's proportions. For one thing, DeVoto was under contract with Little, Brown, and an arrangement would have to be made with them if he were to write for Houghton Mifflin. He was "loaned" to the latter firm for the project, but the happy result for him was that he was so pleased with Houghton Mifflin's handling of the book that he shifted to them permanently. The other two obstacles were Reves and Porter. Although Reves was "an operator," as Stegner characterizes him, a character worthy of one of DeVoto's books, he did have impressive connections in the literary world and a valid record as a publisher. But DeVoto distrusted him for what appeared to be his scheme to use his Hyperion Press, which existed on paper only, as a lever to gain, through "collaborative" publishing with Houghton Mifflin, more than the agent's fee to which he was entitled. Eventually, through complex negotiations, Reves's interest was bought out for a lesser fee, and his involvement ended. Mrs. Porter, whom DeVoto found to be the rankest of amateurs as a historian, continued to the end of the project as DeVoto's putative "collaborator" because of a packet of "research material" she had provided on Miller and the fur trade at the beginning of the project, material DeVoto soon discarded as being too uncritical and inaccurate to be helpful. Although her sole contributions to the project were making the paintings available to DeVoto and writing a foreword recounting her acquisition of them, DeVoto found himself bedeviled by her claim to a share of the Pulitzer and Bancroft prizes. He sharply rejected this claim in a letter reprising her limited role in the making of the book. If DeVoto had not regarded himself as almost predestined to write the book, his frustrations with Reves and Porter might have caused him to abandon the project. Fortunately he persevered, and history is much the richer for it.

Although the literary devices that had characterized *The Year of Decision* also appear in *Across the Wide Missouri*, the second book provoked much less criticism and elicited more admiration. Its more favorable reception was probably because the shock of the earlier volume had dissipated, and fair-minded readers had come to accept the validity of some of DeVoto's methods. *Across the Wide Missouri* also covered a longer period, from 1832 to 1838, and the device of synecdoche this time appears in the form of the Stewart expeditions over several years rather than in one year, 1846. The seven-year period seems to be an optimum scope for DeVoto's methods. While the narrow focus of the earlier book permitted an impressive mastery of the sources, it overplayed the historical significance of the single year it treated. On the other hand, *The Course of Empire*, the last volume in the trilogy, which is global in scope and sweeping in time span, is necessarily based in large part on the secondary literature, and the intimate knowledge of characters and events that is the hallmark of the earlier volumes is lost.

In *Across the Wide Missouri*, DeVoto's methods have their own virtues and weaknesses in comparison with their application in *The Year of Decision*. The larger synecdoche tying the whole story together in this case is the expeditions of the Scottish sportsman William Drummond Stewart, who journeyed repeatedly to the Rocky Mountains in the 1830s. The trips themselves were of such minor historical significance that they seem a frail reed upon which to rest the whole story of the fur trade, geographic exploration, missionary work, race relations, and other themes DeVoto treats. That the reed does sustain the weight is evidence that the synecdoche does not express a dubious thesis, and that DeVoto's readers had learned to recognize a literary device for what it was and not to yield to the temptation to make it into something larger.

DeVoto's narrative technique, if anything, demands more of the reader here than in the earlier book. Even though the simultaneity of *The Year of Decision* required visualization of several different developments at once, one was aided by the differences among those developments: it was impossible to confuse the Mormons with Zachary Taylor's expeditionary force or the Bear Flaggers or the mountain men. Confusion is more likely in *Across the Wide Missouri* because much of the story is about the competition among the various fur companies, their field parties, forts, and supply trains. All of these groups were made up of the same types of people, and their personnel sometimes shifted from one group to another, so that the reader almost needs to keep a scorecard. Moreover, DeVoto employs flashbacks, not a conspicuous feature of the earlier book, which further tax the reader's attention, particularly the lengthy one at the beginning of the book. While the reader is trying to get acquainted with the characters of 1833, the scene steps back to stage-setting events in 1832 for two entire chapters before returning to the first date.

The case that *Across the Wide Missouri* is a masterpiece can be made by examining several themes that were present in *The Year of Decision* but which achieve full development in the second book. Although no scholar has yet noted it, DeVoto's interpretive perspective in *Across the Wide Missouri* is more compatible with the so-called "New Western History" that emerged in the 1980s than with the historiography of his own day. For one thing, although DeVoto admired the work of Frederick Jackson Turner and used his ideas in his interpretation of Mark Twain, he largely ignored the Turner thesis in his books about the far West, focusing instead, as we shall explore in a supplementary essay, on the West as a place rather than a process. Also, DeVoto treats the women in his story, both Indian and Anglo, as full human beings rather than simply as companions to their husbands. From Susan McGoffin in *The Year of Decision* to missionaries Narcissa Whitman and Eliza Spaulding and the often nameless Indian women who played a vital social and economic role in the Indian communities and trappers' camps in *Across the Wide Missouri*, he is careful to explore the uniqueness of their experiences in the West. Further, DeVoto was already developing his thesis of the West as the "plundered province," whose natural resources and indigenous inhabitants were victims of exploitation by eastern economic and religious interests with no regard for ecological imbalance and cultural destruction. Finally, DeVoto realized that a major part of western history was Indian history, that Indians were human beings with rich cultural traditions and valid claims to self-determination rather than simply obstacles to the progress of Anglo-American civilization.[39]

DeVoto's view of the Indians, to be sure, was not enlightened even by the anthropological standards of his own day and certainly not by those of ours. He saw them uncritically through the eyes of the mountain men and emigrants, and he achieved a critical objectivity only when examining the motivations and consequences of the missionaries and their work. Characteristic of DeVoto's view was an evolutionary hierarchy that placed Indians on a scale of worth according to how closely their culture resembled Anglo culture. Thus the Shoshonean peoples to whom the mountain men referred as "Diggers" were lowest on the scale, the more "civilized" Maricopas and Pimas of southern Arizona occupied a sort of middle position, and the Indians of the plains and Rockies were highest of all. It was exactly the kind of prejudice, placed on another scale, for which DeVoto excoriated Parkman, whom he accused of looking for Cooper or Rousseau among the Sioux.

DeVoto made no attempt to conceal his contempt for the Diggers or to find anything redeeming in their culture. "Theirs was the most miserable life lived in North America since the ice retreated," he tells us, and, while deploring the wholesale massacre of a group of them by mountain man Joseph Reddeford Walker's men, he recognized its necessity. "It is hard to see what else he could have done. Some of his men who had killed no Indians before enjoyed this cheap victory and that is repulsive. But it does not diminish the fact that Walker's action was necessary." When the Donners passed through the same country they could expect no succor from the Diggers, whose "half-gram brains [were] vibrating with the remembered murders of hundreds of kinsmen and with desire for oxen and other plunder." DeVoto considers their culture analogous to that of unskilled factory workers—"the technologically unemployed"—losers in competition with other Indians and whose loss had included loss of cultural and even physical vitality. Passing over to the western slope of the Sierras, the Walker party slaked their hunger on giant acorns harvested "by the somewhat more developed Diggers who lived here and whom Joe did not slaughter." (One generosity begets another.) Jumping ahead once again to 1846, Stephen Watts Kearny's men found the next step on the hierarchy represented by the Maricopas and Pimas, "jovial, sedentary Indians who had established about the best social adaptation to this country that has so far been worked out." His men "decided that they surpassed many of the Christian nations in agriculture, were but little behind them in the useful arts, 'and immeasurably before them in honesty and virtue.'" (Here, then, is where Parkman should have been looking for his noble savages.) Finally, reaching the pinnacle of Indian evolution in the plains and Rockies tribes, DeVoto acknowledges that "a modern student knows that he cannot avoid using a white man's measuring rod" in evaluating the Indians, and so he plies it with a vengeance, creating a cultural hierarchy even among those tribes. "[T]he Crows, the Cheyennes, and the Arapahos outranked the Sioux," and the top rung of the ladder was occupied by the Nez Perce, who were "superior Indians." Why? Because "they made no trouble, they liked and admired white men."[40]

Though he held a high opinion of the Indians of the plains and Rockies, DeVoto had no sympathy for the guilty white liberals who idealized them in order to make the white man's destruction and dispossession of the Indian appear more deplorable than it was. "I feel to the full the barbarous injustice of the white man's dealing with them and especially that of the American white man," he wrote to art critic Holger Cahill. "At the same time," he added, "I believe that up to a very small tolerance of possibility, what happened was historically inevitable. . . . [W]hat did happen, or something only very slightly different from it, must happen." While accepting the integrity and validity of the cultures of the various Indian tribes, DeVoto refused to idealize them. "I respect and honor the Indians' fight for their country and I have tried whenever I have written about them to do justice not only to their cause but also to their ways of thinking. I do believe that we tend to make many mistakes about the Indians out of our own sense of guilt and that some of the most liberal and advanced ideas about Indians today are in fact sentimental and unsound."[41]

In the same letter, DeVoto focuses much of his wrath about the inhuman treatment of the Indians on the Protestant missionaries who play a large role in *Across the Wide Missouri*. "I believe the Spanish were the worst, the French the best, and the English and the Americans the most non-human if not inhuman [in their treatment of the Indians]. I instinctively despise all efforts to Christianize primitive peoples but especially those whose real motive was economic." Clearly he is referring here to missionaries like the Methodist Jason Lee, whom he considered to be "the missionary as advance guard of empire. . . . It was

Jason Lee who gave the orders but it was Manifest Destiny that cast the vote." In contrast with the Presbyterians Marcus Whitman and Samuel Parker, whom DeVoto tentatively accepts for their willingness to bring medical care and other assistance to the Indians while attempting to convert them, Lee saw that cultural destruction had to precede religious conversion. Therefore, according to DeVoto's interpretation, Lee set up his mission in the Willamette Valley as a station where Indians could be turned into white people "by transforming a migratory society to a sedentary one, shifting a hunting economy to agriculture, and thereafter erasing everything in the neolithic consciousness so that nineteenth-century white culture and the grace of God could flow across it like the color in a wash drawing."[42]

One of the most delightful aspects of *Across the Wide Missouri* is the generous collection of paintings and drawings by Alfred Jacob Miller and others such as Charles Bodmer and George Catlin that are interspersed in groups throughout the volume. It was those paintings, after all, that inspired the book, and it is easy to see why DeVoto and his many readers have found them so engaging. They are all the more remarkable when one recalls that they were not conceived as finished works, and in fact many were tossed off in a hurry under pressure of time or other circumstances unfavorable for art. Although they were only sketches intended to serve as visual reminders for finished oil paintings Stewart had commissioned Miller to paint for his Scottish castle, the watercolors, some dark and moody, others bright and open, are aesthetically pleasing in their own right. Moreover, they are unique and invaluable primary sources that document the history of the fur trade at its peak, some of them providing the only views we have of the original Fort Laramie, the young James Bridger, the mountain man Joseph Reddeford Walker, and the daily life and work of various Indian tribes.

Equally instructive, if not even more so, are the almost excerptible essays DeVoto includes on various aspects of life in the Rocky Mountains. They are little verbal cadenzas, displays of virtuosity, in which DeVoto exhibits his expertise while he vividly instructs. Similar essays, such as DeVoto's answer to the taunt of the Whigs, who in 1844 had asked, "Who is James K. Polk?" regarding the dark horse Democratic presidential candidate, or his "Outline of American history" on the continental career of mountain man James Clyman,[43] had been part of the narrative technique of *The Year of Decision*. The essays were rapid-fire recitations of facts, like a violinist's cascade of sixty-fourth notes, at the end of which DeVoto could proudly stand back with his arms folded and say, like the orchestra's final fortissimo chord, "That's who James K. Polk was." In *Across the Wide Missouri*, the essays do not generally focus on individuals as they did in the earlier volume, but rather on institutions and ways of life within which the chronological narrative takes place. They are instructional rather than exhibitionist—little tutorials in which DeVoto takes the reader by the hand and leads him out into a clearing in the woods and explains the way things are. One thinks in particular of chapter four, "Paul Bunyan's Fair," in which he explains the annual rendezvous—not only its drinking, fighting, and copulating so dear to so many popular accounts of the fur trade, but also its hard-fisted economic exploitation, complete with prices and profit margins. Or chapter seven, "The Winter Lodge," in which DeVoto details the bone-chilling realities of setting a beaver trap in a wintry mountain stream and preparing pelts and curing provisions for the winter, with acknowledgement of the vital role of the Indian women who took up with the trappers not only as wives or concubines but also as business associates. The essays provide a break from the rigors of DeVoto's fact-permeated narrative, and they give wider view of the context within which his characters operated.

Like *Across the Wide Missouri*, the last volume in DeVoto's trilogy, *The Course of Empire* almost did not get written, though the problems DeVoto faced were nothing like the troubles he had had with Reves, Mrs. Porter, and the publishers. DeVoto conceived his book to be about Meriwether Lewis and William Clark and the significance of their expedition in the creation of America's transcontinental empire—the basic theme, as we have seen, of the entire trilogy. The problem was that John Bakeless, who had been DeVoto's classmate at Harvard, published his *Lewis and Clark: Partners in Discovery* just as DeVoto was finishing *Across the Wide Missouri* in 1947, and it seemed that Bakeless's excellent study, which has become a standard work on the subject, had stolen his thunder.[44] Upon further reflection, however, there was no conflict, for DeVoto's plan was to give only a skeleton narrative of the expedition (and as it turned out, only of the outbound leg) while devoting most of his book to the larger theme of European expansion across the American continent, of which Lewis and Clark were the culmination.[45] So Bakeless's book no more pre-empted *The Course of Empire* than a biography of Alfred Jacob Miller would have obviated *Across the Wide Missouri*. In both of these DeVoto volumes, the frame upstaged the picture.

Because it embraces the whole of European colonization in North America to 1805, *The Course of Empire* is a different book from the others in the trilogy. As Wallace Stegner points out, the scale of the undertaking removed from DeVoto's hands most of the novelistic devices that had distinguished the other volumes: synecdoche, simultaneity, the dramatic scene, the colorful characters over which DeVoto could linger and exploit their literary potential. Nor, of course, could he hope to exhibit his usual mastery of sources.[46] Thus it is the least characteristically DeVoto and few of his readers have ranked it as their favorite; in fact, it might be recommended to readers who can stomach no other DeVoto.

The Course of Empire is not necessarily a lesser book, however, nor are the novelistic devices of the earlier books entirely missing. The basic thesis of the series, that the creation of an American transcontinental empire was geographically logical and inevitable, is developed more impressively here simply because such a sweeping thesis requires a sweeping scale to achieve its full persuasive potential. The book is about nothing less, DeVoto says, "than the transformation, in response to the continent, of Europeans into Americans."[47] And DeVoto pursues his goal, as one would expect, at full speed. *The Course of Empire* taxes the reader's stamina perhaps more than either of the other two books because its factually detailed narrative covers so much ground, geographically and chronologically, that almost any reader is going to find himself in unfamiliar territory much of the time.

On the other hand, DeVoto drops enough enticements along the way to keep the reader happily trotting along like an Appaloosa under a Nez Perce warrior. Even though DeVoto lacked the space for character sketches like his memorable portrayals of James K. Polk and

John C. Fremont, his verbal virtuosity produces turns of phrase nothing short of Shakespearean in their brevity and vividness, creating unforgettable uniqueness in a few words. Of the infamous Jeffrey Amherst, for example, DeVoto says, "No libel ever accused him of intelligence." Or the boastful Kentucky frontiersmen, who "were the first half-horse, half-alligator Americans, Nature's premature attempt to create Texans."[48]

One of the devices that had distinguished *Across the Wide Missouri* reappears in the final volume: the incidental essay. Witness, for example, his treatise on the birch bark canoe and its role in the way of life of the *voyageur*, the primary institution of French and later British imperialism in Canada as the missionary had been for the Spaniards in the Southwest.[49] The visual counterpart of the Miller watercolors this time is the maps at the head of each chapter drawn by cartographer Erwin Raisz to summarize the collective geographic knowledge of North America to that point in DeVoto's narrative. The crude artistic level of the maps is no match for the aesthetic appeal of Miller's paintings, but as an educational device they provide a nice supplement to DeVoto's prose.[50]

The environmental (as we would call it now) outrage that increasingly dominated DeVoto's attention during the last decade of his life is apparent in *The Course of Empire*. Retracing the route of Lewis and Clark, for example, DeVoto comes to the Great Falls of the Missouri, which he finds scarred in the name of progress. "Nowhere in the entire length of the river," he interjects, "has industrial civilization, if the noun be permitted, more hideously defaced the scene than a power development has done here." Thus the activist DeVoto built a historical context for his case of the West as the "plundered province." Another aspect of *Across the Wide Missouri* that seems historiographically modern appears once again here in DeVoto's concern that the Indian portion of American history be told fully and sympathetically. DeVoto, unlike many western historians of his generation, was well aware that at the same time the West was being won, it was also being lost. "A dismaying amount of our history has been written without regard to the Indians," he observed, "and of what has been written with regard to them much treats their diverse and always changing societies as uniform and static. . . . But also, I believe, there is some inherent tendency to write American history as if it were a function of white culture only."

Although DeVoto never got to write the definitive study of the Lewis and Clark expedition that he had once hoped to, he did create the definitive abridgment of their journals, with a lengthy introduction, which he published in 1953.[51] And in some ways, *The Course of Empire* might be considered even more of a tribute to the achievement of the captains than a book only about their expedition might have been. The historical mural of the book he did write places them in the grandest context imaginable, as the culmination of the struggle for a continental American empire. Unless the Lewis and Clark expedition was "just some soldiers that Mr. Jefferson sent to find out how he could protect the sea otter trade from British sea power in case of war," he wrote to Garrett Mattingly, "it was a turning point in world history."[52] Lewis and Clark are certainly the heroes of the book, for they represent not only the spearhead of Manifest Destiny (before the term was invented), but also the application of science, of reason, and of humane sensibility to comprehension of the American West that DeVoto found so lacking in his own day.

Apart from the purely scientific accomplishments of the expedition, to which DeVoto gives ample space, the almost flawless record of positive diplomacy the captains achieved with the Indians they met was especially appealing to him, particularly in view of the tragic failure of the explorers, trappers, and settlers who followed them to emulate their amicable precedent. Their success, as DeVoto sees it, was evidence that most Indians were willing to meet white intruders at least halfway if the whites would treat them as human beings. Those whites of the frontier era who had the best relations with Indians were those who *liked* the Indians, who respected their way of life and wished to help them protect it, and Lewis and Clark were the first. Clark, in particular, had a "genius for handling Indians—he liked them and he understood the primitive mind. . . . And Indians liked him." Accordingly, DeVoto found most tragic those instances in which later white men betrayed the same Indians whom Lewis and Clark had most tried to befriend. Manifest Destiny may have been inevitable, but the experience of

Lewis and Clark offers a tantalizing hint of a more humane way it might have reached its ends.[53]

DeVoto's admiration for Lewis and Clark equaled his feelings for the other heroes who march across the pages of his trilogy—the James Clymans, the James Bridgers, and the Stephen Watts Kearnys. But in this last great historical narrative of his career, he was able to resist the temptation to turn his admiration into caricature. Although his research turned up nothing unsavory about either of the captains, it did disclose a complexity in Lewis that made him a quirky hero, though no less heroic for it. Lewis was a character type in western exploration, "the complexly introverted personalities who turned to the solitude and beauties and challenges of nature to satisfy a need that human association could not assuage. . . . Though solicitous about the welfare of his men, he lived in the recesses of his own personality and had no deep interest in people."[54] It was a nuanced psychological interpretation that found its way into few other character sketches in DeVoto.

Where to place DeVoto in American cultural history? To find a counterpart worthy of comparison with DeVoto, one would almost have to go all the way back to the great poet of the expansion of American democracy, Walt Whitman. "Democracy! near at hand to you a throat is now inflating itself and joyfully singing."[55] If Walt Whitman's line had anyone but himself in mind, it most likely prophesied a Robert Frost or a William Carlos Williams. But is it stretching Whitman's expansive imagination too much to speculate that he may have envisioned a Bernard DeVoto? DeVoto's project to Explain America was certainly an enterprise of Whitmanesque proportions, and one could easily imagine Whitman's delight if he could have witnessed DeVoto's continental vision, his extravagant language, and his easy trespasses across the boundary lines of literature and history. To be sure, the Romantic historians of Whitman's own day, such as George Bancroft, created prose hymns to American nationalism, but perhaps no others, then or since, took the same risks in form, in concept, and in language that would evoke a Walt Whitman as much as Bernard DeVoto did. If Whitman was the poet of American democratic nationalism, surely DeVoto was its historian. "'Leaves of Grass,'" Whitman asserted in his old age, ". . . [was] an attempt, from first to last, to put *a Person*, a human being, . . . freely and truly on record. . . . I say no land or people or circumstances ever existed so needing a race of singers and poems differing from all others, and rigidly their own, as the land and people and circumstances of our United States need such singers and poets to-day, and for the future." Not only singers and poets, DeVoto might have added, but historians as well, historians who can write prose that sings. No American historian has put his Person more unmistakably, more Whitman-like, on record in his writings than has DeVoto. And for those of us who can admire DeVoto's achievement while casting a skeptical eye on some aspects of it, our inspiration is Whitman's reminder that "all really great poetry is always . . . the result of a national spirit," and that "the strongest and sweetest songs yet remain to be sung."[56]

ENVIRONMENT AS EXPLANATION

One of the most complex, not to say baffling, strains of Bernard DeVoto's thought is his treatment of the question of whether the individual or the environment is the primary causal force in history. Although historians differ on the weight one should place on one or the other, most agree that both are important and that no fully satisfying historical explanation would ignore either. DeVoto also recognized the significance of both forces, but he seemed unable to bring them into balance in any given instance. Instead, he moved back and forth, placing all his weight on one or the other as best seemed to fit the case at hand. Nor was he always able to agree with other scholars on the consequence of a particular environmental force nor upon the decisive personality trait or profile.

The environment as a determinative force in western history was the idea of two theorists who stand among the founding fathers of the field, Frederick Jackson Turner and Walter Prescott Webb, whose works had become the bedrock of western studies by the time the historians who are the focus of this book began their work. For Turner, the expansion of Anglo-American civilization onto available lands in the West created American democracy through the social leveling of the frontier. Westward expansion also perpetuated democracy through a "safety valve" that offered disgruntled eastern workers a fresh start in the West, keeping wages high and social discontent down in the East.

For Webb, as Anglo-American civilization moved from the humid East onto the arid Great Plains, it was forced to make fundamental innovations and alterations in technology and institutions in order to survive.[1] Although the other historians of this study showed little awareness of Turner and Webb nor made any effort to incorporate their interpretations, DeVoto was well aware of both and admired their ideas. In several letters, for example, he speaks highly of Turner and defends him against the criticisms that had begun to mount in the 1930s and 1940s, and his introduction to *The Portable Mark Twain* uses Turnerian ideas and terminology. When agricultural historian Fred Shannon published a withering assault on Webb's *The Great Plains* in 1940, DeVoto, who detested both Shannon and his ideas, barely restrained himself from taking up the cudgels in Webb's defense. He expressed himself so forcefully on the matter in private that it cost him his friendship with Arthur M. Schlesinger, Sr., a Shannon partisan.[2]

And yet DeVoto was unable to use the ideas of either Turner or Webb in a central or consistent way. Webb's ideas about the adaptations forced upon Great Plains settlers were largely irrelevant to DeVoto, whose coverage of western history ended in 1846, before any substantial settlement of the Great Plains had begun and before the forces described by Webb had begun to assert themselves.

Similarly, he found the frontier described by Turner largely irrelevant to the West of his own interests. To be sure, he accepted Turner's idea of democracy as a product of the frontier. Both Abraham Lincoln and Mark Twain, for example, "absorbed the midcontinental heritage: fiercely equalitarian democracy, hatred of injustice and oppression, the man-to-man individualism of an expanding society." And DeVoto recognized a Turnerian process at work in the Mississippi Valley frontier (though his terminology owes more to Webb than to Turner). "When the tidewater culture came to the Great Valley it necessarily broke down: new conditions demanded adaptations, innovations, new combinations and amplifications. The new way of life that began to develop there had a different organization of feeling, a different metabolism of thought."[3]

For DeVoto, Turner's ideas had limited utility in explaining Twain, however, because the Hannibal, Missouri, where Samuel Clemens grew up was no longer a frontier. Although it was still a culturally rough-hewn environment, it "had passed the pioneering stage. It must be seen as a later stage that characterized all our frontiers east of the great plains, after the actual frontier of settlement had pushed westward, after the farms had been brought in and functional communities had been established, but while the frontier crafts and values and ways of thinking lingered on, a little mannered perhaps, a little nostalgic, but still vital."[4]

What of his trilogy of histories, where he *was* writing about a frontier and where Turner's ideas would have been relevant? Here DeVoto abandons Turner completely and even tacitly refutes him. DeVoto saw in the early history of the far West the development of an empire, not a democracy, a history much more useful to his contemporary thesis of the West as a "plundered province" than as evidence of Turner's democratic nationalism.[5] More precisely, perhaps, DeVoto accepted and even applauded the imperialism of Manifest Destiny as the means of spreading democracy, while at the same time recognizing that imperialism is inherently undemocratic. Regarding the mountain men, for example, who are the focus of a major part of *The Year of Decision* and all of *Across the Wide Missouri*, DeVoto emphasizes their individualism and gives full play to the libidinous anarchy of the annual trading rendezvous. Their larger significance, though, is that they were wage slaves of a greedy capitalism, "the agents of as ruthless a commerce as any in human history; they were its exploited agents." Outside their economic function, DeVoto sees them as forerunners of empire, not democracy—collectors of geographic data, guides of emigrant parties, and spearheads of territorial acquisition. As trappers and hunters, they began the thoughtless depredation of natural resources that became a headlong rush during the Gilded Age and threatened total destruction of the West in DeVoto's day. DeVoto admired, even idolized, the mountain men's competence and resourcefulness, but he had to deplore their servitude and the environmental consequences of their work. And Indians were not the beneficiaries of any westward-moving democracy. The missionaries "thought they came to bring Christ but in thinking so they were deceived. They were agents of a historical energy and what they brought was the United States. The Indians had no chance. If it looked like religion it was nevertheless Manifest Destiny." After quoting William Clark on the hospitality of the Nez Perce, DeVoto cynically remarks, "So every white man who ever wrote about the Nez Perces till it was time to steal their lands."[6]

The theses of Webb and Turner aside, what was the role of the environment in western history and culture? DeVoto's analysis of the West of Mark Twain and the West he himself had grown up in discloses additional ambiguities. As we have seen, Mark Twain's West, in DeVoto's analysis, was not the frontier of Frederick Jackson Turner, but rather a post-frontier phase of rural life on small farms and towns. (He does, though, use the terms "West" and "frontier" inconsistently and sometimes does seem to mean the Turnerian frontier between European civilization on the one hand and the wilderness and the Indian on the other.) That rural America, in DeVoto's view, was the real heartland of American culture, of unself-conscious ferment, as new indigenous forms and traditions grew out of the mixing of ethnic cultures, including that of the slaves. There was, then, at least a minimal agreement between Turner and DeVoto that in some sense American uniqueness had to be found in the West. To Explain America, one first had to explain the West, and that was the self-appointed task to which DeVoto directed the major works of his career.

The first part of the West DeVoto attempted to explain was his own part—the post-frontier village of Ogden and its larger context, Utah culture as a whole. We have seen how DeVoto grew up alienated within both, an intellectual and an individualist in what he considered a "herd-minded" culture smugly content in its commitment to bizarre and oppressive Mormon doctrines and institutions. We do not know when DeVoto first became acquainted with the works of Mark Twain, whether as a boy in Ogden or as a literature student in college, but it is clear that he discovered Twain early and returned to him often. It is easy to see, at least in part, why DeVoto chose Twain as the subject of his first major scholarly work. The two writers came from similar backgrounds, both had undertaken the task of explaining the West to the rest of America, and DeVoto would have found an echo of his own experience in several of Twain's characters. DeVoto had been ignored and ultimately rejected by his hometown, and once he came into adulthood and his full intellectual and verbal powers, he turned those guns around to wreak revenge. Like the man that corrupted Hadleyburg in Twain's story, he was "a bitter man and revengeful" against the smugness of the village that "was sufficient unto itself, and cared not a rap for strangers or their opinions." He sought to bring that village down in a way that "would comprehend the entire town, and not let so much as one person escape unhurt." He was Ogden's version of Twain's Pud-d'nhead Wilson, "a cipher in the estimation of the public, and nobody attached any importance to what he thought or did. He was liked, he was welcome enough all around, but he simply didn't count for anything." Like Wilson, the free-thinking rationalist who knocked the very foundations out from under the smug society of Dawson's Landing with the application of his apparently quirky hobby of fingerprinting—in other words, science--DeVoto would take Ogden down in an equally dramatic act of "calculated mayhem" by applying reason to its antiquated folkways.

Probably during the process of developing his thesis for *Mark Twain's America*, DeVoto realized that if he wanted to explain the West properly, he first had to do a better job of explaining his own particular part of the West—Utah—than he had done. Mark Twain's West had turned out to be much more than just the Hadleyburg or the Dawson's Landing that DeVoto had made of his native Ogden. It was also the St. Petersburg of *Tom Sawyer* and the real-life Hannibal of Samuel Clemens. Exposing an inconsistency in the judgment of literary critics like Van Wyck Brooks of the value of a rural environment for a writer, he exposed himself to charges of a similar inconsistency. "One wonders why an environment held to be commendable for Thoreau is thought unfortunate for Mark Twain," DeVoto says in his excoriation of the literary critic Van Wyck Brooks.[7] One could wonder with equal validity why an environment he held to be commendable for Twain was thought so unfortunate for himself (and, as we shall see, also inadequate to explain the Mormon prophet Joseph Smith), for the Hannibal, Missouri, of Samuel Clemens's youth, the Palmyra, New York, of Joseph Smith's, and the Ogden, Utah, of DeVoto's would seem to represent comparable stages of cultural development somewhere between the frontier and the industrial revolution. And yet it was the thesis of DeVoto's book that the heart of Twain's literary energy had come from his immersion in the folk culture of Hannibal, whereas DeVoto's articles on Ogden and Utah had lambasted them as devoid of culture and stultifying to anyone with cultural aspirations. Joseph Smith, to DeVoto, was merely a paranoiac whose creativity had originated within his own internal delusions, and his cultural environment was irrelevant.

The answer to this inconsistency may lie in the possibility that two things had happened to DeVoto during his years of study for the Mark Twain book (roughly 1928–32). For one thing, as he eventually admitted, he had begun to outgrow both his early literary recklessness in which he simply fired away with no concern for ricochets into crowds of innocent bystanders, as well as his adolescent lust for revenge on those who had made things tough for a young man with literary yearnings. Also, DeVoto's study of small-town culture in early nineteenth-century Missouri must have opened his eyes to a greater complexity in small-town Utah culture early in the following century. Small-town life exposed a basic "dilemma of democracy," DeVoto came to see, a dilemma which "has been insoluble to more minds than Mark Twain's. . . . One would record the idyll. . . . [T]hen, after a time, there would be something else. St. Petersburg would grow into Hadleyburg and Dawson's Landing, for the dilemma had another horn."[8] In his Utah articles, DeVoto had been Ogden's version of Pudd'nhead Wilson and the man that corrupted Hadleyburg, but he had failed to appreciate that his hometown was also the idyll of Tom Sawyer's St. Petersburg.

Even then, DeVoto was slow to make amends, evidently because, although he came to regret the caustic tone and sarcastic language of the articles, he found nothing factually in them that required repentance. In his 1930 letter to Robert Elliott of the *Salt Lake Telegram*, DeVoto repented of nothing, and suggested instead that the future of Utah cultural life depended on the ability of Utahns to learn to accept criticism from outsiders and to generate criticism from within.[9]

By 1943, though, after a series of articles about Utah with a generally favorable theme, and especially with the appearance of *Year of Decision 1846*, in which he expressed a forthright admiration for Mormon social cohesion and endurance under the leadership of Brigham Young (though he maintained his scorn for Joseph Smith's bizarre theology), DeVoto found it worthwhile to issue both public and private statements modifying his earlier views. In his public statement, a letter to Jarvis Thurston of Ogden, which he gave Thurston permission to publish in the *Rocky Mountain Review* (a bowdlerized version appeared in the Mormon magazine *Improvement Era*), DeVoto called his articles "ignorant, brash, prejudiced, malicious, and what is worst of all, irresponsible." Privately, to Dale Morgan, he explained that "I was young, bumptious, intoxicated with print. Also I was full of resentment of an environment that had been unfriendly to me always and sometimes actually contemptuous or even hostile. Also I thought I knew a lot more than I really did, and had not learned that gaps in one's knowledge should be filled, not bridged over with romance."[10] But in a masterful piece of invective penned late in life, DeVoto reaffirmed his caustic view of Mormonism. Responding to a person who had been approached by a Mormon missionary and who wanted background information to guide him, DeVoto advised him that Mormonism contains "ten thousand cubic feet of patent and puerile imbecilities," and that discussing religion with a Mormon is futile. "If someone tells you that he holds nightly conversations with Napoleon and Zoroaster and has with his own eyes seen some chimpanzees constructing a television set, you do not, I hope, argue with him." On the other hand, he said, "The Mormons are an admirable people, kindly, open-hearted, hospitable, bigoted, in terror of things that happened a hundred years ago, with a tremendous inferiority complex, and they have made a hell of a lot of money, and they have performed one of the prodigies of American sociology. But their doctrines," he concludes, "are simply preposterous. Anybody who can believe any of them can believe any nonsense that human idiocy could invent."[11]

As mentioned above, DeVoto's view of Joseph Smith as a paranoiac, a view he had developed in his early writings about Mormonism and advanced once again in a review of Fawn Brodie's biography *No Man Knows My History* in 1945, marked a turn away from environment as explanation. As a result, Dale Morgan initiated a testy exchange of letters in which he called DeVoto to account, for in previous cases DeVoto had seen environment as everything. This time it was Morgan's thesis. During research for his own history of Mormonism (posthumously published in fragmentary form) and in helping Brodie on her book, Morgan had come to the conclusion that Joseph Smith was fully a product of the popular religious hysteria and materialistic ambitions of his environment. "He is merely the Jacksonian common man permitted an extreme development." DeVoto's theory of paranoia was wanting in factual support. Brodie had produced evidence that Smith's claims of visions were after-the-fact attempts to bolster his authority over his followers, that he did not become wilder and wilder in his claims as one would expect a paranoiac to do, and that his claims to revelation almost completely ceased as his authority became accepted. DeVoto's complaint that Brodie had minimized Brigham Young's role in early Mormon history was equally invalid, for Young had indeed been a minor figure until Smith's death opened an opportunity for him to assert his talents.[12]

DeVoto's reply is an example of his less-than-admirable tendency to assert his authority when challenged rather than answer his critic on the merits of the criticism. He began by yielding to Morgan's expertise on the factual details of early Mormonism. "I can fairly claim to be a student of Mormon history, but I cannot claim to be a specialist in it or an authority about it—I have nowhere made such a claim, in fact I have repeatedly denied it in public and at the top of my voice."[13] The substance of his position beyond that was simply to assert his expertise in psychiatry and his ability to recognize a paranoiac when he saw one. "I read psychiatry. I associate with psychiatrists: in twenty years there has never been a time when I was not hashing out the actual behavior of actual neurotics and psychotics with several psychiatrists who were intimate friends of mine." As to the merits of the argument, DeVoto gave up hope of communicating with Morgan. "Permit me to hazard a guess that you are a spoiled [frustrated] sociologist—at least it appears to me that when you have found an environmental explanation for something you are content," he wrote. "Well, I am a spoiled psychiatrist." The spoiled sociologist and the spoiled psychiatrist apparently could not bridge the gap between them. "I can't . . . hope to meet your mind," DeVoto complained. "What seems to me to weigh a pound seems to you to strike C-sharp and there is no way of bringing us to discuss things in the same terms."[14]

On any other issue, the two probably would not have been that far apart. In fact, Morgan was willing to acknowledge some kind of psychological abnormality in Joseph Smith while rejecting DeVoto's rigid insistence upon paranoia. But even in the face of Brodie's factual research and Morgan's remonstrance, DeVoto was unable to back down. His rigidity no doubt stemmed from his prior publications in which he had propounded the paranoia thesis.

A greater matter was also at stake, however: DeVoto's overall thesis about early Mormon history. It held that Joseph Smith was a wild-eyed visionary who had written a crazy book and invented a bizarre theology. There were dozens of failed religious and utopian experiments growing out of the fertile soil of the "burned-over district" of western New York at the same time as Mormonism, and Smith's theology in time would have inevitably doomed Mormonism to a similar failure. He was "a man drunk on deity whose mind swooned with apocalyptic splendors but who could produce no effective leadership, no effective government, no effective social organization." Brigham Young, on the other hand, "was a much greater man than Joseph. . . . It was Young who saved the Saints. Without him Mormonism would have become exactly what its heresies became, a series of dividing sects dwindling to handfuls of gaffers remembering Joseph in their sorrow and waiting for the sky to open and show him come again." Smith's death, in DeVoto's view, was fortuitous, for it brought the iron-fisted organizational genius Brigham Young to the leadership of the church. It was Young who imposed a group cohesion and rationality on Smith's delusional theology and saved Mormonism. "Deseret [the Mormon utopian state in Utah founded by Brigham Young] is seen to be . . . what happens when Brook Farm comes into the hands of those fit to build Brook Farm," DeVoto wrote in *The Year of Decision 1846*.[15] Joseph Smith, then, was one of DeVoto's caricatures like, as we shall see, Lansford Hastings, John C. Fremont, and James Bridger. Once DeVoto had painted Smith as irrational, he could not blur the lines by allowing him to share any of Brigham Young's canniness.

Even by DeVoto's day American historians were moving beyond the idea that a plausible historical explanation has to consist of a key, a single decisive factor that unlocks all the apparent complications of causation. As the environmental explanations of Turner and Webb came to appear simplistic, so the psychological biographies by the likes of Freud and Erik Erikson seemed less and less compelling. Although DeVoto's interest in psychology and psychiatry continued, and he even wrote a book, *The World of Fiction*, about the psychological basis of literature, Joseph Smith was the only historical character he ever attempted to explain purely in terms of psychological abnormality. He expressed frustration at the lack of interest of scholars in attempting a psychological study of Francis Parkman, but only because he thought such a study would help explain Parkman's hypochondria and lack of self-confidence and not because DeVoto thought it would constitute a complete explanation for Parkman's work. DeVoto himself regarded Parkman's roots in New England culture and his reading in romantic literature on the Indians as useful in understanding *The Oregon Trail*.[16] DeVoto, in other words, was apparently moving toward a position similar to that of most modern historians, who are generally aware that both interior and exterior factors need to be taken into account in constructing a plausible profile of human motivation.

MANIFEST DETERMINISM

THROUGHOUT HIS CAREER, Bernard DeVoto liked to cast himself as a hard-headed empiricist, the man of facts whose research would rebuke the precious theories of library-sequestered intellectuals who disdained to venture forth into the workaday world. During the 1920s his attacks became focused on the so-called Young Intellectuals such as Van Wyck Brooks and Lewis Mumford, who developed an unflattering view of American culture as banal, materialistic, intolerant, and anti-intellectual. Although DeVoto himself, during his Menckenesque phase, had shared some of the Young Intellectuals' scorn for part of America (Utah), he considered his criticisms to be based on an intimate acquaintance with the object of his scorn, whereas Brooks and his associates were basing their ideas purely upon literature, on the assumption that literature was a universal cultural barometer. Literature, DeVoto maintained, was a barometer only of literature, not of life as a whole, and the "literary fallacy," as he called it, had deceived the Young Intellectuals into a seriously wrongheaded appraisal of America at large. As his contempt for such hothouse theorizing mounted, he began calling it "Great Thinking" or "Beautiful Thinking," and dismissed the ideas it produced as "metaphysics." DeVoto cast himself as the Aristotle to Brooks's Plato, the earthbound empiricist for whom reality existed solely in the concrete Thing itself rather than in some ethereal Ideal of which earthly things were merely dim reflections. It was a posture well suited to

DeVoto's personality, to his mocking wit, and to the outsider perspective he been forced into as a child in Mormon Utah and as a westerner at Harvard.

Unfortunately, it was a poor fit for one who aspired to Explain America. One who sets goals of that magnitude must traffic in ideas of that magnitude, and those ideas inevitably become further and further removed from their empirical base as they increasingly concern themselves with great themes and ignore the complications and complexities that are the essence of empiricism. As a result, DeVoto's books are packed from cover to cover with Great Thinking, with metaphysics, with Beautiful Ideas as beautiful as anything Brooks and Mumford were capable of at their most expansive. To DeVoto, his large ideas were conflations of fact that materialized as naturally as a genie expands out of a bottle, but a reader who casts as jaundiced an eye on DeVoto's work as he cast on Brooks's can find as much metaphysics as ever emanated from Brooks's cloistered study. Consider, for example, the following passage from *The Year of Decision 1846*, in which DeVoto speculates: "Sometimes there are exceedingly brief periods which determine a long future. A moment of time holds in solution ingredients which might combine in any of several or many ways, and then another moment precipitates out of the possible the at last determined thing." Any readers who still have their heads above water at that point are certain to be submerged when they learn that the book is about "a period when the manifold possibilities of chance were shaped to converge into the inevitable, when the future of the American nation was precipitated out of the possible by the actions of the people we deal with."[1] The meaning of this murky metaphor of unstable emulsion seems to be that inevitability somehow emerges from the action of free will—a mysterious proposition at best, and one that not only is ungrounded in any body of empirical data, but is impossible to demonstrate. It is Beautiful Thinking at its most beautiful.[2]

DeVoto's metaphysics of American history was grounded in his understanding of the ideas of Italian sociologist Vilfredo Pareto, whose *Traite de Sociologie Generale* (as the title appeared in its 1917 French translation) became an obsession to DeVoto and his circle of Harvard friends beginning in about 1928 after his return to Cambridge. "The

Pareto flu hit Harvard," Arthur Schlesinger, Jr. recalled of his student years, and the metaphor of a contagion is apt. By 1937, Schlesinger continues, "the elaborate Paretian machinery began to weary DeVoto," but in the full flood of his enthusiasm for it, he considered Pareto "the prophet of a new revelation."[3] The basic thesis of Pareto's lengthy and difficult book is that society is basically driven by irrational folkways called "residues" that become implanted in the group psyche. When challenged, those folkways are defended by appeal to equally irrational sources called "derivations," such as authority or accepted "principles." DeVoto found Pareto appealing because he seemed to supply a scientific basis for two fundamental ideas toward which DeVoto was instinctively moving: that society is so mired in irrational self-justification that change can occur only at a glacial pace, thus dooming the facile social reform programs offered by intellectuals out of touch with the popular mind; and that vast subcutaneous energies, the real determinants of social behavior, can be discerned far below the rational. In order to Explain America, then, the historian must somehow recognize those unconscious forces and show how they have worked themselves out in chronological events. Clearly this is not the inductive method DeVoto claimed to be following. It is, rather, a completely deductive method in which one begins by establishing—by a method DeVoto does not explain—the basic "residues" to which a society is responding, then interpreting events in that light. Thus it is natural for DeVoto to point at what he considers to be inevitabilities and to refer to his characters as the agents of history or some similar force.

Historiographically, Paretian analysis carried a high price tag, as we shall see. But it also paid handsome dividends. In DeVoto's skillful hands, history became a vast arena in which momentous forces grew from barely discernible beginnings, built to immense size, and rolled to collisions on irreversible courses. Here was a history that *meant* something, a history in which each development had a vital function in bringing vast forces to a logical (indeed inevitable) denouement. Told with the vigorous narrative techniques, the inerrant eye for the telling detail or anecdote, the vivid characterization, and the other novelistic tools he brought to bear so masterfully on his historical subjects, DeVoto's histories proved irresistible to readers.

The most fundamental Paretian "residue" motivating American history, to DeVoto, was expansionism. Rooted in a basic restlessness inherent in European culture, expansionism, expressed in a hunger for land, for domination, for untrammeled scope of individual action, was the force that drove European discoverers, explorers, and conquerors to the New World. As European political regimes extended their authority across the Atlantic, expansionism caused some of the British colonies to seek and achieve independence. As the new United States spilled across the Appalachians to the Mississippi and established a beachhead on the Pacific, promoters of expansion during the mid-1840s claimed it was America's "Manifest Destiny"—that is, it was manifestly the will of God—that the United States should become a transcontinental empire.

Manifest Destiny, in one form or another, was the basic theme of all three of DeVoto's histories. In his analysis, there were both irrational and rational defenses for Manifest Destiny. At the irrational level, Americans appealed to a typical Paretian "derivation," the will of God, as justification. At the rational level, DeVoto evoked Thomas Jefferson and Abraham Lincoln as proponents of the idea that there was a geographic logic to the United States, a continental unity the pursuit of which was a logical end of diplomacy in Jefferson's case, and of political unity, in Lincoln's.

To consider the rational argument first, DeVoto cited Jefferson's letter to Robert Livingston during the negotiations over Louisiana, a letter that made the case that American possession of the Mississippi Valley was a necessary condition of national independence. "There is on the globe one single spot," Jefferson wrote, "the possessor of which is our natural and habitual enemy." That spot was New Orleans, which, being located at the mouth of the Mississippi River, controls access to the interior of the continent. Permanent French control of New Orleans would, in effect, force the United States to become once again a colony of Great Britain. "From that moment [when France should establish such control] we must marry ourselves to the British fleet and nation," he concluded.[4] Lincoln, in his second annual message to Congress in 1862, extended Jefferson's argument by urging the indivisibility of the continent, which was unified by geographic logic. Division of the nation would violate that logic and render both parts vulnerable to foreign domination. "There is no line straight or crooked," he asserted, "suitable for a national boundary upon which to divide. Trace through from east to west, upon the line between free and slave country, and we shall find that a little more than one-third of its length are rivers, easy to be crossed and populated or soon to be populated thickly on both sides; while nearly all its remaining length are merely surveyors' lines, over which people may walk back and forth without any consciousness of their presence." Those rivers, he continues, cannot be divided among more than one political entity because they are the lifeblood of the continent and in an important sense dictate its unity. "There is no possible severing of this but would multiply and not mitigate evils among us. . . . In fact it would ere long force reunion, however much blood and treasure the separation might have cost," he concluded.[5]

Upon such statements of the geographic logic of expansion DeVoto rested the rational side of his case. "It is not conceivable—or at least I cannot conceive—that anything could have stayed the progress of American settlement of the Far West, including New Mexico and California," he wrote to defend his thesis against the objections of Oliver LaFarge, who protested the imperialism of *The Year of Decision 1846* when it was serialized in *Atlantic*. "I do not believe that anything known to history or philosophy could have prevented this development. . . . There was no military opposition to it, there was damned little cultural opposition to it, and over ninety percent of the West there was no opposition to it at all—except the Indians. . . . There I stand, and if that makes me an imperialist, then I am one."[6]

Most nineteenth-century Americans, as DeVoto realized, did not comprehend the issue of expansion at a rational level. For them, expansionism was more of an instinct than a thought, and DeVoto chose to deal with it at that level through Paretian analysis of "residue" and "derivation," though he employs only the concepts and not the terminology. He was much less interested in Paretian "derivations," or rationales, which in the term "Manifest Destiny" appealed to the Divine Will, a theological force DeVoto did not find useful, than he was in the "residue" of expansionism, the unconscious drive at the base of cultural aspiration. That drive appears in his books as a mysterious deterministic force, ultimately irresistible in its power. That force radically limits freedom of will, so that his characters are doomed to failure if they choose to resist.

Thus one finds in DeVoto's books such deterministic statements as "American history in the person of Jim Clyman had told the Donner party not to take the Hastings Cutoff from the California trail," and Methodist missionary Jason Lee was "like the mountain men and Nathaniel Wyeth, an instrument of the national will. . . . It was Jason Lee who gave the orders but it was Manifest Destiny that cast the vote." The Protestant missionaries like Lee "were the vortices of force thrown out in advance by the force to the eastward that was making west. They thought that they came to bring Christ but in thinking so they were deceived. They were agents of a historical energy and what they brought was the United States. The Indians had no chance. If it looked like religion it was nevertheless Manifest Destiny." The popular reports of John C. Fremont "were adventure books, they were charters of Manifest Destiny." Finally, American geographical features "compose an articulation, a pattern, an organic shape. It is not a perfect symmetry nor a perfect unity, but it is incomparably closer to being both than the physical matrix in which any other modern nation developed. The American teleology is geographical."[7]

Not surprisingly, in a history in which human will is directed by an invisible, irresistible force, inevitabilities abound. In fact, everything is inevitable. The election of Abraham Lincoln was inevitable at the moment of the introduction of the Wilmot Proviso in 1848. "Slavery was out of the closet, and it was going to stay out." The Civil War had become inevitable even earlier than that. Lincoln's second annual message to Congress in 1862, discussed above, told America, as DeVoto put it, "that the achieved West had given the United States . . . an internal, domestic empire, and he was telling them that Yesterday must not be permitted to Balkanize it. . . . Too late. At some time between August and December, 1846, the Civil War had begun. . . . They had done that, the people of this book: they had brought in that empire and made that war inevitable."

Inevitability, in fact, was nothing new even as early as 1846. The British ministry, in the Proclamation of 1763, "supported furs and the

Indian trade as against land. Just long enough to make the Revolution, for still another reason, inevitable."[8]

To be fair, DeVoto, in various places, rejected this interpretation of his idea of historical causation. In *The Year of Decision* he referred to "the naive mythology called economic determinism," though that is not a rejection of determinism *per se*. More specifically, he warned at the beginning of *The Course of Empire* that giving due place to the limits geography places on history's possibilities is

> not to set up a determinism: no one who reads my book can suppose that I believe in historical predestination. Men are masters of their societies, society's will is free, and history is not geography, it is men and the events they produce. But the natural conditions in which men live help to shape their societies. . . . Meanwhile though no one can say to what degree the physical and psychological forces of our continentalism have conditioned our history, no one can avoid seeing that they have conditioned it to some degree. Nothing in history is more visible than the transformation, in response to the continent, of Europeans into Americans.[9]

Although the Turnerian twist in the last sentence, to the effect that it was their "response to the continent" that transformed "Europeans into Americans," has been debated at length, few historians would question DeVoto's assertion that geography influences history. In view of the previous quotations, however, one finds it difficult to accept his claim that that is *all* he was asserting. The force he calls "continentalism," which one assumes means the expansionist drive that he sees as an unconscious "residue" underlying American culture, appears in his narrative as an irresistible determinism. Finally, when DeVoto repudiates determinism, one cannot be certain that he realizes, when he says that History is acting through someone or that someone is an agent of the national will or of Manifest Destiny, that he is making a deterministic statement. "History abhors determinism but cannot tolerate chance," he says in another place.[10] One feels compelled to ask if determinism and chance are not antonyms; if there is no such thing as determinism, then chance must exist, and if chance does not exist, then some force of determinism must have canceled it.

Determinism exists in a myriad of forms, from a religious determinism in which humans are pawns in the working out of God's will, to a Marxist determinism in which they are passive agents of economic forces, to almost anything where some force is amplified until it consistently trumps the human will. And of course the existence of free will is one of the classically unprovable propositions. Most people find, however, that assuming the existence of free will is a risk worth taking, for only then does human striving have any meaning. And extending that assumption into the past seems an equally productive basis for writing history. Engaging as DeVoto's characters are under his creative touch, they are much less engaging when they are spokesmen for History instead of for their own wisdom or folly, much less engaging as agents of Manifest Destiny instead of agents of the values and assumptions of their church or their political leaders, who are equally subject to wisdom or folly. There are, to be sure, inarticulate cultural values that underlie much of human activity, but realistic historical explanation is not required to turn those inarticulate motives into deterministic forces, and should not do so.

Geography may place limits on human activity, although mainly as a passive entity upon which the human will works rather than an active force that shapes that will. DeVoto's argument that the geographic features of the American continent predetermined political unity is *post hoc, ergo propter hoc*: the United States has remained a unified, transcontinental empire, therefore the continent's geography caused political unity. But looking at American geography without looking for features that promote political unity, one can see many features that promote disunity: the mountain ranges that impede east-west travel; the rivers that allow travel downstream but impede it upstream and discourage crossing; the Grand Canyon, the Great Salt Lake Desert, Death Valley, and similar forbidding features that seem to promote isolation rather than community. DeVoto was not the first to think he could read a message in the mountains, a culture in a continent, for much land-use legislation and environmental policy, good and bad, has been grounded in readings of that kind. How much better such policies would be, historian Patricia Nelson Limerick points out, if we realized that humans impose their will on geography rather than vice versa.

> Nature does not legislate; nature does not write policy; nature does not decree what kind of settlement can occur in which place. . . . Responding to and interpreting the conditions presented by nature, human beings legislate, write policy, and determine which settlements will occur where and how they will get their water. . . . But the assumption that nature carries political and economic messages and mandates is finally a failure of self-consciousness, a failure of a recognition that humans implant and install the meaning in these messages and mandates.

Environmental activist Edward Abbey, as one might expect, puts the matter even more starkly. "What does the desert say?" he asks, then gives the brutal answer: "The desert says nothing. . . . What is the heart of the desert? . . . I am convinced . . . that the desert has no heart, that it presents a riddle which has no answer, and that the riddle itself is an illusion created by some limitation or exaggeration of the displaced human consciousness."[11]

One of the features of DeVoto's historical writing that has won and held an audience through many changes in historiographical fashion is the absolutism of his thunderous pronouncements. The reader who is carried away by the flow of DeVoto's sequences of causation as they lead to their inevitable results feels that Truth has been presented in irrefutable form. But the more skeptical reader, who may see in life fewer inevitabilities than dubious battles, more nuance and uncertainty than eternally resolved victories, will often find DeVoto's historical explanations unconvincing. The tentative hypothesis, the qualified conclusion, may have less crowd-rousing potential, but it seems more persuasive as reflections of the lack of absolute certitude with which most of us have to go through life.

1846: YEAR OF CARICATURE

VIVID CHARACTERIZATION ALWAYS has an ambition to caricature. In fiction, where the author is creating a character out of whole cloth, exaggeration is limited only by the reader's willingness to suspend belief, but in history (and to a lesser degree in historical fiction) the author is limited by the factual record. Historians who write well happily accept that limitation and create vivid character portrayals by selective underlining, as it were, of their sources—emphasizing the apt quotation or the revealing anecdote, for example, among the less telling facts. That underlining is an act of interpretation in which the historian emphasizes those parts of the factual record he or she believes are most significant, and as all students of historiography know, disagreements are frequent. Thus the historian bears the burden of being as judicious and balanced as possible so that facts that modify or even contradict an interpretation are not ignored or suppressed, but instead appear, in the hands of the most skilled historians, as evidence of the complexity of human nature.

Bernard DeVoto's characters are among the most vividly portrayed in all historical literature. If George Bancroft had, as Richard Hofstadter said, an "exceptional ability to marshal a mass of facts and set them into motion,"[1] DeVoto could take a mass of facts and set them into *orbit*. Somehow the realization that history is about real people excited a passion within him to reveal the real-life drama in his characters that he never reached when he was creating them from nothing in his novels. Unfortunately, his immense literary power and his hyperventilating enthusiasm for his material often dragged DeVoto over the line between vividness and distortion. DeVoto can rarely be accused of factual inaccuracy in his character portrayals, but can be charged with smoothing off the rough edges and ignoring facts contradictory to an image he was trying to build. Couched in his vivid language and fueled by his love of controversy, his interpretive distortions sometimes cross the line into caricature.

None of his three volumes about the far West is completely free of caricature, but the first one, *The Year of Decision 1846*, is particularly ridden with overdramatized characters. There are two possible reasons for this. First, DeVoto's first volume was the most experimental. He was fully aware of the uniqueness of what he was attempting, and he looked for the biggest bricks he could throw to break the most glass in the windows of the historical profession. DeVoto's story was one of vast proportions and dramatic contrasts, and he wanted to make sure his readers missed none of its dimensions. Second, DeVoto's didacticism has never been properly emphasized. His combativeness and his crusading (he would have hated that term, but his role as a conservationist merits it) were all part of a lifelong compulsion to teach, and to teach what he could so clearly see to be the truth. History, to DeVoto, had meaning; it was a story with a point. Fearful that his readers might miss that point (he needn't have worried!), DeVoto painted his characters in primary colors, in dramatic hues that caught the eye and would not let go. Although little if anything was factually inaccurate in his character portrayals, his emphases were so simplistic that history's complexity, the baffling contradictions in human nature that make the study of the past so challenging, got left out of DeVoto's cartoon version.

In *The Year of Decision*, the heroes and villains of DeVoto's melodrama often come in pairs. For every poison there is an antidote; for every soft-minded dreamer there is a hardheaded realist; for every egotistical self-promoter there is an objective empiricist, and so on. Sometimes the pairs appear in unmistakable opposition: Lansford Hastings crosses the California trail with James Clyman, one dreaming of the urban splendor of Los Angeles and the agricultural bounty of the San

Fernando Valley, the other obsessed with the salt flats and the snows of the Sierra; the high-minded dilettantes of Brook Farm contrast with the regimented Zion of the Mormons; the delusional prophet Joseph Smith contrasts with the authoritarian social engineer Brigham Young. At other times the pairing is less proximate: the consummate soldier Stephen Watts Kearny is the antithesis of at least three incompetents, Zachary Taylor, Robert Stockton, and John C. Fremont; and the Puritan and Boston Brahmin Francis Parkman, his hypochondriac head filled with fears of his own frailties, with romantic notions of the Indians, and with aristocratic loathing of the proletarian Mormons, is counterbalanced by the class of omnicompetent and omniscient mountain men.

California promoter Lansford W. Hastings is one of DeVoto's most tightly drawn caricatures. An Oregon emigrant with the Elijah White party of 1842, Hastings saw that Oregon already contained competitors for his promotional genius. So he journeyed south to California, which, though still loosely held by Mexico, offered irresistible potential both for American imperialism and Hastings's personal ambition. California, then even more than now, offered much to tempt the emigrant, and Hastings's *Emigrants' Guide to Oregon and California*, published in 1845, painted the province's very real potential in luridly exaggerated colors.[2] The California one finds in its pages is a paradise in which "December is as pleasant as May," where disease is virtually unknown, where meat can be cured in its pure atmosphere for weeks without rotting, where wild oats with stalks suitable for walking sticks can be cultivated merely by fencing them off from the animals.[3]

Although brim full of such obviously inflated advertising rhetoric, Hastings's *Guide* also contained practical advice for the potential emigrant, advice based on personal experience on the overland trail and vindicated by subsequent emigrants, both those who followed it and those who ignored it. The gist of his advice was to travel light, with small, sturdy wagons carrying a minimum of baggage and provisions along the lines of a list he provided.

Unfortunately, the *Guide* also included a suggestion that led to tragedy. "The most direct route, for the California emigrants, would be to leave the Oregon route, about two hundred miles east of Fort Hall;

thence bearing west southwest, to the Salt Lake; and thence continuing down to the bay of San Francisco, by the route just described."[4] Some of Hastings's readers, their literary acuity no doubt dulled by the hyperbole of the *Guide's* descriptions of California's Golden Shore, missed the subtlety of the subjunctive mood in this passage and interpreted it as a recommendation of a cutoff that would save them several hundred miles of arduous western travel. Among those were the Donner-Reed party, mostly Illinois farmers, who followed what came to be known as the Hastings Cutoff to a tragic denouement in the Sierra that left many of them dead and the remainder surviving mostly by cannibalism.[5]

Bernard DeVoto was among those who missed or ignored that and other subtleties and complexities in the history of the Hastings Cutoff that we shall discuss below. Instead, he leaped to the conclusion that Hastings's propensity to let his enthusiasm run ahead of his facts had led him to play with the lives of the hapless emigrants who took him seriously, and that the Donner tragedy can be laid entirely at his door. In his view, Hastings was "a Fremont in miniature [no compliment in the hierarchy of DeVoto's cast of characters], . . . a smart young man who wrote a book—it is not a unique phenomenon in literature—without knowing what he was talking about." Fair enough so far. But where other smart young men (one can see Van Wyck Brooks standing in the wings here) only made fools of themselves by writing ignorant books, Hastings's *Guide* led its readers to gruesome deaths. "If the young man, stuffed with vision, ignorance, and the will to lie for empire's sake has had any romantic appeal so far," DeVoto observes at the point in his narrative where Hastings begins recruiting volunteers for his Cutoff, "he now loses it."[6]

Hastings, the overenthusiastic and irresponsible promoter, is one-half of DeVoto's caricature. The other half is James Clyman, "the thirty-third degree mountain man," the exemplar of "the continental mind" who is one of the central heroes of *The Year of Decision*. Hastings recruited Clyman in California to join his eastward journey to meet the overland emigration of 1846, which he hoped to turn aside from the established California Trail and take his new shortcut under his leadership. During that journey, Clyman and Hastings fell into disagreement over its desirability as an alternate route. Hastings's judgment, which DeVoto characterizes as "that of a real-estate booster selling lots to suckers," so appalled Clyman "that he would set up as a one-man bureau of more reliable information."[7] Accordingly, once he began encountering emigrant parties on his eastward journey, including the party of James Frazier Reed, whom he had known in Illinois, Clyman warned them of the perils of the Hastings Cutoff. DeVoto, as is apparent from his rhetoric quoted above, found himself totally on the side of the omniscient mountain man and totally opposed to the peddler of hot air, Lansford Hastings.

DeVoto's sources, unfortunately, contain complications that seriously blur the sharp lines of his caricature. First, although it is undeniable that Hastings's book proposed a cutoff that was nothing more than a line on a map, Hastings had replaced that theoretical line with first-hand knowledge of the cutoff by the time he met the overland emigration of 1846. As a promoter of overland emigration, then, Hastings stands out among the likes of Hall Jackson Kelley and Nathaniel Wyeth in not only advertising the benefits of settlement in Oregon or California, but also in his willingness to lead them personally over the recommended route. Furthermore, most of the 1846 parties who took the Hastings Cutoff found it difficult but passable, costing them the life of animals but not of humans. The Bryant-Russell party, to be sure, hardly counts because they had abandoned their wagons for saddle mounts, but the Harlan-Young and Lienhard parties made it with wagons. Only the Donner party met with tragedy. Why?

An amazing convention of Donner historiography, beginning with Charles McGlashan and proceeding through Charles Kelly, George R. Stewart, and DeVoto to most present-day scholars, has been to look for almost every possible agent for the Donners' demise other than the Donners themselves. Some of this oversight no doubt issues from sympathy with their gruesome fate, for which one would like to find some exterior cause or villain. But there is compelling evidence that suggests the Donners should take a major part of the blame for their own fate. The Donner party was made up of naive Illinois farmers who had never seen a western river, mountain, or desert and who had poorly investigated the ruthless testing to which western geography could put them.

They had ignored much of the advice in Hastings's *Guide* that could have saved them—the recommendation of light wagons and minimal supplies and baggage. Instead, their leader, the imperious and stubborn James Frazier Reed, had insisted upon bringing what he called his "family wagon," otherwise known as the "Pioneer Palace." This vehicle was reputedly of such monstrous dimensions that it can be blamed for the party's delayed crossing of the Wasatch Mountains and the salt flats weeks after the previous parties—weeks that spelled disaster in the early snows of the Sierra.[8]

And what about the other quotient in the caricature, the infallible mountain man James Clyman? DeVoto had said of his kind: "They had mastered the last, the biggest, and the hardest wilderness. Give any of them a horse and a pack mule, a half dozen traps, a couple of robes, a bag of possibles, and a rifle—and he could live comfortably among privations that broke the emigrants' spirit and safe among dangers that killed soldiers like flies in the first frost. They had learned not only to survive the big lonesome but to live there at the height of function"?[9]

The Hastings Cutoff was an arduous route—in fact, not a good one—and an honest disagreement over its utility need not have meant the violent rift DeVoto saw between the two men. Clyman did argue against the cutoff in his conversations back along the trail after he left Hastings, but we do not know how adamant he was. Clyman had to have recognized Hastings's superior experience in overland travel with wagons, and some of the emigrants with whom Clyman discussed the route—most notably the Donners—chose to ignore him. Further, as we have noted, Clyman was wrong in the cases of the Harlan-Young and Lienhard parties, who took the Hastings Cutoff with hardship but no loss of life. Finally, if one tabulates the votes of all the mountain men discussed in DeVoto's book who commented on the Hastings Cutoff, one finds more in Hastings's camp than in Clyman's: those opposed to the route include only Clyman and Joseph Reddeford Walker, whereas those who recommended it include James Bridger, Louis Vasquez, and James Hudspeth, who had crossed it eastward with Clyman and Hastings and stayed with Hastings to help shepherd the emigrants across. Bridger, who DeVoto thought was such an expert on western matters that he should have been preceded everywhere by fanfares of trumpets and drums, incurred "the heaviest sin charged against Old Gabe in his entire career" when he expressed a favorable opinion about the Hastings route.[10] (One wonders why the young Bridger's sin of leaving Hugh Glass to die either of the wounds inflicted by a grizzly bear or under the lances of the hostile Indians in whose country he had had the bear encounter was somehow of lesser gravity. Both incidents would seem to be black marks on Bridger's otherwise immaculate record in DeVoto's telling of it.)

Other caricatures stand out as well. One is Francis Parkman, a Bostonian who conceived the idea of writing the history of the French and English empires in North America. As part of his research, he journeyed to the Great Plains in 1846, where he hoped to observe real Indians in their natural setting and with their culture little altered by European influences. The experience was to help him understand the ways of life of the eastern Indians whom the European explorers, missionaries, and settlers had encountered in previous centuries. A result of his trip was Parkman's first book, *The Oregon Trail*, a classic of American historical literature. DeVoto acknowledges Parkman's book as "the most considerable achievement by an American historian," but it is a mysterious accolade when placed alongside his assertion that "[i]t was Parkman's fortune to witness and take part in one of the greatest national experiences, at the moment and site of its occurrence. It is our misfortune that he did not understand the smallest part of it."[11]

How, then, is *The Oregon Trail* "the most considerable achievement by an American historian"? Many historians have found many good things to say about the book, but few if any good things are to be found in DeVoto's writings. All DeVoto could see in Parkman was another ignorant Bostonian whose provincialism blinded him to everything significant about the westward movement even when he had it right under his nose—a prototype, in other words, of Van Wyck Brooks. Well, almost. Although "it was the narrowness, prejudice, and mere snobbery of the Brahmin that insulated him from the coarse, crude folk who were the movement he traveled with," Parkman outdid his twentieth-century counterpart (Brooks) in that he did at least visit the West. In fact, he proved himself equal to the physical vigors of the region if not to its cultural and intellectual challenges. "[T]hough the Brahmin was indifferent to Manifest Destiny [the original sin in DeVoto's historical metaphysics], the Puritan took with him a quiet valor which has not been outmatched among literary folk or in the history of the West."[12]

A full explanation for DeVoto's hostility to Parkman lies in DeVoto's psyche and probably eludes exact delineation. Don D. Walker observes that in DeVoto's mind Parkman stood between him and the West much as Brooks stood between him and Mark Twain. Psychologically, DeVoto "needed Parkman's book, not as source but as target." In order to make room for his own book, DeVoto needed to demolish Parkman's. Having a definable point of view toward one's materials, Walker continues, does not necessarily invalidate one's interpretation. "Certainly he [Parkman] brought with him the educated-in assumption that Harvard and New England were close to, if not actually the hub of the universe, that they represented a civilization from which the Western white settler and the Indian alike could only seem culturally down there, at best on the slow way up. Still *snob* is too strong a word, too personal a word. It implies an individual arrogance and blindness which I do not think the biography can wholly prove." No one, Walker concludes, is free of bias, and for DeVoto to condemn Parkman's implies an arrogance of his own. "No one surely would argue that Parkman left his cultural preconceptions back in Boston when he set out in March. Who did when he went west? Or for that matter, who did when he went east? One might as usefully argue that Bernard DeVoto could have understood Francis Parkman better if somehow he could have left his Western preconceptions, his Western snobbishness back there in Ogden."[13] Finally, DeVoto's condemnation of Parkman indicates a fundamental misunderstanding of the nature of historical (or literary, for that matter) interpretation. In his preface to *The Life and Adventures of James P. Beckwourth*, DeVoto asserted that "*The Oregon Trail* is a grand book; it is not the West." This statement reveals an assumption that a historical interpretation can be so profound, so definitive, that the book and the subject become one. In the nature of things, however, a book can never be more than a book. And the West will always remain as complex, as challenging, as perplexing, and as elusive of explanation as human nature itself. An honest book, Walker concludes, "tries to be true to its object, but the subject is there too. Anyone as aggressively present as Bernard DeVoto ought to have realized that even the most thorough of realism is tainted by the knowing presence. Any other view would be naive indeed."[14]

There are other caricatures in *The Year of Decision*. In fact, virtually none of DeVoto's characters appear in the full, baffling complexity and contradiction that other historians have seen. Military caricatures, to pick one example, abound in DeVoto's account of the Mexican War, which occupied so much of Americans' attention in 1846. Stephen Watts Kearny appears as the paragon of military competence. "In the vaudeville show of swollen egoism, vanity, treachery, incompetence, rhetoric, stupidity, and electioneering which the general officers during the Mexican Way display to the pensive mind, Kearny stands out as a gentleman, a soldier, a commander, a diplomat, a statesman, and a master of his job, whose only superior was Winfield Scott." (Scott's virtues are treated only in summary, for his contribution to the war, the capture of Mexico City and the capitulation of the Mexican government, came after 1846.)

Arrayed on the other side are the likes of John C. Fremont, "Major Jinks of the Horse Marines" (whom DeVoto previously called "Childe Harold" and "The Conqueror"), whose California command was "like some militia known to American humor as the Talapoosy Vollontares," and whose strategy "set a high value on the delayed attack. . . . He did not reach this war till it was over." Another was Commodore Robert Stockton, who "had Fremont's gift for multiplying the opposition by twenty-five whenever he calculated his chances." Where Stockton was a fool, Fremont "was worse than a fool, he was an opportunist, an adventurer, and a blunderer on a truly dangerous scale." Stockton, however, draws DeVoto's blame for passing on to Kearny what turned out to be the mistaken judgment that southern California had been pacified. This judgment led Kearny to leave two-thirds of his command in New Mexico and forced him, as a consequence, to fight at San Pascual with dangerously diminished (as well as starved and exhausted) manpower. Stockton unfairly bears the brunt of what was more likely inefficient communication. DeVoto conveniently forgets that mountain man Kit Carson, who was one of his paragons of wisdom and competence and who carried Stockton's message to Kearny, also believed both that southern California was indeed out of the fight and that the *californios* would not fight at San Pascual.

Zachary Taylor, even though he fought the Mexican army to a standstill in several victories along the Texas border (wherever one interpreted that as being), was incompetent in DeVoto's view for his subsequent passivity. "The victor sat in his attakapas pantaloons under a tent fly and grew great." President James K. Polk, who, DeVoto barely mentions, was doing his best not exactly to sabotage his Whig generals Taylor and Scott, but certainly to keep them from succeeding brilliantly enough to encourage presidential ambitions, "could get neither plans nor information from Taylor, who had none. His hard mind bogged in the softness of what cannot be called Taylor's intelligence."[15]

Some of DeVoto's characterizations are at least partly valid. Fremont's bungling in California was only a piece of a larger vaudeville show featuring actors from both sides, and his true dangerousness perhaps did not appear until his Civil War generalship—which DeVoto is probably reading back into 1846. Taylor may have been both lucky and indecisive, but he would fight when the chips were down, and Lincoln might have wished for such a general in northern Virginia in 1861–62.

The point here, though, is that DeVoto could only see one side of his characters—or in the case of Fremont, to whom he did give his due as an outdoorsman and explorer, one side at a time. The result is history as a cartoon feature, in which unmodulated characters go about their preordained tasks in their preordained ways to effect a preordained end. It makes an entertaining story, but it achieves its effect at the expense of a larger realism, a realism possible only through respect for the flawed virtues, the redeeming exceptions, and the pyrrhic victories that are the real object of history: life itself.

Dale Morgan

Dale Morgan

THE MENTOR

An arresting irony of Utah historiography is that thirty years after Dale Morgan's death, no biographer has yet attempted a full-scale study of the life of perhaps the state's best and one of its most prolific historians, himself a master biographer.[1] The irony is deepened by Morgan's readily available correspondence, which documents his life more elaborately than virtually any other comparable scholar's. And it is deepened even further by Morgan's life, which was, for a historical scholar, full of human interest and color. Out of personal poverty and national depression, he earned a university degree and made a career for himself as a book reviewer and historical writer, he triumphed over the devastating handicap of total deafness, and he was several times unlucky in love. He was an artist of professional skill, a championship chess player, a reader of endless breadth and depth, a researcher of bottomless energy driven by a relentless work ethic, and a prose stylist of breathtaking lyrical gifts.

No one writing in Morgan's specialties of the fur trade, overland trails, and the Mormons during his lifetime could have escaped his influence. Few would have wanted to, for while he was straightforward in his criticism, particularly of inaccuracy in factual detail, he was even more generous with his help, and his letters are filled with elaborate and often unsolicited assistance to other scholars. Morgan is the one thread that runs through the present book, for he was the only person well known by all the others and the one person who appears in the acknowledgments of all of their books on western history. It was Morgan, more than any other person, who taught the generation that matured in the 1940s how to write history, and his strengths and weaknesses as a historian were also their strengths and weaknesses. One would have to go back to the Romantic historians of the nineteenth century, the Francis Parkmans and the George Bancrofts, to find similar examples of historians who wrote history without academic training. But one can find few examples better than Morgan of one who could have profited from such training, who ignored and disdained it to his peril.

Morgan was born in Salt Lake City on December 18, 1914, and given the name Lowell Dale Morgan, which he used until adulthood, when he reversed the two given names. He was the oldest of four children born to James Lowell and Emily Holmes Morgan, who lived on Hollywood Avenue in a modest middle-class home just north of 21st South. The first of several tragedies in Morgan's life came in his fifth year when his father, a business machines salesman, died of appendicitis, leaving Morgan's mother with no way to support her young family. In a remarkable exhibition of the spirit and tenacity that became the hallmark of her oldest son, Emily Holmes Morgan worked her way through college and became an elementary school teacher.

As a boy, Dale Morgan gave every indication of a promising future. His good looks, topped by a head of thick curly hair that he retained throughout life, and his warm smile and sense of humor made him popular at school. His quick intellect brought him top grades, and he exhibited modest athletic ability. In the general optimism and prosperity of the 1920s, there was every reason for him to expect a first-rate education, a good marriage, and professional success.

In August 1929, just before his fourteenth birthday, the second tragedy in his life threatened to wipe out all those hopes. Morgan contracted spinal meningitis and lost his hearing, throwing him into an abyss of devastation for which as a young boy he was totally unprepared. Morgan's papers contain highly moving autobiographical accounts of the emotional turmoil he suffered as deafness approached, and how he experimented, in both the first and third person, with ways of telling of his hearing loss. The onset was apparently not sudden, yet it was terrifying in the speed and completeness with which it engulfed him. Lying in bed in the darkness, neither fully awake nor asleep,

> It seemed that I was dead. Strangely I was floating upward from the far dark earth toward an unforeseeable but queerly anticipated existence that was after-life. I began to say to myself in puzzled realization, incredulous of this experience, "I'm dead! I'm dead!"

Either in reality or in a dream, he heard his mother's voice asking,

> What's the matter? Dear, what's the matter? . . . Staring at the dark indeterminate ceiling, I began to hear the tolling of a locomotive bell. The sound grew louder and louder, insistently more harsh and more brazen. I had often heard trains pass by night on distant tracks, but never had there been such a savage clamor. . . . That sound is the last I was conscious of hearing. My mother's voice is the last voice I recall. I slipped into a haze from which I came, many hours later and without realizing my loss, bereft of my hearing.[2]

Deafness was not an unprecedented consequence of meningitis, but Morgan's doctors hastened to assure him (without intending to create false hopes) that it was sometimes temporary. But there was no way for them to know whether his hearing would return or not, and all they could advise was to wait and see. In the meantime, his life had to go on, but it could hardly continue as before. His mother kept him out of school for a year so Dale could wait for the return of his hearing, learn ways of coping if it did not, and avoid having to face his old schoolmates with this devastating handicap. "When I did return to school in the fall of 1930," Morgan recalled, "I knew very few kids, mostly those coming from my own neighborhood, and I was glad of it." But things were of course very different.

> I can see that I did remarkably well in school that year I returned. . . . But all my social relationships had changed. . . . The effect of the loss of my hearing was to deprive me of a little of the pre-eminence I had had scholastically, though less than might have been supposed in most respects. But socially life became a kind of quiet desperation for me, because I felt myself now relegated to the outer fringe where before I had been at the heart and center of everything.[3]

Still, Morgan had not reconciled himself to permanent deafness. As time went by and it became less and less likely that his condition was temporary, the social, academic, and personal frustration of his loss of hearing created an ever-mounting tension, and the necessity of coming to grips with a life of deafness became more immediate. Matters came to a head one unforgettably horrible evening in March 1931, when a minor altercation with his mother ignited a paroxysm of hysteria:

> Some trivial conflict with one of my younger brothers led Mother to bawl me out, unjustly as I then felt, and that blew [the] top, emotionally, off the whole thing. I was in a semi-hysterical state for a couple of hours, and during the course of it for the first time admitted to my mother as well as to myself the state of my feelings about the world I was having to make for myself.
>
> Later I could appreciate that that night marked a turning-point in my life. It took me a long while to work things out for myself at all satisfactorily, another seven or eight years, really. But that night I reached bottom. I began to face the future instead of wasting myself in bitter regret over a past that was beyond my reach. That was the beginning of my adjustment to the fact that my hearing was gone and would probably never return. No one ever settles anything in his life absolutely or permanently, but there are significant turning points, and this was the first and greatest one for me.[4]

Once he had begun to reconcile himself to permanent deafness, Morgan started studying lipreading as a means of communication, but it was not successful. The inevitable element of guesswork in lipreading frustrated Morgan's love of precision. He never learned to live with factual ambiguity, and although that tenacious demand for accuracy became his hallmark as a historian, it was his downfall as a lip reader. Even though he studied lipreading intensively enough to develop considerable competence, and probably used it to some degree in his daily interactions, none of his close friends recall much if any reliance on it. There is no evidence that he ever secretly used it as one might feign incompetence in a foreign language to gain an advantage over an interlocutor. Nor does Morgan ever seem to have studied sign language. Nowadays, American Sign Language experts provide interpretation at many public lectures and on television, but in Morgan's day it would have been useful only in conversing with other deaf people, of whom there were few, if any, in his circle of professional and personal acquaintances.

Instead, one communicated with Dale Morgan in writing, which could be a taxing experience. William Mulder remembered "using up a pad of note cards in conversation with him once on a park bench in Washington, D.C., when he sat by the hour like a patient academic Bernard Baruch sharing his wisdom." Roderic Korns, on an automobile ride with Morgan revisiting historic trails in Emigration Canyon and Parley's Canyon, reported that "I wore myself out trying to write my conversation and found it quite wearing and difficult to clear the points I wanted to make." And Morgan was not always sensitive to the burden he placed on his interlocutors. His friend Jarvis Thurston recalled that during chess games with him, Morgan would turn to Thurston's wife while Thurston was contemplating his next move and ask her what she thought of *Madame Bovary*—not a question easily answered in writing. Morgan would deliver his part of a conversation in "a high-pitched monotone," according to Mulder, in which, as Korns observed, he "talked fairly well and it was not often that I had to ask him to repeat." But talk was obviously much easier for Morgan than writing was for those with whom he was conversing.[5]

Other than rendering conversation difficult, the effects of Morgan's deafness on the personal and professional levels were profound but difficult to identify and measure. A common opinion is that his deafness partly accounts for his vast research and literary productivity because it rendered him immune to distraction. But it would be easy to ascribe too much importance to that; although Morgan's deafness certainly isolated him, most libraries and archives have few distractions anyway, and productive writers learn to find places where they can work undisturbed. Writers who have trouble focusing on their work often admit that they create their own distractions to avoid working and to mask a basic laziness. When one envisions Morgan spending his lunchtimes in the National Archives in Washington, D.C., transcribing newspaper articles on the Mormons and the far West, it seems more convincing to ascribe his productivity to his work ethic, an inner drivenness, than to the absence of distraction.

Careful speculation might suggest other possible effects of his deafness. Although Morgan was famously generous with his time in helping other scholars, and although his personal charm brought occasional social invitations, his deafness inevitably would have drastically attenuated his social life (a form of distraction, to be sure, if one cares to see it that way), thus lengthening the already long hours he spent on reading, writing, and correspondence. Further, because Morgan's deafness shifted his communication with the external world entirely to the written word, his world became a literary world, and the long hours of practice with the written word turned him into a virtuoso of English prose in the same way that musical practice produces virtuosity.

A third misfortune took place in Morgan's life simultaneously with the onset of his deafness. The stock market crash in the fall of 1929 and the ensuing Great Depression cast a huge shadow over Morgan's adolescent years. Jobs became scarce, and the prospects of Morgan's employability as a deaf person appeared grimmer still. Significantly, it was his literary ability that opened up his future. An admiring high school English teacher found college funds for him in a vocational rehabilitation program, and he entered the University of Utah in 1933. Although he had long been interested in history and writing, Morgan chose to major in art, his other area of talent, as a more promising avenue to eventual employment. It was an ironic choice: although he tried unsuccessfully again and again to secure work as a commercial artist, it was as a writer and historian that he found a career.

Morgan's choice of a major in art rather than history is understandable, both because of the employment prospects and also because the history department did not, perhaps, offer the university's strongest program. The department's best faculty members, Harold Dalgliesh and Jacob Geerlings, both had Ph.D.s in European history. American history was taught by Andrew Love Neff, who died in 1936 and was replaced during Morgan's senior year by Leland Creer and by an instructor named Madge Howe. Western history, Morgan's interest, was taught by Levi Edgar Young, whose pro-Mormon bias, like Neff's, was notorious, who possessed only a master's degree, and whose scholarship was shaky at best. Creer in 1937 was still an unknown quantity, but his dissertation, published as *Utah and the Nation*, showed promise. As we have seen, that dissertation turned out to have been the high point of his career rather than the beginning, but no one could have foreseen that at the time. One assumes Morgan took no classes from him because 1937 was already his last year and he was solidly committed to art.

The year following Morgan's graduation was a frustrating time, as it was for Utah and the entire country, which were still caught in the economic doldrums. Morgan had assumed that his talent and training in art would lead to employment, but it did not, both because there was little work available and because employers were unsure of how to deal with a deaf worker. Although his university writing experience led to a minor stipend as a weekly book reviewer for the *Salt Lake Tribune*, he spent most of his time playing chess, reading, and working around the house.

By the summer of 1938, though, Morgan's deepening friendship with college classmate Jarvis Thurston, who had found a job teaching high school mathematics in Ogden, led him toward new opportunities. The first one came to an unhappy conclusion. Morgan became infatuated with Thurston's wife, Madeline Reeder Thurston, a bright, aspiring writer who had studied with Bernard DeVoto at the annual Bread Loaf conference in Vermont. She and Morgan moved from intellectual to physical intimacy. As one could predict, the Thurston marriage eventually broke up, but Madeline rejected Morgan's suit and instead married Tom McQuown, a railroad worker and relative of Morgan's. But Morgan held out hopes of winning her back, and for years he continued to exchange thoughts on literary subjects with her and to promote her writing.[6]

The Thurston friendship also produced a much happier result. In July 1938, Maurice L. Howe, director of the Utah Historical Records Survey, one of the programs under Harry Hopkins's Works Progress Administration (WPA), approached Jarvis Thurston about coming to work for him. Thurston decided his teaching job offered a better future than the temporary work relief program, but he recommended Morgan for the position. Although Morgan was not on the relief roll and thus was not qualified for WPA employment, he impressed Howe and Ogden WPA office director Hugh F. O'Neil so much in an interview that they found a way through the red tape and hired him. Morgan was allowed ninety hours of work per month, for which he was paid seventy dollars, "by no means a fortune," he observed, "but it is pretty good pay, considering the time expended for it." The hours were flexible, too, which gave Morgan time to pursue his own writing projects as best he could.[7] The roughly four years Morgan spent with the WPA, first on the Historical Records Survey (HRS) and later as director of the Writers Project, were his apprenticeship in the historical profession. In later years Morgan sometimes referred to himself as "a product of the WPA graduate school."[8]

The Works Progress Administration, created in 1935, was one of the best-known but also one of the most controversial of President Franklin D. Roosevelt's New Deal programs.[9] Its five-billion-dollar budget was to be spent on work programs designed to get three-and-a-half million people off relief funds and back to work on worthwhile projects that nevertheless would not compete with private enterprise or established government functions. WPA jobs were part-time positions at slightly less than prevailing wages in private industry, which would enable workers to earn a living wage rather than simply receive a government dole, but the wages were low enough to be an incentive to find better-paying jobs in private enterprise. Although some WPA jobs "were make-work assignments of scant value," as William E. Leuchtenburg calls them, others, like the HRS and Writers Project, were useful, popular, and of permanent cultural value.[10] The Historical Records Survey in Utah, where Morgan was first employed, created inventories of various county and church archives, collected and copied personal diaries and autobiographies of historical merit, and interviewed pioneers whose lives were otherwise undocumented. The program had its shortcomings, however. Some county inventories were not completed, and no attempt was made to provide for proper storage and preservation of deteriorating records. In addition, many of the pioneer interviews, which were done by means of a standard list of questions, were perfunctory at best. Nevertheless, the county inventories that were completed proved useful, and the hundreds of personal diaries collected, which became the basis of the manuscript collection of the Utah State Historical Society, are still one of the state's monuments of historical documentation.

The Writers Project, at the national level, produced hundreds of publications. The book-length *Guides* to each of the states and territories were the basic product, but compilations of folklore and studies of regional and ethnic culture also resulted. The Utah project, which Morgan eventually directed, published one of the best of the state *Guides*, as well as Morgan's histories of Ogden and Provo and his edited version of the constitution and laws of the Mormon State of Deseret, among other things. The Writers Project was one of the most popular New Deal programs, a fact demonstrated in 1939 when every state in the union raised one-fourth of its share of the WPA budget as a condition of continued federal funding.

In 1938, when Morgan went to work for the WPA, the agency and the New Deal itself were at a point of crisis. The optimism at the outset of President Roosevelt's second term, which had begun with his 1936 landslide re-election victory, quickly vanished in the setbacks of 1937. Instead of the expected economic quickening in response to the millions of dollars expended in New Deal recovery programs, a frustrating economic downturn occurred. Roosevelt could not blame this recession on the policies of the previous administration, as he had the Great Depression itself, and it was derisively dubbed the "Roosevelt Recession" by his Republican opponents. Roosevelt then lashed out at the Supreme Court, which had declared the Agricultural Adjustment Act and the National Industrial Recovery Act—the two foundation stones of the First New Deal—unconstitutional. Characterizing the court as "nine old men," Roosevelt launched the misbegotten Judicial Reorganization Bill, which would have allowed him to add Democratic justices to the court. This "court-packing" bill, perhaps the worst political move of the longest presidential administration in American history, struck even congressional Democrats as a violation of the separation of powers, and they refused to pass it. Finally, the WPA fell under attack for the notorious and even deliberate wastefulness of its work programs, which were more concerned with getting paychecks into employees' hands than with the efficiency or even the usefulness of its projects. The federal Writers Project in particular, which had in some places been perceived as a tax-supported haven for left-wing writers, was investigated by the House Un-American Activities Committee under Rep. Martin Dies and suffered funding cuts at the hands of an increasingly conservative Congress.

To help justify its existence, the Writers Project seized upon the sesquicentennial anniversary of the writing and ratification of the Constitution (1787–89) and urged directors of its state affiliates, like Dale Morgan, to produce something that would affirm the principle of federalism. Not only would such projects reassure Congress of the patriotism of the WPA, they would also reassure the American people in that time of crisis of the inherent soundness of the American federal system.[11] Morgan realized that Utah history offered a unique and fascinating experience with federalism in the abortive State of Deseret, the Great Basin empire of the Mormons. Deseret had applied for statehood several times beginning in 1849 and remained in existence as a "ghost" government for more than two decades after Congress created the Territory of Utah as part of the Compromise of 1850.

The State of Deseret, to Morgan, was historically significant for at least two reasons. For one, it pointed to an essential ambiguity in the Northwest Ordinance of 1787. In that law, Congress created the territorial stage as an "apprenticeship" phase through which an emerging political entity could work its way toward admission to statehood as an equal member of the federal union. The drafters of the ordinance had left considerable room for debate over which entity, Congress or the people of the territory, should initiate the statehood process, in other words, whether the territorial phase under congressional tutelage was mandatory, or whether a political entity could apply directly for statehood. Historically, the power had come to reside with Congress, and those areas that had hoped to bypass the territorial process and apply for statehood on their own had not fared well. The putative State of Franklin (the trans-Appalachian portion of western North Carolina that eventually became Tennessee) was the first to fail, followed eventually by the State of Oregon (eventually carved up into the three states of the Pacific Northwest), the State of Deseret, and the State of California. Of those, only California attained statehood outside the territorial process.[12]

Morgan saw that the State of Deseret was also significant as an instance of the Mormon counterpoint to mainstream American history.

The impulse behind the Mormon emigration to Utah was self-determination, including not only the right to their own religious, social, and economic institutions, but also the hallowed American right of self-government. Statehood would provide self-determination, whereas territorial status would place them under the governance of officials designated by Congress. Although there were members of Congress and other Americans in high places who supported Mormon self-determination through statehood, reports of Mormon theocracy and polygamy convinced others of the essential un-Americanness of Mormon institutions. Those hostile congressmen insisted upon creation of Utah Territory and repeatedly defeated statehood bids by the State of Deseret.

An unstated but equally powerful undercurrent beneath Morgan's interest in the State of Deseret was his frustration with the by now limited and overworked body of primary source material for Utah history. The Historical Records Survey was turning up an immense number of diaries, personal interviews, and other primary materials that promised to revolutionize Utah history. Morgan saw that the publication of the constitution and early ordinances of the State of Deseret, with their historical context given in a lengthy editorial introduction, could add substantially to the body of primary materials on early Utah political and social history. Sponsored by the Writers Project and Salt Lake City, the Utah State Historical Society published Morgan's *The State of Deseret* in the 1940 volume of the *Utah Historical Quarterly*. It was his first substantial historical publication directed at a general audience and, with *Utah: A Guide to the State*, which he edited, partially wrote, and published in 1941, it was one of the two literary culminations of the WPA program in Utah.

Though it was sponsored by public institutions and supported by public funding, *The State of Deseret* was perhaps Morgan's least accessible book for general audiences. It was his most analytical and academically styled book, likely to be popular only among those who would regard poring over legal documents as light reading. For Morgan, who had done his professional training in the "WPA graduate school," *The State of Deseret* was his dissertation. Like Father Dwyer, who also realized he was opening up source materials that had never been used,

Morgan salted his narrative heavily with primary source quotations and documentation. With his *West From Fort Bridger*, which he edited in collaboration with Roderic Korns and Charles Kelly, and his collaboration with Carl Wheat on the multivolume *Mapping the Trans-Mississippi West* toward the end of his career, *The State of Deseret* represented Morgan's scholarly side. The WPA *Guide*, *The Humboldt*, and *The Great Salt Lake*, on the other hand, showed Morgan's skill as a popular writer who could synthesize a great deal of scholarly research, yet present it in appealing and accessible prose. With the other writers who are the focus of this book, Morgan helped create a tradition of the scholar-writer in western history who could reach both professional and popular audiences.

Utah historians before Morgan had been aware of the State of Deseret, but they had treated it as little more than a curiosity, a quixotic and abortive episode that was tangential to the real story of life in the territorial period. For them, the real story was exploration, colonization, population growth, and institutional development on the one hand, and emerging conflict between Mormon and Gentile and between Mormon Utahns and territorial officials on the other. Morgan saw more in the statehood bid and the persistence of the ghost government of Deseret. For one thing, the State of Deseret manifested something unique about the Mormons in the context of western history. "The *Ordinances of the State of Deseret* fully indicate the political and social maturity of the people who created them," Morgan asserted. Although other western settlers brought with them "potentialities for political activity," the Mormons possessed "an immediate capacity for comprehensive organization." It was their ecclesiastical cohesion and regimentation that made such political maturity possible, for "the Mormons very simply had elaborated their ecclesiastical machinery into a political government." Outside observers of Mormon politics, particularly Gentile critics, might emphasize its essentially undemocratic nature, but Morgan saw another side to that as well, a politics that was grounded in an organic relationship between leaders and followers. "In criticizing Mormon authority, opponents usually failed to take into account the specific trust of the Mormons in their leaders, and the sense of responsibility held by the leaders toward their people—a conception of inter-responsibility and mutual faith, which was certainly a more vital ethical relationship than is ordinarily observed between governors and governed."[13] Morgan was also the first historian to study and to perceive the significance of the ghost government of Deseret that persisted for more than twenty years after the establishment of Utah territorial government. Unwilling to affirm the political immaturity territorial status indicated, the Utah Mormons continued to run their own "state" government parallel to the Gentile territorial regime, passing the same laws passed by the territorial legislature and electing their own officials, all the while repeatedly applying for the statehood they asserted that their political maturity justified. Far from representing political disloyalty, as anti-Mormon observers claimed, the State of Deseret represented to Morgan's mind nothing more than a demonstration of Mormon capacity for self-government that lay at the heart of American federalism since the Revolution.

It is important to note that *The State of Deseret* includes not only the constitution, but also the entire body of ordinances, so far as they have survived, that were passed by the ghost government. In them, one can see the ongoing, day-to-day demonstration of Mormon self-government that lifts the State of Deseret out of the realm of wishful thinking or reckless rebellion. Moreover, the ordinances are a fertile field for social and economic history as one sees the government wrestling with matters of irrigation, timber cutting, stock raising, and other settlement issues. In this, one finds another of the main themes of Morgan's later career as a historian: there is no history without sources, so a necessary precondition for history is the collecting, cataloging, editing, and publishing of primary material. Surveying Morgan's bibliography, it is apparent that he spent as much time editing and publishing source material as he did in synthesizing it into his own interpretive narratives.[14] Historical editing was an enterprise to which Morgan's passion for detail and accuracy ideally fitted him, and western historical writing owes even more, perhaps, to Morgan for that than for his own histories, vitally important though they are. Finally, *The State of Deseret* exemplified the perspective on Mormon history that Morgan held for his entire career. Although he had been an active Mormon as a boy, he lost his faith and quietly apostatized during his teenage years. Thereafter, he refused to accept any explanation of Mormonism in any but naturalistic terms. *The State of Deseret* demonstrated Morgan's interest in the secular effects of Mormon theology on Mormon history and institutions even as he turned his back on its religious content.

Historically important though *The State of Deseret* was, the preparation of a state guide was always the primary goal of the Writers Project, in Utah as in every other state. The state guides were supplemented by guides to major cities and regional guides, which swelled the total number of WPA guides to more than fifty. They were conceived as American *Baedekers*, directed toward an audience of intelligent readers and tourists in whom would be instilled a sense of patriotism (though the guides were not to avoid discussion of bad things as the *Baedeker* guides were notorious for doing) and an enticement to travel. The guides appeared just as wartime mobilization was beginning to pull the country out of the Great Depression (the Utah guide was published in 1941), but the rationing of gasoline and tires required by the war effort caused the hoped-for tourism to be postponed. Nevertheless, the needs of the anticipated dual audience of reader and traveler were addressed by the format imposed by the national Writers Project office. A first section would survey the state's history, natural features, economy, and other fundamental facts. This would be followed by sketches of major cities, and finally an elaborate mile-by-mile tour guide for each of the state's major and minor roads. In the case of Utah and other states rich in national parks and monuments, a concluding section covered each of those. The final product was to be a straightforward, up-to-date, factually accurate source of information. "For God's sake," expostulated Bernard DeVoto in advising preparers of a model guide for the series, "make the New England volume a guide. I never yet saw a tourist who wanted to be preached at or even lectured to. He wants to know where the old mill used to be, how far it is to East Twinflower and where is the comfort station."[15]

The Utah guide was a huge success and widely applauded as one of the best in the series, in no small part because it exhibited Morgan's unique talents as a researcher and writer. As historian Ray Allen Billington, director of the Massachusetts Writers Project, observed, the

Utah guide excelled "not only because [Morgan's] perfectionist instincts drove his staff to check and recheck every fact for accuracy, but because his graceful style endowed the volume with a literary grace that many lacked." The utility of the volume is attested by the multiplication in our own travel-happy day of revisions or acknowledged imitations of the WPA guide.[16]

Within the context of the historical and descriptive literature of Utah at the time, the *Guide* was the first serious attempt to present the state objectively and in its entirety, with no special biases for or against, in particular, the Mormons. Billington's characterization of Morgan's objectivity in *The Great Salt Lake* applies to the *Guide* as well: "Today's readers, even those best informed on the Church of Jesus Christ of Latter-day Saints, will not be able to determine whether Dale Morgan when he wrote these pages was a Mormon, a 'Jack Mormon,' or a Gentile."[17] The book's coverage is equally unprejudiced, from the state's main thoroughfares to the merest backcountry road, from the ornamental arts of the Cliff Dwellers to the Mormon Tabernacle Choir, and from the stories of Wallace Stegner to the witticisms and tall tales of rural characters like Buck Lee and Zeke Johnson. Most notable to the historian is the book's coverage of "The Contemporary Scene," not only in Morgan's gracefully written section of that title, but throughout the book, where recent developments in most aspects of Utah life are fully considered.

The *Guide*, then, represented a vast improvement on existing Utah literature, but this is not to say that it fully succeeded in portraying all significant aspects of Utah life. For one thing, Morgan's awareness of Utah's ethnic diversity was barely better than that of writers like Milton R. Hunter. Although the dazzling diversity of Utah's mining districts like Bingham Canyon and Carbon County was conspicuous even to the most untrained eye, the *Guide* notes the fact only once, in passing, in its description of Helper, where "the narrow street is crowded with American, Italian, Greek, Austrian, Japanese, and Chinese miners, who depend upon the twenty-eight mines in the area for a livelihood." Otherwise, the colorful aspects of Bingham Canyon and Carbon County are limited to the wildlife of saloons and whorehouses in the first instance, and the exploits of outlaws like Butch Cassidy in the second.

Although the baffling escape of the Hispanic outlaw Rafael Sanchez is recounted in connection with Bingham Canyon, the hundreds of members of ethnic minorities like him are passed over in silence.[18]

Utah Indians fare a little better in the *Guide* than they do as Levi Edgar Young's romantic primitives or Andrew Love Neff's "Indian problem." The Basketmakers and Cliff Dwellers of the southeastern Utah receive ample coverage, as do the historic Utes, Shoshones, and others. But what modern readers would regard as the tragic dispossession of the Indians and the poverty of their reservation life are almost completely ignored. The travel guide to the Uintah-Ouray reservation, for example, flatly mentions that the Indians' annual per capita income is $187, but it does not point out that the statewide average per capita income was $482. "The Utah Indians have retained little of their original culture," the guide adds, as though that were the Indians' fault, and it credits the federal government with encouraging a revival of traditional arts "because of the current demand for hand-made goods," rather than because of the inherent value of those "goods" as part of a functioning culture. This information concludes on a partial page the rest of which filled with a caricature of an Indian with a drooping feather in his hair and a couple of crooked arrows in a quiver, gorging himself on raw fish. On the other hand, although Mormon-Indian relations are described in benevolent terms, including the "surprising" finding within western history that the Indian wars in Utah were relatively brief and that "conflict between whites and Indians was not without 'some show of justice' on the part of the Indians, as Brigham Young admitted."[19]

Morgan's WPA years, as we have seen, were his apprenticeship in history, his "WPA graduate school." Measuring his stature as a historian in about 1942, it is clear that he had indeed matured and had taken on most of the characteristic strengths and weaknesses that marked his subsequent career. For one thing, the WPA encouraged and utilized his immense capacity for work. However inefficient and unproductive some of the other WPA projects were—and American mythology is full of WPA work crews leaning on shovel handles—the Writers Project was no refuge for drones. Even though quantity and quality do not always go hand in hand and in fact are sometimes in competition, the hundreds of Writers Project publications maintained a remarkably high quality while impressively demonstrating that WPA workers could make ink and paper fly.

Furthermore, the Writers Project created a new base upon which Morgan had a free hand to build his brand of history untrammeled by the outworn traditions of other Utah historical institutions. "In significant ways," Charles S. Peterson points out, the Utah Writers Project "looked beyond the conventions of antiquarianism and history that governed established Utah writers, including historians of the Mormon Church, professors at the state universities, and members of the historical society."[20]

Less happily, the "WPA graduate school" curriculum included no philosophy. What we call "public history" in our own day is mostly carried out by academically trained historians with graduate degrees and a clear sense of the larger cultural benefits and implications of historical study. The Writers Project workers generally lacked such background (many, in fact, had only tenuous qualifications even as writers); their only concerns were factual accuracy and production in pursuit of a largely utilitarian end such as providing background data for tourists, as in the state *Guides*. In a sense, Morgan's later historical career was only an individual continuation of the Historical Records Survey and the Writers Project in which he discovered, edited, and published collections of primary sources on the one hand, and assembled them into factually accurate narratives on the other, with virtually no concern for interpretation or any other larger dimension of his craft. Finally, the WPA also developed Morgan's inherent cockiness and egotism. Always possessed of a sure sense of his abilities, Morgan used the WPA as a base for a kind of intellectual demagoguery in which the amateurs outdid the pros. Writing to thank University of Utah biologist Ralph V. Chamberlin for a couple of his book-length forays into history, Morgan began with a typical jab at the historical establishment, noting about academic books "the quality of intellectual curiosity they display in their author, the sore lack of which is my most serious charge against Utah's historians today. Sometimes I think that those who do not profess to be professional historians are the only ones who exhibit this important quality, without which a work of history is a mere parody of what it ought to be." Writing to Charles Kelly to complain of the shortcomings of one of Leland Creer's articles, he wrote, "Sometimes I get awfully discouraged about the state of scholarship in Utah. The non-academic scholars like two I could name are the only ones worth a damn." And commenting evidently on a caustic reception of one of Bernard DeVoto's books by an academic reviewer, Morgan objected to

> the same guff about "history." I guess when you come right down to it, the term "history" had better be redefined to mean, "a species of writing produced by or enroute to a Ph.D." I have had enough troubles trying to break a path alongside this main-traveled road to know something of the snobberies at work here, and the ways in which the academic world and even the world of learning are geared to these attitudes. Yet I think it would be instructive to make a survey of every field of American history and note how many of the major works in those fields have been produced by mavericks, or someone working outside his formal specialization—Elliott Coues, for example. Or Henry R. Wagner. Or Charlie Camp.[21]

Quotations like these could be multiplied many times over from Morgan's correspondence. There is certainly more than a kernel of truth in them, for as we have seen, Utah historical writing at the time Morgan came on the scene was largely inadequate, and Morgan cannot be faulted for insisting on exhaustive research and factual accuracy. Several things, though, are unseemly about comments of this nature. They ignore, for one thing, the existence of academically trained historians of unchallenged competence. Father Dwyer, for instance, had been a prominent figure in Utah history while Morgan was still doing his WPA apprenticeship, and the 1950s saw a flood of them in the persons of A. Russell Mortensen, Everett Cooley, Brigham Madsen, and others. Furthermore, in his realistic moments Morgan had to admit that the historical "amateurs" were not producing any better history than were the academics. Morgan's letters are full of condemnations of the work of nonacademic historians such as Paul Bailey, Stanley Vestal (Walter Stanley Campbell), and J. Cecil Alter. Even Charles Kelly, as Morgan admitted to Bernard DeVoto, was prone to damaging bias and factual error.[22] Finally, there is an irony in what must be called Morgan's anti-intellectualism. While standing outside the ivy-covered walls and scoffing at the admittedly status-seeking stuffed shirts who dwelt behind them, and promoting do-it-yourself history as the only valid kind, Morgan was cutting himself off from developing the dimensions most lacking in his own writing, the want of which kept his books from acquiring the larger meaning they should have had. Morgan's books lack the sense of history as a cultural activity, as an avenue to understanding, as an ever-changing process of conceptual reconstruction, a means by which each generation answers its own questions about the nature of the world it inhabits rather than just corrects the factual errors of past historians. He who most scorned academia was most in need of what academia could have provided.

As the world slipped closer and closer to war during the late 1930s, the New Deal work programs shifted more and more toward war mobilization activities. The Civilian Conservation Corps, for example, which had employed thousands of young men on forestry projects, had always been run on a paramilitary basis, and increasingly it provided actual military training. WPA crews also helped build military bases such as Hill Air Force Base in Utah. Once the United States actually entered the war in December 1941, the shift from work relief to war mobilization accelerated. As that happened, Morgan became increasingly frustrated with his job, which was neither effective defense work nor the literary work he relished. "I confess . . . I am becoming a little fed up on WPA and all its red tape," he wrote to Juanita Brooks, "especially now that we on this project are losing all individual identity, and are being merged into a sort of anonymous 'War Service' program. (Technically there has been no Utah Writers Project for the last week or so; we are now merely a 'phase' of the War Service Division, like all the other white collar projects.) And the constriction of our activities somewhat gets on my nerves. If I have to spend all my time on defense stuff, I'd like it to be big, rather than piddling, defense stuff." He began talking of leaving Utah for a large metropolitan center where he could deepen his historical background and pursue his research in better libraries and archives than Utah could afford. Also, he wanted "to become external to Utah for a while and look the place over from a distance."[23]

In the fall of 1942 he found a way to accomplish both goals when he accepted a job with the Office of Price Administration, a federal agency created to control wartime inflation. The position took him to

Washington, D.C., where he had immediate access to the Library of Congress and the National Archives and was within reasonable distance of both New York City and the region where Mormonism had originated. Before long, historian and friend Nels Anderson found Morgan living "just over the Potomac in Virginia across the Francis Scott Key Bridge. Got a new one-room apartment and lives alone with his typewriter. He was able to get a job in spite of his deafness and is well liked." Even the work was congenial, as Morgan reported to Charles Kelly:

> About my job, it is in the Trade Services Branch of the OPA Press and Campaigns Division of the Info. Dept. We write for retailers, wholesalers, and the trade services bulletins setting forth in more simple language the provisions of the highly technical and legalistic Regulations. My own job is to edit the copy of four other writers, simplifying and dejargonizing it. While hardly so interesting as the Writers' Projects, the job is instructive, good discipline in factual writing, and not so dull as it sounds.[24]

During the years Morgan spent in Washington, D.C., 1942–47, he found himself in a historian's heaven. While he honed his writing and editing skills at his OPA job, he spent his noon hours, evenings, and weekends doing research, writing, traveling, and developing his friendship with Fawn Brodie. Brodie was at that time completing her biography of Joseph Smith with extensive help from Morgan, and her husband Bernard was transferred to Washington as a Navy intelligence officer at about the same time Morgan arrived there. Morgan's Washington years saw the beginning of what he called his "tool books"—bibliographies and compilations of primary sources such as his "Mormons and the Far West," which consisted of transcriptions of newspaper articles in the eastern press during the first half of the nineteenth century.[25] The "tool books" are awe-inspiring testimony to Morgan's capacity for grueling work. As John Phillip Walker reminds us, they "had to be pounded out by hand on a standard typewriter" in those years of primitive duplication methods. Although some of them, like his newspaper transcriptions, are, as Walker observes, "sadly ignored by most researchers today," they were the groundwork of the almost omniscient command of Mormon and western history exhibited in the works of Morgan's maturity.[26]

Morgan's first book produced by a commercial publisher and unaffiliated with the WPA was *The Humboldt, Highroad of the West* (1943), which Farrar & Rinehart had commissioned as part of their Rivers of America series.[27] Morgan wrote the book during his WPA tenure as the beginning of a bridging of his government employment and his career as an independent historian. Even though the University of Nebraska Press reissued the book in paperback in 1985, it has not been one of Morgan's more popular titles. Students of his work often give it little more than a nod as his entry into the historical profession and a stepping stone on the way toward the works of his maturity. The relative lack of interest in the book might be a result of a lack of interest in its subject, for today we view the Humboldt River through sunglasses in stereo-equipped and air-conditioned comfort at 75 MPH on Interstate 80 across central Nevada. From that perspective the sluggish little stream and the small, remote settlements it supports seem insignificant indeed. One needs a fair degree of historical imagination to see the river in Morgan's terms as a great thoroughfare of western emigration. Morgan himself had little expectation of success for the book. As he neared completion of the manuscript, he wrote Juanita Brooks that "damned glad I'll be to have it over and done with. It won't add to my reputation appreciably, but it will never detract from it either, I think, and that's a lot to ask of anyone's first book."[28]

And yet one could easily argue that *The Humboldt* was Morgan's real masterpiece. Charles S. Peterson's judgment that "few have possessed a sense for issues, an instinct for sources, and a capacity for precision and grace in historical writing to the happy degree that Dale Morgan did" is borne out by a reading of *The Humboldt*, which reveals all three of those virtues in perhaps better balance than Morgan ever again achieved. It is true that *West From Fort Bridger* (1951) better shows Morgan's grasp of the factual minutiae of overland trails geography, and his *Jedediah Smith and the Opening of the West* (1953) shows a better mastery of a vast body of primary sources and secondary literature. But the narrative in both of those classic works tends to bog down under the weight of Morgan's awe-inspiring scholarship.[29] The trail along the Humboldt, by contrast, simply follows the river plain and requires little unraveling of geographic riddles, while the sources, which Morgan's industrious research expanded significantly, are less extensive and problematic than those supporting his later works.[30] Consequently, Morgan's animated prose (*The Humboldt* is surely his best-written book) easily buoyed the weight of his research down that crooked stream. *The Humboldt* is a masterful historical synthesis and an unforgettable literary experience.

In *The Humboldt*, the author and the subject are perfectly matched. As the subtitle indicates, the river's historical significance was as a leg of the California Trail, furnishing a route across the western Great Basin in the mid-nineteenth century, a place and a time that Morgan was carving out as his field of expertise. One of the book's most notable features, though, is Morgan's effort to cover the entire history of the river. The bulk of the narrative concerns the nineteenth century, but the story extends, at least in some fashion, up to the early 1940s. Writing contemporary history presents a particular set of problems that historians have only in recent decades begun to master, and in Morgan's day it was rarely attempted, especially in western history. The influence of Frederick Jackson Turner, the father of western history, was still dominant, and even though Turner himself had recognized the importance of more recent history, his thesis that the frontier was the main theme of western history and that the frontier had closed by 1890 kept scholars' focus on the pre-twentieth-century era. And, as we have seen, the Mormon historians familiar to Morgan in his youth rarely extended their vision beyond the pioneer period. But Morgan's apprenticeship with the WPA, where history was made to serve contemporary concerns, had broadened his view. Even though his specialties—early Mormonism, the fur trade, and overland emigration—were all nineteenth-century subjects, Morgan often extended his narratives into his own century; the WPA state guide, *The Humboldt*, and *The Great Salt Lake* were only some examples. His was an unusual and forward-looking perspective on western history.

The Humboldt also established a precedent: Morgan never short-changed his readers. He always took the broadest possible view of his subject and never left geographic or thematic loose ends. Thus his history of the Humboldt River is more than just a narrative of one portion of the California Trail (although it is that magnificently), but rather the story of the exploration and development of various routes to California. Chapter 3, for example, almost amusingly exhibits Morgan's early fascination with the mountain man Jedediah Smith. Morgan gives an elaborate account of Smith's two journeys across the Great Basin to California in 1826–27, including such far-flung events as his cordial reception by Father Jose Bernardo Sanchez at San Gabriel, his journey up the coast to the Hudson's Bay Company country in Oregon, and the disastrous Umpqua massacre. Morgan devoted an entire chapter to all this in a history of the Humboldt River—which Smith never saw! To be sure, Smith's experience is anything but irrelevant because it vividly illustrates the near impossibility of crossing the Great Basin in its northern latitudes *without* water from the Humboldt. Another scholar, though, might have confined his discussion of Smith to a paragraph or two.

The Humboldt is unforgettable for its literary brilliance. Though it was his first real book, Morgan was already in full possession of his literary power, like an eagle emerging from its shell fully fledged and ready to soar. The felicitous turn of phrase, the telling example, the vivid description, leap out from every page as they do only in the works of his contemporaries Bernard DeVoto and Wallace Stegner, and as they do nowhere else in his books with such profusion. Morgan begins his narrative conventionally, with a description of the geography of the river, but there is nothing conventional in his handling of that apparently unexciting subject. Morgan felt the novelist's obligation to get his hooks into his readers on the very first page and to hang onto them on every subsequent page until his story was done. This he does by emphasizing, through anecdote, poem, and descriptive detail, the essentially inhospitable nature of the river for human purposes—its alkaline brackishness, its odor, its circuitous course inhibiting direct progress, its ultimate death in the fetid Humboldt Sink, and the Indians who frustrated emigrant travel not by direct confrontation but by skirmish that niggled away one's patience or by the arrow that often wounded rather than killed. "This is the paradox of the Humboldt,"

Morgan proposed, "that it was almost the most necessary river of America, and the most hated." One could scarcely cross the Great Basin without it, but one prayed for the end of its course, when the bugs, the heat, and the lye-tasting water gave way to the forest coolness and the tumbling streams of the east slope of the Sierra. "The Humboldt. The goddam Humboldt! This is its story."[31]

Nor did the ordeals inflicted by the Humboldt end with the emigrant crossings. The country proved as inhospitable to settlement as to travel. In Morgan's words, "few settled here until they had to, until greener lands were occupied." Overweening optimism became the downfall of many would-be settlers who succumbed to boosters' blandishments here as elsewhere in the arid West. Near the end of the book, Morgan describes his own visit to Metropolis, Nevada, north of Wells on the upper reaches of the Humboldt tributaries. A dryland development company had lured gullible would-be farmers, mostly from Salt Lake City, to attempt agriculture without sufficient water during the first decade of the twentieth century. To Morgan, the failure of that utopian back-to-the-land scheme was vividly symbolized by an infestation of Mormon crickets that were busily eating the last of the meager crops as he arrived. As a metaphor for the horrors of the Humboldt, his description of the crickets is unsurpassed:

> Imagine a loathsome grasshopper without wings, a grasshopper leaden black or bedbug red, a grasshopper as thick and long as a powerful man's thumb, a grasshopper that leaps and skitters along the ground or pauses to stare with an unutterable malignance. . . . Looking at a Mormon cricket, you suddenly disbelieve the stories the Mormons in Utah tell of sea gulls that came miraculously in 1848 to gorge upon them and save the crops. It is unimaginable that a sea gull could find courage to look a cricket in the eye, let alone actually pick a fight with one and eat it. A Mormon cricket looks strong and mean enough to jump on sea gulls and rend them limb from limb, feather from feather.[32]

Morgan continued to exhibit an eye for telling and colorful detail and a gift of narrative throughout all his books. The last one he wrote primarily for a popular audience, *The Great Salt Lake*, which appeared in 1947 as part of Bobbs Merrill's American Lakes Series, was an obvious attempt to follow up on Farrar & Rinehart's Rivers of America series, for which Morgan had written the Humboldt book. The Great Salt Lake book contains many examples of the wit and color of the Humboldt history, but it is a much more substantial book. Morgan was able to bring into it more of the basic themes of western history in which he had become a virtuoso. In fact, the major delight as well as the major flaw of the book is that it fairly bursts its bindings with factual detail on the entire westward movement, much of which bears little relationship to the Great Salt Lake. The lake, in other words, became a metaphor for western history largely conceived, and it proved to be too small a canvas for the larger picture Morgan was eager to paint. No reader could complain of not getting fair value for the cover price, and the appearance of two reprint editions in recent years by university presses in Utah and New Mexico is eloquent testimony to the book's economic as well as its intellectual appeal.

Ray Allen Billington has given us a revealing glimpse into the pressures under which Morgan wrote *The Great Salt Lake* during the last years of his service with the Office of Price Administration.[33] The paradise of access to the historical resources of Washington, D.C., had begun to give way to the purgatory of government work. The agency, under congressional attack, was forced to eke more productivity out of its workers by requiring full days and even Saturday shifts, which ate into Morgan's research and writing time. Ready to strike out on his own at last as an independent historian, in 1945 Morgan had applied for and received a Guggenheim fellowship which he wished to activate in 1947 to work on his projected multivolume history of Mormonism. The Great Salt Lake book was to be a potboiler for Morgan, a quick synthesis of the western history materials he had been gathering that would provide additional financial support while he traveled around in search of Mormon materials.

It was not to be. Not only did his employer raise the number of hours he was expected to put in, but unexpected houseguests and the arrival of his mother took up still more of his writing time. On the other side of the equation, Morgan could not resist the temptation to include as much as possible of the fruits of his reading and research, and the manuscript began growing to gigantic proportions. In the end, it was only by dint of almost round-the-clock efforts that threatened his health that Morgan was able to deliver the finished manuscript on November 11, 1946, well after the April 1 date previously agreed upon with the publisher.

The book was worth waiting for, not only because of its fact-crammed panorama of western history, but also for its balanced and judicious interpretations. Morgan's impartial perspective on the Mormons, for example, amazed Milo M. Quaife, his editor, who professed to be unable to tell what Morgan's religious affiliation might be. And once again Morgan demonstrated his mastery of contemporary issues and history, as he had done in the WPA *Guide* and the Humboldt book, as well as his awareness of scientific fields and folklore many historians would slight. Like the WPA *Guide*, the book would be as useful to the tourist as to the reader. Finally, Morgan impressively demonstrated, perhaps with more detail than some readers would prefer, his vision of the West as a whole, comprehensible only within an international perspective and over the broadest chronological scope.

The Great Salt Lake, though, marked a turning point in Morgan's career. Never again would he write, at book length at least, for a purely popular audience. He had discovered, as Billington points out, that he was "by inclination and instinct, a historian's historian, less concerned with reaching a wide audience than with locating a revealing document, refuting hoary legends, and recording the events of the past as they had actually happened, however few those who cared to read."[34] Morgan was fully prepared, then, both in preparation and orientation, to begin the work upon which, more than any other, his reputation as a western historian has rested.

Having gotten the manuscript for *The Great Salt Lake* off to the publisher, Morgan began what must have been one of the happiest years of his life. He had received a Guggenheim fellowship to complete the research for what he had planned as his magnum opus, a multivolume history of Mormonism, and he hoped to get a one-year renewal to do the writing. With that $2,000 stipend in his pocket, he quit his government job and embarked on an automobile tour that took him to historic sites associated with Mormonism and hitherto unvisited archives in the East and the West. It took most of the winter of 1947–48.

Arriving at his mother's home in Salt Lake City in 1948, though, his hopes came crashing down when he learned that his Guggenheim renewal application had been denied, and also that the archives of the Mormon Church would not be opened to him. Desperate for money, Morgan sought and received an advance of $750 from Farrar & Rinehart for the Mormon history, which he unwisely, as it turned out, promised to deliver to them in 1949. Although he had no job to return to in Washington D.C., he went back anyway, evidently because of better job and research opportunities there than in Salt Lake City. He was never to live in Utah again.

The next couple of years were financially tight for Morgan. He pieced together an income reviewing books for the *Saturday Review of Literature* and cataloging manuscripts for a New York City dealer. Realizing he was not going to be able to deliver the Mormon book and falling under increasing pressure from the publisher to produce something in return for the advance, Morgan turned to Bobbs Merrill and asked for an advance of $750 to pay off Farrar & Rinehart. For *that* advance, he promised to write a biography of Jedediah Smith. What became his best book was written, ironically, on the spur of the moment out of notes he had been stockpiling over the years, as a stopgap to keep food on his table.

Jedediah Smith and the Opening of the West which appeared in 1953, is not only Morgan's masterpiece but a classic of western history as well. Although discoveries of new sources like Smith's journal of his 1826–27 journey to California[35] have rendered the book no longer definitive (Morgan was planning a revised edition at the time of his death), it is universally acknowledged as one of the best books on any aspect of western history, and for almost a half-century it has occupied an unimpeachable place on the reading list of nearly every western history course.

Its virtues are not hard to discover. In fact, Morgan listed most of them in the preface and at greater length in an unpublished letter to his publisher who was looking for dust jacket copy. It is, for one thing, an adventure story, for Smith was the most intrepid explorer of all the mountain men, traveling immense distances across terrain known only to the Indians and enduring incredible risk and privation. And Smith was a highly unusual character who stood out even among a breed of unusual men, engaging and yet mysterious as well. The biography is also an American success story, as Smith rose from the greenest hand to fur company entrepreneur in only three years, after which he made a considerable fortune and retired after only eight years in the mountains.

Morgan's doggedly persistent research, his exhaustive reading, and his mastery of a galaxy of factual details reveal themselves on every page. There are few books in any field of history more tightly packed with facts than *Jedediah Smith*. For the first time in the historiography of the fur trade, Morgan examined the financial ledgers, determining prices, margins, profits, and losses. He kept a consistent focus on the interrelationships between fur trade competitors, not only rival American companies but international rivals as well, and he avoided what he called "the frankly nationalistic kind of writing about the fur trade which puts the British and American trade in the West in separate compartments." The preface to the book underscores the point yet again: "I shall be satisfied if those who read my book gain from it an organic sense of the West, the play of cause and effect marvelously intricate on occasion, but always a whole."[36]

And yet some of these acknowledged virtues contain problems as well. First, the book as an adventure tale. "Jedediah Smith's life in the West was a sustained adventure, yet it always added up to a great deal more than a simple adventure," Morgan tells us in the preface, "and this biography is written with an eye to the symbols."[37] One wonders what "symbols" Morgan had in mind. It is all too easy for the historian to claim too much for his subject by failing to establish the ways in which the part represents the whole or the individual represents the species. This case is especially perilous, for Smith was unique in so many ways that he symbolized nothing but himself. True, he symbolized the entrepreneurial possibilities of the fur trade, but he succeeded so spectacularly better than almost anyone else in the business that he is hardly a representative symbol. The same can be said of his explorations. Although they symbolize the ability of all mountain men (those who survived, anyway) to make their way through uncharted country, Smith's explorations were of a different order from anything attempted by his colleagues. There were many other mountain men of more typical abilities and conventional careers that Morgan might have chosen to symbolize the basic themes of the fur trade, although some of the best possibilities—James Bridger, James Clyman, and Thomas Fitzpatrick—had already been done.

Morgan was forthright in acknowledging Smith's extraordinary abilities and his atypical career. "Jedediah Smith is an authentic American hero," he tells us, "a man who packed a staggering amount of achievement into the time between his twenty-third and thirty-third years." In fact, Smith ranks among the best of explorers. "In the exploration of the American West, Jedediah Strong Smith is overshadowed only by Meriwether Lewis and William Clark."[38] Thus Morgan's biography succeeds best as the adventure story he was trying to transcend, with the heroic figure of Jedediah Smith and his almost superhuman deeds at its center, rather than a symbol of larger themes, where Smith's life and career are only occasionally usable. How unfortunate, then, that Morgan proved unable, as we shall see in a later essay, to plumb the depths of Smith's personality beyond the surface piety of his Methodist religion. Smith's religion, although interesting and unusual enough, seems insufficient to account for his drivenness, his egotism, and perhaps even the torments indicated in some of the personal documents Morgan includes in the appendices to the book. The inner Jedediah Smith was a deep pool into which Morgan was unwilling to stick much more than a toe. Wading much deeper would have required a willingness to venture informed speculations about the meaning of the source texts, and Morgan, the man of hard facts, found himself unable to do that.

The clash of empires in the far West had begun long before Jedediah Smith arrived on the scene. The eighteenth century had seen the Spanish mission network spreading up the California coast as the Russian trading posts had expanded southward from Alaska and British explorers had moved into western Canada. The United States was a player as well, beginning with Capt. Robert Gray's discovery of the mouth of the Columbia River in 1792, the Lewis and Clark expedition of 1804–1806, and the brief life of the Astoria trading post on the eve of the War of 1812. More than any other individual American, though,

Smith represented the ever-increasing pressure the United States began putting on its European rivals, which culminated in the Oregon settlement of 1846 and the Mexican War of 1846–48 and left the United States in uncontested possession of an immense transcontinental empire. Even though Smith's two California expeditions in 1826–28 (preceded in 1825 by his poorly documented visit to the Flathead Post of the Hudson's Bay Company) were wonderful adventure stories, Morgan correctly perceived that they were also important as the beginning of a sustained American challenge to European claims to the Pacific coast.

Morgan is not so forthright in acknowledging the disastrous loss of life and the lack of immediate economic gains of those expeditions, although these can be calculated from disparate data in his book. No other leader of a trapping party lost more men than Smith did in the Mojave and Umpqua massacres. His financial return was equally deplorable. Smith's beaver catch on the west slope of the Sierra was remarkable, especially considering the limited number of traps he had, but he traded most of the catch for an immense herd of more than three hundred horses and lost most of the rest (and most of the horses) at the Umpqua massacre. Thus his ironic achievement was to show Americans that California's real bounty lay in horses, which could be purchased cheaply or stolen and sold at immense markups at the annual trapper trading rendezvous or in New Mexico. Although trappers operating out of Taos found profitable quantities of beaver in the tributaries of the lower Colorado River that Smith had explored, most mountain men who went to California went there in quest of horses rather than furs.

After Morgan completed the Smith biography, the last decade and a half of his life found him happily ensconced at the Bancroft Library, which hired him in 1954 to work in the manuscripts department. It was the perfect job for him, for his great expertise in western history found the ideal environment in one of the great western history collections. From then until his untimely death from cancer on March 30, 1971, at age fifty-six, Morgan devoted most of his scholarly labors to a succession of editorial projects, perhaps most notably *Overland in 1846: Diaries and Letters of the California Trail* in two volumes, and a long collaboration with geographer Carl I. Wheat, beginning with *Jedediah Smith and His Maps of the American West* and including their six-volume *Mapping the Trans-Mississippi West, 1540–1861.*[39]

At the time of his death, Morgan left three major projects unfinished. The first was a single-volume history of the fur trade, which apparently did not get beyond the planning stage, although his voluminous notes and vast knowledge would have enabled him to write it quickly had he not been pressed with other projects. The second was an exhaustive bibliography of Mormonism that he had begun in the 1940s on file cards and continued to augment over the years. For a time it was taken over by the Utah State Historical Society, whose staff members kept it largely current but whose budget would not permit publication as Morgan had intended. After his death, Brigham Young University librarian Chad J. Flake completed and published it as *A Mormon Bibliography, 1830-1930.*[40] It is an indispensable reference book, perhaps the best work of Mormon scholarship ever created.

Morgan's third unfinished book was his history of Mormonism, which he began in the mid-1940s but had to abandon for financial reasons in 1952. Happily for Morgan scholars and students of Mormonism, John Phillip Walker assembled the extant fragments of the manuscript and published them in 1986 with selected correspondence that further illuminates Morgan's thinking on Mormon history. There are seven chapters altogether. The first four in more or less finished form, with notes and an appendix, were discovered in the papers of Madeline McQuown at the Marriott Library, University of Utah, and the last three, in various drafts, and a second appendix were skillfully edited by Walker from the Morgan papers at the Bancroft Library. Taken together, the seven chapters constitute a biography of Joseph Smith from his birth to the publication of the first edition of the *Book of Mormon* in 1830.

Writing in 1943 to S. A. Burgess of the Historian's Office of the Reorganized Church of Jesus Christ of Latter Day Saints in Independence, Missouri, Morgan stated that his "viewpoint about Mormon history is that of the sociologist, the psychologist, the political, economic, and social historian." As such, he went on, he could not expect that "the average Mormon will accept in its entirety" his interpretation of Mormon history, but that the Mormon will have to respect Morgan's intellectual integrity. "On such a basis we can get along very equably, and we may find that my interpretation of Mormon history will not, after all, do such violence to Mormon ideas of that history."[41] After reading the extant fragment of his history, one wonders what Morgan might have had in mind in thinking that even the most skeptical Mormon would find any part of his interpretation acceptable. It is about the most direct frontal assault imaginable on Joseph Smith's personal integrity and the veracity of the *Book of Mormon* as a revealed narrative of prehistoric America. To someone not already disposed to accept Smith's claims at face value, however, it is highly persuasive.

Morgan begins with the environment into which Smith was born in 1805 to an impoverished farm family unsuccessfully attempting to cope with the harsh Vermont agricultural conditions. Those conditions were so forbidding that the Smiths not only fled to what they hoped would be the more favorable climate of western New York in 1816, but they also questioned the basic Protestant (and American) faith in the efficacy of hard work as the way to success. Many superstitious scions of New England Puritanism like the Smiths began looking instead to preternatural intervention for their economic salvation, by such occult means as divining and visions that would disclose the location of buried treasures.[42] In addition to treasure seeking, another element that fascinated pioneers who moved out onto the New York frontier was the remains of prehistoric Indians, the Mound Builders, whose elaborate communities suggested a much more sophisticated culture than that of the now-degraded Iroquois whom the pioneers encountered in the region. It was the imaginative young farm boy Joseph Smith, seeking an easier way to wealth and status than following a plow around an unproductive farm, who found a way to weave those two local enthusiasms together into a lurid and elaborate tale of buried golden plates containing a narrative of sophisticated prehistoric peoples engaged in devastating conflict and promise of redemption by the resurrected Jesus.

Morgan's view of Joseph Smith and the *Book of Mormon*, then, was completely naturalistic: Smith's creative imagination found everything necessary in his cultural environment for creating the *Book of Mormon* without any recourse to angelic visitations and golden plates. In fact, Morgan shows Smith's claims to such visitations to have been inconsistent and after the fact, originating only after he had decided to use his prehistoric fable as the foundation for a new church. "It is impossible to grant them [Smith's visions] any standing," Morgan asserts, "to accept them as an adequate accounting of Joseph Smith's youth, a history standing fierce in contradiction against what has been remembered about him by those who knew him so well." Instead, Morgan tells us, the *Book of Mormon* "evolved naturally from the circumstances of Joseph Smith's growing up, the world he lived in, his interests and his needs." The appeal of the book was not its originality, but rather the familiarity of its ideas and themes. "[T]he distinguishing feature of Joseph's church was not to be the novelty of its doctrines but the authority with which it seized upon the floating ideas of its generation." Thus, the *Book of Mormon* in Morgan's view "is a great deal more useful to a student of the intellectual preoccupations and the folkways of New York State in the third decade of the nineteenth century than to a scholar who would reconstruct the pre-Columbian history of America."[43]

Morgan's belief, as expressed in his letter to S. A. Burgess, that faithful Mormons would find little to object to in his history of their church, must have applied exclusively to what he had planned to say in subsequent chapters, where he would narrate the historical working out of Smith's ideas using external facts, a way to which no impartial reader of any religious persuasion could object. The extant fragments of his history, however, could hardly have elicited anything *but* objection from faithful Mormon readers who accepted Smith's writings at face value.

Looking back over Dale Morgan's life and career, there is much to admire. As a tale of triumph over adversity, it is flawless. He succeeded despite being stricken with a debilitating physical handicap, then robbed of employment opportunity by the Great Depression. Morgan availed himself, it is true, of New Deal programs, but more important, he redealt his own cards by training himself in history and charting his own career in largely untracked territory. Morgan's life is much more than just a success story, though. He not only survived, but he excelled at what he did, to the point where he is recognized as one of the few real masters of western history. Both in his day and ours, historians have lavished praise on him. Morgan's "compulsion for thoroughness and accuracy," says Ray Allen Billington, "make his . . . books models of scholarly precision." His books possessed "a literary grace that many lacked." Charles S. Peterson, as we have seen, observes that "[f]ew have possessed a sense for issues, an instinct for sources, and a capacity for precision and grace in historical writing to the happy degree that Dale Morgan did." Will Bagley and Harold Schindler, preparing an updated edition of Morgan's *West From Fort Bridger*, assert that he could "write on virtually every aspect of western history with authority far and above that of any other scholar."[44]

All this praise is surely justified. And yet the adulation Morgan has elicited has kept us from looking as critically at his work as we should, and as he himself—the most searching of critics—surely would have wanted us to. Although the "WPA graduate school" developed Morgan's work ethic and his critical judgment, it did not encourage him to consider the larger meanings of his factual syntheses, that history's highest potential is in answering questions that emerge within each generation and to consider perennial questions about human nature and capacity. Morgan thought instead that historical facts contain their own meaning, and that the historian's intellect ought to be active only in internal and external criticism, establishing the authenticity and credibility of sources, yet passive when it came to establishing the larger significance of a factual infrastructure. Although he considered his perspective, as we have seen, to have been that of "the sociologist, the psychologist, the political, economic, and social historian,"[45] his work in fact was almost totally innocent of any theoretical structures in those fields. He could observe psychological abnormality but not explain it; he could statistically quantify class conflict without calling it that. The following brief essays are among the first attempts to explore some of those blind spots and shortcomings in Morgan's work.

HISTORY WITHOUT HYPOTHESIS

Don't you think we have had enough books about the Mormons which started with the conclusions and worked around to the facts? It seems to me that this is what you say when you say that if a writer holds Joseph Smith to be untruthful or visionary, it is bound to color the history; and that if the writer believes him to tell the truth, that this likewise influences the character of the history. I think it is time that we tried another angle of approach, marshalling all the available facts, and then going on from there.

—Dale Morgan to John A. Widtsoe, January 24, 1949

PERHAPS NOWHERE IN Dale Morgan's published or unpublished works can one find a more concise manifesto of his solidly fact-based empiricism, nor a more nakedly stated assault on the apologetic Mormon historiography he was determined to supplant, than this outburst to Mormon Apostle John A. Widtsoe. There were other such statements of Morgan's method. To quote one more to confirm that he was accurately stating his ideas, "Mine becomes an essentially inductive method," he wrote to fellow historian Juanita Brooks. "I put together the facts that I can find, after assessing them according to what I think their worth may be, and thus slowly and painfully I build toward central conceptions." Brooks's method, by contrast, was an essentially deductive one, which in Morgan's description sounds similar to Widtsoe's apologetics. "You start with central conceptions," Morgan wrote, "and (all the while testing your facts by those conceptions) work toward a factual structure that will articulate those conceptions and give them life and meaning according to our everyday standards of objective reality—'historical facts,' in other words."[1] In the method Morgan is ascribing to both Widtsoe and Brooks, in other words, facts play a secondary role to conclusions.

To the modern professional historian, trained in and committed to the inductive method, Morgan's comparison inspires a condemnation of Widtsoe and his truth-evading apologists to a historiographical nether world. Morgan unfairly ignores the empiricism of Brooks's research, but his placement of her with Widtsoe in the camp of Mormon apologists is roughly accurate. Be that as it may, a closer consideration of the way historians, including both Brooks and Morgan, actually work suggests that Brooks and perhaps even Widtsoe, if Morgan is accurately representing his position, had the better conception of the process of historical synthesis.

Morgan's conception of the function of the historian represented, as we have previously noted, a reversion to the "scientific" history of Hubert Howe Bancroft—an association that would have seemed uncomplimentary to Morgan. Bancroft produced his histories the way Henry Ford later produced Model T automobiles, on an assembly line along which researchers and writers extracted factual data from raw source material and mechanically assembled it into a secondary narrative. The resulting history was absolutely objective, as devoid of "interpretation" as Ford's automobiles were of idiosyncratic contributions of his workers. Bancroft's histories all came in black, like Model T Fords. "I would have it clearly understood that it is my purpose, here as elsewhere in all my historical efforts," Bancroft warned, "to impart information rather than attempt to solve problems."[2]

Bancroft's naivete on the possibility of avoiding interpretation is understandable. It was the prevailing assumption of the "scientific" historians of his generation. Historians of the late nineteenth century like John W. Burgess at Columbia and Herbert Baxter Adams at Johns Hopkins were envious of the claims to scientific finality being advanced in the newly emerging social sciences. They were also embarrassed by the Romantic historians of the preceding generation like Francis Parkman and George Bancroft, who had pleaded in behalf of the apparently ephemeral religious and philosophical systems that had governed their writing. In response, the scientific historians attempted to limit their work simply to assembling incontestable factual data into what they hoped would be definitive reconstructions of the past.[3]

Morgan's attempt to resurrect the idea a half century after Bancroft, though, is nothing short of astonishing. The historical profession had long since followed the lead of the historical relativists of the Progressive Era in recognizing the inevitability of interpretation even in the act of factual selection. Morgan's reversion to an ideal of scientific objectivity thus represented an act of intellectual paleontology. Nothing, perhaps, shows the high cost of Morgan's lack of academic training in history more than his commitment to the no longer tenable enterprise of scientific history. Whatever virtues Morgan derived from his experience with the WPA—its high standards of critical rigor, its workmanlike production schedule, and its demand for accessible prose, among others—the arrogance of his preference of the "WPA graduate school" to an academic school prevented him from developing an adequate theoretical basis of methodology that could have immeasurably improved his work.

Denied academic training in history, Morgan might have made up for much of it by joining one of the professional organizations like the American Historical Association or at least dipping into some of the profession's ongoing theoretical discussion, which, to his detriment, he apparently held in disdain. Todd I. Berens, a history teacher who shared Morgan's passion for overland trails, once attempted to probe beneath Morgan's immense expertise in factual detail to see if he had deeper thoughts on the larger significance of those facts. His question raised Morgan's eyebrows:

> Your more abstract question, how I would answer the philosophical questions, "What is history?" takes me somewhat by surprise. They say that poets are entitled to whatever readers can get out of their poems, and I suppose the same applies to historians. But I have never been much concerned with a philosophy of history as such. I have been more interested in practical questions, straightening out the enormous distortions of the record that I have found on every hand; and beyond that, being continuously interested

in the causes that produce certain effects, and the effects that are produced by certain causes. Historians seem to have trouble enough getting at these elementals, to say nothing of wrestling with large abstractions.[4]

Morgan's distaste for "large abstractions" included ignoring the work of two of the founding fathers of his own profession, Frederick Jackson Turner and Walter Prescott Webb. He mentions both almost within the compass of a single page in a letter to Bernard DeVoto. "I decline to let academic historians . . . require me to declare myself on the Turner hypothesis in relation to Mormonism." And "you may remember what Walter Prescott Webb had to say in his The Great Plains, that none of his facts was new but that we should look at them in new ways. I think the idea is perfectly applicable to the Mormons."[5] It is amazing for a historian to maintain the position that the Turner thesis is a trap to be avoided, like being caught backing the losing team in the World Series, rather than an opportunity to find larger meaning in one's own materials, and that Webb was useful only as a proponent of the idea that old facts can be looked at in new ways, rather than as the creator of a thesis about the significance of the Great Plains in American history, a thesis Morgan might have found useful in understanding the Great Basin. Morgan's abdication of what most academically trained scholars regard as an obligation to reflect upon the larger meaning of their craft makes him one of what J. H. Hexter characterizes as "a few aborigines in the historical hinterlands [who] have been able consistently to shove into the back of their minds the question, 'What the devil are we, am I, up to? And why?'"[6]

Carl Becker's 1931 AHA presidential address, "Everyman His Own Historian," was a devastating obituary to the illusions of scientific objectivity that Morgan was just getting ready to dust off. It was not that Becker objected to the "scientific" school's commitment to factual accuracy.

One of the first duties of man is not to be duped, to be aware of his world; and to derive the significance of human experience from events that never occurred is surely an enterprise of doubtful value. To establish the facts is always in order, and is indeed the first duty of the historian; but to suppose that the facts, once established in all their fullness, will "speak for themselves" is an illusion.

Interpretation, Becker went on to warn, is unavoidable:

> Thus the scientific historian deliberately renounced philosophy only to submit to it without being aware. His philosophy was just this, that by not taking thought a cubit would be added to his stature. . . . Hoping to find something without looking for it, expecting to obtain final answers to life's riddle by resolutely refusing to ask questions—it was surely the most romantic species of realism yet invented, the oddest attempt ever made to get something for nothing![7]

It would be hard to imagine any history written by the simplistic process Morgan suggests; that is, merely throwing a myriad of historical facts out onto the table like a gigantic Scrabble game and then recording the patterns into which they fall. Morgan certainly did not write *his* that way. To be sure, starting with *conclusions* and working back to facts, as Morgan accuses the Mormon historians of doing, is indefensible. But starting with a *hypothesis* that one proceeds to check against the facts is a cornerstone of the scientific method. Surely the historian begins as the scientist begins, with questions or hypotheses in mind, then looks for facts that bear upon those questions. The interpretive patterns exist in the historian's mind, not in the facts themselves. That is manifestly the process Morgan himself followed, whether he realized it or not, and evidence is abundant that he was one of those who, in Becker's words, "renounced philosophy only to submit to it without being aware."[8]

The narrative of his Jedediah Smith biography is clearly assembled with the goal of answering a list of questions about Smith's significance in the fur trade in the American West in the early nineteenth century. They include: what were the economic returns from the fur trade; what techniques of trading or trapping and administrative organization offered the best chance of realizing those returns; and at what risks from natural and human hazards were those returns accumulated? Of particular importance to Morgan was the accumulation of geographical knowledge through Smith's travels. Moreover, Morgan's books are full of interpretive judgments and even imaginative reconstructions of episodes with no hard documentary basis.

In a remarkable letter to his publisher suggesting ideas for dust jacket copy for the publication of the Smith biography, for example, Morgan showed a keen awareness of his contribution to historiography. "The stories of individual events, firms, and personalities have all been told in isolation before;" Morgan begins, "now they are tied all together, so that the relationship of one to another becomes apparent. . . . Moreover, the book abandons the frankly nationalistic kind of writing about the fur trade which puts the British and American trade in the West in separate compartments, showing how the whole was tied together." The details of the economic history of the fur trade, he concludes, are a third major historiographical contribution. "The returns of [William H.] Ashley and later of Smith, Jackson & Sublette have hitherto been distilled in the histories out of the purest moonshine; this book presents the detailed facts, and also attends to the economic basis of the relations between the American free trappers and the entrepreneurs—which in turn affected the future course of mountain history."[9]

To most modern historians, these and other questions Morgan tacitly poses are compelling in their interest, and Morgan documents his answers to them so elaborately that we are often tempted to forget that they are highly selective in their focus and that Morgan in answering them ignored more facts than he used. One has only to pick up, for example, Don Russell's *Firearms, Traps, and Tools of the Mountain Man*[10] to realize how many of the quotidian realities of Smith's life Morgan dismissed as trivial in his pursuit of answers to the larger questions that captivated his attention. Surely the weight and price of a #3 Oneida beaver trap, or the muzzle velocity and reliability of his Hawken rifle, were of greater importance to Smith than the issues of Mexican-American relations in California or the price of beaver pelts in St. Louis, issues that concern Morgan. Yet Morgan barely mentions traps or rifles, instead focusing his attention on the larger issues.

Morgan's book, furthermore, is laden with interpretive comments that, however cogent and well-documented we may find them, are nevertheless judgments originating in Morgan's mind rather than emerging from the facts themselves. The era of the fur trade, he tells us for example, "was a golden age in the history of the West, and all the Ashley men have something of the stature of culture heroes. That Jedediah Smith emerged head and shoulders above them all is in itself a measure of greatness." In another place Morgan invests Smith with an almost metaphysical significance that rivals some of Bernard DeVoto's hyperbolic assessments. In his 1824 rediscovery of South Pass, the passage through the Continental Divide over which American emigration would pass, and with it most of the American claim to the far West, "in his own person [Smith] is the American oncoming, the long-delayed frontal challenge to the maintenance of the British position in Oregon."[11] The very title of the book, *Jedediah Smith and the Opening of the West*, expresses an interpretation of Smith's significance: the explorations of the mountain men represented an opening rather than a closing. Modern historians, especially those who call themselves the New Western Historians, see the fur trade era just as much as a closing when looked at from the standpoint of the native inhabitants and the European colonists, whose presence in the far West was greatly diminished by the work of the mountain men.

Nor did Morgan shrink from adding imaginative detail to fill the silent spaces in his sources and enhance the literary appeal of his narrative. Witness, for example, his imaginative reconstruction of Smith's role in the pitched battle of 1823 between Ashley's trappers, which included Smith, and the Arikara Indians on the Missouri River. The conflict, which at the time was a disaster for the trappers, turned out to be a pivotal moment in the history of westward expansion, for it led the St. Louis fur companies to abandon the Missouri as an avenue to the mountains and look for a more southerly route without hostile Indians. It was that decision that led to the rediscovery of South Pass. Since Smith was a participant in that turning point, Morgan's sense of biographical proportion required that he give the battle as much emphasis as possible. Unfortunately, contemporary documentation of Smith's role in the fight, Morgan acknowledges, is completely lacking, so he is required to rely upon a reminiscence written nine years later. A stale memory penned by a contemporary admirer, it is not the ideal source the historian would want, nor is it abundant in detail. "When his party was in danger, Mr. Smith was always among the foremost to meet it, and the last to fly; those who saw him on shore, in the Riccaree fight, in 1823, can attest to the truth of this assertion." Lacking the documentary detail required by his biographical purpose, Morgan employed his literary skill to provide the necessary weight. "We can picture him ramming one last ball home and firing at the Rees spilling down on him while the men of his party splash into the water toward the boats. Then himself abandoning the beach, thrusting the muzzle of his rifle into his belt, and running into the river, swimming for it with the balls from the Ree fusils reaching angrily after him . . . . This day Jedediah Smith made his reputation."[12] It is as unforgettable a passage as anything in Zane Grey, and it is every bit as much a creation of the author's imagination as anything in Grey, a complete contradiction of Morgan's professed commitment to the facts and the facts alone.

Coming to grips with the other Smith who concerned Morgan—Joseph Smith—involves the same requirement of testing hypotheses against facts. Who was Joseph Smith? Many interpretations are possible: one could take Joseph's statements of divine revelation at face value, as all orthodox Mormons do; one could take a "naturalistic" view advanced by Morgan, that Joseph had everything he needed to write the Book of Mormon and create the Mormon Church within his own cultural environment without any recourse to divine intervention; one could consider Joseph as laboring under paranoid delusions of divine visitations, which was the thesis of Bernard DeVoto; one could regard him as Fawn Brodie did, as a cynical imposter who consciously lied in order to gain power--and these still do not exhaust the possibilities. Note, however, that none of these theses—including Morgan's—can be derived by collecting random facts and reading them as a fortune-teller might read tea leaves. All are *a priori* hypotheses toward which facts can be marshaled to either prove or disprove.

In the extant draft chapters of his history of the Mormons,[13] Morgan provided impressive evidence of inconsistency in Joseph's accounts of his supposed divine visitations, evidence he adduced to question the veracity of those accounts. Such inconsistencies, to Morgan, proved instead that Joseph's claims of divine visitations were after-the-fact attempts to add divine weight to ideas he had derived from earthly materials ready at hand in his cultural milieu. But how, one must ask, does one prove or disprove claims of private revelation? Even if Joseph's narratives of his experiences can be proved inconsistent or after the fact, his claims to revelation themselves can no more be proved nor disproved than any other intensely personal experience. One begins, that is to say, with a hypothesis, which one then proceeds to examine in the light of relevant factual data. In the case of Joseph Smith's claims to revelation, even the issue of what constitutes a fact becomes important. Are Smith's own claims to be taken at face value or in some other sense?

Morgan's predilection to reject supernatural explanations of Mormon origins in favor of naturalistic ones appears to be so deeply rooted in his own teenage apostasy that he could no longer recognize it as a bias as deep as the orthodox Mormons' inclination to accept Joseph's claims at face value. Widtsoe was right: if one is predisposed to accept Joseph's claims of divine visitation, then one will write a certain kind of history; if one is not so disposed, then one will write his history very differently. It is clearly not a simple matter of gathering facts and reading the patterns they reveal, but rather of interpreting the factual record in the light of various possible hypotheses. Trying to write history without hypothesis is like trying to navigate without using the ship's rudder. The ship will move, and it will reach some destination, but that destination is as likely to be calamitous as happy. History without hypothesis leads to history without interpretation.

THE ENIGMATIC TRAPPER

Maurice S. Sullivan, to whom history is indebted for the discovery and publication of the diaries of Jedediah Strong Smith and for the first full biography of that mountain man, paints an engaging literary picture of Smith's winter camp on the Wind River in 1829–30.[1] Among the details in his description, two are significant. The first is a detail of omission. Unlike most of his colleagues in the fur trade, Smith was never known to take up with an Indian woman in the winter, and upon that and other personal idiosyncrasies hang much of Smith's character. The other is the presence of a half-dozen baby beavers wandering around the camp, one of which wore a red collar and was Smith's special pet. Their presence in the camp of one whose explorations had led to the destruction of many thousands of their species is unusual enough, but in this case they are important as symbols, for Smith's life was taking an abrupt change of course. He was leaving the mountains the following summer and planning to take the little beavers east to remind him, presumably, of the source of the considerable wealth he had won in the mountains.

Perhaps those symbols of his past, his future, and his atypical nature were not lost upon him, for he was clearly in a reflective mood regarding each of those matters. Because William Sublette was leaving for the East on Christmas Day and could deliver letters for him, Smith wrote three. One was a lengthy report to William Clark of his recent explorations and tribulations at the hands of Indians, one was to his parents, and one was to his brother Ralph.[2] Perhaps the lengthy recitation of his record in the mountains helped trigger his reflections on its meaning. The two family letters reveal some of the inner Jedediah Smith—his character, his motives, his attitudes toward civilization and the civilized obligations of a free-ranging trapper. Together with another letter to his brother the next year, they seem to offer almost the only sustained look into the inner life of one of the most enigmatic personalities in the history of the fur trade. But historians who have tried to deal with Smith's personality have found that they only deepened the enigma, and scholars have largely failed to resolve the puzzle of this unusual man.

The character of the mountain man has become one of the stereotypes of western history: the hard-living, hard-playing fatalist who wrests a perilous living from icy mountain streams under frequent risk of Indian attack, only to blow it all in a week of riotous release at the annual rendezvous and return for the fall hunt with a newly mortgaged outfit. The mystery of Jedediah Smith is that he exhibited all the mountain man's virtues but none of his vices. His deep Methodist faith kept him from drinking, smoking, swearing, and consorting with women. If the opportunity to live a life free from civilized constraint held no lure for him, then what was it that sustained him through the three worst Indian massacres in the history of the trade, near-death on a waterless crossing of the Great Salt Lake Desert, and untold other risks and privations?

Men have endured that much for money, but Smith never hints that material gain is an end in itself. Instead, his letters are filled with religious regrets and remorse, and the desire soon to quit the mountains to take up once again a life of regular religious observance. "I feell the need of the wa[t]ch & care of a Christian Church," he wrote to his parents, "–you may well Suppose that our Society is of the Roug[h]est kind, Men of good morals seldom enter into business of this kind–I hope you will remember me before a Throne of grace." And to his brother, "As it respects my spiritual welfare, I hardly durst speak[.] I find myself one of the most ungrateful; unthankful, Creatures imaginable[.] Oh when Shall I be under the care of a Christian Church? I have need of your Prayers. I wish our Society to bear me up before a Throne of grace." Finally, after informing his brother that "Providence has made me Steward of a Small pittance" (in fact a rather considerable fortune), Smith gives instructions for dispensing that money for the benefit of his family and Dr. Titus Gordon Vespasian Simons, his old teacher. Smith then offers this explanation for his tribulations as a mountain man:

> It is, that I may be able to help those who stand in need, that I face every danger—it is for this, that I traverse the Mountains covered with eternal Snow—it is for this that I pass over the Sandy Plains, in heat of summer, thirsting for water, and am well pleased if I can find a shade, instead of water, where I may cool my overheated body—it is for this that I go for days without eating, & am pretty well satisfied if I can gather a few roots, a few Snails, or, much better satisfied if we can affo[r]d our selves a piece of Horse Flesh, or a fine Roasted Dog, and, most of all, it is for this, that I deprive myself of the privilege of Society & the satisfaction of the Converse of My Friends.[3]

What to make of all this? There is much in it, certainly, to tempt the psychohistorian: the man driven by religious guilt, courting privation, suffering, and perhaps even death to expiate some unspecified sin. But for any biographer seeking the marrow of the man, these passages are frustratingly oblique, yet arresting in their frankness and passion, and one would think the literature of the fur trade would be laden—if not overladen—with analyses of this enigmatic trapper.

As a matter of fact, no scholar to date, including Dale Morgan, author of the most complete biography of Smith, has attempted to penetrate much below the surface of the man. In Morgan's *Jedediah Smith and the Opening of the West*, the subtitle is the tail that wags the dog. Morgan is more interested in plotting, as it were, every last hoofprint of Smith's horses in exploring the American West than he is in probing for the reasons that drew—or drove—Smith there in the first place. With few exceptions, the book is the story of movement through space and time, with only the most perfunctory account of ideas, personality, and motives.

For example, after fully quoting the letters excerpted above, Morgan ventures a scant two paragraphs of general observations and speculations about Smith's personality, without explicating the passages themselves or wrestling with what they might indicate about the man and his motives. "There was a sternness and austerity to his life," Morgan observes flatly, citing as evidence Smith's lack of interest in women, liquor, and tobacco, and his cleanliness in body and speech. "He may have been entirely humorless," Morgan continues, but adds that there was honesty, directness, and openness that won him friends in spite of it. Finally, Smith stood apart from other mountain men, who all had courage and survival skills, because of a high level of intelligence that, Morgan observes, "has never been commonplace, in the West or anywhere."[4] And with that, Morgan is back in the next paragraph to his narration of Smith's travels.

In fairness to Morgan, one must note that he was not the only student of Jedediah Smith to have failed to rise to the bait of Smith's introspective passages. It is testimony to the depth of the enigma of Smith's personality that those students have been so consistently intimidated by what one would think is a biographer's central obligation. The poet John G. Neihardt, for example, treated Smith's faith sentimentally, as simply a comfort in tribulation:

> *There'd be a freshness in his face and eyes*
> *When he came striding from a spell of straying*
> *Off trail somewhere. I know now he'd been praying.*
> *You'd swear he knew a spring along the way,*
> *And kept it for himself! . . .*[5]

Without questioning the comforting power of prayer, one might find it even more compelling, given what one could persuasively read as an anguish in his letters, to place Smith in the company of the great saints throughout history. For many of them, faith was as much a driving, even a tormenting, force as it was a comfort.

Maurice S. Sullivan quoted extensively from Smith's letters as well, but failed to venture even a sentimental explanation. He compounded the sin when he listed the books found in Smith's possession after his death and speculated that Smith may have read them aloud in the evenings to illiterate companions—as we know literate trappers often did—but then failed to analyze the values contained in them that may have shaped Smith's personality and character.[6]

Only Harrison Clifford Dale, among the major students of Smith's life, made even a tentative effort to probe beneath the surface and sentimental aspects of Smith's religion. "His letters," Dale observed, "express his spiritual longings and the crushing sense of his own sin and unworthiness. . . . The same sense of unregeneration and of unsatisfied groping after spiritual justification" in the environment of western New York during Smith's youth that led another Smith—Joseph—down the road toward creation of the Church of Jesus Christ of Latter-day Saints.[7]

Western literature scholar Don D. Walker almost offhandedly ventured the boldest speculations on the mountain man's personality in an article that only partially concerned Smith. In so doing he suggested some directions Morgan might have gone in his biography, even while exonerating Morgan for not having done so. "If one asserts that Jedediah Smith was a thoughtful man," Walker begins, "he does so as an act of biographical faith, for the documented thoughts that we have are remarkably few, and most of these are commonplace, proof of piety and good sense but scarcely of original insight." Following this, Walker quotes passages from Smith's journal indicating a renewed realization of the vanity of earthly wealth and glory when faced with imminent threat of death, and, commenting on two of Smith's letters, including the one to his brother given above, Walker observes that "it may be the key to the man, if a key is to be found." Unfortunately, Smith's biographers have found a meaning in the letter that it does not contain: "[The letter] does not support the image of Smith as 'the pious, but none the less vigorous fighting Knight in Buckskin.' [Maurice Sullivan's words] No, instead it ties the mountain hunter to his Puritan ancestry. It makes the rigors of mountain life another form of worldly asceticism. For this passage in its detailing of self-sacrifice is no more genuinely modest than the diary of Cotton Mather." Maybe, in other words, Morgan should have dismissed the letter as pious posturing in front of his family, whom Smith wanted to impress with his religious faithfulness, and the pious journal passages in the face of death as some kind of deathbed conversion. The real Smith, perhaps, was the one who took the pursuit of glory and of wealth all too seriously and kept running against the end of the tether of the disapproval of those motives in his Methodist upbringing. But "the biographer . . . would be reluctant to reconstruct Smith in this pattern, for the full body of biographical evidence is lacking," Walker concludes.[8] "Better to detail Smith's movements as they can be documented from his own writings and those of others and leave the heart in mystery." Perhaps. It was certainly Morgan's decision. But how much better if Morgan had been venturesome and creative enough to advance some of the tantalizing speculations Walker suggests, even while admitting that a rounded and convincing account of Smith's personality is not possible? It would seem more fulfilling to the reader than simply to leave Smith's intriguing expressions without substantial comment.

Along with several other projects that remained unfinished at his death, Morgan had planned a revision of the Smith biography to incorporate new sources that his and others' research had turned up since the appearance of the first edition. One of those sources was Smith's narrative of his 1826–27 journey to California, which George R. Brooks was editing and preparing for publication with Morgan's assistance at the time of Morgan's death. The narrative offers interesting evidence of Smith's psychology and motives that includes no religious element. Instead, he names the conventional motives of material gain and adventure and even exhibits a touch of egotism.

> In taking charge of our S[outh] western Expedition, I followed the bent of my strong inclination to visit this unexplored country and unfold those hidden resources of wealth and bring to light those wonders which I readily imagined a country so extensive might contain. I must confess that I had at that time a full share of that ambition (and perhaps foolish ambition) which is common in a greater or less degree to all the active world. I wa[nted] to be the first to view a country on which the eyes of a white man had never gazed and to follow the course of rivers that run through a new land.[9]

Equally intriguing was a reference provided Morgan by the historian LeRoy Hafen in a letter of September 28, 1952, which Morgan incorporated in a footnote. It was a statement by a descendant of Smith's brother Ralph that Jedediah had been in love with Ralph's wife, Louisa Simon, which had been a dark family secret. Morgan declined to make anything of the idea. "There is not the slightest suggestion of such feeling in Jedediah's letters," he pointed out, "nor did he make any special provision for her in his will." Besides, he continued, many mountain men married late, and his celibacy may simply have meant that he had not yet found the right woman. He wrote to Hafen, "I think she [Louisa] would have been a considerably older woman than he, and he probably never saw her after leaving home at the age of 22, but this is not to say that the idea is impossible, human nature being what it is, and I shall look into it further." He goes on to note that he had been unable to find any evidence of Smith's sexual interest in Indian women, an omission he speculates could have been a result of religious inhibition, or that Smith may have been "a sexually inactive type." In any event, if a love for his sister-in-law had existed, "[o]ne does not see how it necessarily reflected any discredit on either. If true, that is merely the way life goes at time[s]." Of course. But it could have helped explain Smith's apparent chastity in the midst of the plentiful temptations of life in the mountains, and Morgan was little interested in exploring that. Instead, he comments blandly, "One of the difficulties of writing about [Smith] beyond the heroic plane is that we have so little information about the wellsprings of his life."[10] That, as we have seen, is hardly the case. What is lacking, rather, is a biographer willing to venture an interpretation, or perhaps alternate possible interpretations, of his subject's personality out of the documentation that does exist.

Morgan's *Jedediah Smith* is an acknowledged classic of western history and biography. Its careful narrative of Smith's travels and measured assessment of his place in the history of the fur trade and western exploration were, given the sources available at the time, definitive. But in another sense it is a curiously shallow book, for Morgan chose to lavish his formidable analytical talents on geography rather than on psychology. Where the controversial issue of Smith's personality came up, Morgan chose to retreat to the solution of Hubert Howe Bancroft:

provide the text of the sources and put the burden of interpretation on the reader. Consequently, one lays down the book with a sense of emptiness, a feeling that one has seen the action, but not the actor. Once again, as elsewhere in his otherwise admirable body of historical writing, Morgan conceived historical writing to be merely establishing an accurate factual record rather than probing for the larger significance of his materials.

CLASS CONFLICT WITHOUT MARX

ONE OF THE curious features of the historiography of the fur trade of the far West during the mountain man era (c. 1822–40) is a relative lack of discussion of the economics of what was, at bottom, a business. To some degree this lack is understandable, for the mountain men offer many objects of study more interesting to the historian. So instead the literature is full of dramatic tales of Indian battles, grizzly bear maulings, heroic feats of endurance, triumphs of geographic discovery, and especially of drinking, wenching, and brawling at the annual rendezvous. If historians have sometimes been accused of pedantic prose and of stumbling over the dramatic potential of their material, surely this is not such a case.

To the reader who eventually becomes sated with the color and romance of fur trade history and wants to try to make some sense of its larger significance, it becomes inescapable that the trappers and those who hired and traded with them were linked in a business relationship. Unfortunately, hard economic data on who was making how much and by what means has been relatively scarce, and the reader is greeted instead by vague assertions that the superiority of beaver felt drove beaver prices up and those who supplied it could become sumptuously rich.

Glimpses of the hard economic facts of the fur trade, to be sure, have not been entirely lacking, both before and since Morgan's writings on the subject. Even Bernard DeVoto, one of the leading romanticizers of the mountain men, tried to include some indication of prices and profit margins in *Across the Wide Missouri*, his study of the fur trade at its competitive peak in the 1830s. Unfortunately his figures, taken entirely from a fragmentary 1833 invoice of goods provided in St. Louis to Lucien Fontanelle of the American Fur Company, do not cover the entire inventory, and the figures he does give directly contradict DeVoto's interpretation of them. DeVoto wanted so badly to see the trappers as tragic heroes heartlessly exploited by greedy St. Louis capitalists that he wrenched his data to show a pattern of price gouging that was probably an exaggeration of the already exploitative profit margin that did exist. He bases his interpretation on the single frail straw of Osborne Russell's angry expostulation that the trappers were having to pay a 2000 percent markup at the 1837 rendezvous. With that as his benchmark, DeVoto cannot understand why the 1833 invoice shows prices that "have not been advanced the full one hundred percent that was customary." Not letting that uncomfortable fact stop him, he rushes on to assert, with Russell's outburst as his only documentation, that "[w]hen the mountain man was the ultimate consumer, he would pay, in beaver, prices which were seldom less than a thousand percent above St. Louis costs for only the most expensive items and which for many items ran up to two thousand percent."[1]

A major turning point in this area of study came in 1979, several years after Morgan's death, with publication of David J. Wishart's *The Fur Trade of the American West, 1807–1840: A Geographical Synthesis*, a book whose many virtues included careful tabulations of pelts harvested and of prices and profits in the fur trade on a continental scale among the various entrepreneurs.[2] Wishart's book began a trend toward examination of the fur trade's significance as a point of contact among diverse cultures and of economic and environmental exploitation, which was a welcome change from worn-out tales of hardship and adventure of earlier books. "After all," he pointed out, "you can only describe the trappers' antics at a rendezvous so many times."[3] Unfortunately, Wishart's data does not go even as far as DeVoto's in examining the first cycle of the spiraling markups, the wholesale prices of trade goods in St. Louis.[4]

Over the years, fur trade historians and their readers have consistently found the colorful tales much more interesting than studies of ledger balances and profit margins, and the older romantic historiography has never lost its appeal. A recent case in point is Robert V. Hine and John Mack Faragher's *The American West: An Interpretive History*, an excellent updating of Hine's imaginative and much-admired general history of the West that first appeared in 1973. Chapter 5, which deals with the fur trade, is extremely impressionistic in its lack of precise data in discussion of the fur trade's economic aspects and consists mostly of awestruck citations of the size of the fortunes made by various fur trade entrepreneurs. John Jacob Astor, for example, "eventually became the richest man in America, with assets at the time of his death in 1848 of some twenty million dollars (the equivalent, perhaps, of four hundred million dollars today). Astor's was the first of the great American fortunes, and it was built on furs." Similarly, Manuel Lisa's Missouri Fur Company "proved a very profitable operation. One happy season Lisa made thirty-five thousand dollars, this in an age when a successful merchant might clear a thousand dollars a year." William H. Ashley cleaned up as well, for "the fabulous cache of beaver brought back the first year made Ashley a rich man." In 1825, the first year of the new rendezvous system, "Ashley brought home furs worth nearly fifty thousand dollars, and in 1826 he made enough to retire with a fortune. The Rocky Mountain Fur Company, as new owners renamed his enterprise [The authors pass over without mention two previous partnerships, Ashley-Smith, and Smith, Jackson and Sublette!], took back 168 packs of beaver pelts worth eighty-five thousand dollars in 1832."[5] And so forth. In this analysis, the beaver business was simply a matter of buy low, sell high, and as long as the demand remained strong, the money rolled in.

A discordant note peals out at the end of the chapter when the authors, reflecting environmental concerns, deplore the near depletion of the beaver, though they finish in a major key with the observation that by the 1850s the beaver population had sprung back. Regarding exploitation of the human participants in the fur trade, they are confusing. "In the flush years of the 1820s," they say, "traders, if not trappers, took in handsome returns at the rendezvous." And yet, even though trappers were not the ones making the money, by the end of the paragraph they have become, in William Goetzmann's characterization, "expectant capitalists." As such, "a third of them left the mountains to pursue other careers. Many became businessmen, investing their money in stores or saloons."[6] One wonders where all that venture capital came from, for the authors' account of the mountain men's profligate blowouts at the annual rendezvous does not suggest a conspicuous frugality.

Dale Morgan's 1953 biography, *Jedediah Smith and the Opening of the West*, contained little on the trappers' rendezvous antics because Smith was a sober Methodist for whom such indulgences apparently held little appeal. Although the book is solidly situated within the earlier celebratory literature emphasizing the heroic dimensions of the mountain men and the positive aspects of westward expansion, Smith's aloofness from the riotous aspects of the trappers' life and his dramatic success as a fur trade entrepreneur gave Morgan an opportunity to examine the economic aspects of the business. "The economic information developed in this book is also something radically new," he wrote to his publisher. "The returns of Ashley and later of Smith, Jackson & Sublette have hitherto been distilled in the histories out of the purest moonshine; this book presents the detailed facts, and also attends to the economic basis of the relations between the American free trappers and the entrepreneurs—which in turn affected the future course of mountain history."[7] Thus *Jedediah Smith and the Opening of the West* stands at the historiographical divide between the older romantic tradition and the kind of social and economic analysis attempted by the likes of David Wishart.

Nevertheless, the book is much more successful in following the romantic perspective than in its economic analysis, which is quite primitive. Following the economic theme through the book, one could wish for more detail and also for more tying together of disparate data. For one thing, passages throughout the book give the same kind of impressionistic, round numbers one finds in books like Hine and Faragher's. Also, if one wants to create a balance sheet for Jedediah Smith's personal production, it is necessary to keep a running tally of furs collected, furs lost to Indians or natural disasters, furs traded for horses, and so forth. This latter point is important, for Morgan explains Smith's amateurishness as an explorer, relative to Meriwether Lewis for example, in economic terms. Although Lewis was well-trained and equipped for the deliberate function of exploring, Smith's explorations, which were even more impressive in their geographic scope than Lewis's, were merely adjunct to his primary role as a businessman. Wherever Smith went, his travel "had to pay its way in beaver," Morgan reminds us.[8] It would be nice to know whether it did. Of course it would be as impossible to place a price tag on Smith's 1824 rediscovery of South Pass as it would be to place one on the Mona Lisa. South Pass was the one passage over the Continental Divide that made possible both the bulk of the Rocky Mountain fur trade and the westward emigration over the Oregon and California Trails. But when one tallies Morgan's data on the immense gains and losses of Smith's two-year attempt to exploit California's beaver streams in 1826–28, which culminated in the forced sale of a small band of horses and a few packs of moth-eaten beaver pelts to George Simpson of the Hudson's Bay Company at Simpson's discount prices, it is obvious that the company was carrying Smith, not vice versa.

Nevertheless, Morgan delivers on his promise of detailed and accurate economic data, if one has the patience to unravel his convoluted explanations and get to the implications of the contractual relations between William H. Ashley and the field partners Smith, Jackson & Sublette. Those agreements (the texts of which Morgan fortunately supplies in full) show both Ashley's shrewdness as a businessman and also the cynical exploitation that lay at the base of fur trade economics. The centerpiece of Morgan's concise discussion of those economics (on pages 230–34) is a revealing table of prices on page 232 that Morgan created himself showing both wholesale and retail prices in 1825 and 1827 of the trade goods for which the trappers exchanged their furs. A remarkable fact emerges from that table and from Morgan's supportive explanations. Although Ashley made most of his money on the beaver pelts he bought at three dollars per pound and resold in St. Louis or in eastern cities at as much as five or six dollars per pound, the field partners—Smith, Jackson & Sublette—made their money on the trade goods they bought at wholesale from Ashley and retailed at ferocious markups to their own trappers. Osborne Russell's outrage at having to pay a 2000 percent markup at one rendezvous may be an exceptional instance, but markups of 50 to 400 percent are well-documented.

Those provided, as Ashley's biographer Robert T. Clokey observes, "incomparable padding to the profits from fur sales in St. Louis"—all profits going into the pockets of the middle men rather than the trappers.[9] In 1827, gunpowder, for example, wholesaled for $1.50 per pound and retailed for $2.50. Coffee and tobacco wholesaled for $1.25 and retailed for $2.00. Vermillion and beads brought a markup of 100 percent, whereas calico cloth wholesaled for $1.00 per yard and retailed for $2.50. From these figures it is easy to see who was making the money and where they were making it, and why trappers like Daniel Potts complained, in Morgan's paraphrase, "that there was a poor prospect of making much money in the mountains."[10]

So much for the trappers and the field partners. How about Ashley, who marketed the beaver in St. Louis? Beaver prices there held fairly steady at five dollars per pound throughout the 1820s, so Ashley, who had bought them at one and seven-eighths dollars, apparently stood to make the fortune for which he became proverbial in the fur trade. Morgan largely deserts us at this point, for Jedediah Smith had little to do with the furs once they left the mountains. Novelist Don Berry, whose one venture into history was a study of the Rocky Mountain Fur Company and its predecessors, fills out that side of the picture through research in the fur trade records at the Missouri Historical Society. Before jumping to conclusions about Ashley's profits, as contemporary newspapers and subsequent historians have done, Berry warns us to look at Ashley's overhead and his risks. "For this profit it is necessary for him to outfit a major overland party (with the consequent great risk of loss to Indians) and make the complete trip to and from the mountains; this means paying men. With horses at a mountain price of $60—and sometimes unobtainable even at that—it doesn't take much bad luck to wipe out the profit." Accepting the field partners' freighting fee of one and one-eighth dollars per pound meant that all the risks were Ashley's, and with the expenses outlined by Berry, that fee seemed little enough. "These factors cut the profit figure down to something a good deal less impressive," Berry concludes.[11] But the fact remains that, after we have given the put-upon capitalists their due, those risks and expenses did not prove risky or expensive enough to keep Ashley and others from running up enormous profits in very short order, and the fact is also inescapable that a large portion of those fortunes came at the expense of their own trappers, whom they conspired to keep in a state of serfdom.

The economic relationships between the trapper, the field partner, and the supplier is strongly reminiscent of the crop lien system among farmer, merchant, and capitalist in the South after the Civil War. That system was, in the words of C. Vann Woodward, "one of the strangest contractual relationships in the history of finance. The seeker of credit usually pledged an unplanted crop to pay for a loan of an unstipulated amount at a rate of interest to be determined by the creditor."[12] Credit was a factor in the fur trade only when a trapper's need for supplies was not met by the value of the beaver he could offer, but, like the southern farmer and also the western farmer of the same era out of whose midst the populist movement emerged, the trapper was forced both to buy and to sell at dictated and ruinous prices.

Although Robert M. Utley's recent history of the mountain men, *A Life Wild and Perilous*, focuses on the trappers as geographic discoverers, it briefly addresses the economic exploitation as well, recognizing that "the supplier made the money. The trapper never got out of debt, never earned enough money to leave the mountains for the comforts of home." Utley distinguishes between the hired men, or *engages*, who were a part of most of the great fur brigades, and the free trappers, who were independent businessmen selling their furs and buying their supplies wherever they chose, and he notes the analogy between exploited southerners and westerners when he refers to the *engages* as "sharecroppers." The free trappers, however, seem to strike him much as they struck contemporaries and most historians, as much better off because of their independence. The free trapper, he says, "looked with condescension from the pinnacle of the social pyramid. He equipped and supplied himself, traveled with a company brigade or not as he wished, and sold his catch to whoever offered the highest price."[13] Utley and apparently Morgan seem seduced by that much-vaunted freedom of the free trapper, and they minimize the inherent exploitative nature of the fur trade, which was applied mostly against the *engages*.[14]

Was the free trapper really free, or was he just as "trapped" in exploitative economics as the wage earner? What were his alternatives if he thought he was being gouged? Not many. Theoretically, he could sell to a competitor. At various times during the 1820s the Hudson's Bay Company, the Missouri Fur Company, and especially Astor's American Fur Company, which began stepping up the competitive pressure toward the end of the decade, were all operating in the mountains as buyers and suppliers. The opportunity to choose among these buyers, however, was largely illusory. The HBC offered its trappers such unattractive prices in comparison with the Ashley companies that desertion sometimes occurred, and the other American companies pretty well held the line in price fixing, much like the infamous "pools" of the Gilded Age. Another apparent possibility would be for the trappers to band together to market their own furs and buy their own supplies, thus eliminating the middle men. The Rocky Mountain Fur Company, successor to Smith, Jackson & Sublette, tried that, but such cooperative buying and selling demanded business acumen and connections few of the Ashley trappers of the 1820s had. It also involved the risk and arduousness of the overland or river journey from the mountains to St. Louis, which few wanted to make. They loved the mountains and were willing to endure the most egregious exploitation imaginable to stay there. Viewed in this light, one could make a case that the *engages* were the truly free trappers, for although their pay was low, it was at least secure—even if life and limb were not—and their supplies came at the expense of the company rather than from their own pockets.

One most misses in Morgan's presentation of fur trade economics, as welcome and original as it is, an awareness of the meaning of the facts he carefully assembles. Once again, the facts do not simply speak for themselves; determining their larger meaning requires the active intellection of the historian to look at those tables of beaver prices, freight rates, and retail markups and see *exploitation*. A particularly cynical and brutal exploitation as well, for the fur trade suppliers made their immense fortunes by using their monopoly powers to force prices up, like the infamous robber barons of the Gilded Age did, but also by turning their own employees into consumers and gouging them as well. That one word, *exploitation*, had Morgan been able to utter it, would have given his book a larger significance beyond the raw economic data it presents. It would have provided an immediate link to similar economic relationships throughout history, from the medieval landowner and his serfs to the storekeepers and sharecroppers of the post-bellum South, to the robber baron and the Kansas farmer, to the labor movement, and even to the Asian sweatshops of the Nike shoe company. The history of the fur trade could have helped us understand those other relationships and they in turn could have deepened our understanding of the fur trade. The closest Morgan ever got to any perception of this insidious circumstance was his bland paraphrase of Daniel Potts's observation that the trappers found it hard to make any money.

It would have required no creative insight on Morgan's part to perceive the heinous dimensions of the fur trade exploitation. Exactly ten years before Morgan's book appeared, Bernard DeVoto had put his finger on it in the most direct and unflinching way in his *The Year of Decision 1846*, a book Morgan highly praised and to which, according to DeVoto's acknowledgments, he had made major contributions of information. DeVoto, who was infamously inclined to express a one-watt idea in hundred-watt language, this time found a crime proportionate to his prose. The mountain men and the Indians as well, DeVoto observed in an indictment as worthy of the courtroom as the history book,

> were the agents of as ruthless a commerce as any in human history; they were its exploited agents. The companies hired them—or traded with the highest order of them, the free trappers . . . —on terms of the companies' making, paid them off in the companies' goods, valued at the companies' prices deep in the mountains. They worked in a peonage like the greasers they despised, the freed Negroes of the South, or the share-croppers of our day. The companies outfitted them and sent them out to lose their traps, their horses, and frequently their scalps—to come back broke and go deeper into debt for next year's outfit. Their trade capitalized starvation, was known to practice land piracy, and at need incited Indians against competitors. It made war on Indians who traded with competitors and debauched the rest with the raw alcohol that was called whiskey in the mountains.

Central to this exploitation, DeVoto goes on to point out, was the companies' awareness of the pride of the free trapper and his determination to stay in the mountains at any cost. "At any evening fire below the Tetons, if they had paid civilization its last fee of contempt, they had recompense in full. . . . The back trail was always there and need only be followed eastward. Few ever took it. They were, by God! the mountain men."[15]

In spite of the title of this essay, one need not be a Karl Marx to interpret properly the class antagonism inherent in the relationship between the trapper and the fur company, any more than one needs to be a Freud to analyze Jedediah Smith's personality. But one needs *some* larger contexts into which to place one's facts if the facts are going to have any meaning beyond the mere adventure story Morgan was trying to transcend. Why bother to compile tables of trade goods prices, of profit and loss margins, unless one can make a point about the basic economic relations they document? Of course it was hard for the trappers to make any money, as Daniel Potts observed, but it is hard to make money in many endeavors, and surely Morgan owed his readers some analysis of the particular forces that the trappers felt themselves to be up against. Some of DeVoto's moral outrage, even diluted by a factor of ten, would perhaps have been too much to ask of Morgan, but the simple recognition of a pattern in the facts does not seem unreasonable.

Juanita Brooks

Juanita Brooks

THE VILLAGER

UTAH HISTORIAN Juanita Brooks begins her autobiography with the story of a Sunday School field trip she made when she was six or seven years old to a hilltop that offered a panoramic view of her hometown of Bunkerville, Nevada, and the lower Virgin River valley. The thought of a field trip for rural Nevada children who spent their daily lives in the "field" might seem ludicrous, but the canny teacher had a purpose in mind that changed the life of at least one of her fortunate pupils. The hilltop vantage point shrank their village and placed it in the larger perspective of "the great, wide, beautiful, wonderful world," as it was called in a poem the teacher recited. Orienting the class at first by identifying the center of their world, the Mormon meeting house, she extended the lesson to other nearby buildings and features. Then she expanded their vision to the neighboring village of Mesquite, five miles to the east and across the river, then to the blue mountains on the horizon, behind which was hidden the town of St. George with its Mormon temple, and in the other direction the fearsome desert that lay between them and Las Vegas, and beyond that, California and the Pacific Ocean. Juanita Brooks's long life would take her far out into that world, which she must have found much wider—and both much more and much less wonderful—than her teacher's imagination could embrace. When she returned home at the end of that day, she found that Bunkerville never looked quite the same again. It is also true, though, that she never saw that wider world through anything but the lenses of her Bunkerville girlhood, a vision that, as we shall see, was at the same time both acute and astigmatic.

The history of the American West is, perhaps more than most other historical fields, a history of place. The dramatic geographical features of the region have placed definite limits on the scope of human activity, as they have tested the spirit and resourcefulness of those who have attempted to live there. Thus one of the hallmarks of western history is a profound understanding of the nature of the country itself and its effects upon human activity. The western environment, that is to say, has shaped its historians as much as it has shaped its history. This is true of all the historians who are the subjects of this book, but it is most true of Juanita Brooks (1898–1989), the great historian of southwestern Utah popularly known as "Dixie." Born, reared, educated, and employed in that far-flung outpost of Mormon country along the middle and lower Virgin River in southern Utah and Nevada, Brooks left her homeland only for brief sojourns and spent her scholarly career collecting sources and writing about little else. Bernard DeVoto's Ogden and Fawn Brodie's Huntsville were Utah's versions of Gopher Prairie—oppressive small-town cultures to be fled from rather than celebrated. Dale Morgan wrote memorably and lovingly about Salt Lake City and the Great Salt Lake, but he rejected his natal Mormonism and found both his major subject matter and dwelling places outside of Utah. Wallace Stegner, similarly, generously acknowledged the formative influences of Salt Lake City upon his adolescence and early professional development, but he located his career and residence elsewhere. A Juanita Brooks, however, would be unthinkable outside of Utah and indeed outside of Dixie, where she found her cultural nourishment. "You know, Juanita, you are always astonishing me," Dale Morgan exclaimed in delight early in their friendship. "You say something quite casually, and all at once I realize what a world of experience you have which you take for granted but which is quite foreign to my own experience. . . . The frontier is right inside you in a way it never has been, and maybe never will be, in me."[1]

A necessary first step toward understanding Juanita Brooks, then, is to understand Bunkerville, Nevada, a nineteenth-century Mormon experiment in communal living under the rules of the United Order of Enoch. A certain utopian communitarianism has always been a part of the Mormon ethos, for the church was born out of the revivalist and reformist zeal of the Age of Jackson, the same zeal that created Brook Farm, Oneida, and many other religious and secular utopian experiments. Mormon communitarianism has seen its ebb and flow, and its most thoroughgoing manifestation was the United Order of Enoch. Implementation of the United Order in Utah in the mid-1870s was Brigham Young's way of fighting back against various forces, both deliberate and inadvertent, that increasingly threatened the Mormon way of life during and after the Civil War. The federal government, for one thing, was using its anti-polygamy crusade as a spearhead to destroy the economic and political power of the Mormon Church, and mining, which had been promoted by Gen. Patrick Edward Connor's troops after 1862, threatened to lure Mormons away from the agricultural economy that Young envisioned as the basis of Mormon self-sufficiency. That self-sufficiency was also threatened by the arrival of the transcontinental railroad in 1869, which diluted the Mormon population with an influx of outsiders and linked Utah to the national economy of capitalism and industry. Finally, the Panic of 1873, a bank collapse that led to a national depression and destroyed the livelihood of many Mormons who worked in the mines or who supplied mining communities,[2] was a catalyst for implementation of the United Order.

Not surprisingly, it was in St. George that Young started the first United Order in 1874, and it was Dixie pioneers like Juanita Brooks's ancestors who led the way in its implementation. The Dixie pioneers, out of their experience in trying to subdue the vicious Virgin River and wrest a living from the harsh Red Rock country, had had the virtues of cooperation hammered into them season after season. Individualism in Dixie meant failure and death. Moreover, they were used to making do with a minimum of worldly goods and comforts. And they had seen firsthand the fickleness of capitalism when the profits of the silver mines at Pioche, Nevada, suddenly dried up in response to the distant economic collapse, a collapse that had cost many Dixie miners and freighters their livelihoods. Dixie was fertile ground for the United Order. "It was in the Virgin Basin," Dixie historian Andrew Karl

Larson reminds us, "that the church initiated its first attempt in its new western empire to establish the United Order of Enoch, and it was in this area where it had its greatest success."[3]

That success, however, even at its greatest, was not very impressive. In most cases, United Order communities held out for only two or three years before passing into what Larson calls "the limbo of forgotten causes." The reasons for the Order's failure are not hard to find. They are rooted, as Larson points out, in the frailties of human nature itself. "The habits of an acquisitive society were too strongly forged [even among the hardy and self-denying Dixie pioneers] to be broken without the utmost devotion and selflessness to the cause, and rugged individualism triumphed over this abortive attempt at communal ownership and communal living here."[4]

The Bunkerville, Nevada, United Order was a last-ditch attempt to make the experiment work at about the time other communities were giving it up. After the failure of the Santa Clara Order, some members, led by their bishop, Edward Bunker, Sr., thought the order could yet succeed if implemented from the ground up in a newly established community. After securing permission from Brigham Young, twenty-three people incorporated a United Order community and set out for a site they had chosen on the lower Virgin River some twelve miles below the mouth of Beaver Dams Creek. They arrived there on January 5, 1877, and founded the settlement of Bunkerville. Dudley Leavitt, Juanita Brooks's grandfather, was elected one of the counselors to Bishop Bunker, though he did not actually join the community for about a year.[5] Leavitt and his polygamous family were all zealously committed Mormons who became cornerstones of Bunkerville. It was that community, one of the remotest Mormon colonies on what Brooks would later call "the ragged edge" of Mormon country, born of communitarian enthusiasm and tempered by the trials of life in one of the world's harshest environments, that shaped the character and defined the identity of Juanita Brooks.

The site chosen for Bunkerville offered some attractive agricultural advantages. There was enough fertile land in the Virgin River bottoms to support a significant community, and there was a growing season long enough to grow cotton, the goal of much of the Mormon colonization effort in Dixie.

Unfortunately, the site offered daunting disadvantages as well. The notorious uncooperativeness of the river had been the bane of earlier colonies further upstream, which had to have water but often got it in dam-devastating quantities. The river at Bunkerville was doubly dangerous because its bottom offered no bedrock footholds to anchor a dam. It was a country, as Brooks termed it in her autobiography, of "quicksand and cactus."[6] Another disadvantage was the infamous unpalatability of the water, particularly late in the summer when it was undiluted by spring snowmelt. "One has to taste it during the hot weather to understand how unpleasant it can be," remarked Andrew Karl Larson. In fact, the Bunkerville water, known unflatteringly as "Virgin Bloat," called forth some of Larson's finest eloquence: it had "a slick, almost greasy taste and feeling to those compelled by thirst to drink this saline, sulphurous liquid that passed for water." It was equally unsatisfactory for laundry. "When soap was placed in it, it produced a suds resembling the sickly curd on a pioneer swill barrel."[7] One of the major utilities projects in Bunkerville became the digging of cisterns to trap and settle runoff water for drinking and cooking. (Brooks's father, Henry Leavitt, hired Dudley Leavitt himself to dig most of theirs, which he did by arduous hand labor for two dollars per day, payable daily and—manifesting the old pioneer's distrust of paper money—in silver!) Even the cistern water took some getting used to. "We don't mind it," Brooks told a stranger who grimaced when she gave him a cup of it, "but strangers always say that it tastes like a dose of epsom salts." She observed that "he drank it quickly as an ordeal to get through."[8]

In terms of simple agricultural production, the Bunkerville United Order gave early promise of success, with impressive yields of cotton, wheat, and molasses during the first year, a production that grew almost fourfold by harvest time in 1879 (Larson reports that cotton was grown in Bunkerville as late as 1915, when Juanita Brooks was in high school). But that production came at such a high price in human tribulation that it doomed the United Order and almost the community itself. The river, as one would expect, was a major source of frustration. It washed out the poorly anchored dams so regularly and caused so much extra work and property loss that the community frequently discussed abandoning the entire experiment. And the regimentation and stifling of individual initiative under the United Order proved unendurable to its members. In 1880 the corporation was dissolved, and each member took an adjudicated settlement in proportion to his labor and investment.[9] The dissolution of the United Order might have saved Bunkerville, which is today a viable agricultural community, for people seemed willing to face the frustrations of the river if cooperation were voluntary rather than mandatory and if they could reap the fruits of their own initiative. In the end, the Bunkerville United Order met with the same kind of failure as most communitarian experiments then and now.

By the time Juanita Brooks was born in 1898, Bunkerville still carried earmarks of its communitarian origins, but for the most part it had become a typical Mormon agricultural village of the type one would find throughout the red rock desert of southern Utah and Nevada and northern Arizona. The Dixie communities were then in the midst of what Charles S. Peterson has called the "middle period" of rural Mormon life, between the colonial period characterized by the heavy-handed direction of Brigham Young that ended with his death in 1877 and the gradual opening of modernizing influences like the automobile and the radio, which began around 1920. During that middle period, the internal dynamics of rural Mormon culture had a free scope of development, largely unaffected by outside forces.[10] Several characteristics of that idyllic era in Mormon life imprinted themselves indelibly upon Juanita Brooks.

One was a peculiar version of Mormonism that was more like the original spirituality of Joseph Smith rather than the institutionalized church of Brigham Young. Although Mormon priesthood authority was largely unquestioned in religious and secular spheres, there was a democratic belief in direct revelation, in dreams and visions, in the validity of peepstones and water witching, in the reality of spirits, good and evil. Brooks's letters and her autobiography are full of stories of the supernatural and of divine intervention in human affairs. A telling anecdote occurs in *Quicksand and Cactus*. While she was a student at Brigham Young University, her young son, Ernest, contracted measles and appeared to be losing his life as he collapsed and the color departed from his face. She hailed a passing Mormon elder (one can do that in Provo, Utah!), who anointed the boy with oil and prayed for his healing. When there was no immediate visible effect, the question Brooks asked was not "why isn't this working?" but rather "why did it take so long?"[11]

Dixie pioneers had a work ethic that became perhaps Juanita Brooks's most remarkable personal attribute. There was little capital available, and large speculative ventures were out of the question. Whatever got done was done under the hot Nevada sun with the muscle power of animals and humans. During her productive years as a historian, Brooks had the heavy domestic responsibility of caring for what she called her "compound-complex" family: her son Ernest from her first marriage that ended in widowhood, the children of her husband Will Brooks, himself a widower, and the children they had together. In addition, she shouldered the obligations all Mormon women had to the Ladies' Relief Society and other church activities. Finally, she felt an obligation to carry out her literary endeavors largely in secret. They were not the kind of toil expected of a woman in her situation, and she did not wish to arouse the suspicions of neighbors who might drop in unexpectedly at any time. Accordingly, she arose in the dark an hour or so before anyone else to do some furtive reading and thinking. After the family was up, fed, and off to their daily activities, she would put in whatever writing time she could squeeze in among household duties, always keeping her ironing board set up as a ruse in case an unexpected guest should wonder what she was doing.[12] A weaker person would have caved in under such pressure (in fact, many would-be writers have capitulated to much lesser pressures), but the Bunkerville struggle against the desert and perhaps the minerals in the water had placed a steel in her backbone that never weakened.

On the other hand, it is common to make too much of the toil inherent in rural life. When there is work to be done, one works hard and long, but such periods are sporadic. Most of the time, rural life is a life of routine, of cooking, cleaning, and eating; of feeding and watering the animals; of taking one's turn at the irrigation water. In such a way of life, even minor reprieves from routine are eagerly embraced. Brooks writes memorably of the social significance of the thrice-weekly arrival of the mail in Bunkerville, and of the wildly enthusiastic reception given a couple who played Edison phonograph cylinders off the back of their wagon as a public entertainment.[13] In such a culture, people made their own entertainment most of the time, and folklore became rich and deeply entrenched. Brooks's autobiography is brim full of such lore, and her early publications drew deeply upon that tradition. Even her biographies, of Dudley Leavitt, Jacob Hamblin, and Emma Lee, are folkloric in much of their content and flavor.

Folklore encouraged the sense of Dixie as a special, unique place and the people of Dixie as possessing a special character and destiny. Much of this, naturally, was a residue of the United Order, with its self-denying commitment and its sense of being the Mormon way at its fullest. There was a concomitant contempt for the softness and luxury of life in northern Utah, where consumer goods and urban amenities were more readily available. In a story Brooks told more than once, Dixie folklore had it that a fancily dressed wife of Brigham Young once visited the southern settlements to promote the Retrenchment Society, a society that advocated a return to self-sufficiency and simple living. Disgusted with the apparent hypocrisy, a woman in the audience clad in a dress fashioned from old flour sacks asked, "Which do you want us to retrench from, Sister Young, the bread or the molasses?"[14]

That Juanita Brooks would relish such a story is evidence of the Bunkerville in her backbone. There is much to be learned from the penetrating characterization of her as a "villager," a characterization made by biographer Levi Peterson, himself a product of such an environment. He recounts a story of Brooks's battle, during the years of her struggle to provide for a large family in St. George, against the arbitrary and inequitable rates imposed by the power company. "One . . . remembers that she was a villager by birth," he observes. "Accustomed to direct, cooperative action in the production of the common necessities of life, she had a native distaste for corporate organization and bureaucracy." Similarly, when she witnessed an impressive local fruit-canning project in St. George during the Great Depression, she found herself forced to modify her skepticism that church welfare programs could effectively substitute for federal relief funds. "It was an instance of classless cooperation of which the village-born Juanita could not fail to approve," Peterson says.[15]

Finally, there was an undercurrent of tragedy in Dixie culture, an unspoken memory of the Mountain Meadows Massacre. The official story of the murder of some one hundred Gentile emigrants on their way to California was that it was perpetrated mostly by Indians whose wrath the emigrants had incurred by poisoning water holes. Although some few Mormons may have taken a hand in the matter (John D. Lee had been executed for his role), most attempted unsuccessfully to restrain the Indians and managed to save only seventeen babies and young children.[16] The truth, which was scarcely passed along even in whispers and never discussed publicly, was not only that the Mormons had taken the major role, but that they had first disarmed their victims with a promise of protection, then betrayed and murdered them in utter cold blood in one of the worst atrocities in American history. The core of the tragedy was not only the bloodthirstiness of the act, unthinkable though that might have been, but that in a deeper sense it called into question the validity of Mormonism itself, the new earthly order that was to follow the restoration of the true gospel through the medium of Joseph Smith. Instead of bringing the Mormon Zion to its culmination, the zeal of the people of Dixie had degenerated into a fanaticism that led to an unspeakable atrocity. It was the most courageous of Juanita Brooks's projects to look into the jaws of that disaster and to try as impartially as possible to unravel the lies and establish the truth.

As Brooks was a product of the culture of the Mormon frontier, she was largely a product of its educational system as well. During her formative years, America's public school system was struggling toward maturity, as universal public education moved slowly from ideal to reality. Even though the quality of education in the schools of rural Nevada and Utah around the turn of the century of course fell far short of modern standards, there is no reason to believe it was any worse than that in rural schools anywhere else in the country, and it may have enjoyed an enthusiasm derived from the characteristic Mormon zeal for self-improvement. Reminiscing in the 1930s about her own family's faith in education, Brooks took pride in the way "we took the adage 'You are saved no faster than you gain knowledge' and 'The Glory of God is Intelligence' so literally that we had books and magazines in the home though we children were barefoot—(I never wore shoes in the summer until I was 14 years old)—Then I think it was mother's love of the beautiful which saw to it that we had a piano, though were still eating from white galvanized plates."[17]

Her family demonstrated its commitment to education by having Bunkerville's first elementary school classes held in the Brooks home while the school building was being built. Although Brooks was too young to enroll, she eavesdropped from the doorway during idle hours and read the textbooks—and other books—in the evenings. Higher grades were added by the time she was ready for them, and she graduated from high school at the normal age. Her desire to become a teacher coincided with a push by the state of Nevada to provide local training for prospective teachers in its rural schools. Accordingly, for the school year of 1916–17, a Miss Mina Connell, a graduate of Columbia University, was hired to run a Normal School training program in Bunkerville for recent high school graduates wishing to teach in rural Nevada elementary schools. Brooks was one of eleven students who enrolled. Miss Connell was not only a gifted teacher herself, by Brooks's account, but an emissary from the wider world as well. Neither a Mormon nor a locally trained teacher, she kept her private life to herself, but she inspired her wide-eyed students not only with high educational standards, but as a role model as a dedicated and cultured teacher as well. Later, when Brooks was offered a sabbatical year in which to seek a master's degree, she bypassed the University of Utah and other regional institutions in favor of Columbia University to emulate Miss Connell.[18]

That, however, was ten hard years away. In between were years of teaching elementary school and two years at Dixie College in St. George, arduously financed by meager savings from her salary and grueling summer jobs. There was a brief marriage (1919–21) to Ernest Pulsipher, which was marred by ghastly treatments for a malignant tumor on his neck that caused his death just a few months after their first wedding anniversary. And there was the birth of a son, Ernest, in 1920, which marked the beginning of her strenuous struggles to orchestrate a life of demanding domestic and scholarly obligations. By means of various creative financial and domestic arrangements, she completed her undergraduate degree at Brigham Young University and returned to Dixie College as an English instructor. It was from that institution that she took the sabbatical that led her to the master's program at Columbia.

Her career as a historian was both facilitated and complicated by her decision to marry Sheriff William Brooks of St. George in 1933. He was a widower with a young family, and she had to integrate herself and her son into Will's family. These new obligations added to her domestic duties and taxed her skills as a psychologist and social worker. On the other hand, Will Brooks was in many ways the ideal husband for an aspiring writer and historian. For one thing, he adored his young bride (he was seventeen years older than she), and in spite of the inevitable increase in domestic duties his family placed upon her, he supported her unwaveringly in her literary ambitions. He was also perhaps the most likeable and best-known man in Utah's Dixie, and Brooks's marriage to him opened innumerable doors in her quest for historical sources.

The decade of the 1930s was important not only for Brooks's new marriage and family responsibilities, but also because it saw the beginning of her concerted program to collect and preserve manuscript sources for history and her first significant publications. The catalyst for both was Nels Anderson, whom Brooks characterized as "the most unconventional mortal you ever saw." Anderson had accidentally arrived in Utah's Dixie in 1908 as a stranded teenage hobo who had been hitching rides on a roundabout route toward Panama, where he planned to help dig the canal. Taken in by a polygamous Mormon family on a remote ranch, Anderson became infatuated with the Mormon way of life, underwent a nominal conversion to the religion, and graduated first from Dixie Academy and then Brigham Young University. He left Utah to study sociology at the University of Chicago, but his interest in hoboes, prisoners, and other socially marginal groups was too unconventional to gain him an academic appointment, so he spent his professional career working for government agencies. In 1934, a research grant brought him back to St. George for four months, where he did the research that led to *Desert Saints: The Mormon Frontier in Utah*, a superb scholarly study of Mormon history and institutions based in large part on the records and experiences of the Dixie frontier.[19]

During his brief return to St. George, Anderson lived adjacent to the Brooks residence and became intimately acquainted with Brooks's knowledge of rural Mormonism. One of the things he learned was that Juanita had developed an interest in collecting and preserving manuscript sources, beginning with the diary of her great-grandmother, Sarah Sturdevant Leavitt, and the diary of her first husband's ancestor John Pulsipher, a Dixie pioneer. When Utah received a generous allocation of funds under the Federal Emergency Relief Administration of 1934, Anderson suggested that she apply for a grant to collect and copy Dixie pioneer records. Her application was successful, and Brooks was able to employ a small cadre of agents to solicit the loan of early diaries in private hands, to be copied in typescript by another cadre of stenographers who plied their craft in a converted bedroom in her home. The original document and a free carbon copy of the typescript would be returned to the owner and the original typescript would then be publicly available for research. It was the beginning of what became a statewide project under another New Deal agency, the Historical Records Survey, which was part of the Works Progress Administration of 1935.[20]

Anderson also asked Juanita to create genealogical data on her own polygamous ancestors to be used in his book, then suggested that she follow up on that by doing some writing of her own about her family history and Dixie folklore. When he left St. George, Anderson gave Will Brooks a slip of paper with his address on it and offered to help Juanita polish and publish her writing, but the shirt with the slip of paper in a pocket got into the laundry before Will remembered he had it, and the address became illegible. No matter; Juanita's determination was enough. She finished the article and sent it to *Harper's*, where it appeared under the title "A Close-up of Polygamy," in February 1934—her first significant publication.[21] It was the beginning of an intermittent stream of such writings—some accepted, some rejected, and one even stolen!—that gradually became a river of original articles, edited documents, and books that established Juanita Brooks as one of the major historians of rural Mormonism.[22]

Her first actual book, a biography of her grandfather, appeared in 1942 under the title *Dudley Leavitt: Pioneer to Southern Utah*.[23] In an "Author's Statement" introducing the revised edition of 1973, Brooks tells the story of the inception of the book. Her father had urged her to shift her research interest from the better-known Mormon frontiersman Jacob Hamblin to Leavitt, Hamblin's long-time associate and relative by marriage. Leavitt, her father insisted, was a better man than Hamblin and often did difficult and dangerous jobs that Hamblin avoided, with little credit for his courage and resourcefulness. Acceding to her father's wishes, Brooks gathered documentary records and interviewed surviving relatives and friends for their reminiscences. The publication procedure was amusing: Brooks contracted with a St. George printer to publish it on an installment plan of fifty dollars down and fifty per month to the amount of six hundred dollars, for which he would produce five hundred copies. Her father donated the down payment, but 1941–42 were lean times in southern Utah, and in the end she and Will had to borrow money to pay off the printer. As she completed each chapter, she carried the draft to the printer, who set it into type individually and bound the whole in a blue paper cover when it was finished. It was a modest book by any standard, but it discharged her obligation to her father and pleased the family. Moreover, it opened the doors of the Huntington Library when she applied there to do research on the Mountain Meadows Massacre, for the librarian, Leslie E. Bliss, happened to be a descendant of the New England Leavitts and had read and enjoyed her book.

There is room for disagreement with the otherwise inerrant judgments of her biographer, Levi Peterson, regarding the merits of *Dudley Leavitt*. Peterson twice calls it "one of her finest books" and supports his assessment by observing that it "is written in a simple, concrete style. Utterly devoid of footnotes and other scholarly apparatus, it convinces through detail. . . . [Leavitt's Mormon zeal and his colorful adventures are] palpable, immediate, and real. He was a credible giant, a believable doer of unbelievable deeds."[24] Peterson's literary judgment is accurate enough. Brooks's style is indeed simple and concrete, and Leavitt's adventures are surely "palpable, immediate, and real," though the style seems more appropriate to a children's story than a historical treatise. And one sees no reason to insist, in a book directed toward a family and local audience, on precise scholarly documentation, especially since Brooks indicates her major sources in the text.

One has more trouble, though, with her invented dialogue, her assured readings of her characters' emotions, and her uncritical acceptance of miraculous manifestations that typically attend pious Mormon narratives. On these points, Dale Morgan's criticisms of her autobiography, *Quicksand and Cactus*, which she began drafting only shortly after the appearance of *Dudley Leavitt*, aptly apply to her earlier book as well: "Conversations are remembered too facilely for them to have been actually remembered, and by 're-imagining' those conversations, you are working in the borderland of fiction. The difficulty is compounded by the fact that you have several chapters in which one strongly suspects the things you describe never happened, that you have merely fashioned your own vehicle for saying some things you want to say."[25]

There is every attempt, in other words, to write the Leavitt family history in a way that makes the Leavitts appear as epitomes of the Mormon story itself. Twice Brooks mentions (uncritically quoting a primary source) that the Leavitts were converted to Mormonism in the mid-1830s merely by reading Parley P. Pratt's *A Voice of Warning* and the *Book of Mormon* "without preaching."[26] Of course this is possible, but it also fits Mormon missionary mythology perfectly—that the truth of the Mormon gospel is so self-evident that missionary explication is often superfluous—and Brooks sees no reason even to lift an eyebrow. Furthermore, on the crucial matter of Dudley Leavitt's participation in the Mountain Meadows Massacre, the scandalous violence of which casts a shadow over the personal morality of the individual perpetrators, even Peterson points out that Brooks "attempted to ameliorate [Leavitt's participation] by stressing the family tradition that he had served as a scout on the periphery of the bloody event."[27] As late as 1962, when the revised edition of her *The Mountain Meadows Massacre* appeared, she was still taking comfort in the agnosticism made possible by the lack of sources on her grandfather's role in the bloody business: "My own grandfather was there. What part he took I do not know, except that in his late life he insisted, as many others did, that he had nothing to do with it. There is evidence that he was in the vicinity at the time and that he knew what was going on. If he did not help with the massacre, he still did nothing to prevent it."[28] At last, then, an accessory before the fact; in *Dudley Leavitt* he is simply "a scout on the periphery."

Sometime during the mid-1940s, Brooks became committed to writing a history of the Mountain Meadows Massacre. Like many major writing projects, its inception was gradual and its process lengthy. Once she had decisively set sail toward the goal, however, Brooks prosecuted the journey with a determined energy and an expertise that made the book her masterpiece and an acknowledged classic of western historiography. Because of her profound involvement in the culture of the region and her dogged persistence in digging out the truth about it, *The Mountain Meadows Massacre* became, as her biographer calls it, "the story she was born to tell."[29]

At the most fundamental level, the story of the 1857 massacre was as much a part of her heritage and that of other Dixie natives as the desert itself. Referred to only in whispers and oblique allusions, it was the ever-present shadow in the Dixie sunshine, like the dark family rumors and feuds of Nathaniel Hawthorne's Puritan Massachusetts. It was the paradox of the region, both inescapable and unacknowledgeable.

As she tells the story, her earliest confrontation with the incident came through her friendship with Nephi Johnson, a grizzled old Dixie pioneer and discoverer of what is now Zion National Park, while she was a young schoolteacher in Mesquite, Nevada. She could hardly have failed to notice him, for, as Levi Peterson's prose indicates, his appearance was unforgettable: "his head bald; his cheeks sunburned; his mouth and chin lost in an effulgent white beard; his countenance wistful and sad, as if he pondered endlessly the probability of his own damnation."[30] Johnson's affinity for the young woman led him to pronounce a patriarchal blessing upon her—a Mormon institution in which a senior member of the church confers upon a younger member a sort of prophecy of her ultimate role in life and in the church. Since she was presumably the best educated and most literary person in the community, he also asked her to write the story of his life, indicating that he had secrets for her ears and pen alone. As a busy young teacher, still in her teens, Brooks had more pressing obligations and more engaging interests, and she kept finding reasons to procrastinate. Eventually, delirious on his deathbed, he called for her a last time, but by then it was too late. He could no longer tell his story, but as it flooded back through his fevered mind, he cried out, "Blood! BLOOD! BLOOD!" in an inarticulate anguish that, it scarcely needs saying, terrified her.

"What is the matter with him"? she asked her uncle. "He acts like he is haunted."

"Maybe he is," came the reply. "He was at the Mountain Meadows Massacre, you know."

"No, indeed, I did NOT know," Brooks thought. But the hair-raising incident put her on the way toward finding out, a way that would lead, more than thirty years in the future, to her most important contribution as a historian.[31]

The Huntington Library played a major role in her research as well. In the mid-1940s it received a $50,000 grant from the Rockefeller Foundation to collect primary sources of western history. Impressed both by her work on the Dudley Leavitt book and by her immense success at locating pioneer Utah source materials during her years with the New Deal programs, head librarian Leslie E. Bliss and Occidental College history professor Robert Glass Cleland, administrator of the grant, offered her a monthly stipend and travel allowance to scout similar materials for the library. After Blanche Knopf, wife of Alfred A. Knopf, indicated an interest in considering the Mountain Meadows Massacre manuscript for publication, Brooks talked Bliss and Cleland into raising her stipend and extending her duties to some research time on the book. In addition, the library provided invaluable sources, transcripts of the two trials of John D. Lee kept by the official court recorder, and eventually Lee's own diaries, though these were not acquired until the first edition of the book had been published.

Gaining entrance to the Huntington Library, where scholarship was the *raison d'etre*, was easy despite her lack of academic credentials in history, which were easily outweighed by her record of scholarly attainments. Gaining access to sources among her own people, especially sources in the hands of the church and of the families of participants in the massacre, was a different matter. Here, despite drawing on her impressive experience and skills of persuasion, she sometimes fell short. Her letters reveal that her basic approach was to convince recalcitrant owners of source material that she held their ancestors in high regard for the totality of their contribution to taming the Utah frontier, and that she regarded the massacre as a temporary moral lapse committed under extreme pressure. Further, she, as a dedicated Mormon and lifelong Dixie resident, was in a position to tell the story truthfully and sympathetically (those two qualities not being in conflict, she thought). To a member of the Higbee family from whom she sought permission to use John M. Higbee's "Bull Valley Snort" statement, one of the major primary sources for the story, she said, "I think that the first place to tell the truth is at home, and I am sure I have a slant on that affair that has not been presented."[32]

Sometimes resistance came from interested family members other than the holder of a manuscript. An aunt and uncle who "are very much opposed to any of it coming to light," for example, were roadblocks to her use of the "Bull Valley Snort" statement, even though the holder of the manuscript trusted Brooks to interpret it properly. Her greatest frustration, however, was in dealing with high officials of her own church. Levi Peterson tells of her repeated attempts to examine a packet of affidavits from massacre participants that had once been in the hands of her friend Judge David Morris of St. George. Morris died before Brooks got around to looking at them, and his widow, afraid they would compromise the church, conveyed them to Apostle David O. McKay, at that time a counselor to President Heber J. Grant and later to President George Albert Smith. Today we would call the behavior of these church officials "stonewalling." At first they pretended not to possess the material, then they stood her up on appointments for which she had ridden the night bus all the way from St. George. Their tactics were designed to wear her down and make her give up, but these men were neither the first nor the last to misjudge the obstinate persistence of the Dixie villager Juanita Brooks. Someone was going to have to face the quiet lioness in the waiting room. Responsibility for that fearsome task slid down the pecking order to Joseph Anderson, secretary to the First Presidency. When, eventually, he faced Brooks across his desk with the envelope of affidavits between them, he could resort only to institutional obstinacy and authority to justify denying her request. She went home empty-handed.[33]

The book that resulted from her research, *The Mountain Meadows Massacre*, was a sea change in Mormon explanations of the incident. In the first chapter of this book we saw something of the way Mormon academic historians dealt with it at the time Brooks began her research. Popular explanations on the Dixie frontier during her youth exonerated the Mormons completely. Brooks recalled at the time of her visit to Nephi Johnson's deathbed:

> I had read and been told our standard story that some emigrants had been massacred at a place called Mountain Meadows, far away from the Mormon settlements, but it was the work of Indians. They were stirred up because some of their number had been killed by these emigrants, and they wanted revenge. A few of our people who lived in the area had tried to restrain the Indians, but were able to save only about seventeen children, who were sent back to their relatives in Missouri."[34]

Why, then, had Nephi Johnson been so distraught when memories of the incident came before him as he prepared to meet his maker? Eventually she learned that a few Mormons had been participants, and one of them, John D. Lee, had been the evil instigator of their participation and had been executed for it. Why only Lee? Because the others had only been following Lee's orders, and Mormon justice, sanctioning the social solidarity based on the authority of the priesthood, accepted what later came to be known in a different context as the "Nuremburg defense," that culpability for immoral or illegal orders rested only upon those who gave them, not on those who obeyed.[35] On the surface, the story seemed plausible enough, but Brooks, the villager who never accepted "official" explanations simply because they were official, distrusted it and felt compelled to dig deeper. The scare Nephi Johnson had given her hinted that there must be more to the story. And no doubt the secrecy in the collective memory of Dixie Mormons suggested that something about the story would not bear honest scrutiny. As she began collecting and studying the personal records of those Dixie pioneers during the 1930s, perhaps a collective character profile took shape in her mind, a profile of group cohesion, of dedication, and religious zeal—all qualities that distinguished the Mormon pioneer character and had made possible the achievements of Mormon settlement in the desert—that turned tragic once the potential for violence came to the surface.

Brooks begins her book by recapitulating Mormon history up to the expulsion from Nauvoo. It is a story of intolerance, persecution, and violence directed against the Saints wherever they located. Even though she acknowledges Mormon clannishness and bloc voting as sources of Gentile suspicion and hostility, her purpose is not to judge between the Mormons and their enemies, but to establish a mentality of persecution that grew out of Mormon history and which the Saints brought with them to Utah. The journey across the plains would be their last move; they would never be driven out of their Zion in the mountains, as Brigham Young promised, if they could have but ten years to establish themselves. Ten years, as things turned out, is exactly what they did have. Friction between the Mormons and the unsavory officials appointed under the 1850 territorial government escalated to the point that President James Buchanan felt compelled to send federal troops to put down what he represented as a Mormon rebellion. Young chose the Pioneer Day celebration in Big Cottonwood Canyon on July 24, 1857—ten years to the day after the arrival of the main body of initial Mormon emigrants in Salt Lake Valley—to announce the dispatch of the troops.

An outpouring of emotion ensued as the collective Mormon memory of persecution came back to the fore. Military preparations were made. Raiding parties left to harass the army supply trains, and snipers' breastworks were erected in Echo Canyon on the troops' approach to the valley, while the people of Salt Lake City prepared to burn the settlement and flee to the south. The religious fervor of the Mormon Reformation of 1856–57 renewed as people responded to emotional appeals to stand their ground against the invasion and defend the Mormon way of life. Such preparations included what Brooks calls "the zealous South," where Dixie emotions were whipped to a fury by the preaching of George A. Smith. Twelve Indian leaders were taken to meet Brigham Young, who exhorted them to prepare for battle on the Mormon side against the Americans, who would surely wipe them out if they did not. The untimely appearance of a contingent of government surveyors on the lower Colorado River under Lt. Joseph Christmas Ives aroused Dixie suspicions of preparations for an invasion from the south, and instructions came from Salt Lake City to prepare for it. Further horrible news of the murder of the beloved Mormon Apostle Parley P. Pratt while serving a mission in Arkansas further heightened the tension. "War hysteria," Brooks calls it, gripped southern Utah, Mormon and Indian alike, as a hapless party of California-bound emigrants from the very state where Pratt had been murdered prepared to leave Salt Lake City via the southern route of the Old Spanish Trail. As Brooks writes, "Exaggeration, misrepresentation, ungrounded fears, unreasoning hate, desire for revenge, yes, even the lust for the property of the emigrants, all combined to give justification which, once the crime was done, looked inadequate and flimsy indeed."[36]

One of the few serious shortcomings of *The Mountain Meadows Massacre* is that Brooks examined the incident almost exclusively from the Mormon point of view, and gave too little attention to the emigrants. She had little more than a document from the Office of Indian Affairs giving a roster of the heads of household, an enumeration of wives and children and their counties of origin, plus a few miscellaneous references from people who had met them on the trail. All agreed that there were two basic contingents: the emigrant families and a party of coarse frontiersmen whom some called the "Missouri Wildcats."[37] Mormon hatred of anything from Missouri dated from their violent experiences there in the 1830s, and the counties of origin of most of the party were on or near the northwestern border of Arkansas adjacent to Missouri and in the region where Parley Pratt had been killed. It would have taken some expert diplomacy to mitigate Mormon prejudice against such a party, but Mormon reports of their progress south indicate a short supply of that commodity. Stories accumulated of emigrant livestock turned into Mormon fields at harvest time, of boasts by the Missouri Wildcats of their complicity in the murder of

Joseph Smith, and even of their poisoning of a water hole near Fillmore that killed some Mormon cattle, some Indians, and one of the Mormon settlers. By the time the travelers reached a spring-fed verdant pasture called the Mountain Meadows some thirty miles southwest of Cedar City, where they stopped to rest and feed their animals in preparation for the long desert drive ahead, the emigrant party was in deep trouble, both with Indians and Mormons.

From this point, the story, even told in the broadest outline possible, indicates that things got out of control almost immediately. As Mormon strategy in northern Utah began shifting from military resistance to negotiation, strategy in the south accelerated in the opposite direction, and slow communication kept one hand from knowing what the other hand was doing. A large contingent of Indians gathered at the Mountain Meadows, and the Mormons at the site made the cowardly decision to let them become the battle-axe of the Lord and to bear the brunt, therefore, of any legal liability for the murder of the emigrants. But the plan backfired when the initial Indian assault failed, succeeding only in getting the emigrants to take up a strong defensive position. Further assaults only enraged the Indians, who began suffering casualties under the experienced fire of the Arkansas squirrel hunters behind the wagons. Even worse, the first emigrant casualty, a young man named William Aiden, who attempted to escape and seek help, was shot not by an Indian but by a Mormon, a fact his companions took back to the emigrant encampment. Now the emigrants had to be eradicated, because any who escaped would tell the tale of Mormon complicity and bring federal punishment upon them for sure.

The Mormons by this time were in a double-ended trap, for the Indians, who outnumbered them by at least two to one and perhaps as much as six to one, warned that they would turn their wrath upon them instead of the emigrants if they failed to help exterminate the wagon party. Accordingly, John D. Lee devised his strategy of convincing the emigrants that their only hope lay in giving up their arms and their defensive position and returning to Cedar City under Mormon guard. The success of his strategy indicates that the emigrants did not know they held the upper hand at that moment, and they paid for their ignorance with their lives. Deployed in a long line with a Mormon "guard" beside each male member of the party, as per Lee's instructions, the emigrants were dispatched in a matter of minutes upon Lee's signal by the Mormons and the Indians, who came charging out of hiding.

The deed was done. The rest of Brooks's story is an equally unlovely one of lying and obfuscation, flight and hiding, perfunctory investigation, and eventually the decision to apply the Mormons' Nuremburg justice to John D. Lee, the ranking Mormon military official on the site. Those who had followed his orders in perpetrating the massacre, as well as Lee's immediate military superiors, who had protected themselves by issuing orders oblique enough to allow for misinterpretation in court, were never brought to trial. The obvious injustice of the all-Mormon kangaroo court that sacrificed Lee produced cultural reverberations that were still vibrating in Juanita Brooks's day. On the one hand, the precarious exoneration of the participants except Lee drove discussion of the affair underground and visited a sense of guilt upon their descendants as well as on themselves. On the other hand, a smoldering outrage was kindled among the Lee descendants who accepted his guilt, but not his alone.

The Mountain Meadows Massacre immediately became the definitive interpretation of the darkest moment of Mormon history. Its thesis is clearly developed and well documented. The massacre was perpetrated, she asserts, not by evil people but by otherwise good people whose judgment was clouded by war hysteria. As she wrote of the Higbee and Haight families, she "found only good things in their lives before and after this tragedy."[38] Although she exonerated Brigham Young of ordering the incident or having prior knowledge of it, she found him an accessory after the fact in inadequately investigating and hiding the truth of the matter, and especially in his decision to sacrifice his adopted son, John D. Lee, as a scapegoat. Lee himself she found guilty, but she pointed out that he was neither the instigator of the atrocity (William Dame, the military leader of the southern region, bore that responsibility) nor its only Mormon participant, and she regarded the sham trial in which he was condemned by his own compatriots and sentenced to death as a tragic miscarriage of justice. Her book was the first study of the massacre conducted with a high level of honesty and of industry in research, and its thesis should have been greeted with a sigh of relief among the Mormon community and a forthcoming belated apology to the Lee family, the surviving family members of the emigrants, and even America itself, from the church leadership.

Sadly, that was not to be the case. Although the book drew favorable reviews in historical journals and enthusiastic congratulations from the likes of Dale Morgan and Fawn Brodie, official Mormondom simply looked the other way. At home, former friends avoided her, and she and Will were shunned when church assignments were handed out, even though she proudly continued to attend church, to pay tithes, and to send her children on missions and to the temple for marriage.[39] Brooks's biographer emphasizes that for all her villager's obstinacy, she found the image of a nonconformist profoundly distasteful and deeply hungered for church approval. The church never took any official action against her (How could it? Her research was irrefutable and her active participation in the church was elaborately documented and well-known.), but it wounded her perhaps even more deeply by simply turning its back. Disfellowship or excommunication would have given her something to fight against; what she got instead was a featherbed for a punching bag.

The Mountain Meadows Massacre was not Brooks's last word on the affair. A second edition issued by the University of Oklahoma Press in 1962 enabled her to incorporate subsequent research, though that research allowed her to sharpen her thesis rather than abandon or modify it. More immediately, however, she began a full-scale biography of John D. Lee, the central figure in the event and the scapegoat who alone took the punishment that should have been shared by others. Brooks took up the biography not only because of her fascination with Lee's complex character and tragic end, but also because of the acquisition of a major portion of Lee's diaries by the Huntington Library, which she was able to supplement by access to other of his diaries in private hands and in the archives of the Mormon Church. The Lee family, too, urged the project upon her out of their admiration for the Mountain Meadows Massacre book that had vindicated their long-held view of Lee's essentially good character and the injustice of his end. They now sought to have their ancestor's story told fully. They wanted him posthumously reinstated in the church, but they also wanted to fill out completely their assessment of his character and to establish a record of his faithful service, often at great risk and sacrifice, to his church.

Although her *The Mountain Meadows Massacre* is deservedly Brooks's most famous book and her most enduring contribution to western history, *John D. Lee: Zealot–Pioneer Builder–Scapegoat*, which appeared in 1961, is in some ways a more impressive achievement, in its size, its sweeping scale, and its meticulous examination of one of Mormon history's most infamous yet compelling figures. As Levi S. Peterson observes, John D. Lee's life is in some ways more interesting than the life of his prophet and friend Joseph Smith because of its authentically tragic dimensions.[40] Smith's violent death, gruesome and deplorable though it was, was more pathetic than tragic, coming as it did from the external factors of betrayal and mob violence rather than from his own doing. Lee's demise, on the other hand, was a genuine tragedy in a Greek sense, for it was rooted in an inherent character flaw—an excess of zeal and a propensity for violence—rather than external forces. Once again, it was a story Juanita Brooks was born to tell, not only because of the expertise brought by her research, but because she was a native to the soil on which Lee had lived and died, and because her literary background opened her sensibility to the tragic meaning of her subject.

The Lee biography enabled Brooks to tell the entire story of Mormonism, almost from its very beginning, through the tribulations in Missouri and Illinois, through the westward migration, and through much of the pioneer period in Utah, emphasizing the expansion of the Mormon empire onto the desert frontier of southern Utah and northern Arizona. It is truly an epic story, with the unforgettable figure of John D. Lee at its center. And Brooks brings her lifelong empathy for the Mormon ethos and institutions, and particularly for the rigors of life on the Mormon frontier, to her task with an effectiveness that few if any others could have accomplished. Like *The Mountain Meadows Massacre*, the Lee biography has become an acknowledged classic of western history.

That said, *John D. Lee* is, for a standard biography of a major figure in western history, a curious book. For one thing, while Brooks's literary background gave her an instinctive sense for Lee's life as a tragedy, it also tempted her to import literary devices to her narrative that are quite at odds with modern historical scholarship. As in her minor studies of Dudley Leavitt, Emma Lee, and Jacob Hamblin, she introduces invented dialogue and imputes emotions to her characters that are not sustained by her sources. Moreover, scholarly documentation is erratic. Only the first chapter is consistently and adequately footnoted; thereafter, footnotes are employed only to add supplementary material to the text, while documentation for her narrative is given entirely in an essay on sources at the end of the volume. Documentation of this sort is not necessarily inadequate, for her main source is the Lee diaries, of which a citation on every page would become a tedious distraction, and Brooks often indicates other sources in the text. But it does render the book something of a curiosity in the context of modern scientific historiographical conventions.

Even more curious, perhaps, from the standpoint of modern secular historical scholarship, is her naive portrayal of the ethos within which Lee—and Brooks herself—operated. Early Mormonism, and the Mormonism of the frontier of both Lee and Brooks, was an enchanted world. It was an apocalyptic world in which signs and wonders abounded, in which people prophesied and worked miracles. Patriarchal blessings loomed over people's lives as the manipulative gods of the Greek pantheon kept dipping into human affairs. Some kind of miraculous manifestation of God's hand pops up, if not on every page, certainly in every chapter. Brigham Young's face lights up with a heavenly glow as he dispenses the word of God; his voice becomes the voice of Joseph Smith as he asserts his authority over the church; fatal illnesses yield to the laying on of hands; people's heads are run over by wagons with no ill effect. And through it all is a profound sense of the End Times, that history is coming to a culmination, that the trumpet of the Lord is about to sound and the sword of the Lord to be drawn, while He dons His boots to trample out the vintage of the grapes of wrath. All this, of course, is readily documented in a multitude of sources, not the least of which is John D. Lee's diaries. There can be no question that the enchanted world of John D. Lee was precisely as

Brooks presents it, and that he was willing to serve and to suffer for the church—and to take blaspheming Gentiles into eternity with him—because Lee's head was in heaven while his feet were on earth, and he was zealously eager to bring the kingdom of God to Earth. What is curious, though, is that Brooks presents all this with a wide-eyed straightforwardness as historical fact. The absence, in Brooks's narrative, of any external, critical perspective on Lee's enchanted world forces the reader to wonder, then, just what was wrong about the Mountain Meadows Massacre. Lee and his compatriots at the Mountain Meadows may have gotten a bit ahead of things, but their apocalyptic vision not only explains why they did what they did, but was in fact *true*, in Brooks's mind. How can one accept the soundness of everything that led up to the massacre, then condemn the act itself? Nineteenth-century Mormonism, she seems to be saying, was a good thing—unless one took it seriously. John D. Lee took it seriously indeed.

Although Juanita Brooks's reputation rests securely on her books on the Mountain Meadows Massacre and John D. Lee, her less celebrated documentary editing projects may be, in the long run, her most substantial contributions to Utah and Mormon history. Locating, transcribing, and editing primary sources, as we have seen, was a particular genius of Juanita Brooks by virtue of her unique background and circumstances, her personality and temperament, and the necessity of such work as a preliminary to any secondary syntheses. Her bibliography shows a string of such projects from the very beginning to the very end of her career, including the diaries of southern Utah pioneers Thales Haskell, John Pulsipher, and Thomas D. Brown, John D. Lee's Mormon Battalion diary, and the diary of Martha Spence Heywood.[41] Her most important and ambitious editing projects, though, were the diaries of John D. Lee and of Hosea Stout, each in two volumes, appearing in 1955 and 1964, respectively.[42] They are arguably the two most important diaries for the Mormon pioneer period in southern Utah (Lee) and northern Utah (Stout). Lee and Stout had much in common and were close friends from Missouri and Nauvoo days. Both were, in a sense, strong-arm men for Joseph Smith, then Brigham Young, as members of the Danite Band, and Stout as chief of police in

Nauvoo. Both were members of the shadowy Council of Fifty created to implement Mormon projects in the secular realm, and Stout was president of the territorial legislature. Both were prolific diarists, vigorous writers, and privy to the inner workings of both church and state government, which allowed them to offer much information unavailable elsewhere.

Both diaries exhibit Brooks at her best, but they also reveal some of her characteristic shortcomings. Brooks drew deeply on her lifelong insider's familiarity with and feeling for Mormon institutions and folkways. Also, Brooks's artistry as a historian was best displayed on small canvases, in digging out minute and sometimes fugitive facts for annotations. Even though Leonard Arrington complained that her dogged fidelity to the rendering of textual vagaries in the Stout diary was "a little on the 'fussy' side," her annotations, another reviewer observed, were "a veritable Who's Who of early Mormon history."[43] Less happily, her disdain for the formal mechanisms of scholarship appear as well. Her annotations, for example, which bristle with information, contain source citations only when they quote directly. Still, her transcriptions and their scrupulous accuracy are an immense service to scholarship. It would be difficult to imagine any history of the pioneer period in Utah that did not draw heavily upon one or both diaries.

It is universally conceded that among Juanita Brooks's major books, her *History of the Jews in Utah and Idaho*, which appeared in 1973 and was the last project she completed on her own without substantial editorial assistance, is her least successful achievement. The project seems to have had its inception in laudatory comments made by Louis Zucker, a professor at the University of Utah and a Jewish community leader, about *The Mountain Meadows Massacre*. As the years passed, Zucker apparently followed Brooks's career as she became a prominent Utah historian. During the 1960s, funding became available from a woman named Myrtle Friedman to have a history of the Jews in Utah and southern Idaho written, and a committee consisting of Zucker, Ben M. Roe, another Jewish leader, and Sterling McMurrin of the University of Utah asked Brooks at the beginning of 1966 to do the research and writing. Unwisely, she accepted.

Juanita Brooks was a fine historian, but her expertise and competence were confined to her own Mormon people, and especially to the history of her Dixie homeland. As her reputation had grown through the years, a false sense of omnicompetence seems to have developed. But the study of Jewish culture and history was far too remote from the realm in which she felt comfortable. Worse yet, her interest in the subject quickly faded. "In the first place, I know little of the Jews and care less," she wrote to archivist Alfred Bush before she had even started the project. After working at it for several years, she felt she was getting nowhere. "The Jews of Utah! I can hardly learn who they were—and are. Truly, Fools rush in where angels fear to tread." When she submitted her first eight chapters for Zucker's review, even he had turned against her, and he rejected them for their lack of feeling for the Jewish character. Zucker, who was himself a writer of some skill, seemed to feel she was trespassing onto his territory. Finally, she wrote to Myrtle Friedman to suggest abandoning the project altogether in spite of the time and labor already spent. "BUT THEN WE'D BOTH BE FREE OF IT!" she urged in capital letters.[44]

Unhappily, Friedman talked her into finishing the book. The result was little short of a disaster. The writing is absolutely pedestrian, with Brooks's apathy apparent in every word. There is little synthesis, little interpretation of any kind, with long lists of members of organizations and congregations, page after page of dreary group photographs of confirmation classes and the like, and facts dryly compiled with little connection between them. Her biographer, although admitting that it "was indeed Juanita's worst book," puts the best possible face on things, recognizing it as properly placing most emphasis on the Jews of Salt Lake City, where there was the largest concentration, her presentation of interesting and significant details, and her excellent portrayal of Simon Bamberger, who, as a prominent businessman and Utah's only Jewish governor to date, was one of the most significant Jews in the region.[45]

Although *Quicksand and Cactus: A Memoir of the Southern Mormon Frontier* was the first major writing project Brooks ever attempted, it was the last to be published. It was finished in the early 1980s by Trudy McMurrin and other staff editors at the University of Utah Press, and

Howe Brothers, who published it in 1982.[46] It was the sharp eye of Dale Morgan that had first discerned that Brooks was a native repository of indigenous source material on Dixie and that she had the literary talent to make it live on the printed page. He worked with her tirelessly as she wrote the book during the 1940s, cashing in his credits with several publishers and with the curmudgeonly editor Bernard DeVoto to try to get it into print. But DeVoto, the ex-Utahn who evidently thought that nothing good could come out of Nazareth, was apathetic about the project, and none of Morgan's publishing contacts paid off. Like most neophyte writers, Brooks became discouraged after these rejections, and one might wonder how she mustered the courage to move on to other things. She put the manuscript away for years at a time, pulling it out only occasionally to cannibalize various chapters for publication in literary or folklore journals. Finally, even as she entered the mental debility that increasingly clouded her last years, she responded to Trudy McMurrin's urgings and skilled editorial assistance to bring the book to something of a conclusion. Even at that, the final version awkwardly tapers off into a version of her article on her manuscript-collecting days with the WPA and a couple of letters from Dale Morgan on the significance of her memoirs.

Still, McMurrin's editorial procedure worked. The book is a treasured memoir of Utah and Mormon history, invaluable for understanding the world out of which Brooks and her historical works emerged. The first section of the book is highly episodic, each chapter a vignette of some event or theme in her Bunkerville girlhood (several of these were published separately). The second section is a more continuous narrative that deals with her education, her teaching career, her marriage, widowhood, and remarriage into the "compound-complex" Brooks family, and the inception of her manuscript-collecting project. If there is a single theme, it is what her biographer calls her "village" values, a combination of hard-headed rural practicality, a driving work ethic and determination, a sense of communitarian obligation, a simple faith in the authority of the Mormon priesthood and a feeling of permeation of the material world by the spiritual, and a firm contempt for dishonesty, pretension, and nonsense. Those village values are the unstated worldview that informs all of her histories, but in *Quicksand and Cactus* they come downstage in full view, leaving us with an unforgettable picture of a woman of gritty determination, yet of humaneness and integrity.

Juanita Brooks was the first historian from within the Mormon community courageous enough to take an unflinching look into the abyss of its darker depths and to put to the test her assumption that nothing but the unvarnished truth was good enough for her church—that its essential soundness could withstand such truth. Today, nearly a half-century after the appearance of her books on the Mountain Meadows Massacre and John D. Lee, as her church still struggles to lay that dark business to rest and to reaffirm its positive programs and sunny assessment of the human condition, her faith has yet to be fully vindicated. On the other hand, there is no question that honesty in Mormon historiography has made great progress, and credit for much of that progress must go to Juanita Brooks. "Because of her," Levi S. Peterson concludes, "the collective mind of Mormondom is more liberal and more at peace with itself than it might otherwise be. . . . Juanita helped make Mormondom a little less suspicious about nonconformity in general." And finally, he observes, "The human race need not apologize for the life of Juanita Brooks."[47]

Though Brooks helped Mormons achieve an honesty about their history that included its dark aspects as well as its triumphs, she was never able to gain a complete objectivity herself. In the essays that follow, we shall look at her struggle to construct a convincing context for the Mountain Meadows Massacre within the optimistic view of human nature inherent in Mormon theology, and to create a believable personality profile for the massacre's most famous participant, John D. Lee. We shall see that she fell short in both endeavors by failing to explain how supposedly saintly people could perform some of the most beastly acts in western history.

ORIGINAL SIN ON THE CALIFORNIA TRAIL

BIAS, AS ALL historians know, is unavoidable in the writing of history. By studied effort, bias can be masked or minimized to an amazing degree, but it can never be fully eradicated. One who writes about his own culture gains the advantage of an insider's empathy for the motivations and the folkways of the people who are his subjects. An outsider, on the other hand, enjoys a critical vantage point from which he can see his subjects as others see them. Historical study has the humanizing potential to enlarge one's perspective as one tries to stand in the shoes of another, but in the end we all see the world through our own eyes.

In writing *The Mountain Meadows Massacre*, Juanita Brooks drew upon her insider's perspective in at least two vitally important ways. One was an access to sources that descendants of the participants would almost certainly have never shared with an outsider. She was the wife of the universally known and loved Sheriff Will Brooks, a conspicuously active Mormon, and a lifelong resident of the Virgin River frontier and descendant of one of its celebrated pioneers. These things—along with her own humble and soft-spoken personality—gave her every possible advantage toward gaining the trust necessary for access to tightly protected sources. Her other insider's advantage was an instinctive understanding of the people and the culture of which she was writing. The desert, as Dale Morgan observed, was indeed inside her in a way that no one without a similar upbringing could have hoped to experience. For these and other reasons, *The Mountain Meadows Massacre* was truly, as her biographer calls it, "the story she was born to tell."

As things turned out, even though she spent every bit of the capital in both of those accounts and borrowed even more at heavy interest, she fell short in both areas. She failed, in the first place, to gain permission to use all the sources she knew to exist. For all the interpretive advantages she possessed as a Dixie Mormon insider, her insider's perspective contained limitations as well, which kept her from doing justice to the tragedy that was her subject. Finally, her interpretation, which is basically a psychological one, is naive and shallow.

It is necessary to understand something of the Mormon theological and intellectual tradition to understand why Brooks interpreted the Mountain Meadows Massacre as she did. Mormonism was born out of the ebullient optimism of the Age of Jackson and developed a worldview that was fully consistent with that environment. A cornerstone of that worldview is an optimistic conception of human nature that Sterling McMurrin, the most profound modern student of Mormon thought, identifies as Pelagianism.[1] Pelagius, a British monk who showed up in Rome in the late fourth century, maintained that Adam's original sin was Adam's alone, with no continuing consequences for humanity, and that human nature was thus essentially good and uncorrupted. Pelagius drew the fire of St. Augustine, who countered that original sin continues as a flaw in human nature and accounts for man's apparent propensity for evil.[2] Although Pelagianism was condemned as a heresy at the Council of Carthage in 411, it has remained popular over the centuries because of its flattering conception of human nature and potential. It is not surprising that it would enjoy a resurgence during a time of optimism like the Age of Jackson, and it reappeared at that time not only in Mormonism but also in New England Transcendentalism and in various other utopian and reform movements. Optimism and faith in human nature, in fact, may be said to be a basic element in the American character.

Pelagianism, unfortunately, became more difficult to sustain during the twentieth century, when the presence of evil was more conspicuous and constant, than it was in the sunnier world of the 1830s. Whatever philosophical strengths it may possess elsewhere, Mormonism's explanation of the persistence of evil in human affairs has not been its strongest suit. Although the official position of the church is to focus more on the means of human improvement and progress, one encounters in "street level" Mormonism, so to speak, a good deal of inadvertent Augustinianism.

That tension between the ideal and the real may be seen in Juanita Brooks herself. Her stepson Clair returned from military service in the Pacific at the end of World War II just as she was beginning to formulate her thesis about the Mountain Meadows Massacre. She was intensely affected by his stories of war atrocities and once blurted out a solidly Augustinian conviction that "in any age war is hell, that it releases the beast in man, and that in spite of our so-called civilization, we have not changed essentially. It is easy to point out the atrocities of our enemies, but we should realize that our own men react in a similar manner to the emotions engendered by war."[3] However persuasive such an explanation of atrocity might be, it is difficult to reconcile with a Pelagian conception of human nature, which denies the existence of any "beast in man" that can be released in any circumstance.

Brooks's problem, then, as she worked out her interpretation of the Mountain Meadows Massacre, was the question of why good people do bad things. Her answer, and probably the only answer available to her within a Mormon worldview, was that external agents had temporarily clouded the otherwise good judgment and moral rectitude of the people of southwestern Utah. Such an answer avoids the obvious question of the source of the evil within those external agents, but at least it protected the essential moral integrity of the Dixie Saints and thus the basic validity of the Zion they were building there. When she wrote to a critic, J. S. Foster, that she had studied the entire history of the Haight and Higbee families and "had found only good things in their lives before and after this tragedy," she was coming perilously close to a judgment on a person's total life permitted only to God, but it was a judgment she was compelled to make to sustain a Pelagian explanation of the incident.[4]

The external agents to which she pointed were, in the first place, the oratorical extremism of the so-called Mormon Reformation. In southern Utah at least, this in turn could be blamed on another external agent, this time a conveniently non-Mormon one, the threat to the existence of the Mormon community presented by the oncoming federal troops. That preaching, exemplified in the northern settlements by the fire-breathing apocalypticism of Jedediah M. Grant and brought to the southern settlements by George A. Smith, was designed to prepare the Mormon pioneers for war. It encouraged a puritanical retrenchment to basic Mormon values manifested by repentance and rebaptism, it raised emotions to a feverish level that would enable peaceable people to fight and kill, and it infected the Indians of southern Utah with the same emotional intensity, making them the "battle-axe of the Lord," which the Mormons hoped to direct against their Gentile enemies. The result of such preaching, in Brooks's view, was a "war hysteria," an abnormal emotional state in which people were willing to abandon their otherwise sane judgments to violent militaristic passion. This hysteria fed upon itself and intensified as it spread among the population through what Brooks calls "mob psychology: . . . men catching fire from each other, uniting under strong emotional stress, carrying out lynchings or burnings or mass murder, which in times of sanity or calmness every one would condemn individually." The resulting "interplay of personality and circumstance, this complexity of motives," she concludes, "makes it difficult to measure individual responsibility."[5]

The other external agent beclouding the settlers' Pelagian will was the alleged provocations of the so-called Fancher party, the Arkansas emigrants who slowly made their way down from northern Utah to their doom in August and September of 1857. Evidence of these provocations, as Brooks admits, is mostly after-the-fact, biased, and exaggerated to the point of absurdity in some places because, after all, the Mormons (and perhaps the Indians) exterminated everyone who could have given the Gentiles' side of the matter. The story, nevertheless, is that the emigrants were apparently spoiling for a fight from the beginning. One contingent of the party was a typical family emigrant group like most who went west to California in the 1850s. But they were guilty by association with a group of roughnecks who styled themselves the "Missouri Wildcats," who, from the moment they entered Utah, set out to provoke the Mormons by rekindling the bad feelings between Mormons and Missourians dating from the 1830s. There was guilt by geography as well, for Parley P. Pratt had recently suffered martyrdom at the hands of Arkansans, in fact in the very region of the state from which the emigrants were coming.

As they progressed southwestward through the Mormon settlements, the emigrants were said to have boasted that they had the pistol that had killed Joseph Smith and that they were spoiling for a chance to use it again. They were said to have turned their animals into Mormon grain fields, to have renamed their draft oxen "Heber" and "Brigham," and to have sworn at them by name. Near Fillmore, they poisoned a popular waterhole as they left, resulting in the death of some of the settlers' cattle, of some Indians who had eaten one of the dead animals (they shot an Indian in an altercation at this point as well), and even of a settler who became contaminated while skinning a cow carcass. At Beaver, only intervention by the bishop prevented the Indians from falling upon the emigrants in revenge; Parowan completely closed the walls of the fort against them, Cedar City refused to receive them, and so on.

Sorting the truth out of such biased and inflammatory evidence heavily taxes the historian's skill and judgment. Realizing that the truth in such conflicts rarely resides entirely on one side, Brooks seeks a middle ground. While faithfully reporting the story of the poisoning of the waterhole, she indicates that Proctor Robison, the skinner who died from rubbing his poisoned hands on his eyes, could have contracted a natural poison from whatever the cow might have been eating.[6] She does seize upon one non-Mormon source, the recollection of one George Powers, another Arkansan and a member of another emigrant party ten days behind the Fancher train. He found the Mormons at Buttermilk Fort (modern Holden) still incensed at the preceding party's offensive behavior when he arrived. Nevertheless, while admitting "the Mormon tendency to exaggerate the offenses of the emigrants," she assigns some credence to their charges and adds it to the external agents that caused the Mormons to jump the moral track at Mountain Meadows.[7]

How valid is this interpretation? And is it the only, or even the best, interpretation suggested by Brooks's evidence? Let us begin with the so-called "war hysteria" hypothesis, asking in the first place what effect the preaching of the "Mormon Reformation" had in southern Utah, and in the second place if something like "mob psychology" had brought the people of that region to a hysterical condition.

The Mormon Reformation began in the northern settlements in 1856, burned brightly for several months, and eventually faded out in 1857. It was motivated by Brigham Young's perception that many of the recent converts to Mormonism were lured more by economic opportunity than religious zeal, and he wished to temper the steel in the Saints' backbones and enable their faith to persevere through the drought, grasshopper infestation, and severe weather they were experiencing. The Reformation was a call to a heightened commitment to rigid standards of righteousness and a weeding out of those who failed to respond.[8] The Jonathan Edwards of this revival was Jedediah Morgan Grant, a tall, thin preacher with a puritanical zeal and immense crowd-moving skills, popularly known as "the sledgehammer of Brigham." On a fateful mid-September weekend, Brigham Young in Salt Lake City and Grant in Kaysville simultaneously launched the Reformation.[9] Among the doctrines they preached was the notion of "blood atonement," under which some sinners are so hopelessly degraded that the only expiation possible is the shedding of their own blood. One of the means they used to effect the Reformation was a catechism, which existed in various forms. It confronted suspected sinners with a lengthy list of transgressions and, if the suspects were guilty, they were to confess publicly and submit to rebaptism as a sign of repentance. Such preaching produced much discomfort and public humiliation among a people who previously had been characterized, as Indian agent Garland Hurt described them, by "peace, sobriety and good order." And, like the preaching of Jonathan Edwards and many subsequent revivalists, it produced what one might consider signs of hysteria, like "weeping in the utterest agonies of soul."[10]

The human psyche can sustain such emotional hypertension for only a short time, and by the time of the church's general conference in April 1857, even Brigham Young had grown weary of the public confessions and told his followers to confine such admissions to private sessions. Grant's overexertions, including baptisms in mountain streams in the winter, led to his early death on December 1, 1856, and the Reformation soon faded into history.

Brooks presents no evidence that the Reformation ever reached Dixie during its heyday except, of course, by word of mouth and reportage in the *Deseret News*.[11] The only preaching of that kind she documents in Dixie was a brief trip through the southern settlements by George A. Smith in August 1857, just days before the massacre—in fact, Smith's party on its return trip camped near the Fancher train and conversed with them at the supposedly poisoned waterhole near Fillmore.[12] It is upon that one journey that Brooks hangs the entire cause of the war hysteria. Smith's preaching, she says, "was of such an inflammatory nature that it roused them to a high emotional pitch," so much so that "the excitement that was sweeping the whole territory at the approach of the army was perhaps most intense in the isolated southern settlements."[13]

If so, Brooks fails to establish anything in the reports of Smith's speeches, by his listeners and himself, to suggest an effect even remotely approaching hysteria. To be sure, he urged military readiness and inveighed against the Mormons' historic persecutors in terms that Rachel Lee described as "full of hostility and virulence," but one struggles to find in Smith's rhetoric anything that goes beyond what would be expected of a leader getting his people ready for invasion (which as he spoke was a reality and not just a possibility). By August of 1857, the Reformation fires had mostly burned out, and Smith had the rational responsibility of making sure the southern flank of Mormondom was protected and ready for war if it should come from the southwest, as some thought it might. With that understanding, the rhetoric of Smith's speeches is striking in its moderation. Smith himself called the trip "a mission of peace to preach to the people," and at one point he poured calming oil on the hotheaded boast of Isaac C. Haight, who said was eager to "use up" the federal troops. Smith told him he probably would not get the opportunity. He urged at one point that "if the Lord brings us in collision with them [the traditional enemies of the Mormons], and if it is His will, let us take hold, *not in the spirit of revenge or anger*, but simply to avenge God of His enemies, and to protect our homes and firesides [italics added]," but one notes that he is counseling cool-headed military action, not trying to whip up hysteria; in fact, he is trying to quell emotions. And who could fault him for encouraging his people to defend their homes against an aggressor? The only truly inflammatory statement Brooks attributes to Smith—his oblique observation to the people of Parowan that bones would make good fertilizer for their fruit trees—comes from an undocumented local tradition and seems completely alien to the tenor of his documented remarks.[14]

The picture one gets from Brooks's evidence is not one of hysteria whipped up by apocalyptic oratory (one doubts the possibility of that on the basis of one rapid speaking tour anyway), but rather of something much more fundamental and much more ugly: a profoundly deep-seated, smoldering grudge lasting for an entire generation, an undercurrent of latent violence waiting to burst forth against the persecutors of the Saints. "Ever since the days of Missouri and Nauvoo," Brooks tells us, "ever since the martyrdom of their prophet, the Saints had been taught that they should never cease to importune the Lord to avenge the blood of the prophet. . . . Always the crimes of their enemies were a favorite theme for testimony, sermon, and even recreation."[15] This hardened spirit, undoubtedly present to some degree in the breasts of Mormons everywhere in Utah, was if anything heightened among the toughened souls on the southern frontier, who, as we have seen, saw themselves as living on the sacrificial edge of Mormondom. Brooks quotes dramatic evidence of that vengeful spirit from Thomas D. Brown's "Journal of the Southern Indian Mission," in a speech given by John Lott on May 14, 1854, more than three years before the Mountain Meadows Massacre. "We suffered from damned Sectarians in Mo., driven, robbed, and murdered. I hope to see the day when the blood of the martyrs will be avenged, and these damnable rebels make restitution, or the children suffer for the wickedness of their fathers." David Lewis followed with the equally bloodthirsty statement that "[m]y Brother Benjamin was killed in Missouri, and I am alive to avenge his blood when the Lord will."[16] One might be inclined to discount such rhetoric when delivered among friendly company with no Gentiles around for hundreds of miles. But when the emigrants were pinned down at Mountain Meadows, these men, or men cut from the same unforgiving cloth, proved that their talk was more than bluster. They had no need for the false intoxication of "war hysteria" imported from Salt Lake City; they contained within themselves all the resources of violence they would need.[17] Furthermore, even though one can sympathize with the earlier persecutions and sufferings of such people and understand their bitterness, harboring a grudge so deep that one vows to pass it on to one's children and to back it up with oaths of vengeance is hardly convincing evidence of the essential goodness of human nature.

What is lacking, in Brooks's delineation of the psychological state of southern Utahns in 1857 is, in short, a convincing psychology. She fails to show the extent to which the Reformation of 1856–57 was preached in the South, by whom it was preached, the state of mind the preaching created in its recipients, and the degree to which that state of mind was still present during the second week of September 1857. Instead of looking into the role of the hotheaded Isaac C. Haight, who had been the prominent preacher of the Reformation in the South and who still burned red hot with bloodthirsty enthusiasm in August of 1857, Brooks ascribes the "war hysteria" to the brief and relatively benign preaching expedition of George A. Smith, a burden that that comparatively frail reed cannot persuasively bear.

Further, Brooks fails to define the symptoms of hysteria and the conditions that would create such a state of mind, and she fails to demonstrate that such conditions and state did exist at the time of the massacre. Proving the existence of such a set of circumstances would require a theoretical grounding in social psychology that Brooks simply did not have. Consequently, the psychological circumstances she attempts to demonstrate are inadequately defined and sketchily substantiated. Simply stated, she fails to explain how a *group* can become a mob and she fails to show that that is what occurred at the time of the massacre. The failure to do so is particularly significant in an essay such as hers on Mormon history, for Mormonism's group ethos and cohesion are ubiquitously cited as among its most characteristic and laudable features. If so, there is a fundamental irony in an event where Mormonism's greatest strength becomes its greatest downfall, an irony Brooks fails to perceive.

Why did she miss it? There are several reasons. One is that Pelagianism is uncomfortable with irony. If one defines irony as an unperceived discrepancy between one's pretensions and reality, Pelagianism can account for it only as a limited ability to bring the ideal into reality, rather than as an inherently flawed or fallen will. Another reason is Brooks's lack of background in social psychology, which would have enabled her to discriminate between group psychology and mob psychology and to offer persuasive evidence that one had become the other. Lastly, the one attempt at a psychological interpretation of history with which Brooks was familiar, Fawn Brodie's *No Man Knows My History*, a biography of Joseph Smith, repelled her. Although she admired the depth of Brodie's research and even accepted that the prophet had done some unsavory things, Brooks could not accept Brodie's larger thesis that Smith was an imposter, a conscious and deliberate fraud. She had seen too much of the good consequences of Smith's life and ministry—the deep loyalties he inspired, the lives transformed, the miracles worked—to accept that they were grounded in pernicious motives. "To me he seems to have a dimension that is quite un-get-at-able," she wrote to Dale Morgan.[18] Perhaps. And perhaps the motives of the Mountain Meadows murderers are equally elusive. But if psychology applies, it must apply rigorously and scientifically, not in vague concepts and sketchy evidence.

But was guilt for the massacre the Mormons' alone? Did the emigrants not provoke their own doom and thus bear some of the responsibility? In spite of Brooks's skepticism about the poisoned waterhole and her awareness of the Mormon penchant for exaggeration of their persecutions—especially after the bloody deed had been done and they were casting about for a way to spread the guilt as thinly and widely as possible—she still believed that the emigrants were not altogether innocent.

And perhaps they were not. A relevant question is who committed the initial provocation that led to retaliation and escalated to murder? Brooks accepts the observations of Eli B. Kelsey, reported by T. B. H.

and Fanny Stenhouse, and of a P. K. Jacoby, both of whom traveled with the emigrant party east of Salt Lake City, who said it consisted of two contingents—a group of families typical of emigrant parties on the Oregon and California trails, and a rougher element—"a rough-and-ready set of men," Kelsey called them, who the Mormons later said called themselves the "Missouri Wildcats." Jacoby reports antagonism between the two groups that was severe enough that he left the party at Fort Bridger.[19] The emigrants, according to Brooks, were spoiling for a fight right from the start. "That this group began to have trouble soon after they left Salt Lake City there can be no doubt."[20]

At this point, where we particularly need reliable information to understand the tragedy, the meager and biased sources become frustrating. It is easy to believe that the emigrants became abrasive, perhaps to an extreme degree as the Mormons claimed, but we must not forget, as Brooks tends to, that the one provocation for which we have incontrovertible documentation is the order prohibiting trade with the Gentiles. Brooks was well aware, at least by the time she revised her book, that Alexander Fancher had been through Utah before and had traded with the Mormons for supplies—and likely was counting on doing so again in 1857. She also knew, and makes a major point of it in her biography of John D. Lee, that the emigrants were carrying a substantial amount of money, primarily for a down payment on a California ranch, but partly, no doubt, for supplies.[21] Any provocation from the emigrants would have been in retaliation for the closing of a vitally important source of supplies, for it beggars belief that any overland party, even a tough bunch of "Missouri Wildcats," would have ridden across Utah, outnumbered several times over, deliberately courting conflict. If they were indeed from Missouri, they would have known of the Mormon hatred for them and recognized the immense threat the well-armed and numerically superior Mormons presented. One marvels at their foolhardiness in retaliating, if in fact they did.[22]

One form of retaliation—the poisoning of the waterhole—may be rejected out of hand. Brooks seems half inclined to give it some credence, though she volunteers other sources of poisoning in the Proctor Robison case. But the episode reeks of implausibility. To begin with, as Indian agent Jacob Forney pointed out during his investigation of the incident, the Indians in the vicinity of Corn Creek, where the waterhole was supposedly poisoned, were not among those at Mountain Meadows, and he wondered further what a party of California emigrants would be doing with a large supply of poison in the first place.[23] And why would they poison a waterhole they knew other emigrant parties close behind them on the trail would need to use? Would the Indians have eaten carrion in the form of dead cattle poisoned at the spring, especially during early fall when natural food sources were most plentiful? And if they had, would they have ingested enough poison to kill them? Would Robison, for that matter, have picked up enough poison on his hands while skinning the animal to kill him? Murder by poisoning is about the most cowardly form of murder one can commit, especially in the indiscriminate form of poisoning a water source, and it takes little imagination to see behind this story a Mormon attempt to create a proportionality that would justify their own heinous crime, a justification which, as Brooks observes, looks "inadequate and flimsy indeed."[24]

It seems reasonable to suggest, then, that Brooks's research might have yielded more plausibly to an interpretation based on her Augustinian moments rather than the Pelagianism with which she felt compelled to reconcile it. Instead of giving us thoroughly good people who became suddenly sidetracked by a highly aberrant moment of hysteria and provocation, she might have probed more deeply into the dark recesses of the Mormon psyche, with its festering resentment, its latent violence, and its readiness to visit the sins of the fathers upon the children. Unfortunately, she was unable to arrive at an Augustinian interpretation because of her felt obligation to explain the tragedy in terms acceptable to her church.

The Mountain Meadows Massacre is often praised for its unflinching examination of Mormon history's most unsettling moment. "In trying to present this subject with a desire only to tell the truth, I believe that I am doing my church a service," Brooks offers at the beginning of her book. "I feel sure that nothing but the truth can be good enough for the church to which I belong."[25] And surely she did tell the truth as well as her understanding of the matter allowed. But in her felt duty to fit her materials into a Pelagian worldview, she gave those materials perhaps less than they deserved. Why? Because she sought an interpretation that her church would find palatable, and she knew that her Mormon readers would not accept motives explained in terms of fundamental personal or cultural flaws. The mere fact of examining the massacre was risky enough within the Mormon Church, and explaining it in terms of an Augustinian theory of human nature would have immediately put her outside the church. It was, in a sense, the same *group* psychology—not *mob* psychology—that held her people together during the 1850s in a commitment to avenge the blood of the prophet even though it meant transgressing a moral code that obtained in other situations.

It would be most unjust in any assessment of Brooks's historical contribution not to credit her immense courage in advancing an interpretation of the massacre that imputed any collective responsibility at all to Mormons, Mormonism, and to Brigham Young, even as an accessory after the fact. It was a huge risk to her, as Levi Peterson observes, to propose any interpretation that "would seriously impugn the moral stature of those cherished pioneers who had established the church in the Rocky Mountains." In staring down the barrel of excommunication, Brooks faced a much greater loss than had Fawn Brodie. Peterson continues, "Unlike Brodie, who had moved out of Utah and married a non-Mormon, Juanita could expect almost no support and encouragement in the event of her excommunication. In overwhelming numbers, the people who were meaningful to her would certainly interpret her ejection as a shocking disgrace."[26] As things developed, she suffered almost as greatly by being silently shunned and excluded from church activities and roles.

Brooks was reluctant whenever she felt obligated to dissent from official church points of view, and Peterson explains this reluctance in terms that seem to explain why she clung doggedly to Pelagianism in this case. "[B]esides fearing excommunication, Juanita suffered the guilt of disloyalty. In certain moods she regarded her dissent as perverse and reprehensible. In short, she was a complex and ambivalent person."[27] Indeed. Complexity and ambivalence often enable a historian to create nuanced interpretations that respect life's untidy and tentative nature. But in Brooks's case those qualities kept her from following her materials to what many would regard as their most convincing interpretation.

THE CONVERSION OF A ZEALOT

Stylistic sophistication is a hallmark of all the historians considered in this book. One of the most dramatic passages in any of their works is Juanita Brooks's account of the conversion of John D. Lee at the outset of her biography. Sitting beside the corpse of his two-year-old daughter, Lee in his emotional distress resumes reading the *Book of Mormon*, which he had begun during her illness. He is engrossed by the book and reads all night, but his emotion reaches its apex when he comes upon the passage in the book of Moroni, chapter 10, that enjoins readers to ask God sincerely for confirmation of the truth of what they have read. The words on the page appear to Lee to have a "lifted, bold, three-dimensional look," and he drops to his knees to follow their injunction. It is a moment of blinding revelation. "Suddenly he was filled with a joy that was a mixture of exhilaration and peace. He knew! Beyond all shadow of a doubt, he knew!" It is important to note that Brooks emphasizes the irrationality of the experience. "Other men might dissect this book, argue as to its geography, search it for evidences of fraud, compare it with contemporary publications, but Lee brushed all these aside. For him, there was but one answer. The book was true!"[1]

It was obviously the crucial experience in Lee's life. Brooks says his wife was also converted when he told her the next morning what had happened, and they immediately began planning to move to be with the Saints. All the drama and tragedy of the rest of his life are contained in that moment: his membership in the Danites and the Council of Fifty, the westward migration of the church, the arduous colonization of southern Utah, the Mountain Meadows Massacre, Lee's Ferry, the arrest, trial, and execution. What forces and events brought him to this crisis? One need not be much of a sociologist or psychologist--or historian, for that matter—to know that such episodes, unforeseen though they may be, always have their antecedents.

Having captured the reader's attention with that dramatic opening, Brooks then flashes back to Lee's birth in 1812 to fill in the more mundane details that brought him to the conversion crisis. It is a pathetic story of orphanage, child abuse, and physical and emotional hardship through which Lee was able to persevere only by a capacity for hard work and a "proud, perverse streak in his nature" that kept external circumstance from getting the best of him. His pride and perversity alienated him from a fiancee who unwisely demanded that he give up gambling as a condition of their marriage. Lee intended to give up the habit anyway, but he required that the initiative come from himself rather than from anyone else. Marriage to another came in time, as did three children and a certain modest prosperity as a farmer.

So much for the external facts and the development of his personality for his first twenty-six years. Brooks's sketch of Lee's religious background is much more brief; in fact, it is virtually nonexistent. Religion entered Lee's life, by her account, only the autumn before his conversion when he had met a Mormon missionary named King. Elder King lodged with the Lees for a time, but Lee forbade him to preach within his hearing. Lee was nevertheless impressed with King's sincerity and character, and his curiosity was piqued by the unusual hostility Mormon preaching provoked in members of other churches. In time, Lee's friend Levi Stewart, whose wife had become a Mormon though he himself was holding out, gave Lee the copy of the *Book of Mormon* that, with little apparent peripheral support, effected his conversion the night of his daughter's death.

Brooks's sketch of Lee's early life is a masterpiece of the kind of persistent search through fugitive local sources—family histories, genealogies, local public records—that is the hallmark of her best work.

This kind of work enabled her to reach insights that eluded less diligent scholars, but those insights rarely penetrated far beneath the surface, so that when she faced the necessity of explaining a psychological and spiritual revolution in a man's life, she found herself out of her depth.

Her response was to retreat to stereotype. She presents Lee's conversion as an almost completely adventitious event of the kind dear to missionary mythology: the gospel as presented in the Mormon scriptures is so true and so compelling that any reasonable person encountering it will be converted. External agencies of persuasion, the subject's background and psychology—all are minor in importance compared to the blinding truth of the gospel.

Furthermore, Brooks's retreat to stereotype in the face of her lack of confidence in dealing with psychological and spiritual themes forced her to ignore potentially fruitful material in her sources and even to falsify facts that did not fit the stereotype. If the sources for the external facts of Lee's early life are fugitive and meager, the sources for his interior development are even more scanty. And they are tainted as well. The only significant primary source we have is Lee's own *Mormonism Unveiled*, the autobiography written while awaiting his execution for his role in the Mountain Meadows Massacre. The title betrays its bias. Written in the full fury of his wrath over his betrayal by his church, prompted in its creation by anti-Mormon zealots who sought to use Lee as a tool for discrediting Mormonism, and based on memories staled by a half-century or more of time, it is not the type of source a historian would like to have. Nevertheless, it contains the seeds from which a more accurate and psychologically persuasive account of Lee's conversion than the one Brooks presents could have grown.

Brooks mentions no religious affiliation in Lee's youth, but there was a strong background in Roman Catholicism. "My father and mother were both Catholics," Lee relates, "were raised in that faith; I was christened in that Church. William Morrison and Louise Phillips stood as my representative god-father and god-mother. It is from that Church record that I could alone obtain the facts and date that referred to my birth."[2] Lee gives no account of the extent of his participation in the Catholic Church, but he does indicate that one Catholic teaching, at least, became deeply rooted in his personal values. "My life was one of misery and wretchedness; and if it had not been for my strong religious convictions, I certainly would have committed suicide, to have escaped from the miserable condition I was in. I then believed, as I do still, that for the crime of suicide there was no forgiveness in this world, or that which is to come."[3] Somewhere along the line, Lee abandoned whatever formal Catholic belief and participation he had ever been part of and retreated to a residual, creedless Christianity. On the eve of his conversion to Mormonism, he says, "I was not a member of any church, and considered the religion of the day as merely the opinions of men who preached for hire and worldly gain. I believed in God and in Christ, but I did not see any denomination that taught the apostolic doctrine as set forth in the New Testament."[4]

Lee's conversion, then, grew not from the religious void Brooks seems to think existed in Lee's mind, but rather from one religion that had grown cold and amorphous to another that seemed to fill a religious hunger he had developed. And that religious hunger began to gnaw at him a good while before the crisis of his daughter's death. The fires of revivalism burned brightly on the Illinois frontier, and Lee's large house was often both lodging and pulpit for traveling preachers of a variety of persuasions. Brooks's story of Lee's initial coldness toward the Mormon missionary, Elder King, is the exact opposite of Lee's own account, which says that he not only allowed King to speak, but invited him to do so one evening following a Methodist sermon, and was so impressed that he ceased allowing any other preachers to speak there.[5]

If Lee's conversion had none of the abruptness of Brooks's account, neither did it have the cataclysmic emotional content she describes. In fact, in a place and time when cataclysmic emotional conversions were quite common, Lee's conversion seems to stand out by its deliberateness and rationality. "I reflected," Lee said, "I determined, as every honest man should do, to fairly investigate his [King's] doctrines, and to do so with a prayerful heart. The more I studied the question, the more interested I became." So rational was Lee's approach to Mormonism that he rejected an opportunity to attend a Mormon meeting where speaking in tongues and other divine signs would be proof of the truth of Mormonism. "I want no signs," Lee told his companions. "I believe the gospel they preach on principle and reason, not upon signs—its consistency is all I ask. All I want are natural, logical and reasonable arguments, to make up my mind from."[6]

By the night of his daughter's death, the crisis on which Brooks hangs his entire event, Lee's conversion was already nearly complete. He indicates that he had by then "left off [his] frivolity and commenced to live a more moral life,"[7] and whatever remained to be done that night seems to have been little more than reading for himself of the *Book of Mormon*, the source from which King had been drawing his doctrines, and confirming that they were indeed what Lee wanted to believe. "The night she lay a corpse," he says, "I finished reading the Book of Mormon. I never closed my eyes in sleep from the time I commenced until I finished the book. I read it after asking God to give me knowledge to know if it was genuine and of Divine authority."[8] There are, in Lee's account, no words standing out on the page; there is no specific mention of the passage from Moroni on which Brooks hangs so much. There is only a general prayer for enlightenment that one would expect from an inquirer into any religion, which came before he had begun reading the book. There is no dropping to the knees, no emotional exclamations. Instead, there is the matter-of-fact statement that "by careful examination I found that it was in strict accord with the Bible and the gospel therein contained."[9]

Levi S. Peterson, author of the definitive biography of Juanita Brooks, asserts that "the primary achievement of the work [the Lee biography] was its depiction of a remarkable personality." Lee's interest, Peterson continues, lies in the tragic dimension of his life, which exceeds even that of Joseph Smith, for Lee's tragic end came not only from "disloyal friends and unfortunate circumstances" but rather because "he was, like many tragic figures of literature, the victim of his own flawed character." Brooks herself was well aware of that tragic dimension and claimed that she had originally "become intrigued with this man Lee . . . because he seems to typify one of the eternal problems. Like Prometheus, who gave fire to man in what he considered a good act, and then bore his sufferings for eons because he would not admit a guilt which was not a guilt, or like Oedipus, who unwittingly offended the Gods, here is a man born to tragedy."[10]

One would like to be able to defend Brooks's account of Lee's conversion on grounds of literary license. Her literary instinct is sound, for Lee's conversion was indisputably the decisive event of his life, even more so than the Mountain Meadows Massacre. It was the fierce nature of his conversion to Mormonism that brought forth the tragic flaw in his character that led to the massacre. Instead, her alteration of factual materials and her invention of others, whatever its scholarly ethics, deprived her of the opportunity to construct an accurate and persuasive picture of the personality that perpetrated the worst catastrophe in Mormon history. If it is true, as the Catholic writer Thomas Merton has said, that the Nazis were able to effect atrocities on such a hellish scale not because they were insane, but rather because they were so ruthlessly consistent in their sanity,[11] then perhaps something similar could be said about personality characteristics of John D. Lee that were first revealed in his conversion narrative. On the eve of the Mountain Meadows Massacre, the Paiutes applied the nickname "Yawgetts" (crybaby) to Lee for the way he wept as he pled for the lives of the emigrants.[12] That the man had a tender, emotional side is well attested by family and friends who often benefited from his kindness. But once the plan was set and the orders given at the Mountain Meadows, it was not Yawgetts who prevailed, but the man of unshrinking commitment to cold, hard reason.

As a result of her biography of John D. Lee and her study of the Mountain Meadows Massacre, Juanita Brooks became a symbol of the courageous, truth-seeking Mormon scholar who dared to look into the abyss of Mormon history's dark side and to follow her evidence to an honest conclusion, whatever that might be. Her reputation is well-deserved, and the younger scholars inspired by her example have advanced Mormon history a long way toward the objectivity that was her goal. On the other hand, it takes nothing away from that reputation to recognize that her courage had its limits in her unwillingness to risk church disapproval. Nor does it taint her achievement to point out that the intellectual framework of the Mormonism in which she was reared placed limitations on her interpretive resources. Anyone's cultural background is a river bank within which one's creativity flows. It would be a poor tribute to Brooks's pioneering work in Mormon history, though, if scholars of the future did not find ways to transcend her limitations and to open the historiographical doors that she first unlocked.

Wallace Stegner

Wallace Stegner

THE NOVELIST

HISTORIAN, BIOGRAPHER, ESSAYIST, short story writer—Wallace Stegner was all of those, but he found his real home as a novelist. His novels won the Pulitzer Prize, the National Book Award, and many other honors. He was almost completely ignored by the *New York Times Book Review* and other organs of the eastern literary establishment even though he had taught at Harvard, been a member of the Bread Loaf faculty in Vermont, and had been published by Houghton Mifflin and other prestigious eastern firms. But Stegner was universally recognized in his own region as a genuine westerner who wrote of the West with deep knowledge and empathy and with almost unparalleled sophistication. Engaged during the 1960s by Interior Secretary Stewart Udall as a special environmental advisor, Stegner also wrote prolifically and critically about western economic development and exploitation of natural resources, and he became, late in life, a guru to the environmental movement. It would be hard to find, in modern American history, a person who has symbolized his region, both as a public figure and as its interpreter in a broad range of fiction and nonfiction works, as completely as Wallace Stegner has symbolized and represented the American West.

It is one of the oldest—but one of the truest—adages that a writer should write what he knows, and Stegner's best novels and stories are all deeply grounded in his personal experience and observation of the

West. "I have written about the kind of people I know, in the places where I have known them," Stegner wrote in a Foreword to his collected stories, though he added yet another warning that they are unreliable as autobiography because "I hate the restrictiveness of facts; I can't control my impulse to rearrange, suppress, add, heighten, invent, and improve."[1] During his conversations with Richard W. Etulain in 1980–81, Stegner repeatedly warned against taking his novels too literally as autobiography. "Everybody reads that [*The Big Rock Candy Mountain*] as straight autobiography," he complained, "which it isn't." Nor, he went on, is the crusty retired literary agent Joe Allston of *All the Little Live Things*, for example, anything more than a literary projection of some of Stegner's traits and attitudes. "He's a construct, a literary figment, a voice, a persona, and I found that I could speak through his voice though I am not he. Neither am I the Lyman Ward character in *Angle of Repose*. . . . You project yourself in various ventriloquisms and various guises."[2] No matter; Stegner scholars have largely ignored the warnings and succumbed to the temptation to extract the real Stegner from his fiction. Even his capable biographer, Jackson J. Benson, treats literature as autobiography in *Wallace Stegner: His Life and Work*, while taking care to make factual corrections where necessary.[3]

Telling Stegner's life story through his books means doing violence to the chronology of Stegner's body of work, for his novels and stories were not created in the order of the events in his life upon which they are based. Also, it means this chapter is more a study of literary than historical works. Unlike Bernard DeVoto, the other novelist whose career we have examined, Stegner worked most naturally in fiction and interspersed his novels and stories with occasional works of history. DeVoto, whose fiction was tone deaf, found his real forte in history.

Stegner's fiction and nonfiction are similarly focused, consistently addressing several basic themes that grew out of his personal experiences with the West. One is a preference for cooperation, for group effort, over the rugged individualism that has characterized so much of western history. This individualism has, in Stegner's view, retarded the development of civilization in the West and has savaged the natural resources and scenic beauty of the region. Another is a preference for science and reason rather than myth or premature optimism as a basis for action. Stegner therefore prefers, historically, the organized, regimented approach of the Mormons to western settlement over the willy-nilly individualism of the Gentiles, and the careful, rational government surveys of Maj. John Wesley Powell over the careless optimism of a William Gilpin or the greedy materialism of a Sen. William Stewart of Nevada. A third theme is the persistence of the past. History is an important guide to present action in Stegner's thought because the present grows out of the past organically. Thus he reserves some of his most caustic language for the rootless, careless presentists of, for example, the youth rebellion of the 1960s. Finally, Stegner, as the scion of immigrants, was interested in the contrasting virtues and vices of Europe and America and of East and West and the question of whether America's freshness and innocence as exemplified by the West are really superior to the deep traditions and cultural sophistication of the Old Country and of the East.

The Big Rock Candy Mountain, Stegner's first major work of fiction and the book that made him a major literary figure, was a thinly fictionalized narrative of his own family history.[4] Told in third person, it is the story of Bo and Elsa Mason—based on Stegner's parents, George and Hilda Stegner—two midwesterners who marry in high hopes of a prosperous life bankrolled by one of Bo's inexhaustible easy-money schemes. But as things turn out, the rainbow leads not to a pot of gold, but to a wandering life—sometimes even on the lam—as Bo's restless quest for the quick dollar leads them all over the West, on both sides of the Canadian border, and on both sides of the law. The enduring friendships begun in childhood, the dusty attic full of family photograph albums and discarded toys and story books—all were missing in this migratory family. "None of these forms of moss clings to a rolling stone," Stegner reminds us, "and I was born rolling. . . . Since I was born in Iowa in 1909 (my hometown held me six weeks) I have lived in twenty places in eight different states, besides a couple of places in Canada, and in some of these places we lived in anywhere from two to ten different houses and neighborhoods."[5]

The fictional union produces two sons, Chet (based on Stegner's older brother Cecil) and Bruce (Stegner himself). It is a classically dysfunctional family. Bo proves to be an erratic provider and an abusive and uncaring husband and father who eventually abandons Elsa completely during her final illness. The athletic Chet is, in the title of one of Stegner's stories, a "Chip Off the Old Block" of his burly and energetic father, but Bruce turns out to be a frail and bookish mama's boy who evokes his father's scorn.[6]

Failing as a farmer on the severe Saskatchewan plains, Bo eventually moves his family to Salt Lake City, where he makes a sporadic income in bootlegging and other nefarious pursuits. The long-suffering Elsa tries to maintain some kind of stable and nurturing domestic life, but Bo sabotages even that by his frequent changes of residence, which place the family just out of reach of the law or his creditors.

Out of such instability and adversity grew the real-life Stegner's famously mellow personality, his generosity and compassion, and his grueling work ethic. The latter was vividly evoked in *Crossing to Safety* in the character of Larry Morgan, a young English instructor, who, despite a pregnant wife to care for, a burdensome teaching schedule, and bales of papers to grade, produces a torrential literary output.[7] The youthful Stegner, obviously learning a reverse lesson in compassion and responsibility from his father, had also learned that his destiny was in his own hands, for he could expect little help at home.

Although he might have employed softer language, it seems not too much to say that Stegner held his father in contempt, nor does it seem too much of a reach to observe that George Stegner appears over and over in his son's writings in various unsavory guises. Bo Mason is of course the quintessential example, but he reappears in Oliver Ward, the wandering mining engineer in *Angle of Repose*, in the boosters like William Gilpin and Captain Samuel Adams in *Beyond the Hundredth Meridian*, whose hyperventilating schemes for western economic development contrast with the measured rationality of John Wesley Powell, and in the twentieth-century developers skewered by the swordlike sarcasm of Bernard DeVoto in Stegner's biography of DeVoto, *The Uneasy Chair*.[8]

A farm near Eastend, Saskatchewan, is the first place the two Mason boys enjoy any stability. While Bo experiences more years of failure than success as a farmer and resorts to poker playing and bootlegging to support the family, the boys find enough respite from the hard work of farming to enjoy the youthful pleasures of hunting, trapping, and general rambling around in the wide open spaces of the northern plains. Even more memorably and elaborately, Stegner returned to those youthful memories in one of his most celebrated books, *Wolf Willow*.[9] Subtitled *A History, a Story, and a Memory of the Last Plains Frontier*, it is all of those elements in an inseparable emulsion that must be, as Stegner mused, the bane of library catalogers.[10] One would be hard-pressed to find a similar broth of history, reminiscence, and fiction, but Stegner's creative genius makes it cohere.

The first section, "The Question Mark in the Circle," is a physical description of the country itself that stands with that of any other nature writer in its evocation of the colors and smells—the character—of the Canadian plains. Stegner also states his theme in a deft phrase that has been quoted by almost every Stegner critic: "I may not know who I am, but I know where I am from."[11] It is the premise of *Wolf Willow* and all of Stegner's best fiction. The second section, "Preparation for a Civilization," contains some of Stegner's best historical writing. Although sketchy and based on secondary sources, it effectively establishes the major themes in Canadian plains history while avoiding most of the didacticism and biases of his more serious histories.

The third section, "The Whitemud River Range," begins with a reminiscence, "Specifications for a Hero," which details the masculine world in which Stegner grew up (and into which he fit poorly). It follows with three stories of the big die-up on the northern cattle range in the winter of 1906–07 based on the recollections of a cowboy, Corky Jones, whom Stegner knew. The first story is a novella, "Genesis," which critics regard as one of his finest pieces of short fiction. It is a sentimental tale of an English immigrant, Rusty Cullen, trying to become a cowboy. Picked on by Ed Spurlock, one of the older hands, Rusty is on the verge of a fistfight a couple of times, but in the end he becomes a hero by saving Spurlock's life in a blizzard. The value of the novella, though, is Stegner's gripping narrative of the cowboys' desperate attempts to save their cattle, their horses, and eventually themselves in the face of one of the infamously harsh Canadian Great Plains winters. A second story, "The Wolfer," was eventually omitted from the book, though its outlines are sketched as part of "Genesis." It is a first-person narrative of a Mountie trying to locate a wolf hunter, who is almost as savage as the immense hound who accompanies him and helps him kill the wolves. A third story, "Carrion Spring," comes full circle to optimism. Ray Henry, foreman of the cattle outfit that lost virtually its entire stock in "Genesis," brings his wife to the ranch during the spring thaw, where they witness the bloated and rotting carcasses. In full view—and smell—of the past winter's destruction, he talks her into letting him borrow several thousand dollars to buy the ranch and start over again. Stegner returns to reminiscence in the last section, "Town and Country," where he recounts his happy boyhood experiences hunting, trapping, and fishing. The main theme that runs through this section is the perennial western optimism, but in the end, he concludes that the natural harshness of the environment not only dooms the residents to a low standard of living, but it creates eccentric characters and promotes the lingering, claustrophobic, deprived nature of small-town life.

Stegner mined his Saskatchewan memories for several other stories, but he found an even richer vein in his adolescent and college years in Salt Lake City. Despite an undercurrent of domestic unease and conflict, those years were otherwise happy and productive. He wrote and spoke about them with unfeigned joy later in life, not only in *The Big Rock Candy Mountain* and *Recapitulation*, but also in "At Home in the Fields of the Lord," and indirectly in *Mormon Country*[12] and in his published interviews with Richard Etulain. His real life existed outside the home, in his participation in Mormon Church–sponsored basketball teams, on outings to the Saltair resort and in the nearby canyons of the Wasatch Mountains, and ultimately in the social, intellectual, and athletic life of the University of Utah. Although the Stegners moved again and again, they were always close enough that Wallace could walk to East High School, though from ever-changing directions, which maintained a certain consistency in his social contacts and teachers. He discovered an aptitude for tennis (and a fierce competitiveness that went with it) that helped him find a way out of the physical awkwardness of adolescence and gave him a social standing apart from his family. An after-school job in a carpet store brought some financial independence as well, though one of his friends recalled an embarrassing moment when Stegner had to go to his father for twenty-five dollars to enroll at the University of Utah and had to endure, in his friends' presence, a caustic lecture about the worthlessness of college.[13]

The University of Utah sparked Stegner's first real intellectual awakening, both in the classroom and in after-hours bull sessions. It was not a first-rate institution, but some first-rate people passed through its faculty from time to time (including, later, a young instructor named Wallace Stegner). But it was the best thing Stegner had yet experienced intellectually, and it got him started thinking and reading seriously. "[T]hat was the first chance any of us had to see minds at work at all," Stegner reminisced. "They weren't great minds, but they were at work, and I think there was a lot of good teaching that went on. . . . My teachers . . . were very kind to me, and they opened up a lot of doors."[14] All in all, during his years at the university, he "was as happy as a shrimp in cocktail sauce."[15]

Stegner majored in English at the university, studying with the as yet unpublished Vardis Fisher, who first began to stretch him as a writer, and developing close personal ties with other professors like Sydney Angleman and writing professor L. A. Quivey. One of those professors, alarmed by the rumor that Stegner was thinking of graduate work in psychology, secured financial aid for him to attend the University of Iowa, where the soon-to-be-famous writing program was then just developing under Norman Foerster. Stegner and the other students often took issue with Foerster's New Humanism during seminars, but student and professor got along well otherwise, and Stegner let Foerster persuade him to stay on for the Ph.D. in literature and seek an academic career.

Among the works Stegner based upon his years in Salt Lake City were *The Preacher and the Slave*, later reissued as *Joe Hill: A Biographical Novel*.[16] Although his interest in the literary potential of labor radical Joe Hill did not emerge until Stegner was teaching at Harvard in the 1940s, he knew the story of Hill's arrest and execution in Salt Lake City during World War I through acquaintance with people who remembered Hill. Hill was a songwriter and labor activist with the Industrial Workers of the World (IWW), a radical labor organization that flourished in the late nineteenth and early twentieth centuries. Its basic program was to gather together all labor unions into one big organization in opposition to capitalist exploitation. Arrested and charged in connection with a robbery and murder in Salt Lake City, Hill became a focal point for conservative Americans' fears of labor radicalism, and his trial took on overtones of persecution. The trial became a legal fiasco in which Hill made no attempt to defend himself, instead challenging the prosecution to prove his guilt and testing the principle that one is innocent until such a proof is made. Although the government's case, based on circumstantial evidence, was unconvincing to impartial observers, Hill was convicted and executed in 1916, a martyr, as he desired, to the IWW cause.

Rather than write a straight biography, Stegner chose instead to produce a slightly fictionalized narrative, which allowed him to probe more deeply into the issues of radicalism in a democratic society. Even at that, after making allowances for Stegner's fictional license, the novel is one of the best of several books on the historical Joe Hill. It was one of Stegner's first uses of historical materials in a novel, and he would repeat the technique with even greater power in *Angle of Repose*. During his research, however, Stegner had come to the conclusion that, though the trial had failed to establish it convincingly, Hill was indeed guilty of the crime and thus not an authentic martyr. Hill, in his view, was nothing more than another western bad man, a character type Stegner could never see in heroic terms, but only as an example of the wasteful and destructive individualism represented by his father. This conclusion won Stegner no friends among Hill's admirers and partisans of organized labor, and it helped form the public image of Stegner as a conservative. In time that image would deepen and eventually single him out as a target of modern student radicals at Stanford in the 1960s.

Recapitulation, Stegner's last novel about Salt Lake City, is a haunting work of maturity and mellowness produced in the twilight of a writer's career. It is a chronological sequel to *The Big Rock Candy Mountain*, but as Jackson Benson points out, it is a "recapitulation" of Bruce Mason's youth in Salt Lake City, told through his memories, rather than simply a chronological extension of the earlier novel.[17] After a long and distinguished career in the diplomatic service, Bruce Mason returns to Salt Lake City, ostensibly to bury an aunt but more profoundly to revisit the scenes and people of his youth, and in particular to try to come to grips with his memories of his father. It is also the story of Bruce's early maturation and emancipation from his dysfunctional family through his first job, his first big love affair, and development of his growing reputation as a tennis player.

Stegner's narrative technique reaches its apogee in *Recapitulation* in his effortless shifts into the past, triggered by the most minor sensations in Bruce's present experience. Not only is the flashback device psychologically realistic, it functions as Stegner's way of showing us that the past and the present are actually one seamless experience. Stegner is also exploring the idea of mortality, reminding us that eventually our lives will have no present and will be entirely history. Bruce Mason is unmarried, so his aunt's death leaves him the family's last member. As he prepares for his own death, he sees the need to reconcile himself with his past, most insistently in the form of his father; their ultimate reconciliation is symbolized by the headstone he places on the father's grave.[18]

The University of Iowa, when Stegner arrived there to begin his graduate work, was beginning to develop a nationally famous writing program under the leadership of literary scholar Norman Foerster and others. For his master's thesis, Stegner was allowed to do a creative writing project, which turned out to be three short stories based on his boyhood experiences in Saskatchewan. Though none of these stories was immediately published, they put Stegner on the path that led to *On a Darkling Plain*, *The Big Rock Candy Mountain*, *Wolf Willow*, and his other Saskatchewan stories.

Unusual as his thesis was, his dissertation was perhaps more adventuresome. While an undergraduate at the University of Utah, Stegner had had to miss a final examination in a geology class. When he approached the professor about making up the examination, the professor suggested instead that Stegner read Clarence Edward Dutton's *Geology of the High Plateaus of Utah* and write a critical evaluation. The experience, no doubt to the surprise of both, was life-changing for the student. Stegner's family had long owned a vacation cabin near Fish Lake in Utah, atop the Fish Lake Plateau, one of the plateaus Dutton had been the first scientist to study. Dutton's report not only dealt with a country familiar to Stegner, but it explained the area to him for the first time with great scientific depth and clarity and in prose he found highly revealing and even poetic. Dutton was not just a geologist, but also perhaps the first masterful nature writer Stegner had ever encountered. So when it came time to propose a dissertation topic, Stegner suggested a study of Dutton as a literary artist.

The dissertation, called "Clarence Edward Dutton: Geologist and Man of Letters," was only 103 pages, but it effectively evoked the man and his relationship to his subject. Aware of the unusual nature of his subject for a literary dissertation, Stegner began by anticipating the objection "that no sincere and competent scientist can also be a poet." His response was that "a large part of Dutton's descriptive excellence comes about not in spite of his accurate scientific mind, but because of it. Fine as are his panoramas and landscapes, it is in his revelation of the scientific *method* as applied to nature writing that his greatest value lies." Recognizing, Stegner continued, in his *Tertiary History of the Grand Canyon District* that the physical size and stunning grandeur of the Grand Canyon's colors and formations would be difficult for eastern readers to grasp, "Dutton specifically stated his intention of attacking the reader through his imagination, so that one unfamiliar with the country would not be left groping among a cold mass of facts. The product of this dual method is a book written in alternating chapters of description and interpretation, with singularly happy results."[19]

Stegner's ultimate assessment of Dutton as a literary artist, supported by generous quotations from his reports, was a positive one. Although he admitted that Dutton was "a second rate literary artist," it was "not because his capabilities, his mind, or his style were inadequate, but because his literary work is all in a field which by its separation from human life must always be considered a minor branch of literature. But within that field he had few rivals." Being limited to the narrow field of geology deprived Dutton of the larger range of vision that energized the nature writing of figures like John Burroughs or John Muir, but "within his range he wrote as well as any American has ever done. As interpretations of the most strictly geological aspects of nature his works are as much a part of American literature as Audubon or Agassiz, and it will be a long day before any one again describes the Grand Canyon as it was described by Clarence Edward Dutton."[20]

Stegner's dissertation already exhibits his own vivid writing, though it is lacking in the maturity he would achieve during the following decade, even in early works like *Mormon Country* and especially in *The Big Rock Candy Mountain*. Although it was a steppingstone on the way to *Beyond the Hundredth Meridian*, the dissertation is tightly focused on Dutton and his literary skill. It telegraphs little of the grand conception Stegner would develop of John Wesley Powell and the Powell survey as symbols of Science applied to the unplanned and unregulated settlement and exploitation of the West.

Stegner held brief Depression-era instructorships at the University of Utah and the University of Wisconsin, during which he made his first significant appearances in print. *Crossing to Safety*, his last novel and mellowest work, is based on his Wisconsin years as a struggling instructor trying to teach, gain tenure and promotion, and write.[21] Like Shakespeare writing *The Tempest* at the end of a long and productive career, but still at the pinnacle of his literary power, Stegner gives an old man's autumnal memories of an academic and literary career and the network of friendships that enriched it. At first glance, the story has little to do with the West, for almost none of it takes place there (unless one counts Wisconsin as the "West," which Stegner does not). Looked at more deeply, though, it has everything to do with the West, for it is a story of two westerners moving progressively eastward and trying to make a life in the East with eastern friends. Like *Angle of Repose* and *The Spectator Bird*, it is at one level a sustained contrast between an older and a younger culture.

Stegner said he never intended to publish the novel, that he wrote it as a memory of a friendship for his wife and their friends Phil and Peg Gray, to whom the book is dedicated, and that he allowed it to be published only when he learned that the Gray family did not object.[22] Like *The Big Rock Candy Mountain* and *Recapitulation*, it is a highly autobiographical remembrance of a long and close friendship between the two couples.

The first-person narrative is the story of Larry Morgan (Stegner), a young literary scholar and aspiring writer, who takes his wife Sally to

Madison, Wisconsin, for his first teaching position, a precarious post during the Great Depression. There they meet another first-year English instructor, Sid Lang, and his wife Charity and form a close friendship. They appear to have much in common: both wives are pregnant, both husbands are desperately struggling to enlarge their toehold on the academic ladder, and all love music, books, and the outdoors. As things develop, the friendship turns out to be enriching as much for their differences as for their similarities. The Langs are both easterners, Charity from a sophisticated literary family and Sid from a wealthy family, whereas the Morgans are impoverished westerners with humble antecedents.

The hard-driving Larry quickly publishes stories, reviews, and even a novel, which he hopes will guarantee his academic future, but they actually prove to be his academic death warrant. Jealous department members see him as competition, and he is terminated at the end of the year. Paradoxically, Sid, who is a poet but not a scholar, is retained. The Langs insist on helping the Morgans through a difficult time by sharing both their Madison home and their Vermont estate while Larry continues to write and to look for another job. The assistance turns out to be mutual. Charity uses a family connection to get Larry a job as an editor with a publishing house, while Larry uses his literary connections to get Sid a position at Dartmouth after his failure to publish costs him his Wisconsin job. Through it all, however, the professional and financial relationships are much less important than the enriching friendships that deepen over the years. Stegner's focus stays on the engaging personalities of his four characters and their evolving relationships.

At the center of that focus is Charity Lang, who initiates the friendship and remains both its engine and its rudder. (It was Peg Gray's death, and Stegner's memories of her at that time, that motivated the novel.) In Stegner's hands, she comes to represent not only eastern sophistication but also eastern intensity in her controlling manipulations, not only of her husband's reluctant academic career, but of the daily schedules of the two couples, right down to the proper way to organize a picnic.

Like his fictional counterpart Larry Morgan, Stegner found himself needing more time for writing than an academic schedule would allow. During the 1930s he successfully applied for fellowships, first at the Yaddo artists' colony in New York, then at Middlebury College's Bread Loaf conference in Vermont, and eventually a Briggs-Copeland Fellowship, which took him to Harvard for six years as an instructor. Bread Loaf was a two-week get-together of both young and established writers, two weeks of intense literary discussions, readings, and hard drinking that introduced Stegner to people like Robert Frost and Archibald MacLeish and strengthened the friendship he had begun with Bernard DeVoto.

Mormon Country, which appeared in 1942, was Stegner's first significant historical publication.[23] Later in life, Stegner was inclined to dismiss the book as an insignificant exercise in nostalgia, tossed off during a period of homesickness by a westerner in exile at Harvard.[24] One could read the book as only that, for its breezy style, peppered with personal reminiscence, and its episodic flitting from one topic to another imparts the appearance of what Jackson Benson calls "an impromptu patchwork." To do so, however, as Benson continues, would be a serious mistake. For one thing, the numerous brief essays are symbols of larger wholes, and they constitute a "cleverly designed tapestry in which many small figures and bits of color come together in a total effect of breadth and depth."[25] Furthermore, the book was biographically important as a link with Stegner's past as well as something of a seed pod that germinated into many of his later nonfiction projects. His portrayal of the Mormons as a cultural minority, for example, led to *One Nation*, his wartime extended essay on America's cultural diversity.[26] He had already written about Dutton, and his essay on Powell and his men, "The Terrible River," would lead to his Powell biography, *Beyond the Hundredth Meridian*.[27] The essay on paleontologist Earl Douglass, "Notes on a Life Spent Pecking at a Sandstone Cliff," would lead to *This Is Dinosaur*, a collection of essays that helped defeat the Echo Park dam project that would have flooded Dinosaur National Monument.[28] His interest in Mormon history led to *The Gathering of Zion*, and his explorations of Utah back roads and rural communities led to *American Places*.[29] All in all, *Mormon Country* was anything but trivial in Stegner's career.

Mormon Country at one stroke enshrined Wallace Stegner in Mormon affection among the handful of Gentile writers to that time—the Howard Stansburys and the Hubert Howe Bancrofts—who had written fairly about the Latter-day Saints. That affection only deepened as his career progressed and books like *The Big Rock Candy Mountain*, *The Gathering of Zion*, and *Recapitulation* extended and reaffirmed his regard for the Mormons.[30] Jackson Benson, once again, rightly ascribes this to "an urge in him to right a wrong, to bring some justice to the Mormons, who had done so much for him, and who had such a bad reputation among Americans generally."[31] "Fair," however, rather than "flattering," is the right word to characterize Stegner's writing about the Mormons; he never blinks at their blemishes. Others might expand on Stegner's list of traits that have made the Mormons obnoxious to their Gentile neighbors from the beginning, but the point is he does paint a sufficiently rounded picture that non-Mormon readers can find justice in the same place where the Mormons can find appreciation. Stegner gives generous space, for example, to the rationality of the Mormon settlement process, its group cohesion, strong families, and courage in the face of persecution and privation, but he also brings to the fore quixotic Mormon elements like the Deseret Alphabet and the United Order of Enoch, and the downright despicable like the rural service station proprietor who stranded Stegner by refusing to sell him a tank of gasoline on the sabbath.[32] Later in life, too, after Stegner had become more aware of environmental issues and better informed about the modern West, he came to see the Mormons' stewardship of the land in a much less favorable light.

> Now, a hundred and forty years after their hegira, they have managed to put only about 3 percent of Utah's land under cultivation; and because they took seriously the Lord's command to be fruitful and multiply, Zion has been overpopulated, and exporting manpower, for at least half a century. One of the bitterest conflicts in modern Utah is that between the environmentalists, who want to see much of that superlative wilderness preserved roadless and wild, and the stubborn Mormon determination to make it support more saints than it possibly can.[33]

Even though Stegner admired, in *Mormon Country*, the Saints' proverbial ability to make the desert blossom as a rose, he eventually came to the conclusion that they had produced quite enough roses, and perhaps it was time to let at least some of the desert simply produce sagebrush.

In ways reminiscent of Juanita Brooks, Stegner's *Mormon Country* exhibits a conspicuous lack of regard for the formalities of academic scholarship. Although trained as a scholar, Stegner wrote his books the way he wanted to write them, with a large popular audience in mind, and he apparently cared little about the reception they might get within the academic community. Like *Wolf Willow*, which moves unapologetically from history to reminiscence to fiction, *Mormon Country* shifts repeatedly from history to description to folklore to reminiscence. Even though striving for as much factual accuracy as possible, Stegner gives little or no indication of his sources. The result might be as frustrating as *Wolf Willow* for library catalogers, but for his readers *Mormon Country* makes for a deceptively light read, an apparent collection of literary bagatelles, until one becomes aware of the comprehensive portrait of the Mormon world that is taking shape and of how lightly Stegner wears his learning.

One of the book's strengths, too, is that it is about Mormon *country*, not just Mormons and Mormonism. The first half of the book, called "The Rock Our Fathers Planted," is, to be sure, about Mormon history, institutions, and folklore, but the last section, "The Might of the Gentiles," is an equally thoroughgoing and objective treatment of the non-Mormons who inhabit Mormon country. This proportionality represents a milestone along the road to modern historians like Dean May and Thomas Alexander, who give great care to presenting a comprehensive picture of Utah life. In their works, women and racial, ethnic, and religious minorities find their place alongside the white Mormon males that were the almost exclusive focus of Utah historical literature before Stegner.[34] Along with the WPA state guide, which was published almost simultaneously (1941), *Mormon Country* remains one of the two best portraits of that region in the early 1940s.[35]

Mormon Country contained a sketch of the life and career of Maj. John Wesley Powell, explorer of the Colorado River and Colorado Plateau and author of what Stegner later called a "blueprint for a dryland democracy," the 1878 *Report on the Lands of the Arid Region of the*

United States.[36] Stegner expanded that sketch into a full-scale biography, *Beyond the Hundredth Meridian: John Wesley Powell and the Second Opening of the West*. Dedicated to Bernard DeVoto, it was the most ambitious and the most scholarly of Stegner's historical works, and it immediately superseded William Culp Darrah's anemic biography and became the standard work on Powell and a fixture on reading lists in university courses in western history. Although it has itself been superseded recently by Donald Worster's definitive work, *A River Running West: The Life of John Wesley Powell*, Stegner's *Beyond the Hundredth Meridian* has unique virtues that will probably guarantee it a place in the literature of western history.[37]

Although Stegner was alarmed at the mindless greed that had been destroying the West for generations, he was, as we shall see later, basically an optimist, an affirmer, a definer, as he put it, of a "geography of hope." In Powell, he found a hero whose career as an advocate for a restrained and rational western exploitation was frustrated by the corporate ravagers and the politicians who represented their interests. But Stegner could use his ideas, nevertheless, to calibrate the compass of the country and point policy makers of his day in the right direction. "Heroes—If not heroes, at least *representative* men," he wrote in his notes on the relationship of biography and fiction. "Models of a sort, rarely warnings. The natural tendency of biography is *positive*, not negative, and this appeals to me. It is otherwise with contemporary fiction. . . . What I suppose I mean is that I wish biographies were more like the sort of novels I like, & novels were more like the kind of biographies I like. . . . Biography & the realistic novel have much in common."[38] Powell as a real-life hero served in Stegner's mind as the vehicle for the same kind of message he might have put into a novel.

Although the table of contents indicates six relatively equal chapters, the book is really two stories. The first is contained in the first two chapters, the adventure of the trips down the Colorado River in 1869 and 1871 and the expansion of scientific knowledge gained in the surveys of the 1870s. These culminated in the merging of the Wheeler, King, Hayden, and Powell surveys in the United States Geological Survey in 1879. The last four chapters is a story of Powell's struggle to promote his idea, first advanced in his *Report on the Lands of the Arid*

Region in 1878, that the settlement of the arid region extending from roughly the one hundredth meridian of longitude to the western edge of the Great Basin was possible only after a systematic scientific survey of its meager water resources. This would be followed by rationally situated cooperative communities that would distribute those resources among small farms, with the rest of the region given up to livestock grazing on much larger tracts. The first section is thus a success story of democracy applied to western exploration and survey, of brave though poorly trained men learning to run the fierce Colorado River and then to conduct systematic scientific studies of the region through which it flows, supported by funds laboriously raised by Powell. The second section is a tragedy in which Powell's dream of rationally organized expansion into the arid West is defeated. Mythmakers disputed his warning that there was not enough water to support a willy-nilly rush to distribute western lands in 160-acre parcels under the Homestead and similar land acts, and Powell was also opposed by powerful corporate exploiters led by Sen. William N. Stewart of Nevada, whose greed refused to be delayed or restrained by science.

Like Stegner's biography of Bernard DeVoto twenty years later, the Powell biography is highly selective in its coverage. Stegner was more interested in the public careers and cultural significance of both men than in the details of their private lives, and he includes only the private details that enable his readers to sense the continuity, background, and motivation of his characters. In Powell (and in DeVoto, as we shall see), Stegner found a hero whose career was an ideal text from which he could preach his fundamental message about the West: that greed, materialism, and individualism cannot build a civilized and humane way of life, and that reason, science, and cooperation are necessary. Stegner had to fit some square pegs into round holes in order to make his structure stand, but Powell has a solid place in Stegner's hall of heroes of rational western living, along with the cooperative society of the Mormons, the scientists of the Powell survey, and the conservationists and environmentalists of his own day. "The 'Second Opening of the West,'" Stegner's biographer observes, "was not so much an opening of territory as it was an attempt to open eyes."[39] An attempt, yes, but one with limited success—a mere battle in a larger war that was still being waged in Stegner's day and that constituted the basic theme of western history.

Stegner's other book about the Mormons, *The Gathering of Zion: The Story of the Mormon Trail*, appeared in 1964 as part of McGraw-Hill's American Trails Series edited by western writer A. B. Guthrie, Jr. Guthrie had become acquainted with both Bernard DeVoto and Stegner through his Nieman Fellowship at Harvard and Bread Loaf participation. He wished to recruit Stegner's lively prose, careful research, and intimate knowledge of Mormon history for his series, which included such distinguished titles as David Lavender's *Westward Vision* (on the Oregon Trail) and George R. Stewart's *The California Trail*. It was a fortunate choice. Stegner's book has achieved a solid place in the literature of Mormon history, and in spite of the limited body of sources upon which he was able to draw, it has hardly been improved upon since.[40] "If *Mormon Country* was written in Cambridge out of nostalgia for the West," his biographer observes, "*Zion* was written by a professional whose research had a solid foundation in previous work and who had, with his usual conscientiousness, mastered all the documents available to him."[41]

Realizing (correctly) that he would probably not be allowed access to the primary sources in the archives of the Mormon Church, Stegner wisely turned to the two best collectors of Mormon materials he knew: Dale Morgan, then at the Bancroft Library, and Juanita Brooks. The vast amount of material to which they directed him enabled him to tell the story accurately, both in its broad outlines and through intimate glimpses into the plodding daily realities and the little heroisms of the humble participants in one of history's great folk migrations. Those primary sources, too, enabled Stegner to establish his own foothold of objectivity in interpreting the Mormon Trail rather than having to rely upon the secondary accounts, which he characterized as "enormous, repetitious, contradictory, and embattled."[42] Stegner was also careful to state explicitly at the outset his own position on Mormonism in order to gain a fair hearing both among the Saints and the Gentiles. "I write as a non-Mormon but not as a Mormon-hater," he stated. As to the Mormon faith, "I do not believe it, but I do not quarrel with it either." He was suspicious of the Mormon hierarchy as he was suspicious of any corporate bureaucracy, but he knew and admired the everyday virtues of the Mormon people. "Suffering, endurance, discipline, faith, brotherly and sisterly charity, the qualities so thoroughly celebrated by Mormon writers, were surely well distributed among them [the Mormon pioneers], but theirs also was a normal amount of human cussedness, vengefulness, masochism, backbiting, violence, ignorance, selfishness, and gullibility."[43]

The basic theme of the history of the Mormon migration, as Stegner saw it, was the group cohesion of Mormon culture and the iron-fisted leadership of the Council of Twelve Apostles and especially its president, Brigham Young. Where other parties on the overland trails were burdened with poor preparation, factionalism, and ignorance, the Mormon parties quickly overcame those problems. They developed a system in which a well-established route, proven equipment and provisions, and experienced leadership combined to move thousands of people over thousands of miles with an amazingly low loss of life and property and without much discomfort. Stegner gives especially high marks to the Perpetual Emigrating Fund, a revolving account that poor European converts could draw on to pay their way to Zion, and which would be replenished by various church investments and repayments by its beneficiaries. He perhaps places too much emphasis on the disaster of the 1856 Willie and Martin handcart companies, which seems to him an indictment of the entire handcart idea, even though there were ten handcart companies altogether between 1856 and 1860, the other eight successfully completing their journeys. Nor, perhaps, does Stegner give enough credit to the "ox teamology" of the remarkable Joseph W. Young, perhaps the best ox skinner in history, who developed the "down and back" church wagon trains that replaced the handcarts in the 1860s and brought in the last overland pioneers before the railroad.[44]

The Gathering of Zion, nevertheless, is vintage Stegner. His promise to give proportional attention to both the greatness and the smallness of Mormon history is perfectly kept. He also writes with compassion about the suffering of the handcart parties stranded in the snow, while keeping a sharp eye out for the occasional callousness of their leaders. Stegner's fictional skill comes to the fore in his deft delineation of character and his eye for the dramatic moment. As Benson points out, "*Zion* may not be as significant a book as the Powell book, but the writing has more zest and bite, and because it comes to a climax toward the end, rather than in the middle as *Hundredth Meridian* does, it is, overall, more dramatic."[45] Like the other works, fiction and nonfiction, upon which his literary reputation rests, *The Gathering of Zion* reaffirms Stegner's faith in social cohesion as opposed to individualism, and his belief in rationalism as opposed to myth and romanticism. Finally, his purview is remarkably modern in its emphasis on the role of the Mormon women, an emphasis that was already discernible in the work of his mentor, Bernard DeVoto, but which would not become a major feature of western history for a decade or more after he wrote. "Their women were incredible," he says at the close of his introduction, and his narrative is as much a women's story as a men's one.[46]

The Gathering of Zion was written after Stegner left Harvard in 1956 to direct the writing program at Stanford. An alumnus of the University of Iowa and the Bread Loaf conference, the two most innovative and successful writing programs in the country, Stegner was an ideal choice to lead the one at Stanford. Recognized by that time as a major literary figure, Stegner turned his hand to helping other aspiring writers become established. By the time he retired in 1971, Stegner's program had produced a stream of first-rate writers, including Edward Abbey, Eugene Burdick, Ken Kesey, Larry McMurtry, and Wendell Berry.

There were tensions at Stanford that painted a dark backdrop to Stegner's tenure at the writing program. In order to get Stegner, the university offered him a full professorship with tenure after the first year, which leapfrogged him over several older faculty members, and this produced jealousy toward him among some. Also, other faculty members disagreed with Stegner's literary realism and traditionalism. The poet and critic Yvor Winters, who directed the poetry writing program, was jealous of Stegner's budget, while Albert Guerard of the English department favored a sort of postmodernist experimentalism in the teaching of writing. Stegner was also frustrated with the present-mindedness of some of his students who had no appreciation for the traditionalism, the commitment to revision, and the downright hard work that were the hallmarks of his approach to writing and teaching. In the end, these pressures won out and forced his early retirement.

In the mid-1950s, though, those stresses and frustrations were mostly in the future, and he and his wife Mary settled on a comfortable estate in the Los Altos Hills. His morning writing sessions in a detached studio were sacrosanct, and he could devote his remaining time to his writing, to his students, and to entertaining students, colleagues, and visiting literary figures at expansive cocktail parties and dinners where Stegner demonstrated his gregariousness, wit, and love of life. Northern California suburbia may have been, both geographically and culturally, a far distance from "his" West of the Saskatchewan short-grass plains or the Utah high plateaus, but it was a good place for a writer to live and work, and he even drew upon it for the setting of some of his most mature stories and novels.

The serene happiness promised by his new situation in California was marred, though, by a widening gap between Stegner and the larger culture in which he lived and worked. His famous essay, "Born a Square," in *The Sound of Mountain Water*, not only identifies some of the features of western cultural life that inhibit production of great literature, but it also defines the conservative values that are conspicuous in Stegner's own life and work.[47] As his biographer puts it, Stegner "believed in all those things we used to believe in."[48] Those values made him an outsider in the northern California of his Stanford days, as the youth rebellion burst forth on and off college campuses. Alienation ran in both directions in those years: the students were disgusted with their professors, and professors like Stegner were frustrated with their students. "It was no fun teaching," Stegner later recalled. "The intolerable [students] came with answers and not questions, and the others came with just confusions. Between them there was no way you could feel you were not wasting your time in the classroom." Although he remembered that that alienation did not apply to his writing students, who generally had their feet on the ground better than the undergraduates, he was forgetting Ken Kesey, the quintessential hippie who was one of Stegner's students. The two had a major conflict and falling out that never healed. Eventually, the frustration led Stegner to retire early at age sixty-two and return to writing.[49]

One of the salubrious literary effects of Stegner's Stanford alienation was his development of the curmudgeonly commentators on the sixties in the characters of Joe Allston and Lyman Ward, and the slightly less crusty Larry Morgan of *Crossing to Safety*. Stegner disliked and avoided conflict and confrontation, but his sublimated feelings about the hippies and sixties radicalism emerged scathingly in those fictional *personae*. Significantly, all three characters appear in first-person narratives, a device Stegner used only in admittedly autobiographical writings. The setting and characters of *All the Little Live Things* were so obviously drawn from the Stegners' Los Altos Hills neighborhood that his neighbors "for years talked about who matched whom." Stegner's sly response to that was simply, "Never have a writer for a friend." In his personal notes, though, he went further in defending fiction drawn so closely from life. "One may be a peeping Tom in literature as in life. There will always be carelessly or carefully undrawn blinds through which these people may peep and peer. This fact does not mean that windows must be nailed shut, blinds taped to the sills, and all the outside garden booby trapped to prevent peeping. Let the peeper beware—Caveat peeptor."[50]

Joe Allston proved to be a durable creation, appearing in three major works. His first appearance was in a lengthy short story (Stegner later referred to it as a novella), "Field Guide to the Western Birds," in *The City of the Living, And Other Stories*, written in 1956, before the sixties. The character fulfills a different function in this work than in *All the Little Live Things* and *The Spectator Bird*.[51] Allston is a retired literary agent living in the hills south of San Francisco, much like Stegner himself. When he first appears in "Field Guide," his retirement has only begun, and he has built an isolated studio down the hill from his main residence, where he can supposedly work on his memoirs without interruption, but where he is frittering away his time on a new hobby of bird-watching. The story concerns a dinner party to which he and his genteel and long-suffering wife, Ruth, have been invited by a wealthy neighbor couple to hear a young pianist the wife has discovered and wants to sponsor for a concert career. She hopes Allston's New York connections may be useful to the young man. Allston, uninterested in the whole idea, takes an immediate dislike to the pianist's *artiste* demeanor, gets drunk, and plans to put the young man down. For the most part, though, the concert is a success. The kid has talent. Afterwards it is the musician himself who destroys the evening and throws away his opportunity. He gets uncontrollably drunk, debates angrily with Allston about parasitic agents and the unjust lack of opportunities for young artists, insults his hosts, and falls into the swimming pool, turning the evening into an irredeemable disaster. "Field Guide to the Western Birds," in spite of the humor in Allston's acerbic running commentary, is a disturbing exploration of the place of the artist in a democratic society, a society in which hard work, a dedicated patron, an effective agent, and even a lucky break do not always guarantee success. It is also a study in human self-centeredness, both Allston's and the pianist's, and its tragic potential to destroy civilization.

By 1967, when *All the Little Live Things* appeared, the youth rebellion was in high gear at Stanford and virtually every other university, and Stegner dusted off the character of Joe Allston as a vehicle for his social frustration. Although that is the predominant focus, the novel covers more ground than just the youth rebellion. As the title suggests, the story explores as well the larger issue of man's stewardship of the earth and its creatures. It is by all odds Stegner's most polemical work of fiction. There are many lengthy passages that consist only of a debate between Allston and one or more of the other characters—or within Allston himself—over a lengthy menu of cultural issues provoked by the youth rebellion, from traditional morality and education to parental roles and environmental management and development. Through it all, though, Stegner's wit and skill in delineating character keep the novel's polemicism lively, and Joe Allston emerges as perhaps his most vivid creation.

The setting once again is the suburban community where the Allstons have retired. Bill and Sue Casement, the dinner party hosts in "Field Guide," reappear in a minor role; this time Stegner builds the story on the Allstons' relations with a full cast of other neighbors. Two are at the center: Jim Peck, an unwashed, bearded hippie on a motorcycle with his long-haired head full of rejection of every establishment idea for which Allston stands; and Marian Catlin, an angelic young mother, open-minded and full of love for "all the little live things" around her. Neighbor Fran LoPresti is a putative artist whose oddball sculptures of assembled junk become the butt of Allston's misplaced jokes, Stegner's gibe at innocent suburban California kookiness. The LoPrestis' daughter, Julie, seethes with teenage resentment against her parents and begins hanging out with Peck and his hippie friends. Finally there is Tom Weld, a tasteless materialist whose bulldozer rips up the beauty of the suburban environment and whose vagrant horses and dog invade and irritate his neighbors. His son Dave joins Peck and Julie in their rebellion.

The story grows out of Peck's request to camp indefinitely on an unused part of Allston's property, a request the generous Ruth Allston pressures her husband into granting, on limited terms. Ignoring those terms, Peck turns his camp into a hippie compound utilizing poached water and electricity and, as previously mentioned, encouraging and focusing the incipient rebellion of the neighborhood kids. Allston and Peck, to whom he refers as "Caliban" and the "incarnated essence of disorder," have their direct confrontations, but much of their debate takes place indirectly through Marian Catlin, whose love of life leaves her open to both sides. She becomes, as Stegner himself points out in a dust jacket commentary, a mediating principle between the oil and water of Peck and Allston. "In Joe Allston and Jim Peck I wanted to pose the antagonism between square parents and hippy children in its most irreconcilable terms. . . . If there is an answer both to Peck's lust for kicks and Joe Allston's impulse to flinch away and retire, it is in Marian Catlin's openness to all experience and her affection for all life."

Marian, it turns out, is both pregnant and dying from cancer, a symbol of the opposing life forces of rebellion and retirement she represents. A race develops between her death and the baby's birth, for she refuses either to abort the baby or to accept radiation treatments that will prolong her life but endanger the baby. "There isn't good life and bad life," she tells the Allstons in her resignation to let nature take its course. "There's only life."[52] The story reaches an apocalyptic, though contrived, finale in an emotionally wrenching and even bloody clash at a rickety bridge at Peck's compound as the Allstons and Catlins attempt to get past Peck, a microbus full of hippies, and Julie LoPresti's horse to get the dying Marian to the hospital.

As our memories of hippies and the youth rebellion fade into history, *All the Little Live Things* is likely to become as dated as its pre–pop top soft drink cans. But it will be redeemed as literature by its larger affirmations of parental and filial love and responsibility, of man's obligations as nature's caretaker, and of the ultimate value of life itself.

Stegner used Joe Allston one last time in *The Spectator Bird*, which won a National Book Award in 1976. Like *Angle of Repose*, it is two stories in one. The first takes place some time after the events of *All the Little Live Things*, and the other some years before. Stegner apparently had the story that became *The Spectator Bird* in mind while he was writing *All the Little Live Things*, for in the earlier novel Allston says, "We smelled our way back to the old country . . . where my mother was born. We learned something, perhaps, but that is another story."[53] The flashback story in *The Spectator Bird* recounts a trip to Denmark that the Allstons had made, told through the couple's nightly readings of his rediscovered journal.

Stegner based the Denmark trip on a similar trip he and his wife made in the 1950s, which included lodging with a countess in her genteel poverty and meeting with Karen Blixen (Isak Dineson). Embedded in the California part of the story as well is Stegner's own feeling of marginalization after his retirement, returning unrecognized to the Stanford campus for a concert, and Allston's being surrounded by ailing and dying friends from his productive years whose sufferings remind him of his own mortality. The title of the novel refers to Allston's sense of the marginal nature of his career as a literary agent: he was only a spectator while the authors, his clients, made the real contributions to civilization. Stegner himself was of course no spectator in his own productive literary career, but he certainly felt, as we have noted, that his teaching career became increasingly futile and unappreciated.

Aging and America's relationship to the Old World are the two major themes of the novel. Neither theme appears very "western" until one remembers that half of the narrative, after all, takes place in

California. Stegner uses California subtly as a metaphor for the rootless presentism of modern American culture, exposing its inadequacy for an elderly man looking for some larger significance for his career. California also symbolizes what Allston imagines to be the shallowness of America's rootlessness in contrast with the Old World, where, to shift to Stegner's own metaphor, people have attics where they can rediscover their past.

Allston's idea of Old World superiority suffers two major blows in the story. The first comes early, in the form of a visit from an Italian novelist whom Allston once represented. Cesare Rulli is a human whirlwind who has apparently exhausted everything San Francisco has to offer in two days of a three-day visit, and his hostess calls Allston in desperation to see if she can kill a little more time by bringing him over. The Allstons invite them for what turns out to be a disastrous lunch, with Rulli proving shallower than anything even California can claim. He bolts Ruth Allston's elegant lunch and Joe's expensive wine without comment, ceaselessly castigating, instead, their decision to turn their backs on the social and cultural scene in the city in favor of a quiet, contemplative life in the suburbs. Joe, in other words, is not to be permitted to grow old quietly and gracefully; all Rulli can see is that Joe has put himself on the shelf. So much for Rulli, one representative of Old World culture.

The Old World fares little better in the flashback story, in which the Allstons reverse the journey made by his Danish peasant mother many years before to try to learn something of her family and background. Joe throws himself into the project with zest, brushing up on his childhood Danish and finding lodging with an authentic, though impoverished, countess in order to experience the local culture firsthand. An unexpected treat materializes when the countess turns out to be related to Karen Blixen and offers to take the Allstons by for a visit. (As indicated above, Stegner's narrative of the visit is based on his own encounter with Blixen, and is a delightful vignette of literary history.) Allston is highly impressed with her sharp features and leathery skin, which give her the look of a witch, an impression reinforced by the coincidence that as the Allstons arrive she has just dug up an ancient rune stone in her garden. But if Allston expects the magic of her witchcraft to open profound secrets available only in the Old World, she disappoints him by asking what if the attics of Europe that contain those supposed spiritual riches turn out to contain something ugly instead.

Blixen's question is prophetic. Allston discovers that his mother grew up on the estate of the very countess with whom they are staying, and that she fled to America to escape some mysterious gothic horror associated with her ancestral property. The horror turns out to be incest. The countess's father had been a geneticist of preternatural skill whose black arts extended to genetic experiments within his own family, a practice being continued, the Allstons learn, by the countess's brother. Blixen was right. Allston's own attic contained a monster, and his assumptions of Old World spiritual superiority are shattered.

Contrasts between the past and present and between Europe and America dominate *The Spectator Bird.* In Stegner's most widely acknowledged masterpiece, *Angle of Repose*, which won the Pulitzer Prize in 1972, he returns to the past-present contrast, but this time the Europe-America contrast is replaced by a contrast between the older, more mature eastern United States and the youthful, optimistic, frontier West. Structurally and technically, the book is a masterpiece because it effectively integrates two independent stories, one set in western mining camps in the nineteenth century, the other in northern California in 1970. Much of the book's effectiveness arises, once again, from Stegner's knowledge of his subject. He wrote the book during his years of frustration with the youth culture at Stanford, and also while doing research on late nineteenth-century scientific exploration and economic development in the West.

Stegner was already an expert on the historical material because of his dissertation on Clarence Edward Dutton and his biography of Maj. John Wesley Powell. This time, though, his interest was piqued by the papers of Mary Hallock Foote (1837–1938), a little-known writer and illustrator whose husband became a mining engineer in the West. Accompanying her husband from one mining camp to another, Foote helped keep the couple solvent by publishing stories and illustrations of life in the West for eastern magazines like *Century*. One of Stegner's graduate students had acquired Foote's papers from her descendants and had proposed a dissertation based on them. The student, however, was an older man who found the magnitude of the task beyond his energy, and he turned the papers over to Stegner, hoping he would be able to do something with them. Stegner first considered writing a biography, but instead chose the greater flexibility of fictionalizing the material. He added a parallel modern story as a device for contrasting American culture of the late nineteenth century with the culture of his own day.[54] For Stegner, too, there were distant echoes of his own father in the wandering engineer in quest of the great bonanza, echoes that had previously sounded not only in *The Big Rock Candy Mountain*, but also in the grandiose vision of western promoters William Gilpin and Captain Samuel Adams in *Beyond the Hundredth Meridian*.

Angle of Repose begins in the study of Lyman Ward, a retired Berkeley history professor who has recently lost a leg. Ward has moved into the Grass Valley, California, home where his grandparents spent their last years, and he proposes to arrange his grandmother's papers and write a book about her. Embittered not only by his physical condition but also by a wife who left him for his physician and by a sociologist son whose present-minded focus rejects the relevance of the history Lyman has spent his life studying, Lyman sees in his grandmother's genteel Victorian values a stick with which he can beat the rootless culture of his own day. The son, Rodman, who is uninterested in any human facts that cannot be reduced to "data" for a computer punch card, turns out to be less of a lightning rod for Lyman's curmudgeonly observations than does Shelly Rasmussen, a braless, long-haired hippie girl fresh from the free love culture and student protests at Berkeley, whom he hires part-time to help him sort the papers. Shelly's bemused interest initially focuses on the grandmother's Victorian reticence about sex and her dogged commitment to an unhappy marriage, both of which contrast dramatically with the casual alliances of the self-indulgent culture Shelly represents. In the end, when she proposes to join her boyfriend in a hippie commune, the debate between Lyman and Shelly shifts to the nature of community in a larger sense. Lyman criticizes the commune participants' naivete regarding human nature and their assumption that they can eliminate greed and selfishness simply by changing the external structure of society. Also, he marvels at their ignorance of the failed utopias of history and their failure to address the forces that doomed those efforts. In his notes for the novel, Stegner expressed his intentions more concisely than in any passage in the work itself. "In some conversation with Shelly, Ward would perhaps make some impassioned plug for *continuance, rootedness*. To him, the young Zen devotees are as phoney as the architects who cope Tudor half-timbered houses. The house of the spirit should be indigenous—and that is the whole trouble in a newly invaded country. One of his reasons for stubbornly writing his grandparents' lives is to save them from neglect, reassert them."[55]

Lyman's acerbic observations and his debates with Rodman and Shelly are not, however, the core of the novel. They fulfill a function similar to that of a Greek chorus, emerging from time to time to comment on developments in the real story. That story is the marriage of Susan Burling Ward and her husband Oliver and their late nineteenth-century travels from one western mining camp to another. Stegner's narrative has two themes: the ultimate failure of the quest for the great bonanza in western history, and the concurrent quest to build a civilized life on the western frontier.

Susan Burling, a New York Quaker woman with literary, artistic, and social aspirations, falls in love with Oliver Ward, a dropout from Yale's Sheffield Scientific School, who proposes to seek his fortune as a self-made mining engineer in the West. Susan envies her friend Augusta Drake, who marries the talented Thomas Hudson, editor of *Century* (patterned on the real-life Richard Watson Gilder), thereby placing herself in the center of eastern cultural life. Oliver's promises of a quick fortune in western mining, plus her fears that she may never marry at all, tempt her to marry him and join him in what she assumes will be a temporary western adventure. That adventure will expose her to fresh experiences and bring her enough money to support a life of leisure and culture in the East.

Oliver's reach, unfortunately, exceeds his grasp. What was to be a brief western sojourn turns into a frustrating migration from one failed venture to another. Repeatedly gulled and cheated by his backers and partners, Oliver rarely makes enough money to support his wife, and she has to support the family with stories and illustrations commissioned by Thomas Hudson.

This is not to say that their life together in the West is unremittingly dismal. For one thing, Susan finds plenty of material for her literary and artistic career. And the two enjoy a reasonably happy domestic life, sometimes lived in spectacular locales that delight Susan (though she finds Boise unrelievably dreary). And Susan does not simply take whatever western conditions dish out. Instead, she creates her own community among the talented scientists and writers whose travels through the West bring them frequently to the Wards' door.

There is nevertheless an undercurrent of frustration, caused not only by the couple's economic privation, but also by their fundamental incompatibility. They are never able to find a common "angle of repose," a geological term indicating the angle at which sliding rock comes to rest. Stegner vividly illustrates their incompatibility in the conversations they have with their scientist guests. When mining, geology, or some other technical subject is the topic, Oliver is engaged while Susan is left out; when the talk turns to books, art, and other cultural matters, he is left out.

The tension comes to a focus in the person of Frank Sargent, Oliver's talented colleague who is able to talk books and art with Susan, and falls in love with her. On two occasions he tries to get her to leave Oliver for him. He could obviously be the escape route back to the life of culture she had originally sought, but she rejects him and stays with Oliver. Did the couple actually consummate an illicit affair? Lyman, studying the incident, chooses to believe Susan's Victorian commitment to marital fidelity kept her chaste, though he admits the evidence is inconclusive. Oliver, however, is suspicious enough that a permanent rift emerges between the couple. They never divorce, but they accept long periods of estrangement while he is on travels, and they are cool to each other when together.

Although *Angle of Repose* is largely based on historical research, it is also a highly personal story for Stegner. It is compelling because the issues raised in the story mattered to him. Although the character of Lyman Ward is based in large part on Norman Foerster, the literary scholar under whom Stegner did his graduate work at the University of Iowa, Lyman's vitriolic indictment of the rootless presentism of the sixties is Stegner's own frustration with the culture that led to his resignation from the Stanford faculty.

But *Angle of Repose* is more than just Stegner's personal indictment of western boosterism and the sixties. His sharply drawn characters are vividly memorable as individuals. The debates between Lyman and Shelly, and between Oliver and Susan, are clear-eyed confrontations over vital issues of culture and history. Finally, Stegner's sustained contrasts between East and West and between past and present are deftly integrated into the two stories that make up the novel. Those issues must matter to us as they did to Stegner, and he sets them before us unforgettably in one of the best of all western novels.

After *Angle of Repose*, Stegner continued his examination of the contrast between East and West in *The Uneasy Chair* (1974), his biography of Bernard DeVoto, and in his collection of DeVoto's letters that followed the next year.[56] Taken together, they constitute one of the most memorable portraits in American literature of a colorful and significant cultural figure, a westerner who lived in the East but who never felt himself completely at home in either place.

Stegner's acquaintance with DeVoto began with a letter of thanks for DeVoto's role, as a member of the prize committee, in getting Stegner the Little, Brown award for *Remembering Laughter*. They met in person at a convention of the Modern Language Association, became colleagues at Bread Loaf and Harvard, and neighbors in Cambridge. As two bright, expatriate westerners who had both passed through the ordeal of a Gentile childhood in Mormon country, they had much in common, and as time passed they became intimate friends. The older man was a mentor to Stegner from the start, helping him get his feet on the ground in the eastern literary and publishing communities and establishing himself as a model of the historian and the "public intellectual," both of which Stegner became after DeVoto's death. If Stegner's father was the dominant negative influence in his life, DeVoto was the dominant positive one, at least in intellectual matters.

Soon after DeVoto's death, Stegner began trying to persuade Avis DeVoto to deposit her husband's papers in the Stanford library. DeVoto had had no connection with Stanford, but it was one of the major western universities, it had a respectable archives program, and was the kind of research center that would be an appropriate repository. No doubt Stegner also had in mind the convenience with which he himself could work with the papers, and at about the time Mrs. DeVoto made the donation, she began suggesting that Stegner write her husband's biography. But Stegner was fully occupied at the time with other projects, especially the writing program, and he declined. After fifteen years, after no one else had come forward to tackle the DeVoto project, and at a point when his involvement with the writing program was ending and he was casting about for a new project, Stegner approached Avis about a biography and received her enthusiastic encouragement and cooperation.

The DeVoto who emerges from Stegner's pages is, like his John Wesley Powell, largely the public person rather than the private one. Also, like Stegner's Powell, his DeVoto is a rationalistic hero who contrast with the mythmakers and the headlong exploiters. That said, however, his DeVoto is drawn much more three- dimensionally than his Powell. This is no doubt partly because DeVoto's papers document his life much more thoroughly than do the papers of Powell, who lost his right hand at the battle of Shiloh and could not write letters. DeVoto's native verbosity and straightforward honesty were given wings by his expertise at the typewriter, and multiple-page, single-spaced letters expressing his ideas and feelings in the most frank detail are strewn throughout his correspondence. Another likely reason for Stegner's deeper exploration of DeVoto's personal life is that DeVoto's neuroses and biases were the gasoline that powered his career as a culture critic, and no explanation of his pugnacity and his emotional extremes would be possible without delving beneath the surface. Finally, Stegner was one of DeVoto's closest friends, and Stegner may have felt that the intimacy of their relationship gave him a surer footing in speculating on his friend's interior dynamics than he had in the case of Powell, a man long dead. Even at that, Stegner gives us only enough of DeVoto's interior life for us to understand his public career as writer, historian, and conservation activist.[57] "Malcolm [Cowley, Stegner's colleague at Stanford] says I made DeVoto the hero of a novel," Stegner recorded in his personal notes. "That's not far from the truth. The subject of a biography should be the hero of a *sort* of novel, the best sort. . . . No reason biography can't utilize the techniques—and pursue the intentions—of fiction."[58]

Although Stegner quoted generously from DeVoto's always quotable letters, and those quotations impart an immense zest to his book, many of them were too long to quote in full. In order to let his readers experience the private DeVoto at greater length for themselves, he put together a collection of 148 of DeVoto's most entertaining and revealing letters in a book-length edition in 1975. The effort that went into assembling the collection is hidden by Stegner's modest introduction and apparently effortless editorial apparatus. The Stegner papers contain a complete archival calendar—an individual summary of each individual letter—that Stegner prepared for the *Letters*, with possibilities for inclusion marked in the margin. Another by-product of the *Letters* are slips of paper inserted by Stegner into the DeVoto correspondence that identify people who were known to both of them but perhaps were not known to others. With that careful selection and arranging, *The Letters of Bernard DeVoto* offers an unfailingly entertaining, enlightening, and provocative look into one of American culture's most original and controversial minds.[59]

As a result of DeVoto's influence during Stegner's mature years as a writer, he found himself, from in the early 1950s until the end of his life, drawn more deeply into the conservation (later the environmental) movement as a spokesman for limiting exploitation of natural resources and preserving wilderness areas. Although always sympathetic to the cause, he was reluctant at first to add his voice to it, largely because his friend Bernard DeVoto had pre-empted the field, although it was in response to DeVoto's prodding that he first stuck his toe into the water. For DeVoto, conservation meant confrontation; where Stegner's style was quiet persuasion through careful reasoning and measured argument, DeVoto waded into the fray wielding a battle-ax. Until DeVoto's death in 1955, Stegner was largely content to let his friend carry the brunt of the battle, but later he felt morally obligated to step forward himself. At the time of his death in 1993, he was spending more time in environmental work than in creative writing.

Always, though, there were tensions. As advocacy groups for wildlife and conservation came under the leadership in the late 1940s of strident young men like Howard Zahniser of the Wilderness Society and David Brower of the Sierra Club, they turned more and more to lobbying and political action groups that dared to challenge directly the corporate exploiters of the West and their governmental representative, the mighty Bureau of Reclamation. Moderates like Stegner and his friend the photographer Ansel Adams cooperated with Sierra Club radicals like Brower and river runner Martin Litton and even served on the organization's board of directors, but they objected increasingly to their radical colleagues' stridency and intransigence.

Stegner eventually resigned from the Sierra Club board, but his writings established him as the most eloquent and reasonable spokesmen for wilderness preservation. Many of his magazine articles on the issue have been collected in book form, beginning with *The Sound of Mountain Water* in 1969 and continuing to his last published book, *Where the Bluebird Sings to the Lemonade Springs*, in 1992. Included in that earliest collection and again in his son's posthumous anthology, *Marking the Sparrow's Fall: The Making of the American West*,[60] as well as photocopied innumerable times and posted on the walls of environmentalists' offices, was his most celebrated environmental essay, "Wilderness Letter." Written in 1960 at Brower's instigation to David Pesonen, a member of a government commission studying wilderness issues, it is a memorably eloquent defense of what he calls the wilderness *idea*, the admittedly intangible and thus difficult to defend notion that the preservation of wilderness is preservation of a spiritual resource even more important to American culture than the material benefits of exploitation. In a much-quoted phrase at the end, he argues that in wilderness preservation is to be found a "geography of hope" for continuation of the moral high ground that has been the foundation for the best of what America has represented. It is arguably the finest piece of writing that Stegner ever created, and fully deserves the attention it has received.

Even during the time in which he became one of the best-known and most eloquent spokesmen for the unspoiled West, Stegner spent more and more time on the property he had purchased long before near the Grays' estate in Vermont. He had loved New England during his years at Harvard and his summers at Bread Loaf and with the Grays in Vermont, and as his native West became less "western" in its urban congestion and pollution, he found more of the leisurely solitude and peace he sought in the East. It was, however, in the West that his life ended. Attending a conference in Santa Fe, New Mexico, at the end of March 1993 with his wife, Stegner entered an intersection improperly and was struck on the driver's side by another vehicle. Though seriously injured, Stegner appeared to have a fair chance of surviving, but pneumonia set in, and he died a few days later. "The December of his life ended in springtime," Ivan Doig noted ironically in a moving tribute to his friend.[61] Shortly after his death, his ashes were scattered, according to his wishes, over the Vermont picnic ground where the Stegners and the Grays had spent so many happy hours and which he had memorialized in the mellow prose of his last novel.

A great novelist, a great teacher, a great public figure, and even a great scholar. How did he fare as a historian? We have seen how deeply many of his fictional writings were grounded in history, and we have noted some of the virtues of his historical works, especially his John Wesley Powell biography and his history of the Mormon Trail. In the essays that follow, we will examine the ways in which Stegner's fictional techniques carried over into his histories and the problems that resulted.

THE GOD THAT FAILED

In *The Uneasy Chair*, his 1974 biography of his mentor and friend Bernard DeVoto, Wallace Stegner included a brief but penetrating defense of *The Year of Decision 1846*, DeVoto's first major historical work and arguably his masterpiece. Although the book had been reviewed respectfully by several eminent historians, it had offended as many as it had pleased. DeVoto had entered the historical profession via caesarian section without passing through the Ph.D., and once there, he set about offending almost every narrative and interpretive convention hallowed by that profession. Some of his hyperventilating prose would have flunked him out of freshman composition, and many of his character sketches were so much larger than life that they belonged on billboards rather than on the printed page. Most offensively, he seemed to be suggesting that only one year, 1846, explained a whole century of western history.

Stegner, who had followed DeVoto into history through creative writing, understood that DeVoto was applying a literary device to his historical narrative, a device DeVoto called "test boring." Stegner knew it by the formal term synecdoche, a figure of speech in which a part (in this case, the year 1846) is made to stand for the whole (nineteenth-century western expansion). Robert Frost, DeVoto's colleague at the Bread Loaf writers conferences in Vermont, had said that all an artist needs is samples, and to DeVoto the historian, 1846 seemed to be a good sample to use in elucidating the forces that had made western history.

Stegner appreciated what DeVoto was attempting not only because of his study of formal literary devices during his doctoral program in American literature, but also because he had himself used synecdoche in an autobiographical novel, *The Big Rock Candy Mountain*, that appeared the very same year as DeVoto's history. In that novel and in other novels and stories, Stegner used his own infamously dysfunctional family as a sample of everything that was dysfunctional in western history.

George Stegner, his father, was the archetype, in Stegner's view, of the footloose, careless, materialistic western booster whose headlong pursuit of one chimerical get-rich-quick scheme after another had brought poverty and instability to his wife and two children. In a larger regional and historical sense, the George Stegners of the West had been responsible for the unthinking waste of natural resources, the destruction of indigenous inhabitants, and the suffering of those who had been lured to the West by false promises of prosperity. Stegner had no choice but to follow his father from one will-o'-the-wisp dream to another, and he saw his own boyhood as a microcosm of the larger tragedy of western history.

Stegner's autobiographical writings, then, are dark tales of family conflict, exploitation, and abuse. Escape came, for Stegner, only as adolescence blossomed into early adulthood and he found a place for himself in a larger society outside the home. That larger society was the University of Utah, where he found social acceptance and a new world of reason and beauty in the classrooms of his nurturing instructors. There was hope, then, for the individual. Was there also hope for the entire West?

During the decade that followed publication of *The Big Rock Candy Mountain* in 1943, Stegner found such hope in the career of Maj. John Wesley Powell. Powell was an explorer of the Colorado River and the Colorado Plateau and was a founder and director of the United States Geological Survey and the Bureau of American Ethnology, as well as the guiding force behind the 1902 Newlands Act, which created the Bureau of Reclamation. Stegner claimed that Powell had urged that regional salvation could come to the West through a public policy of development based on science, not on unfounded myth. This is the thesis of his admiring 1953 biography, *Beyond the Hundredth Meridian: John Wesley Powell and the Second Opening of the West.*

It is no accident that Stegner dedicated the biography to Bernard DeVoto, for *Beyond the Hundredth Meridian* was clearly inspired by *The Year of Decision 1846* and contains many of the same characteristics. Both are books of heroes and villains, dramatically (if sometimes simplistically) drawn characters who represent the mistakes of the past and the hope of the future. Both tell their stories through dramatic narrative and sometimes high-flown prose that presents western history as high adventure and seeks a wide popular audience. Finally, both books promote reason and science, in the form of an on-the-ground knowledge of the West, as the only possible basis for an enlightened public policy of western development.

The villains of Stegner's book—the George Stegners, to practice some garage sale psychology—are William Gilpin, governor of Colorado Territory, and Captain Samuel Adams, promoter of a water-level railroad route along the Colorado River that would link the Rocky Mountains with southern California. Gilpin advocated headlong agricultural development of the apparently arid Great Plains on the theory that "rain follows the plow"—that agricultural development would generate its own precipitation by unlocking through evaporation vast resources of water supposedly held in the virgin soil. It was, of course, such unfounded theories that led thousands of naive pioneer farmers into poverty through dry-farming attempts and eventually to the Dust Bowl of the 1930s. Adams attempted, using bogus credentials, to take over Powell's Colorado River expedition and, through underpreparation and overoptimism, met with one disaster after another in his own brief attempt to explore the river. Stegner saves his strongest vitriol for Adams, "a preposterous, twelve-gauge, hundred-proof, kiln-dried, officially notarized fool, or else . . . one of the most wildly incompetent scoundrels who ever lived." Like Gilpin, "his spiritual relative," Adams's "career is a demonstration of how far a man could get in a new country on nothing but gall and the gift of gab, so long as what he said was what people wanted to believe. He was one of a tribe of Western adventurers and imposters and mountebanks."[1]

Powell, on the other hand, was Stegner's hero for demanding that our understanding of the West and our policies for western development be grounded in science and reason. As Stegner writes, "It was to be [Powell's] distinction and in a way his misfortune that in an age of the wildest emotionalism and nationalist fervor he operated by common sense, had a faith in facts, and believed in system. . . . He brought eventually science where Gilpin brought mythology, measurement where Gilpin brought rhetoric."[2]

In Stegner's view, then, Powell was the anti-Gilpin, the anti-Adams and, it seems clear, the anti–George Stegner (that unnamed but ever-present villain). Where Gilpin and his ilk had brought illusion, frustration, waste, and poverty, Powell would bring his people to the Promised Land, a "dryland democracy," a heaven-on-earth utopia grounded in the application of science and reason to natural resource management. "Somewhere in Major Powell's small, maimed, whiskery person," Stegner asserts, "there burned some of the utopian zeal of Brook Farm and New Harmony. His vision of contented farmers controlling their own timber, grass, and water clear to the drainage divides, and settling their problems by an extension of the town meeting, is touched with a prophetic, perhaps a pathetic, piety. Science and Reason have always been on the side of Utopia; only the cussedness of the human race has not."[3]

Stegner's Powell, then, held science to be a sort of god and expected it to transform human nature and society in ways normally done by religion. Note, for example, in addition to the utopian expectations quoted above, Stegner's interpretation of the significance of Powell's *Report on the Lands of the Arid Region.* The report, he says, "offered a blueprint for laws and human institutions that would, if adopted, remake society and thought in the area they affected." And in another place Stegner presents Powell as "an evolutionist in every cell. He never despaired, apparently, of that final Perfection that to [Henry] Adams was a mirage, and he was sure of the method that must be used to find it: experimental science." And again, in Powell's mind, "All science must eventually be practical; the Science of Earth and the Science of Man led to the same end, the evolving and developing of better political, artistic, social, industrial, and agricultural institutions, 'all progressing with advancing intelligence to secure justice and thereby increase happiness.'"[4] It is science, then, not religion, that will bring about the new man and the new earth.

That Stegner intended to elevate science to a religion is apparent in the rhetoric he employs in referring to it. Powell, for example, "was not merely an explorer, an opener, and an observer, he was a prophet." In another place, Stegner refers to Powell as the "High Priest of Science," with the term science capitalized as though indicating a deity. Several environmental catastrophes in the late 1880s seemed to confirm the principles of Powell's Arid Lands report, and they led to the election to the Senate of pro-irrigationist William Stewart of Nevada. Stewart "fitted the plot like a St. John the Baptist, saying, 'Prepare ye the way of the Lord.'" When Powell joined Stewart's Senate Irrigation Committee on a tour of the West in 1889, "resumably he went not only to refresh his information but to do what he could as a missionary, to explain to Westerners the broad needs of their region and the ways in which the survey hoped to serve them."[5]

Stegner's treatment of Powell as a prophet of science and his view of science's possibilities raise two fundamental questions: to what degree is Stegner's Powell the real Powell, and what are the consequences of expecting science to do the work of religion? The Powell of the arid lands report, the Geological Survey, and the Bureau of American Ethnology had certainly become more of a scientist than the Powell of the river surveys. It seems clear that the major scientific achievements of the Powell surveys came in the later years, after Powell had turned the fieldwork over to trained scientists like Clarence Edward Dutton and Grove Karl Gilbert and assumed for himself a bureaucratic function in Washington, D.C. And yet it is in the early river explorations from 1869 to 1872 where Stegner says the quintessential scientist in Powell is most clearly in evidence. Stegner devotes approximately one-third of the biography to those years. "I have been able to conclude only that Powell's party in 1869 survived by the exercise of observation, caution, intelligence, skill, planning—in a word, Science. A man or a civilization could do the same."[6]

Looking at the Powell river trips, even through the evidence presented by Stegner, it is difficult to see much Science. The design of the boats, for example, might have come from the mind of William Gilpin rather than a supposed scientist like Powell. Heavy, narrow, and limited in maneuverability by a keel and tiller steering, the boats were suited for the Ohio or the Mississippi, but they were totally unsuited to the Colorado whitewater. Even more amazingly, after Powell had made the first trip, he made no design changes and returned to the river in 1871 with exactly the same type of craft, differing mainly by the addition of a deck chair for himself, which raised the center of gravity and increased the boat's instability.

When it came to the crew members and the overall scientific achievement of the river expeditions, even Stegner had to admit some damning facts that seriously eroded his thesis. "The river boatmen of 1869," he acknowledges, "were recruited about as haphazardly as Falstaff picked up his squad of ragamuffins, and they were equipped almost off the hedges." But again, on the second trip, which was much better funded and supported and which should have given Powell "the chance to pack his expedition with brains and skill," the major lapsed into his previous hiring procedure. "Nepotism and an acquaintance among the schoolteachers of Illinois explained them all. There was not a real scientist in the lot except the leader, and he was unproved." The results of Powell's two river trips, then, were about as disappointing as one would expect. Stegner writes:

> Scientifically, Powell had not yet done anything. He had gathered data to correct an empty or inaccurate map, but he had produced neither map nor report of his own, and the scientific results of two expeditions to the Rockies and a hundred days on the river amounted to little more than an incomplete and crude reconnaissance marked by inadequately checked latitudes and longitudes, some tables of elevation and barometric fluctuations, some geological sections of the cliffs, and some boxes of miscellaneous collections, still mainly unclassified and unlabeled.[7]

So much for the Science of the river expeditions.

Even the later Powell, after he had come into his own as a scientist, is noticeably modest in his claims for that science. The prose of his arid lands report, for example, is as arid as its subject and utterly devoid of any theological implications. Powell was advancing an irrigation proposal, not a utopia. The utopia was Stegner's.

A much more fundamental problem—one that Stegner by his own admission came only slowly to realize—is the necessary separation between science and religion. Scientists simply cannot, as scientists, make moral pronouncements, any more than theologians, as theologians, can make scientific statements. To realize the perils of the latter, one need only examine the Scopes trial or, in our own day, the Kansas State Board of Education. The perils of the former are most visible in our current environmental problems. We Americans have so easily accepted the proposition that science can create utopia that we have allowed scientists to define that utopia as well, with disastrous consequences. We believe, for instance, that because we are capable of building the Glen Canyon dam, we *should* build it. We have allowed the technologically possible to become the morally possible, with frequently disastrous environmental consequences.

Stegner told Richard Etulain that at the beginning of his career he had no idea that science had its dark side, and that, unrestrained by moral considerations, it could destroy the West as easily as make it habitable. "When I was beginning to work on Powell—I suppose because reclamation was a kind of fulfillment of his ideas—I looked upon the Reclamation Bureau as being really a big savior [another religious term] in the West. A lot of the modern West would have been impossible without it. But I think the West is going to be short-lived, too, partly on account of it."[8] This, of course, is a reminiscence of an older and wiser man who had become a guru of the environmental movement.

But Stegner had already begun to grasp the dark side of unrestrained reclamation by the end of the Powell biography. At the conclusion of a book that has consistently promoted Science as the potential creator of a western utopia, a utopia frustrated only by what he calls "the cussedness of the human race," he imagines that Powell, had he lived to see the excesses of the Bureau of Reclamation, would have turned against unrestrained science. One may question whether Powell's commitment to Science was as consistent or ambitious as Stegner indicates, but to turn him, in the end, into a potential recruit for the Sierra Club—as Stegner does—borders on the absurd. This was a new Powell who, as Stegner portrays him, "might agree that considerations such as recreation, wildlife might sometimes outweigh possible irrigation and power benefits." Historian James Aton responds that "[i]f Powell ever said this in a publication (more than 200 of them), a letter, a journal or a speech, I have never read it."[9] What Powell did say, as Donald Worster's biography points out, is that Florida's Lake Okeechobee should be drained so that cotton or sugar cane could be grown on its bottom, and that the Missouri River should be dammed and so completely diverted to support agriculture that it would be dry at its mouth.[10] Imagining what Powell would have thought of the Glen Canyon Dam and the Central Utah Project is a delightful parlor game, like speculating about how Napoleon might have used tanks and airplanes. We earthbound historians are restricted, though—except in our off-duty hours—to the documentary record, and that record gives no encouragement to Stegner's attempt to move Powell into the environmentalist camp.

How much better, surely, to let Powell stand at the head of an ambiguous legacy, in which science is only science. Such a legacy would remind us of the need for both science and religion, and the perils of allowing one to trespass onto the other's domain.

Although Stegner could legitimately maintain that the West needed better science than it was getting from the Gilpins, the Samuel Adamses, and the George Stegners, the reclamation-run-amok ethos that was emerging in his own day forced him to recognize that the West also needed a morality that science could not provide. As the Bureau of Reclamation proposed more and more dubious dam projects, Stegner spoke more and more for restraint. The god of Science had failed, because a god with no moral capacity is no god.

STAGE MANAGING A MIGRATION

In his recent study of the friendship between Bernard DeVoto and Wallace Stegner, John L. Thomas calls attention to one of the characteristics of Stegner's narrative technique in *The Gathering of Zion* (it applies to *Beyond the Hundredth Meridian* as well). "Stegner's presence as stage manager is constant as he arranges the experiences and reactions of his successive emigrants, many of them women, as they recorded them in their diaries and journals."[1] Thomas puts his finger on both the book's highest virtue and its characteristic weakness in one sentence. The virtue is its deep roots in the diaries and other personal writings of the common people who participated in the Mormon migration, and the weakness is that Stegner cannot resist manipulating those sources, moving his characters around to suit his script and weighing them down with the meanings he intends for them to have.

We have seen, in *Beyond the Hundredth Meridian*, how Major Powell stands for all that is rational and scientific in the westward movement, while the William Gilpins, the Samuel Adamses, and the William Stewarts stand for everything unscientific, overoptimistic, and greedy. The same type of symbolism—synecdoche, if you will—appears in *The Gathering of Zion*. There is Brigham Young, the calculating rationalist versus the whining William Clayton, the mystics Wilford Woodruff and Eliza R. Snow, the airy optimist Franklin D. Richards, and especially the disorganized Gentiles, whose haphazard planning and personal dissension contrast poorly with the systematic and regimented Mormon emigration. Young is the hub around which *The Gathering of Zion* rotates, just as Powell is the synecdoche for rational western exploration and exploitation. Although Stegner was aware of Young's personal shortcomings—his temper-driven tongue-lashings of Erastus Snow, Parley Pratt, and Franklin D. Richards, and his emerging autocracy once the Saints were safely out of reach of secular law—the Mormon migration emerges in Stegner's pages as an extension of Young's will and personality. When Brigham is present, things happen; when he is absent, they fall apart. It was their recognized dependence upon their leader, in Stegner's view, that enabled the Mormon people to put up with his shortcomings and idiosyncrasies and give him an obedience that few other leaders in American history have had. Commenting, for example, on Parley Pratt's meek acceptance of a tongue-lashing from Brigham, Stegner says, "It is a constant astonishment to an outsider how submissive even the apostles could be to this man who united with his own hard capacity for command the ultimate authority of the priesthood. . . . Like him or not—and many in his own time hated him as they hated the devil—he was an extraordinary leader."[2]

Brigham's authoritarianism and organizational genius spread to the rank and file, and the primary characteristic of the Mormon emigration became order and regimentation around a group enterprise. As Stegner points out,

> Whatever the variants of the myth may say, their story is not a story of hardship. It is a story of organization, foresight, and discipline. Over the next twenty years, trail lore would be codified and regularized until the procedures of a Mormon wagon train achieved the precision of a skilled trade. Gentile trains, except for their guides, were essentially amateur; but in all later Mormon trains there was a good number of professionals who had been back and forth between Salt Lake and the Missouri from five to forty times.

Illustrating this Mormon bent for meticulous organization, Stegner emphasizes Howard Egan's inventory of Heber C. Kimball's outfit, which Egan carried down to the last half cent ($1,592.87½). And the pinpoint accuracy of William Clayton's *Emigrant's Guide* actually was appreciated "more by Gentile than by Mormon, for the Saints, sheep guided by careful shepherds, had no need of a guidebook except to satisfy their curiosity about where they were."[3]

But Stegner cannot sustain the synecdoche consistently. By his own admission, Brigham Young sometimes succumbed to overweening optimism. The Thirteenth General Epistle of 1855 was his hyperventilating handcart proposal that Stegner calls "the statement of a man who wanted something to be possible, not of one who knew it to be."[4] When the hapless Franklin D. Richards encouraged the tardy handcart companies of 1856 to proceed, thus dooming many of them to death in the snow, he was only promoting Brigham's overoptimistic estimate of the speed at which such a company could travel, but his unwise zeal earned him a rare public rebuke and exclusion for many years from any real power in the Mormon hierarchy.

Further, Stegner mistakes the unifying authority of Brigham's personality for an ethos of the Mormon emigrants as a whole. Disunity, for example, characterized the Big Company of 1847: "Through nearly the whole thousand miles of uncomfortable travel it kept breaking out again as bickering, road-hogging, and angry clashes of will."[5] Stegner blames the absence of Brigham Young for that disunity, yet there were Mormon apostles in the party, and if the group ethos had penetrated as far into the Mormon people by that time, as Stegner wants us to believe, their authority should have been sufficient to hold things together. In spite of this disunity, he writes, referring to the Mormon rank and file, "Only their faith, the authority of the priesthood, and the peculiarly coherent social system that their faith encouraged made them different from the adventurous, independent, and violent men who made the trip under other auspices." Yet, he tells us that the mere absence of Brigham Young found the returning parties of 1847 "close to mutiny and violence through a good part of their return journey, and [they] arrived not as austerely disciplined companies but as a rabble of backbiting stragglers."[6]

Abandoning Stegner's synecdoche appears to make possible a much more plausible explanation of the Mormon migration. Both Mormon and Gentile emigrants learned through bitter experience that careful planning and tight organization were necessary for a successful trip. Rather than the ragtag individualists that Stegner—and some Mormon observers—wished to make them, most Gentile wagon trains were well-organized, with elected leaders and regimented camp routines. The necessities of the trail and the experienced guides they hired encouraged at least a minimal level of organization.[7] Both Mormon and Gentile emigrants learned the necessity for organization, but it seems the Mormons actually learned it later, on trips where the iron fist of Brigham Young was absent and they had to draw upon other resources. In time, the Mormon priesthood, especially those with the experience of many trips, asserted the leadership that Gentile parties created by democratic election.

Stegner's interpretive error at this point is an overemphasis on Mormon exceptionalism. After growing up in Utah but later living in other parts of the country, Stegner was impressed by the uniqueness of Mormonism and the Mormon people. And he had learned from Bernard DeVoto that the frontier was a place where exceptional people did exceptional things. Finally, Stegner's concern that his work would not be well-received among the Mormons led him to let them have their history their own way insofar as it could be made to fit his critical assessment of the sources. In his quest for a sympathetic readership among the Mormons, Stegner followed the example of the Fort Laramie trader James Bordeaux who, he says, "diplomatically . . . made [the Mormons] feel what in fact they were—disciplined and well-behaved—and demonstrated what has become a truism since: that no one is so popular among the Saints as a Gentile who expresses a good opinion of them."[8]

Dramatization of his subject is another insistent problem in *The Gathering of Zion*. Stegner's basic assumption is that a reality exists beneath historical facts that the facts themselves cannot adequately convey. Therefore the facts presented must be carefully selected and even shaped through a poetic license to convey that reality. Nothing, perhaps, is wrong with this assumption, but it is the assumption of the novelist, not the historian. "You choose to play up one scene because of its dramatic or thematic value," he told Richard Etulain, "and tone down others." When dealing with major public figures like Abraham Lincoln or John C. Fremont, Stegner says, the historian has to stick to the facts, for they are "public events, historical events that are almost everybody's property," but in dealing with more obscure characters, "one has more latitude in straying from fact to get at a larger truth."[9]

The Gathering of Zion, which largely concerns the obscure, common people who made up the bulk of the Mormon migration, often exhibits this fictional license. Stegner speaks of his characters as though they were in a stage play and he is the director. He introduces imagined details to flesh out the historical record and he strays from the past tense into the present and future, giving the impression that he holds the characters in his hands and is shaping them for the role he has predetermined for them.

As the Mormon wagons approached the Mississippi ferry taking them from Nauvoo out onto the first stage of the trail, Stegner says, "They come in an irregular procession, horses humped back in the breeching down the slope, oxen heaving to drag loaded wagons through the mud, men with whips and goads, boys driving loose stock, women tight-mouthed on the wagon seats, children peering out from the bows or darting between the wheels.[10]

This is a vivid scene, and a delight only Stegner could create. But it is imagined detail, and the historian's craft simply does not allow for such flights of fancy. We have to make our delight out of the data the records provide.

And Stegner telescopes time in a way that suggests a Calvinistic predestination. Consider Charles Coulson Rich, for example, one of "Brigham's dependables, a six-foot-four Tennessean, . . . a fighter and doer." After recounting his marital history (five wives dutifully, if not emotionally, wed), Stegner goes into Rich's future without so much as a paragraph break. He will take another wife on the trail, become a member of the Quorum of the Twelve, play a large role in western history, and co-found the city of San Bernardino.[11] Stegner's characters stagger around under the weight of their future as well as of their past and present.

Stegner's Calvinism also gives him a predictive power over his characters. Once he has established their basic nature, he can predict their behavior in any circumstance, real or not. The ever-optimistic Ursulia Hascall impressed Stegner so much that his confidence in her ability to make do in untoward circumstances became unbounded. "In a people remarkable for the capacity to survive, Ursulia had a special knack for survival. She could have existed, if she had to, in places and on food that would have let others starve. She could see plenty in a barren prairie. She would have learned the Omaha trick of robbing the nests of field mice of their hoards of wild wood-pea seeds.[12]

That Hascall never tested Stegner's hypothesis and actually did these things disturbed Stegner not in the least. Having established survival as her nature, she could not have acted otherwise.

Finally, *The Gathering of Zion* contains an anti-Turnerian interpretation of the frontier that Stegner only sketched out and never returned to in his later writings. Late in the book, he focuses on Sir Richard Burton's caustic portrait of Dawvid Lewis, an atavistic Scottish Mormon who, with two equally degraded Irish sisters as wives, ran a way station at Ham's Fork, Wyoming. Stegner presents them as examples of the frontier process at work.

> Their often-slovenly humanity teaches us that much is lost when civilized people go out upon a frontier. The original Mormons were, as Thomas Kane testified, more civilized, better behaved, and cleaner than their neighbors. That advantage tended to dwindle under conditions of hardship and deprivation, and the influx of the underprivileged of Europe. . . . [By 1860] the human race had begun already to pollute its new environment; frontier naturalness and health and freedom had begun already to give way to the second stage of settlement, which is generally merely backward, dirty, and deprived.[13]

In other words, the frontier did not produce the self-reliant, democratic yeoman of Jeffersonian myth, but rather the shiftless, degraded hillbilly memorialized in American history and literature in such figures as Thomas Lincoln and Pap Finn.

Although not immune to that frontier atavism, as Dawvid Lewis and his wives prove, the Mormons had a quality that, according to Stegner, enabled them quickly to recover the higher level of civilization they had originally brought to the frontier. Tracing the Mormon overland route backward in the last chapter of *The Gathering of Zion* brought Stegner eventually to Nauvoo, Illinois, where the migration had begun. There he found evidence of a high civilization that the Mormons eventually replicated in Salt Lake City. "Though some early

Mormons were born poor, and many achieved poverty, and many more had poverty thrust upon them," he tells us, "indigence was not their natural state, and they recovered from it with great promptness when left alone."[14]

This is an intriguing if not original idea, and one is disappointed that it appears in *The Gathering of Zion* more as a grafted-on afterthought than as a vital interpretive framework. But it belongs perhaps more properly in a general study of Mormon civilization than in Stegner's book, which is a tightly focused history of the Mormon Trail. Stegner overburdens his skimpy evidence by asking one isolated example of an atavistic rural Mormon family, contrasted with the civilized attainments of their urban brethren in Salt Lake City, to sustain an entire theory of the frontier.

One may legitimately object that Stegner's literary devices—synecdoche, collapsing the past and the future into the present, and fictionalized detail—ought not to be banned from historical exposition. Are not historians proverbially unimaginative writers? It is true that most historians could learn something about writing from Stegner, but there are also major perils in bending the rules in casual pursuit of literary elegance. Regarding synecdoche, for example, although a novelist or a poet may need nothing but samples, as Robert Frost said, the complexity and nuance of historical detail are both the glory and the usefulness of history.[15] Historical figures are not characters in a morality play, and Stegner's judgmental assessments have given history, as Marc Bloch warns us, "the appearance of the most uncertain of disciplines. Robespierrists! AntiRobespierrists! For pity's sake, simply tell us what Robespierre was."[16] Just as Major Powell's role in western history is more comprehensible if we stop looking at him as a synecdoche of some larger idea like science or a proto–Sierra Clubber, but as a complex human being, so the complexities of Mormon history and culture come forth when we stop seeing them as simply a synecdoche for organization.

And how much better it is to allow a person's future to unfold through chronological narrative than to weigh him down with it in the cradle. If the future is predetermined, we are writing physics, not history, so why not let the real alternatives, the real uncertainties we face each day confront our historical subjects as well? Looking west from the banks of the Mississippi, C. C. Rich undoubtedly had his apprehensions as well as his ambitions, and it seems more realistic to let his struggles with those contradictory forces emerge as time passes.

The field of history has traditionally embraced historical fiction, popular history, and serious, scientific history. Stegner functioned admirably in the first two genres, but less successfully in the third. While nervously denying professional competence in the field of history, he nevertheless wrote what he wished to be taken as serious historical exposition. But he never got both feet planted firmly in scholarly historical study. Those who do are uncomfortable with two apparent primary assumptions beneath Stegner's historiography (and DeVoto's as well): that history is fundamentally boring, and that it is incomprehensible. In this view, history needs help from the historians, and Stegner could therefore not resist stage managing the facts, downplaying or ignoring some things, throwing a full spotlight on others, and providing imaginary connective tissue whenever the excitement seemed to flag. On the other hand, history for both Stegner and DeVoto had to be relentlessly and accessibly didactic. To make sure we did not miss its lessons, they employed cartoon characters and primary colors, something Stegner would never have resorted to in his fiction. Nuance, complexity, and ambiguity are all qualities we expect in fictional characters, and one wonders why Stegner thought the real people of history deserved anything less.

Fawn McKay Brodie

Fawn McKay Brodie

THE EXORCIST

No Man Knows My History, Fawn McKay Brodie's classic biography of the Mormon prophet Joseph Smith, opens with a humorous anecdote about Sharon, Vermont, Smith's birthplace, that may well have applied to her own birthplace of Huntsville, Utah. An old gazetteer, she reports, suddenly loses its enthusiasm when it comes to Sharon and describes it as "the birthplace of that infamous imposter, the Mormon prophet Joseph Smith, a dubious honor Sharon would willingly relinquish to another town."[1] No such opprobrium in any Utah gazetteer is attached to Huntsville, birthplace of one of Mormondom's best literary figures but also one of its most infamous apostates. Perhaps this is because it was also the birthplace of Thomas E. McKay, her father, a Mormon stake president (an important regional authority) and majority leader in the state senate, and her uncle, David O. McKay, one of the most beloved presidents of the Mormon Church. This contrast within the McKay family was one of the fundamental conflicts in Fawn McKay Brodie's life.

Huntsville, Utah, is situated in one of the state's most picturesque settings, a verdant mountain valley east of Ogden on the west slope of the Wasatch Mountains. An agricultural community near the south fork of the Ogden River, Huntsville has never boasted a population of more than about five hundred. A beautiful place to visit, it is a harsh place to live. The thin mountain air at 4,900 feet provides little shelter from the sun's rays in the summer and little to hold in the heat as the temperature plunges below zero in the winter. One of Huntsville's main attractions today is the Catholic monastery, Our Lady of the Holy Trinity (ironic since the population was uniformly Mormon in Brodie's youth), founded in 1947 by the Trappists (Cistercians of the Strict Observance), which now occupies some two thousand acres of highly productive and highly coveted farmland.[2] Both groups, willing to endure privation to achieve their ends—the Mormons an earthly Zion, and the Trappists a life of work, prayer, and penance—have found an ideal home in Huntsville.

Brodie was born in Huntsville at a crucial time. Calling any time a "time of transition" is often meaningless, for history itself is a never-ceasing process of change. But Mormonism, at the time of Brodie's birth in 1915, was in the midst of a fundamental cultural transition from the world of Brigham Young to the world of . . . David O. McKay. Politics that had been divided along religious lines between Mormon and Gentile was yielding to divisions along national party lines; the authoritarian leadership of the days of Brigham Young was giving way to a more democratic ethos in which the church would find subtler ways to exert influence; the cooperative Mormon economy was breaking up into competitive free enterprise; polygamy had been outlawed and was practiced by only a few die-hard fundamentalist sects; a secular public education system was replacing the old Mormon ward schools and Protestant missionary academies. Utah, which had in the nineteenth century prided itself on its cross-grained opposition to mainstream American culture, was now on the way to becoming its embodiment. It was surely one of the most thoroughgoing cultural reversals in history.[3]

If there could have been such a thing as a conventional Mormon upbringing in those unsettled times, Fawn McKay experienced it. Life in the huge McKay farmhouse made for "an idyllic childhood," Brodie recalled, "as far as the freedom and the affection and the sense of belonging to a community was concerned." But, she added ominously, "it was also very parochial." She must have been aware of the tensions within the larger culture, for they were present in her own family. Her mother, Fawn Brimhall McKay, was what Brodie would later call "a kind of quiet heretic," trying to play a supportive role as wife of an apostle in a religion she no longer could accept. As her daughter's religious doubts began to emerge later, she found a silent sympathy in her mother, but for the mother it was a desperately stressful existence that exploded late in her life in repeated suicide attempts.[4]

Fawn was a precocious student from the beginning of her formal education, which began at home because of a whooping cough epidemic. Her mother taught her and her older sister according to a system recommended by Dean Brimhall, her mother's brother, who held a Ph.D. in psychology from Columbia University. By the time Fawn was ready to enroll in school she was already reading far above her age level and was able to skip several grades. Upon completing elementary school in Huntsville and high school in Ogden, she was a confirmed bookworm and one of the class intellectuals.

A member of the Mormon aristocracy like Fawn McKay would ordinarily have attended Brigham Young University, especially since her maternal grandfather, George Brimhall, had been its president. But she had reasons to begin at Weber College in Ogden, a two-year Mormon institution, then to finish at the University of Utah. Both were closer than BYU, a hundred-mile journey from Huntsville, where Fawn was needed for farm work. And BYU had dismissed George Brimhall, unjustly according to the family, and there was still a grudge against the flagship Mormon university.

Although the student body at the University of Utah was perhaps five times that of tiny Weber College, it was still a very small institution of only six buildings clustered around the u-shaped "circle" with the Park Building at its apex. Fawn's experience at both colleges shows that an institution's size is irrelevant to its educational quality, for she found teachers and programs at both places that nurtured and challenged her powerful intellect. She read widely—the core of any authentic higher education. Also, she traveled. As a member of the debate team at both schools, she journeyed as far east as Indiana (with a visit to Chicago) and as far west as California. Finally, at the University of Utah, she encountered a cosmopolitan faculty and student population that began challenging the parochial certainties of the Mormon culture of Huntsville.

At the university, Fawn barely missed meeting Wallace Stegner, although they became good friends later. He had graduated in 1930 and did not return as a faculty member until the year she graduated, 1934. And apparently she also missed Dale Morgan, who was a freshman during her senior year, even though they had a mutual friend in Jarvis Thurston. Her friendship with Morgan, which began in 1943 when she was half finished with her Joseph Smith biography, was of incalculable importance for her budding career as a historian and biographer during the early 1940s when they were both living in Washington, D.C. They were both researching early Mormon history, though their friendship grew less intimate when her interests broadened beyond Mormon and western history.[5]

Fawn was a popular English teacher at her alma mater, Weber College, during one school year, 1934–35. With her older sister, Flora, who was teaching elementary school in Ogden that year, she rented a house that was big enough for the entire McKay family to escape the Huntsville winter. Her academic promise led her to pursue a graduate degree in English for the following year, and she chose the University of Chicago. Chicago offered several attractions, scholarly and personal. It was a long way from Berkeley, where a boyfriend for whom her family had lukewarm enthusiasm was studying entomology. Also, Fawn's father happened to be a friend of Robert Maynard Hutchins, the ambitious new president of the university, who was beginning a career as a leader in American higher education. Lastly, the already famous divinity school at Chicago had attracted many Mormon students, and they formed a community Fawn's parents thought would protect her so far from Mormon country.

Alas, it was at Chicago that she lost whatever was left of her Mormon faith, married outside that faith, and began the research that would lead to her biography of Joseph Smith, the most frontal scholarly assault ever made on the foundations of the Mormon religion. Fawn had maintained at least an outward involvement with Mormonism during her college years, even though doubts had entered through her reading, her classes, and discussions with non-Mormon students. She was known to bear eloquent witness to her Mormon faith from time to time in church meetings. But those doubts grew at

Chicago into a quiet apostasy. A roommate, for example, ridiculed the story of the golden plates from which Joseph Smith claimed to have gotten the Book of Mormon, but which had later been taken away from human view by an angel. This story, difficult for any skeptic to accept, was particularly unpalatable to students at the University of Chicago, where Hutchins and Mortimer Adler were developing the Great Books program, which was based on reading original texts directly. Fawn herself might perhaps have been willing to accept the disappearance of the stone tablets of Moses during many centuries of warfare, captivity, and destruction, but not the golden plates of Mormonism. It all smacked of obfuscation and improbability.

As the remaining foundations of her faith were being knocked down, Fawn was also swept off her feet by Bernard Brodie, a fellow student and Chicago native, and a non-practicing Jew. After completing a doctorate in international relations, Brodie went on to become an expert on defense strategy and a confidant of diplomats such as Henry Kissinger. He was bright, extroverted, and romantic, and he apparently struck Fawn as a gateway to an exciting new cosmopolitan life of intellectual stimulation and love. After a lightning courtship of six months, they were married on the day she received her master's degree in English literature.

Brodie's first two biographies, of Joseph Smith and Thaddeus Stevens, were written while her attention was divided among her literary endeavors, supporting her husband in his doctoral work and moving to various places to advance his career, and keeping house and raising children. But Brodie was energetic and clever at turning the family's various moves into research opportunities. The first opportunity was right at the University of Chicago, where she landed a night job at the library circulation desk while Bernard worked on his doctorate. With few late-night patrons to wait on, Brodie had plenty of time for reading, and she soon learned that the library had a magnificent collection on American religious history, including Mormonism. What may have begun as idle reading spurred by doubts about her childhood religious certainties soon turned into systematic and energetic research into the life and character of Joseph Smith. What she learned both appalled and enraged her, for she came to the conclusion that Smith's stories of angelic visitations, scriptural writings on golden plates translated magically by various occult devices, and his eventual claim to have been a prophet of God were all an immense fabrication. Brodie felt cheated—violated—by Smith and his successors in the Mormon Church who had led her to believe in its divine origin.

By the time he finished his doctorate in 1940, Bernard Brodie was already developing an impressive reputation as an expert on defense strategy, a reputation that led the Brodies to Connecticut, where he accepted a position at Yale, then to Washington, D.C., and finally to Los Angeles. Fawn, having exhausted the Mormon collection at Chicago, used the Yale move to investigate the local New England sources on Mormon origins and the Washington move to exploit the National Archives. She also made occasional trips to the headquarters of the Reorganized Church of Latter Day Saints in Independence, Missouri, and to the archives of the Mormon Church in Salt Lake City.

No major research project is a solitary venture, and Brodie drew upon many friends in her Joseph Smith research.[6] Her uncle, Dean Brimhall, was a major confidant within her own family. Although he had been raised in the Mormon Church and had served a mission to Germany, he had undergone a quiet apostasy of his own. Yet he was close enough to Fawn's family to act as mediator and advisor and an intelligent and knowledgeable sounding board for her ideas. Bernard Brodie, though coming to a knowledge of Mormonism for the first time, was a bright and sympathetic critic who, with Dale Morgan, worked hard to help her mitigate the anger that burst out in early drafts. They helped her understand that a measured tone and a reasoned argument would convince more readers than would an emotional diatribe. Although Morgan helped Fawn with sources, his major contribution was to help refine her arguments as well as mitigate her tone. Three Utah women writers, Vesta Crawford, Claire Noall, and Juanita Brooks, provided data from their own research on Joseph Smith's plural wives. Finally, she secured institutional assistance in the form of a fellowship from Alfred A. Knopf, who eventually published the book.

No Man Knows My History is what Brodie, Dale Morgan, and Bernard DeVoto all referred to as a "naturalistic" biography of the

Mormon prophet, that is, a biography that attempts to explain its subject purely in terms of his personality and environment, with no recourse to supernatural factors.[7] Brodie came to this approach through a study of Smith's boyhood and the culture of poverty and superstition in New England and upstate New York in which he was nurtured, concluding that he "was as much a product" of that region "as Jonathan Edwards."[8] Farmers there, chained to the drudgery of following a plow to eke a living from the sterile soil (a fate young Smith found particularly unappealing), were eager to hear stories of buried treasure and to learn ways of locating that treasure and escaping a life of farm work. By the time he was a teenager, Smith had acquired a reputation as "a likable ne'er-do-well who was notorious for tall tales and necromantic arts and who spent his leisure leading a band of idlers in digging for buried treasure." It was an unproductive enterprise, but probably harmless, and it brought out the salient characteristics of the young man's personality that set him on his particular road to greatness. "He was a gregarious, cheerful, imaginative youth, born to leadership, but hampered by meager education and grinding poverty. . . . Nimble-witted, ambitious, and gifted with a boundless imagination, he dreamed of escape into an illustrious and affluent future."[9]

After his family's move to New York in 1817, Smith found new material upon which to exercise his imaginative powers in the form of ruined remnants of the prehistoric Mound Builders. The Mound Builders were among the first prehistoric Americans to come to the attention of European settlers, and they were a source of endless fascination and speculation. The prehistoric mounds were obvious evidence of large cities, and casual excavation turned up well-crafted artifacts and evidence of metallurgy, which indicated a high level of sophistication. None of this evidence of high civilization, to the untutored mind, could have been the work of the Iroquois culture, the only indigenous people still occupying the region. The Iroquois, stripped of most of their original dignity and cultural integrity by three centuries of white contact, were seen only as drunkards and beggars. If not they, then who were the Mound Builders? New England refugees like the Smiths, steeped in the Biblical culture of Puritanism, speculated that the Mound Builders might have been the Ten Lost Tribes of Israel, who had supposedly vanished from history at the time of the Babylonian Captivity. This theory turned out to be one of anthropology's smelliest red herrings, but it was understandable given the ignorance of the far East and of American Indian cultures and their roots in Mongolia. The prehistoric Ten Tribes offered irresistible temptations as prehistoric Americans. They were Middle Eastern, they were culturally sophisticated, and best of all, they were lost. Among those who proposed this popular theory was one Ethan Smith (no relation), whose *View of the Hebrews* appeared in 1823 and was available to the future Mormon prophet either directly or through popular discussion of its contents.

Brodie's thesis was that all the materials an imaginative young man would need to create the *Book of Mormon* were present in the cultural environment of upstate New York in the 1820s, and that Smith's conception of his own role evolved from that of a simple rural scryer searching for hidden treasure to that of the prophet of a new religion. That evolution took place during the writing of the *Book of Mormon* itself, which began as the story of two groups of Jewish immigrants, the Nephites and the Lamanites, who had crossed the Atlantic several hundred years before Christ. Smith claimed that this story appeared on a set of golden plates he had unearthed on the Hill Cumorah near his home, and that he had translated it by means of various occult implements. He used a "seer stone," which glowed with the true meaning of the ancient writing and could be seen when placed in the bottom of a hat, or a breastplate with lenses that had similar capabilities, which he identified as "Urim and Thummim." Part of the story was that Jesus had visited America after the Resurrection and revealed himself to the ancient inhabitants. America, after a protracted period of apostasy, was to be the site of a restoration of the pure primitive Christian church through the agency of a prophet named Joseph. Thus Smith had combined, in an impressive act of imagination, the occult superstitions of transplanted New Englanders, an explanation of the prehistoric Indian mounds, and a reconciliation of the religious confusion created by the repeated revivals in upstate New York's infamous "Burned-over District" of the early nineteenth century.

What sounds to modern readers like an ungodly slumgullion of popular cultural themes designed to address the yearnings of a particular locality at a particular moment turned out to have a widespread and profound appeal. Smith found his church growing more rapidly than his fertile imagination and ambition could have foreseen. A new indigenous American religion had been born, a religion that has continued to grow to the present day. Along with the growth of his church, Smith grew into the role of religious leader. In his evolution from occult scryer to prophet, Smith first discarded the peepstone and the Urim and Thummim in favor of direct revelations from God, which, as his personal authority over his followers grew, he then largely abandoned in favor of simple personal dictates. "He was transformed," Brodie explains, "from a lowly necromancer into a prophet, surrounded no longer merely by a clientele but by an enthusiastic following with common purposes and ideals."[10]

Brodie's portrayal of Smith as the author of the *Book of Mormon* rather than simply the agent of its translation reveals an interesting and essential irony: She held Smith in higher esteem than his own followers did. Mormon apologists point to Smith's youth and lack of education as evidence that he could only have transmitted the *Book of Mormon* rather than created it, and thus it must be of divine origin. One such apologist, Francis W. Kirkham, said that the translation process occurred at a speed "far beyond his natural ability." Brodie asserted that that speed "was evidence of his ability," adding that "to belittle his creative talent is to do him as great an injustice as to say that he had no learning—a favorite Mormon thesis designed to prove the authenticity of the book." This was not to claim, however, that his literary talent matched his imagination, "for his book lacked subtlety, wit, and style. . . . His characters were pale, humorless stereotypes. . . . [But] there was plenty of bloodshed and slaughter to make up for the lack of gaiety and the stuff of humanity." His "prose style was unfortunate. Joseph's sentences were loose-jointed, like an earthworm hacked into segments that crawl away live and whole." The *Book of Mormon* "clearly reveals in him what both orthodox Mormon histories and unfriendly testimony deny him: a measure of learning and a fecund imagination. . . . The book can best be explained not by Joseph's ignorance nor by his delusions, but by his responsiveness to the provincial opinions of his time." Laziness, it is true, could be charged to him. "He had neither the diligence nor the constancy to master reality, but his mind was open to all intellectual influences."[11]

Brodie's acknowledgment of Smith's creative imagination notwithstanding, her ultimate appraisal of the man's character and significance is devastating. Writing a bad novel is a literary sin with presumably benign ultimate consequences. But passing such a novel off as truth is a transgression of a vastly different magnitude when done for the enhancement of the author's ego as the prophet of a new religion, and at the expense of deceiving thousands of followers who suffered untold expense, privation, and death following the lie. Even the energetic labors of Bernard Brodie and Dale Morgan in mitigating the harshness of Brodie's tone throughout most of her narrative could scarcely conceal the fury of a woman scorned (she had been, as a girl, a victim of Smith's deception) in her summation of the significance of Joseph Smith and his church. Smith's "martyrdom," as his followers are fond of calling his death, was not, Brodie insists, the apotheosis of his prophetic ministry as was, say, the crucifixion of Jesus. His death "was a chance event, wholly incidental to the creed that he created." His lynching has obscured among his followers the simple fact Brodie insists upon, that he died not in the interest of the truth, but in perpetuation of a lie. When William Law published, in the one issue of his newspaper, the *Nauvoo Expositor*, that polygamy was being practiced at Nauvoo by Smith and his followers with his blessing and encouragement, Law was simply telling the truth—a truth that Smith could not permit. Smith, in Brodie's words, "was a builder of temples and cities and kingdoms—most of all, a constructor of continuing fantasy. William Law attacked this fantasy with his simple, almost gentle exposition of reality. A man called Law had called him to account, as his parents never had, and he reacted with lawlessness. It was all extraordinarily symbolic."[12]

Nor was Brodie any easier on the religion he created. With a "ranging fancy, a revolutionary vigor, and a genius for improvisation," Joseph Smith "created a book and a religion, but he could not create a truly spiritual content for that religion." What Mormonism most conspicuously lacks, in Brodie's judgment, is a new and revolutionary spiritual initiative that one finds in each of the great world religions. "Within the dogma of the church there is no new Sermon on the Mount, no new saga of redemption, nothing for which Joseph himself might stand." In that failure Mormonism fell short of becoming "a real religious creation, one intended to be to Christianity as Christianity was to Judaism: that is, a reform and a consummation." Instead, Smith "grafted only two things on New Testament Christianity, himself and his book. Out of the fusion came a new growth, drawing its strength from the great moral code of the old church, and its novelty and flavor from the man."[13]

In the face of words like those, no one, least of all Brodie, could have expected neutral reactions when the book appeared in the stores.[14] Mormon writers Albert E. Bowen, Francis W. Kirkham, Milton R. Hunter, and Hugh Nibley rushed into print with attacks that were heated but lacking in substance. Nibley's *No Ma'am, That's Not History* became a classic of Mormon polemical literature and for years was sold in Utah bookstores alongside the book it was attacking. Dale Morgan called it "something of a slapstick performance" and pointed out that Brodie could "change, say, 20 phrases in your book and you have eliminated nine-tenths of their criticisms [Nibley and the others] without in any way impairing the structure of the biography." Brodie herself observed that if Nibley's critique "is 'a scholar's answer to Mrs. Brodie' then Mormon scholarship has fallen lamentably low, and the contrast with my own leaves nothing to fear. It is as shallow and superficial a piece as has yet appeared." As late as 1996, Reorganized Church of Jesus Christ of Latter Day Saints scholar Roger D. Launius could refer to Nibley's statement that none of Joseph Smith's doctrines had ever undergone the slightest change as "one of the most asinine statements ever written about Mormon history."[15] If the Mormon reaction was shallow and even "asinine," however, it was nevertheless heated and deeply felt, with momentous consequences for Brodie. When she failed to appear before her local church court to answer charges of apostasy, she was formally excommunicated on May 23, 1946, an action that received national press attention but was downplayed in the Utah media.[16]

Non-Mormon reviewers were much more generous. Dale Morgan,

who had been deeply involved in the creation of the book and should have disqualified himself as a reviewer, was predictably enthusiastic, praising Brodie's exploration of Smith's "infinitely complex and steadily enigmatic" personality as a religious figure. Smith's prophetic role, however, was one that he could put on and take off. Morgan emphasizes Brodie's point that "a prophet is a prophet only while he is working at the job," and that while off the job, so to speak, Smith was "an eminently human and entirely understandable being." On the negative side, Morgan thought Brodie understated the role of Brigham Young and let her anger at Smith's deceptive nature show through too conspicuously.[17] The other major reviewers, Vardis Fisher and Bernard DeVoto, properly concentrated their comments on the book's weakest point, the question of Smith's motive. Simply pointing out that Joseph Smith had all the makings of the *Book of Mormon* in his own lively imagination and the cultural materials around him without needing angelic visitors or golden plates skirts the issue of why he wrote it, for other imaginative people had access to the same materials without making such use of them. It is the most necessary and yet the most difficult question for any student of Mormon origins, for writing a fantasy novel of several hundred pages and creating a new religion is an elaborate work avoidance strategy for a lazy farm boy.

Both Fisher and DeVoto scored Brodie (ironically, for one who eventually became a famous psychobiographer) for failing to explore a psychological basis for Smith's actions. Fisher, an Idaho novelist of Mormon background and former director of the Idaho WPA Writers Project, was the author of *Children of God: An American Epic* (1939), a highly regarded novel of early Mormonism. She faulted Brodie for rejecting epilepsy as the source of Smith's delusions.[18] Brodie had found epilepsy in Smith's grandfather, Solomon Mack, but noted that it had been caused by a blow to the head from a falling tree and would not have been passed on to his descendants. "Actually the Mack family," Brodie said, "was marked neither by psychoses nor by literary talent, but rather by a certain nonconformity in thinking and action," or in other words by an entirely rational tradition of religious dissent which Smith had followed.[19] That was not good enough for Fisher, who observed that epilepsy and psychosis are not necessarily synonymous.

Without some psychological explanation, Brodie's thesis of Smith's transformation from prankster to imposter is "a pretty strange metamorphosis" for readers to accept.[20]

For his part, DeVoto was already in print advocating paranoia as Smith's problem, and he stuck to it in his review. While praising the biography as a "brilliant and largely satisfying book" that "has raised writing about Mormonism to the dignity of history—for the first time," DeVoto quickly zeroed in on the question of motive. "In the end everything hinges on his [Smith's] visions, his revelations and his writings," DeVoto insisted, and Brodie explains them on the basis of "an odd and inadequate theory" that Smith was simply a literary artist, "that the medium of prose fiction was the natural expression of his fantasies and religious perceptions." DeVoto then moves into the strange argument that the *Book of Mormon* is of such poor literary quality that it does not qualify as a novel ("The book is not a novel to any literary critic.") and that therefore Brodie's thesis of literary invention is invalid. Having established that to his satisfaction, DeVoto then asserts that "the chapter on paranoia in any standard textbook on psychiatry can be checked against the prophet's career paragraph by paragraph. He was a paranoid personality in process of becoming a paranoiac—and this is wholly without prejudice to his personal magnetism or his religious teaching." Smith had hallucinations, DeVoto claimed, which is indicative of paranoia. "His paranoia was intermittent and in the beginning was slight, but it grew and finally it overcame him."[21]

Perhaps it was the condescending tone of DeVoto's review as much as its dubious psychology and literary theory that led Dale Morgan, ordinarily no controversialist, to abandon his previous reverence for the older man's status as a historian and literary figure and to initiate the exchange of letters discussed in chapter 3.[22] It was an exchange that showed both men at their worst. Morgan, in demolishing DeVoto's paranoia theory, proposed no alternative explanation of Smith's motives and threw the baby out with the water by implicitly rejecting even the need for such an explanation. It was a rejection that, as we have seen, left his own biography of an almost equally enigmatic personality, Jedediah Smith, interpretively thin. For DeVoto's part, what had had a faint scent of *ex cathedra* in his review ("The chapter on paranoia in any standard textbook. . . .") became a full-blown case in his correspondence: "I read psychiatry. I associate with psychiatrists: in twenty years there has never been a time when I was not hashing out the actual behavior of actual neurotics and psychotics with several psychiatrists who were intimate friends of mine."[23]

Brodie by this time became a bystander in the debate over her own book. DeVoto's review delighted her at the same time it outraged Morgan. "I can't pretend to be anything but elated by it," she wrote to Morgan. "I glow a little inside every time I look at it." At the same time, she referred to DeVoto as "a quarrelsome devil, and I marvel that a person of his explosive temperament can be as good a historian as he actually is." Even though DeVoto abandoned the vitriol in his direct communication with her, only chiding her gently that "I think you are not wholly justified in excluding the [paranoia] hypothesis," she confided in Morgan that, according to her reading of the literature on paranoia, DeVoto simply did not know what he was talking about. "I read not only several textbooks on paranoia but also several hundred case histories when I first started research on the book," she claimed. "And it was the case histories in particular which drove me away from DeVoto's thesis." At a later date, she relayed to Morgan a story told her by her husband. "He said that some years ago DeVoto reviewed Nicholas Spykman's book on geopolitics, and apparently tore into it in his usual furious fashion. Ted Dunn wrote a reply, and DeVoto replied to Dunn in much the same manner he replied to you, only this time his theme was, 'I spend all my leisure reading geopolitics. I live with geopoliticians, etc., etc.' "[24]

At the same time Brodie rejected DeVoto's paranoia thesis, she acknowledged that his "passionate plea that a psychological analysis of some sort is essential makes sense," though she also admitted to "a feeling of helplessness on this point."[25] No doubt she felt some of this feeling of helplessness because psychoanalysis was not a fully developed field. Although Sigmund Freud had died in 1939, the total corpus of his work was still more theory than empirical fact, and thus the theorizing of students of Mormonism such as Fisher, DeVoto, and Kimball Young were more in the realm of cocktail party psychologizing than accepted science. Brodie was aware of these shortcomings and was wary of employing psychoanalytic theory in a carefully researched book. Nevertheless, she remained interested in psychology, for DeVoto's review of her book showed the need for probing beneath the surface in a biography of an enigmatic person like Joseph Smith. The field of psychobiography grew up along with Brodie's career; if anything she was slightly ahead of it. Her biographies of Thaddeus Stevens and Sir Richard Burton were both informed by psychoanalytical concepts, and in 1971 she returned to Joseph Smith to apply newly developed psychoanalytical insights to the biographical data she had assembled three decades earlier.

Few biographies in American historiography have had the dominance and staying power of *No Man Knows My History*. To some degree, observes Marvin S. Hill, this is because of the timidity of potential competitors. Mormon scholars have justifiably feared angering their church, whereas non-Mormons have been slow to learn of primary sources in church archives and to take advantage of them. To Brodie's credit, though, Hill adds that the book exhibits a powerful narrative skill, impressive research, and mastery of the secular context within which the Mormon Church began and developed. The book's shortcomings, according to Hill, are its secular point of view, which underestimates Joseph Smith's consciousness of himself as a religious leader in favor of seeking secular or psychological motives. Also, what Hill calls Brodie's sectarianism restricts her focus to the essential rightness or wrongness of Smith's claims often to the exclusion of an examination of their consequences, both in the lives of his followers and in the larger world. Roger Launius emphasizes the latter criticism, pointing out that later historians of Mormonism have allowed Brodie's tight focus on the validity of Smith's claims to restrict their own definition of the range of valid topics of investigation, and in that have made Mormon history a peculiarly insular field.[26]

If stability and tranquillity are necessary elements in a writer's environment, Brodie's second biography, *Thaddeus Stevens: Scourge of the South*, would never have been written. Her life from 1946 to 1959, when it was conceived and created, was perhaps the most turbulent time in her life, and a less determined writer would have found many reasons to give up.[27] The Brodies had four different homes during that time. They moved from the government housing project in New Haven to their rural home in Bethany, Connecticut, to Washington, D.C., and finally to the home in Pacific Palisades, California, where they spent the rest of their lives. Despite the domestic turmoil such moves entailed, they did place Brodie near the two main repositories of Stevens material: Yale University and the National Archives. Also, Brodie's work as a scholar and writer took second place, by her own choice, to her role as wife and mother. Besides her support of Bernard's career and her housekeeping and meal preparation, she had two small boys who were jealous of her time at the typewriter. The Brodies' desire to enlarge their family resulted first in a traumatic miscarriage and then in the birth of another baby, Pamela, who placed even more demands on her time. Finally, Brodie's mother's suicide attempt in 1956, along with her father's declining health, necessitated a visit to Salt Lake City. Her father's death in 1958 brought still more emotional turmoil.

The making of the Thaddeus Stevens book itself was an equally rocky process. Brodie's personal involvement with the Joseph Smith biography, not only in its writing, but in the self-discovery it brought, the distancing from her family and her excommunication, and the strident emotions it aroused in reviewers, engaged her attention so completely that she had little time to make plans for a subsequent project. When at last she began looking for a project, she had trouble finding one of sufficient interest that her competency and access to source material could sustain. Fiction would not impede her as much as history, where she had to leave the home for research, but in the end she realized that her talents and interests were in nonfiction, particularly biography. Her research into the occult during her investigation of Joseph Smith led her for a time to the Fox sisters, the popular spiritualists of the early nineteenth century, but she realized that reporting their seances would not hold her interest for long. Because Brodie was an ardent New Dealer, she admired Eleanor Roosevelt, both for her politics and social activism and for her feminism. Roosevelt, however, was still alive and active, and Brodie realized that she would probably not have the unrestricted access to her papers that she would need. Her attention turned to the Reconstruction era, first through a fascination with the complicated personality and rancorous presidency of Andrew Johnson, and then with his nemesis, Thaddeus Stevens.

An adequate biography of Stevens presented some hurdles. For one thing, it meant mastering a vast literature on one of the most controversial periods in American history, from the Jacksonian era and the abolitionist movement, through the rise of sectionalism and secession, to the Civil War and Reconstruction. Some of the material was already familiar to Brodie, for Joseph Smith had been a sideshow in the cultural and political ferment of the Jacksonian period, but she still faced a great deal of basic reading. Further, as she summarized in the introduction to her book, the controversies surrounding Thaddeus Stevens pursued him beyond the grave and throughout the historical literature so consistently that there was no middle ground on the man and his legacy. Some biographers admired his idealism and uncompromising commitment to his reform goals, whereas others detested him for his puritanical rigidity and punitive wrath against the South. Brodie would be moving into uncharted territory in pursuing an interpretation that would show both the greatness and smallness of her subject.

The book took a laborious route before finding a publisher. The contractual agreement by which Alfred Knopf published the Smith biography gave him the right of first refusal to Brodie's next book, a standard practice in commercial publishing. Knopf at first was eager to see a new Brodie manuscript, but as Brodie's domestic obligations delayed the writing and pressure from Knopf could not get things moving, he gradually lost interest. Her decision to work on Thaddeus Stevens had aroused only a tepid enthusiasm from Knopf, who saw limited sales potential for a biography of a character so reviled as Stevens. As Brodie summarized Knopf's fears to Dale Morgan, "The Democrats won't buy it because it is about a Republican; the Republicans won't buy it because it is about a Radical; the Southerners won't buy it because I am more inclined to defend him than to make him out the monster history has pronounced him to be. The Northerners won't buy it because they don't really give a damn about Negro rights; and the Negroes won't buy it because they don't buy books, anyway."[28] Furthermore, popular writer Ralph Korngold announced that he was also working on a Stevens biography, introducing competition to Brodie's book, even though it turned out that Korngold had no intention of producing something definitive.[29] Finally, the unenthusiastic reviews of Knopf's referees, coupled with his own lack of interest in publishing anything on American radicalism (Brodie suspected), led Knopf to reject the manuscript. Brodie then turned to Princeton University Press, where she had developed a warm relationship with editor Herbert S. Bailey, and it appeared that they would accept the book. But Princeton also turned it down, and Bailey recommended that Brodie submit it to W. W. Norton, who finally brought the book in September 1959.

Initially, Knopf's judgment seemed sound. The book sold poorly—only 1,500 copies in seven months, after which Norton allowed it to go out of print. The reviews, however, told a different story. The book elicited almost universal praise, including accolades from eminent Civil War historians David Donald and Richard N. Current (whose own 1942 biography had been the most recent academic study).[30] In time the book became recognized as the definitive biography of one of American history's most prickly and controversial characters, a deft navigation through the hazards of a biased and polemical literature, and a profound probing into the roots of a famously cross-grained personality. Responding to this favorable assessment, Norton reissued the volume in paperback in 1966.[31]

The success of *Thaddeus Stevens* results from Brodie's delivering on two promises made at the outset: to explain the psychological roots of her subject's personality, and then to construct an interpretation of his personal and political life that explains both his triumphs and his failings. Brodie was inspired and assisted in studying Stevens's personality by a group of psychoanalysts, particularly Ralph R. Greenson, with whom Bernard had become acquainted after their move to California and his own investigation of the psychological roots of the Cold War and nuclear armaments. Psychoanalysis, as her biographer points out, "was very much in vogue" at the time, "with treatment sought not just by individuals in genuine mental or emotional crisis but also by those who felt this therapy was useful in handling life's ordinary demands."[32] In time, both Fawn and Bernard Brodie went into analysis, Fawn for her chronic depression and sexual timidity, and Bernard for his insomnia. It proved more successful for her than for him, and it also led to her new professional orientation toward psychobiography.

That said, *Thaddeus Stevens* could not by any stretch be considered a psychobiography. Brodie's goals were "to suggest what may have been the basis of Stevens' extraordinary capacity for hatred, . . . to explain Stevens' radicalism not only in terms of his activist role [in Reconstruction]. . . but also as an outgrowth of his own desperate inner needs,"[33] but the psychologizing in her book is mostly common sense, devoid of the concepts or terminology of psychoanalytic theory. Thus Brodie sees Stevens's "desperate inner needs" as functions of two childhood disasters: his birth with a club foot and his father's abandonment of his family before Stevens was yet a teenager. Her development of the psychological effects of those events is largely confined to one chapter, though of course she sees these events as affecting the rest of Stevens's life.

In a superstitious New England environment (Stevens was born into a devout Baptist home in Vermont), a club foot was a curse, a sign of the cloven hoof of the devil. How unfortunate for Joshua and Sarah Stevens, then, that their eldest son was born with both feet deformed and their second, Thaddeus, with one. And how ironic (but yet fortunate) that Joshua Stevens happened to be a cobbler by trade, a skill he taught to both his sons. It takes little psychological theorizing to conclude, as Brodie does, that such a physical deformity, which set Stevens apart as an object of ridicule as a child, gave him both a deep-seated pessimism regarding the perfectibility of man and a compassion for the underdog and downtrodden minorities. That pessimism, she goes on to emphasize, was deepened and reinforced by the Calvinist doctrine of his childhood religion, which saw God's separation of mankind into the elect and the damned as quite arbitrary and inexplicable.

During his young adulthood as a lawyer in Gettysburg, Pennsylvania, Stevens maintained pews both in the Presbyterian Church and the Gettysburg College chapel, but rarely occupied either, and in fact lost all interest in organized religion. But, Brodie emphasizes, he never lost his basically Calvinistic view of human nature and its fatalistic conviction that life contained a quotient of inexplicable and unmitigatable tragedy.

On the other hand, that fundamental inconsistency of Calvinism—a belief in an absolutely sovereign God who predestines man's ultimate fate, side by side with a severe work ethic in which man is obligated to make the most of his lot in life—was fully present in Stevens. From his earliest years, Stevens was an implacable opponent of entrenched privilege, whether it was the Phi Beta Kappa honor society or the Masonic order, into both of which he failed to gain admittance, or the feudal caste of white southern planters who unjustly held an entire class of people in slavery. Stevens believed that social injustice could not only be mitigated, it could be obliterated by legislation and litigation, and the pessimistic Calvinist became a crusading idealist in pursuit of that end.

Brodie's *Thaddeus Stevens* gives full play to both sides of the conflicted man, who could hate with a profound and puritanical immovability, yet execute acts of unsolicited and unheralded charity, who could punish white southerners with a relentless fury, yet promote the advancement of black southerners with a boundless idealism. Although disapproving of the man's bottomless capacity for hatred and vindictiveness, Brodie could enjoy his sardonic wit and his serene aloofness from public opinion. Disappointed in Stevens for his nearsighted support for tariffs and other government subsidies for big business that laid the groundwork for the abuses of the Gilded Age, Brodie at the same time admired Stevens as a founder of the social reforms that came to fruition in her own day.

Newell Bringhurst, Brodie's biographer, hits the mark in pointing out that "Brodie's presentation of Thaddeus Stevens as an enlightened reformer clearly reflected her own liberal Democratic orientation."[34] In her introduction, Brodie emphasizes Stevens's dogged pursuit of racial equality, which made Stevens's career seem strikingly relevant to the reform issues of her own day, such as President Truman's integration of the armed forces, school desegregation in *Brown v. Board of Education*, and the civil rights acts of the late 1950s that were being passed even as her book appeared. Stevens's career was worth studying, she asserted, "because he used all three weapons—persuasion, legislation, and force—which are under scrutiny as solutions for the racial problems of our own time," and because the Supreme Court, in the

Brown decision, was at last showing signs of revitalizing the original goals the Fourteenth and Fifteenth Amendments as tools to implement racial equality.[35]

But Brodie's admiration for Stevens as a reformer went far beyond his status as a founding father of the modern civil rights movement. Although she only hints at the analogy, Brodie saw Stevens, with his broad reform program, as something of a proto–New Dealer, an archetype of Franklin D. Roosevelt in both his programs and his basic philosophy of government. Indeed, harbingers of the New Deal appear throughout the book, and Brodie never misses a chance to vote for FDR. If one is looking for a predominant theme in the biography, it is Stevens as a New Dealer rather than a subject of psychobiography.

Brodie uses Stevens's banking policy as an example. When the second Bank of the United States, because of Andrew Jackson's 1832 veto of its recharter bill, ceased to be a national bank in 1836, Stevens pushed through the Pennsylvania legislature a bill chartering it as a state bank (its head office was located in Philadelphia), but at the same time taxing it heavily for the support of free schools. Its director, the canny but twice unfortunate Nicholas Biddle, having met defeat at Jackson's hands, now had to dance to Stevens's tune and accept the tax if he wished to continue in operation at all. And Stevens's idea of financing the Civil War by issuing inflationary greenback dollars was, in Brodie's view, a farsighted means of taxing the American people in the least painful way, an expedient that was followed in the First and Second World Wars. In both of these instances, one can see Brodie's vote for the Banking Act of 1935 and the centrally controlled and flexible Federal Reserve system.

The Freedmen's Bureau, which Brodie calls "the nation's first large-scale experiment in social welfare," is another example. Andrew Johnson, in this case, plays the role of Herbert Hoover by advocating a do-nothing policy regarding southern economic and social problems, trusting instead in the old white leadership to resolve them. Stevens is Brodie's FDR, insisting that the magnitude of the problem and the apathy of local leaders makes it imperative to assert federal authority. The planters themselves are the callous capitalists waiting for things to return to a *status quo ante bellum*, while Bureau director General O. O. Howard, "an imaginative and able administrator, compassionate toward white and black man like" is an 1860s Harry Hopkins.[36]

Only in his land redistribution policy, in which Stevens succumbed to anti-planter vindictiveness, did Brodie find him falling short of the creative vision of an FDR. In contrast with Abraham Lincoln, who thought blacks were incapable of living together in equality with whites and who advocated deporting blacks to Africa or the Caribbean, Stevens was an ardent proponent of complete social, economic, and political equality. Such a policy, Brodie points out, would have kept the South's primary labor force in the South and thus would have made Stevens more of a friend to the southern white man than Lincoln, the perceived moderate. But Stevens wanted to create small farmsteads for the Freedmen out of plantation land confiscated from the rebels. It was a dangerous policy, as demonstrated at Port Royal and other sea island land redistribution projects. It failed to give the Freedmen adequate title to the land and enabled whites to take the land back by legal chicanery. Much better, Brodie thinks, to have resettled them on unoccupied western lands (like the Resettlement Administration) or granted them small, low-interest loans to purchase southern property (like the Farm Security Administration).[37]

Finally, Brodie emphasizes that again like FDR, Stevens found his belief in the checks and balances doctrine of the federal government sorely tested by an uncooperative Supreme Court. In the Milligan and McCardle cases,[38] the Court threatened to upset the foundation of military authority in the South and the civil rights legislation upon which Stevens had based his entire Reconstruction program. Protecting that program taxed the wily old lawyer and legislator's resources to the limit, and it even brought him to propose, in an eerie premonition of FDR's unfortunate Judiciary Reorganization Bill of 1937, to enlarge (i.e., "pack") the court to fifteen justices and offer fully paid retirement to justices over age seventy.[39] Unlike FDR, however, who sought an enlarged executive authority at the expense of the legislature and judiciary, Stevens sought an enlarged legislative authority at the expense of the other two branches, something along the lines of the British parliamentary system.[40]

Brodie's skill in establishing a balanced view of her controversial subject is the chief asset of *Thaddeus Stevens*, which lacks the anger and cynicism that mar her Smith biography. Stevens's uncompromising pursuit of his utopian dream of full racial equality was a noble goal, but it was vitiated by his oratorical invective and harshly punitive measures. Because of his unreasoning zeal, Brodie likens him to a Robespierre without the guillotine.[41] The pathological element in his zeal also inhibits admiration. "Like all Utopians, he could not be content with any triumph, however complete, because his political visions were largely an escape from his own desperate hungers." Nevertheless, she gives the whole of his career in high marks as a steppingstone toward modern America. Stevens "pushed vigorously toward the centralization and consolidation of the federal power, and helped transform what was a sprawling, invertebrate country into a unified nation, responsive to strong central leadership."[42]

Brodie's next biography, *The Devil Drives: A Life of Sir Richard Burton*, focused on the colorful and eccentric English explorer and linguist.[43] Burton would seem an awkward choice of subject for Brodie, who was making her name as a biographer of Americans, but she came to Burton quite naturally through his *City of the Saints*, his narrative of his 1860 journey to Salt Lake City. Alfred Knopf had asked Brodie to prepare an introduction to a modern edition of *City of the Saints*,[44] and she became quite taken by Burton. She recalled, "I found I was doing twice as much research as I needed to for an introduction and realized very quickly that I was lost to this man, who was fascinating beyond belief." Her son went even further, asserting that she became, quite literally, "passionately in love" with Burton. She decided to extend her research to a full-length biography, a book she said "was, in every way, a fun book to write and to research."[45]

It is not surprising that Burton, the archetype of the dashing European explorer, would sweep Brodie off her feet and into her sole biographical venture outside America. Noted in his day for his bohemian life and frank speech, frontal assaults against European respectability, for the heart-throbbing romance of his expert swordsmanship and frequent disguises as an Arabian merchant or holy man, and for his dangerous entries as a pilgrim into the holy cities of Islam, Burton, with his dark good looks and his famous demonic gaze, was a magnet to women on several continents. Nor was his appeal solely on the surface. Burton was one of Europe's foremost linguists, with a command of more than forty tongues and dialects, a pioneering anthropologist and folklorist, and an accomplished poet and translator with several dozen books to his credit. It is no wonder, then, that Burton has exerted a hypnotic appeal (he was expert in that art as well) over biographers before and since Brodie and even to filmmakers. He was memorably portrayed in a BBC series, "The Search for the Nile," in the 1970s, and Bob Rafelson's 1987 movie "Mountains of the Moon," features the arrestingly handsome Patrick Bergin, who plays Burton to a fare-thee-well.[46]

There are more reasons why Burton would have appealed to Brodie, such as his scorn for religious hypocrisy and his interest in the nature of race and of race relations. But Brodie's biographer, Newell Bringhurst, perceptively observes that Burton, the sexual adventurer, the fearless translator and publisher of Oriental erotica in Victorian England, and partner in a troubled and perhaps sexless marriage, offered Brodie an irresistible avenue through which she could explore, in her Mormon upbringing and difficult marital relations, the roots of her own repressed sexuality.[47] Although she had made her first ventures into psychobiography in *Thaddeus Stevens*, psychoanalytical tools are conspicuous throughout *The Devil Drives*. They appear in her examinations of Burton's relationship with his parents (particularly his mother), of his marriage with the sexually repressed Isabel Arundel, of Isabel's own psyche and duplicity that were equal to Burton's, and in her sometimes tediously detailed recounting of Burton's studies of literary erotica and of sexual customs and deviancies. Even to a twenty-first-century reader jaded by the ubiquity of sex in the culture and the eroding barriers between the normal and the deviant, Brodie's preoccupation with the latter theme seems a bit more than is necessary to a well-rounded biography.

A recent Burton biographer, Edward Rice, praised *The Devil Drives* as "the first attempt at a scholarly biography" of the complex explorer and credited Brodie for having "unearthed material previously unpublished, lost, or unknown." But he criticizes her application of "twentieth-century Freudian analysis to an individual of another century whose world was not West Coast suburban and academic America but revolutionary Europe, colonial Asia, unknown Black Africa, and a Muslim Levant in turmoil."[48] It is an interesting criticism, more than a mere lack of appreciation for psychobiography, and it deserves more serious consideration. To what degree is Freudian analysis applicable to members of non-Western cultures like Burton, whom Rice considers to have "gone native" (in the nineteenth-century phrase)? The world of Freud himself, of course, was not "West Coast suburban and academic America" either, though it seems reasonable that Freudian analysis is more apt in diagnosing the ills of the modern Western world than in diagnosing those of the Third World—as are the economic and political diagnoses of his contemporary Karl Marx. Brodie, however, considers Burton, for all his profound immersion in various non-Western cultures, to have remained at bottom a man of the West, a man who "was primarily intent upon bringing the East to the West, and he was at his best in showing the impact of one culture upon another."[49]

Brodie's fascination with Burton's interior life enabled her to bring another dimension to the biography. No Burton biography, she acknowledged, could fail to emphasize his amazing feats as an explorer. "In a world where there seemed to be very little left to be discovered, he sought out the few remaining mysteries." In her view, what really distinguished Burton from other explorers, in addition to his un paralleled linguistic facility, was his constant focus on the diverse perspectives on human nature and experience that his geographical explorations made possible. "Burton's real passion," she insists, "was not for geographical discovery but for the hidden in man, for the unknowable, and inevitably the unthinkable." It was that aspect of Burton's intellect that placed him ahead of his fellows and indeed ahead of his time. "In this respect he belongs more properly to our own day. . . . Precursor of Havelock Ellis and Sigmund Freud, he anticipated many of their insights." Those insights were possible to Burton because he possessed a capacity for objectivity in his observation of non-Western cultures that his contemporaries lacked. "Burton could be more detached a commentator than most of his fellow officers because he was no longer in any sense a practising Christian, and in fact deplored the Christianization of native peoples."[50] But Burton paid for those insights with alienation from his own culture caused by his scorn for Christianity, and with his troubled relations with his devoutly Catholic wife.

As a devoted disciple of Dale Morgan, Brodie left no door closed in her dogged pursuit of Burton sources, feeling spurred, no doubt, to extraordinary diligence by the knowledge that Isabel Burton had put the torch to virtually all of her husband's half-century accumulation of personal journals. A brief sojourn in France in 1960 had permitted no time for research, but a return trip in 1963 enabled her to exploit archives and private collections in England and to visit Greece, Turkey, and Egypt on Burton's trail. Her efforts were productive, uncovering Burton correspondence, marginal notes, and even a few pages of his journal of the trip to Salt Lake City. With similar documents discovered in California and her acquisition of an almost complete set of Burton's writings, Brodie was the master of more Burton materials than any previous writer.

Like the good Freudian she was, Brodie found the roots of Burton's personality in his relations with his parents. His father, a minor Irish aristocrat and former soldier, spent most of his time during Burton's youth in indolent living on the continent apart from his wife. His influence was negligible except for the opportunity he provided his son to learn French and Italian (he had already been studying Latin and Greek since ages three and four) and develop his famous love for travel. Like his father, Burton became a professional soldier. Burton's mother, however, was profoundly influential, mostly because of the mixed messages she gave Burton and his brother, on one hand exposing them to temptations, for example, of foods that she would then forbid them to eat, but on the other hand taking delight when they rebelled against her. Brodie also makes much of an execution by guillotine of a woman who had killed her children, which Burton's French schoolmaster allowed his class to watch. In the boy's developing psyche, he associated his punishing mother with violence and death.

Burton's rebellion against his mother's punitive behavior took the form of lying, a pattern Brodie would also note in Joseph Smith and Richard Nixon. All were imposters, though she capitalized the word as a psychoanalytical term only when applied to Smith in the appendix to the revised edition of *No Man Knows My History*.[51] Lying was no less fundamentally a part of Burton's personality than Smith's (nor, as we shall see, of Nixon's). "Burton never wholly abandoned lying," Brodie tells us; "he lied to shock, to amuse, and above all to catch and hold an audience. And in a deeper sense, since his lying made all reality relative, it also made the truth he could not bear to face less painful." Because Burton also had to represent himself as a scientist, juggling truth and fiction became more desperate a necessity for Burton than for Joseph Smith, who, Brodie contends, was able to create a huge lie and then live inside it. Burton could manufacture a large deception like the disguise under which he entered the holy cities of Islam, but he then had to distance himself from that lie to report as scientific truth what he had learned there. "The struggle against fakery was always with Burton, the master of disguise," Brodie observes, "and though he was guilty of some dissimulation about himself, it was never true of his descriptions of native peoples. Here he wrote with exactness," even burdening his books with elaborate appendices and footnotes "as if to show that as a writer if not as a man there must be no doubt of his integrity."[52]

The self-created legend of Burton as a rake and sexual adventurer was one place where truth and fiction mingled. Beyond his good looks, Burton had a charisma that attracted women, and there is no reason to doubt his reports of liaisons with various Asian women during his travels. Brodie is also inclined to accept the suspicions of Burton's army superiors in India that in carrying out his assignment to investigate the male brothels of Karachi, he personally availed himself of their services—a rumor that nearly ended his military career and dogged his reputation for the rest of his life. But Brodie also sees Burton's obsession with Oriental sexual practices and sexual acts that were regarded as deviant in his own culture as rooted in personal sexual inhibitions and failures. "A conviction was born in him—perhaps intensified by failures in his own life, or by sampling the wide variety in the sexual market—that there was in the East a reservoir of experience against which the West, especially England, foolishly barricaded itself with dams of false modesty and shame. One day he would loosen the floodgates." Burton's translation and publication of Oriental erotica seems to have had little if any effect on the dammed-up prudery of Victorian England, but resistance only fueled his determination. "Whatever was most forbidden," Brodie notes, "he felt compelled to describe."[53]

Burton's openness to new languages, new cultures, and new experiences, however tangled its roots may have been, was the key to his greatness as an explorer and scientist and the cause of his greatest personal frustrations—the feud with John Hanning Speke and his complicated marriage. Both Speke and Isabel Arundel began as Burton acolytes, intoxicated with his intelligence, his audacious courage, and his bohemian disregard for convention. Each, however, came to realize that requiring those qualities in his disciples, which Burton did, was a big order. Speke was the first to fall away in the rarefied air of Burton discipleship, and it happened during their celebrated joint expedition to find the central African source of the Nile. Brodie points out that Burton became contemptuous of Speke's helplessness caused by his linguistic limitations, which included no real facility in any foreign tongues and only a bare smattering of Hindustani, which was useless in Africa. And Speke's theory of the racial inferiority of blacks to whites, which was grounded in the Biblical curse on Ham, struck Burton as ridiculous. Burton himself suspected the black race might be inferior to the white, but he suspended judgment and sought scientific data that would support or refute the notion. Speke, in short, was simply too bound up in Western culture and prejudices to make him suitable as a Burton companion, and a rift developed between the two. Speke "was inhibited and prudish," Brodie asserts. "Burton was like a sponge, Speke a stone." Speke perhaps sensed that "Burton held his own solid British virtues in contempt, and found him after six months to be not only a dull fellow but also an intolerable prig. If so, it was Africa first of all that came between them."[54] Speke's credulity as an explorer, in maintaining that the Nile flowed northward out of Lake Victoria without actually having seen it, precipitated the break with Burton and their eventual debate before the Royal Society in London that led to Speke's apparent suicide. Brodie's explanation was that the basic rift between them was cultural at its roots, between East and West.

Burton's marital problems with Isabel were also cultural at bottom, but this time because, as Brodie put it, he was a man of the twentieth century and she was a woman of the Middle Ages.[55] Devoutly Catholic, she avoided debating religion with Burton while she secretly prayed for his conversion, surreptitiously baptized him while he was unconscious, and subjected his remains to two elaborate Catholic funerals. On the other hand, she railed against her subordination as a wife in the marriage and longed to ride by her husband's side as an equal in his explorations. Psychoanalyzing a dream Isabel reported having during a visit to Jerusalem, Brodie sees in it "her rage, contempt, and longing for power." During Burton's consulate in Trieste, Isabel founded The Society for the Prevention of Cruelty to Animals and referred to herself in her marriage as an abused animal. Brodie speculates that Isabel's tragic destruction of her husband's papers after his death was motivated by a fear that his journals, because of what she knew to be their absolute honesty, would "give the lie to the idealized romance she had made their marriage out to be." Burton never fully understood the wellsprings of his wife's nature. "Master of disguise, he never fully comprehended that he had married a woman with whom dissimulation was a way of life. He knew far better than most men of his time the punishing effects upon a woman of frustration and frigidity, but he had no special insight into the capacity for unconscious revenge of a woman with a blighted sexual life."[56]

It does not seem too long a reach to see in Brodie's portrayal of the Burtons' marriage (as her biographer does) an examination of her own marriage, her struggles to find her role as partner to the urbane, intelligent, and successful Bernard Brodie, and to come to grips with what she saw as her own medieval background in rural Mormonism. The tools of psychoanalysis, which were not available to the Burtons, helped the Brodies through their similar problems. Nevertheless, it is possible to see echoes of her own marriage in Brodie's summation of the Burtons' relationship. "The Burtons did not live with each other, as an ordinary couple; they lived through each other, both providing a component the loss of which would have been intolerable."[57]

Brodie's last two biographies, of Thomas Jefferson and Richard Nixon, are her least satisfying ones, mostly because there is so little of the subjects in the books and so much of Brodie. At the forefront in the Jefferson book are the family and cultural issues with which Brodie was struggling during the 1970s: adult sexuality both within and without marriage, the relationship of parent and child, and the issue of race relations, as well as the efficacy of psychoanalysis in dealing with those issues. In the Nixon book it is Brodie's liberal politics and her fascination with congenital liars, which had been a focal point of each of her books from the beginning of her career.

Thomas Jefferson: An Intimate History is an uncharacteristic Brodie biography.[58] It is not a comprehensive biography like either her previous books or the monumental Jefferson works of Dumas Malone or Merrill Peterson, the depth of which would have made an attempt at another such exhaustive portrayal superfluous in her day.[59] Instead, as the title indicates, it is a study of Jefferson's intimate circle of family members, friends, and lovers. Brodie's examination of these was intended to shed light on his inner life, the life of emotions and of motives, which would then help explain his exterior life, the life of action. The power of Jefferson's ideas, particularly as stated in his memorable prose, Brodie argued, has influenced previous biographers to focus on Jefferson the rationalist to the exclusion of examination of his interior life. "Almost every scholar who has . . . written about this philosopher-statesman has centered upon his luminous mind and its impact on society." By contrast, she indicates, "this is a book about Jefferson and the life of the heart."[60]

The other uncharacteristic feature of the book is its relentless psychoanalyzing, which is both overt and conspicuous on virtually every page. One would expect it in a book billed as "an intimate history," but it is a jarring departure from Brodie's previous books, in which psychoanalysis played a subordinate role. *Thomas Jefferson: An Intimate History* bristles with psychoanalytical jargon, and it raised hackles in Brodie's audience like none of her other books. A Jeffersonian gentlemanliness kept all of the first-echelon members of the "Jefferson establishment" (Julian Boyd, Merrill Peterson, and Dumas Malone) from reviewing the book. All liked Brodie personally, but they did not like what she had done to Jefferson. Lesser luminaries in the Jefferson world excoriated the book. Lois Banner criticized Brodie's "questionable speculations," pointing out that psychobiographers sometimes forget that with some people "there is less (rather than more) than meets the eye." T. Harry

Williams thought the book "badly set back the calling of psychobiography." Brodie was even swayed from her ordinary aversion to public controversy by an opportunity to debate Garry Wills, which turned into a verbal donnybrook at the Kennedy Center in 1975. Wills accused Brodie of being "the worst thing to happen to Jefferson since James Callender" (the pamphleteer who first accused Jefferson of a liaison with his slave Sally Hemings).[61]

The Jefferson establishment rejected both liaisons of which Jefferson had been accused—Maria Cosway and Sally Hemings—during his long life as a widower. Brodie accepted both, but it was her defense of the Hemings affair that evoked the greatest wrath from Jefferson scholars. Until recent DNA tests established the virtual certainty that Jefferson did father children by Hemings, the evidence for such paternity was entirely circumstantial. Hemings had been with Jefferson every time she conceived, there was a noticeable physical resemblance between her children and Jefferson, and there was a strong tradition in the Hemings family that they were descended from the president. The Hemings case was something of a chestnut in Jefferson scholarship, but the Jefferson establishment had chosen to reject the evidence as circumstantial. Brodie not only gave the evidence a new airing, but also added her own psychologizing. She observed Jefferson's repeated use of the adjective "mulatto" to describe European scenery after the onset of the Hemings relationship, which proved, to Brodie's mind, that he had the slave constantly on his mind.[62]

Annette Gordon-Reed, in a 1997 re-examination of the Jefferson-Hemings case, admits that Brodie's psychological speculations are the weakest part of her case, but argues on the other hand that historians who reject as merely circumstantial the evidence supporting the case are not playing fairly. Historians often accept such evidence as proof, as do courts (Gordon-Reed is both a historian and a law professor). Gordon-Reed accuses the Jefferson establishment of timidity (not to say dishonesty) in refusing to accept compelling circumstantial evidence in order to protect a false saintly image of the third president. Fawn Brodie, she observes, may not have made the case in the most effective way, but she at least "did not hide the ball."[63]

The Jefferson book also sold far better than any of her others. Its thesis that one of our most sanctified founding fathers had been a sexual libertine and had fathered children by a comely young slave woman was well-received during the new climate of sexual liberation in the United States during the 1960s and 1970s. In that and in Brodie's other explorations of Jefferson's intimate life, the book is more about Brodie than about Jefferson. Some degree of involvement of biographer and subject, she urged, "is *essential* to great biography. . . . The good biographer does, however, bring some degree of self-understanding so that he can separate his problems from the problems of the man or woman he is writing about—and keep a bridge of relative detachment between them."[64]

It requires little psychoanalyzing of Brodie herself to see how the main themes of the Jefferson book grew out of concerns in her own life at that point. Parental and marital relationships dominate the book: Jefferson's relationship with his cold and autocratic mother and his stifling wife; his own domineering parenting of his daughters; the issue of his continuing sexuality during his long widowhood, expressed in his relations with Maria Cosway and Sally Hemings. Finally, there are the roots of the civil rights movement of Brodie's day (in which she was deeply involved) in Jefferson's struggle with the hypocrisy of his status as a slaveholding philosopher of democracy.

Brodie's examination of Jefferson as son and as parent was driven by her struggles with her own children during the 1970s. Richard Brodie, the eldest, became a hippie who wandered from one place to another and from one career possibility to another, remaining all the while, as Bernard put it, "committed to be uncommitted." Such indecision was frustrating to both of the boy's high-achieving parents and often led to shouting matches between father and son. Fawn admitted that "part of the problem is that I have always known what I wanted for myself . . . and I am impatient with young people who cannot seem to find a direction in their life." In her Jefferson book, Brodie quotes Merrill Peterson's observation, based on the fact that Jefferson seems to have erased virtually every record of his mother's life, that she was "a zero quantity in his life." With no transition, Brodie explodes with the categorical assertion that "no mother is a zero quantity in any son's life."[65] Similarly, the Brodies agonized over their daughter Pamela's unfortunate marriage that ended in divorce, which echoed the marriage of Jefferson's daughter Martha.[66]

Brodie's fascination with Jefferson's postmarital sexuality was rooted in problems in her own marriage. At about the time she was working on the book, her husband Bernard had a brief extramarital affair. The sexual aspect of their marriage had always been problematic, evidently because of Fawn's difficulty in acknowledging and expressing her own libido while Bernard remained both sexually interested and attractive. Fawn decided the marriage was good enough in its other aspects to be saved, but that counseling for the sexual side would be necessary. Thus her examination of Jefferson's continued sexuality, both in the case of the beautiful, bright, talented, and unhappily married Maria Cosway and in the forbidden liaison with his slave Sally Hemings, was in large part her struggle to understand the continuing sexuality of Bernard Brodie and an exploration of the ability of psychoanalysis to shed light on both of Jefferson's relationships.[67]

Conversely, this justifiably maligned book also deserves praise. It is difficult to find fault with her basic premise that Jeffersonian historiography before her time had been unduly influenced by Jefferson's rationality. Previous books had explored only the rational aspects of his life to the exclusion of his emotions and passions that, as a human being, he had to have shared with the rest of the human race. "The idea that a man's inner life affects every aspect of his intellectual life and also his decision-making should need no defense today," she observed, a claim she was able to substantiate at that point in her career with her previous ventures into psychobiography. "Once one accepts the premise that a man's inner life has a continuing impact upon his public life," she added, "then the whole unfolding tapestry of Jefferson's life is remarkably illuminated."[68] Some of the reviewers' hostility can be explained by the jarring effect of subjecting an icon of rationality to the examination of psychoanalysis. If so, then perhaps any offense taken by the Jefferson establishment was overdue.

Also, although many of Brodie's psychoanalytic "insights" badly miss the mark, some of them score direct hits. It may be impossible to ascertain, as Brodie concludes, that Jefferson and Maria Cosway actually consummated their love affair. Maria's fiercely devout Catholicism would have placed inhibitions upon such behavior even in the notoriously libertine world of aristocratic Paris in the late eighteenth century. But there is no question of the reality of their love and even of their sexual desire for one another. And Brodie's exploration of Jefferson's probably poisonous relationship with his mother also seems persuasive. He reported her death in a casual way, almost in a subordinate clause, and he put off for an entire year payment to the clergyman who preached her funeral. Most damning, however, is Jefferson's farm book, the combination diary and ledger in which he kept his records of plantings and harvests, receipts and expenditures for the combined estate he managed for her and himself. Brodie notes that some of the most banal entries of expenditures are given in second person, intimating that she was looking over his shoulder virtually every minute of the day.[69]

Brodie's last book, finished only shortly before her death and edited in its final stages by her children, was her biography of Richard Nixon.[70] Undertaken against the advice of her family, it is perhaps her least fortunate book. Her liberal political position had enabled her to bring fresh insights to the career of Thaddeus Stevens, whom she saw in some aspects as a forerunner of the FDR and the New Deal, and to Richard Burton, whose farsighted views on race contributed to enlightened anthropology. But when she came to Nixon, biography became vendetta. Richard Nixon, both personally and politically, embodied Brodie's deepest hatreds, and she made little apparent attempt to avoid painting him in poisonous colors. Few readers after reading the book will disagree with J. Phillip Rosenberg, who commented that it aroused in him "an urge to demand that psychobiographers be barred from writing about people they dislike."[71] It is a bad book about a bad person.

To be fair, the book is not without redeeming value. "Good research, dubious interpretation," which has been the basic theme of this entire study, applies to Brodie's portrayal of Nixon. As one would expect of the Freudian that Brodie was, she focuses on Nixon's Whittier, California, childhood and his relations with his parents and brothers, in which a pattern of Nixon's pathological lying was established that carried on consistently throughout his adulthood and political career. Although the book frequently jumps ahead to the presidential years to illustrate a point, the basic narrative ends with the assassination of John

F. Kennedy. To have carried the story beyond that point, through the "New Nixon" and the presidential years, would have required release of all the White House tapes rather than just the ones transcribed for the Watergate hearings, to which Brodie had access. At that future point, Brodie said, historians might be able to build a mitigating view of Nixon if the tapes should reveal that there was "a responsible decision-maker as president" rather than simply the "shabby, pathetic felon" that was all that came across in the sources to which she had access.[72] Within the limited scope of her survey, however, Brodie plied her characteristic energy in uncovering every relevant scrap of evidence. Most impressively, she interviewed nearly 150 people who had information on Nixon's formative years, though regrettably Nixon himself and Henry Kissinger declined to appear before her tape recorder. It is a body of data that Roger Morris enjoyed access to while building his own more moderate interpretation of Nixon in his multivolume biography.[73]

Unfortunately, in her haste to compile her list of Nixon's pathological prevarications, Brodie sometimes misreads her own facts and gives them the most invidious possible construction. Quoting a Nixon speech in France, for example, in which he claimed to have majored in French in college, but forgotten most of it through subsequent disuse, Brodie calls it a lie, pointing out instead that Nixon had majored in history. His Whittier College transcript, however, which she gives in its entirety at a later point, appears to indicate a French major, with twice as many courses in that language as in history.[74] At another point, Brodie cites Hannah Nixon's recollections of her son's extensive reading in literary classics, particularly Voltaire and Rousseau, and Nixon's own memory of having spent an entire summer reading Tolstoy, particularly *Resurrection*, which he called his favorite novel. "He seems to have read only to forget," she observes, though she then goes on to cite a couple of superficial references to Rousseau and Tolstoy in his presidential speeches.[75] To a less vindictive reader, this seems unfair. Who among us, including Brodie, would like to be held to close account for books we read in college, books whose cumulative effect shaped our intellect and values even while their specific content may have faded from our minds, like Nixon's French? That Nixon retained even a superficial memory of Rousseau and Tolstoy seems praiseworthy, and one wonders further where his sagacity in dealing with a specific political or diplomatic issue would have been enhanced by a closer command of such writers.

The key to Nixon's personality, in Brodie's view, is to be found in his childhood desire to avoid displeasing his hot-tempered and abusive father Frank Nixon, who may have punished his children by kicking them (Brodie notes the frequency of kicking as a metaphor for abuse in Nixon's speech, as in his drunken press conference after losing the 1962 California gubernatorial race to Pat Brown: "You won't have Dick Nixon to kick around anymore."). Hannah Nixon, his mother, was also abusive in her quiet humiliations of her children, and because of their psychological nature those punishments may have created even greater scars than those inflicted by his father. From these parental relations Nixon's lying was born, out of attempts to create a version of reality that would avert punishment. Competition with his popular and talented brother Harold, who succumbed to tuberculosis as a young man, bred in Richard a craving for power and success at any cost, as well as an irrational sense of guilt for his sibling's demise. He also developed a fixation on violence as an avenue to success, which he realized during the time of his nearness to the presidency because of Eisenhower's precarious health, and after Kennedy's assassination, which eventually brought the presidency within his grasp.

Brodie sees in Nixon's life and career, then, little more than a sustained lie. She could see both Thaddeus Stevens and Richard Burton as men of paradox—Stevens with his puritanical rigidity and capacity to hate on the one hand, and his love for minorities and his liberal politics on the other; and Burton's use of deception to gain an audience and to gain entrance to Mecca and Medina, then reporting his scientific findings with scrupulous accuracy. She sees the paradoxes in Nixon's life, however, as simple hypocrisies: a Quaker who orders the dropping of more bombs than any other president, and the Quaker who denies amnesty to those who protest war—a traditionally Quaker response. In pursuit of her thesis, too, Brodie accepts anti-Nixon reminiscences at face value while psychoanalyzing pro-Nixon statements, as if the real truth is always negative and hidden. And she blames Nixon for things a less hostile observer might regard (without approving of them) as simply endemic features of American politics. She points out, for example, that when he was first asked to run for Congress in 1946, Nixon protested that he had never thought of such a thing, when actually he had already been making campaign speeches. What politician has never tried to make his decision to seek office look like a draft by the people or the party? And although Nixon undeniably was lying in his infamous "Checkers" speech about the existence of a "slush fund" out of which he had enriched himself from money donated for campaign expenses, Brodie admits that Adlai Stevenson acknowledged having a similar fund, as did several other legislators from Nixon's own state of California. Even Nixon's infamous secretiveness was not unique to him as president, either in nature or degree; a recent student of Nixon's predecessor, Lyndon Johnson, who installed the White House recording system that Nixon first removed before reinstalling an improved version, has said that LBJ, "more even than most Presidents, . . . was famous for concealing himself."[76]

Psychobiography, to readers accustomed to more "exterior" biographical approaches, often seems strained. Much of it depends on the biographer's ability to read minor facts as symbolic or symptomatic of larger points. Fawn Brodie, because of her avoidance of clinical terminology in favor of standard literary and humanistic diction, avoided much of the skepticism often heaped on more openly psychoanalytical biographers like, say, an Erik Erikson. In *Richard Nixon*, though, Brodie uses "Freudian slips,"—a dangerous form of evidence at best—to drive the last nails into the already well-secured lid of Nixon's coffin. As if to confirm suspicions that Nixon in 1962 was only interested in the California governor's mansion as a motel on the way to the White House, Nixon referred to the post he was seeking as "Governor of the United States." And his wife Pat, the long-suffering victim in Brodie's portrayal, had to endure what Brodie imagines was the humiliation of her husband's thrice-repeated admonition in the fourth television debate with Kennedy that "the country can't stand pat."[77]

Brodie, who once indicated that she was a quiet rather than a militant feminist, especially empathizes with Pat Nixon, in her college days an actress of promise who chose to abandon her aspirations to stand forever in the wings while her husband took the stage. Much of Nixon's hostility to Helen Gahagan Douglas, his 1950 opponent in the race for the U.S. Senate, a race notorious in American political history for Nixon's dirty tactics and unfounded allegations, was rooted, Brodie asserts, in Nixon's attitude toward women. Brodie writes that "not only was Nixon contemptuous of women's intellect generally, but he was also oblivious to women as individuals."[78] Pat Nixon, of course, had to live with that attitude daily. Even though there is no reason to dispute Brodie's reading of Nixon's residual misogyny, it is also true that skepticism regarding women's abilities was more common than uncommon in America in 1950, and it would be difficult to brand Nixon the worst offender. No doubt it was a particular sore point with Brodie, who also was trying (successfully, one would think) to maintain her own identity and career in a marriage with a nationally recognized expert on defense and diplomacy who was on a first-name basis with the likes of Henry Kissinger.

Finally, it is perhaps an oblique compliment, at least, to Brodie's thoroughness as a historian that one can sometimes use her own evidence against her, for she was careful to present facts contradictory to her thesis. There is plenty of evidence, for example, that is contrary to her portrayal of Nixon as a withdrawn paranoiac, an uptight and humorless recluse who could never let his hair down and present himself in public without a carefully crafted facade. Brodie always wants to see Nixon in apposition to "the exuberant, fun-loving charmer" like his brother Harold or John F. Kennedy. But she herself recounts Nixon's popularity in high school and college when he was running for student body office and appeared (perhaps falsely) to have had many friends, his hilarious parody of a political speech in favor of "Social Insecurity," and his partying with other Duke University law students.[79]

Brodie's last book, then, was an attempted exorcism of that dark presence of American politics in the mid-twentieth century. There were other exorcisms as well in her career, which began with an exorcism of the First Liar of her life: Joseph Smith and the Mormon Church in which she had been reared. Thaddeus Stevens, who also lived a lie in his domestic intimacy with his black housekeeper, performed his own exorcisms of his abandoning father and his physical deformity and emerged in Brodie's biography as a hero (though admittedly a tarnished one) for his farsighted political programs and his dogged insistence on protection of former slaves. Finally, in Richard Burton and Thomas Jefferson, Brodie exorcized her personal sexual inhibitions and family frustrations while attempting once again to exorcize our great national demon, the legacy of slavery. Through it all, she repeatedly reminded historians of the necessity of exploring the inner and intimate lives of our subjects. It was not a mean achievement for a rural Mormon girl with a degree in English and an aspiration to become a novelist.

"DANGEROUSLY LIKE COMMON SENSE"

READING FAWN BRODIE's biographies, one gradually becomes aware of her natural gift for psychology. Although the original edition of *No Man Knows My History*, for example, contains no psychoanalytical terminology, it fairly bursts with psychoanalytical insight. Someone said that St. Augustine had all the concepts of Freudian psychoanalysis and the only thing he could have learned from it was the terminology. Similarly, Brodie's biography of Joseph Smith was a psychobiography with all the data in place, just waiting for the psychoanalytic concepts to catch up. When the literature finally did catch up, Brodie applied the concepts to the biographical data in most of her books with an appropriateness that made her analysis almost invisible. As Erik H. Erikson, one of the founders of psychobiography, observed after describing his theory of the "identity crisis," it all sounded "dangerously like common sense."[1]

A psychological genius like Fawn Brodie is ultimately inexplicable, but a partial explanation might be found in her rebellion against the psychology of the Mormonism into which she was born. There is no original sin in Mormonism, and thus no "dark night of the soul" that informs so much of the world's great literature as well as the discipline of psychology itself. Mormon psychology is thus entirely rational, entirely on the surface, and entirely uniform in its applicability. That uniformity and rationality of Mormon psychology is the foundation of the Mormon group ethos; the same set of institutions, the same programs, the same cultural values apply to everyone everywhere.

As we have seen, in Juanita Brooks that rebellion was never complete. One sees a deeper psychological insight bursting forth almost involuntarily, only to be forcibly packed back into the box of officially acceptable explanations for tragedies such as the Mountain Meadows Massacre. For Brodie that tension between observation and dogma had already become unacceptable by the time she began her writing career. Brodie, who early in life abandoned the Mormon village for life in the big cities of Chicago, Washington, and Los Angeles, thus proved to be more of a villager than Brooks in her intolerance for nonsense and her commitment to empirical determination of truth.[2] In the Mormon worldview, the truth is always on the surface; for Brodie, the truth was *never* on the surface. It had to be dug for in psychological depths un-known to Mormonism. In excommunicating Brodie, the Mormon Church certainly had things right; heresy can hardly go further than this.

Fawn Brodie and the field of psychobiography grew up together. Sigmund Freud had worked out the main outlines of psychoanalysis in his clinical practice and theoretical writings by the late nineteenth century, but his pioneering attempts to apply them to historical figures like Leonardo da Vinci, Fyodor Dostoyevski, and Woodrow Wilson had met with limited success and much criticism, and others were slow to follow him into psychobiography.[3] As Bernard DeVoto and Vardis Fisher pointed out, the most serious shortcoming of Brodie's biography of the enigmatic Mormon prophet was its lack of a convincing psychology. While she did a magnificent job of linking elements in Joseph Smith's cultural environment with the *Book of Mormon*, she failed to establish a motive that would have led him to create his fantasy novel and place himself at the head of a new religion. Less careful scholars like DeVoto and Fisher had proposed, respectively, paranoia and epilepsy as the force that drove Smith, but Brodie, whose reading in the limited literature of abnormal psychology at the time was probably as extensive as either of her critics, found both wanting. "I read not only several textbooks on paranoia but also several hundred case histories when I first started research on the book," she told Dale Morgan, "and it was the case histories in particular which drove me away from

DeVoto's thesis. But I'm still not satisfied with my own, at least not with the presentation of it." Her own thesis, as she described it, was that the *Book of Mormon* was simply a novel based on locally interesting themes that got out of hand and became the basis of a religion. "I had hoped to make the 'literary' explanation suffice, but it didn't," she added. "I can't help feeling that there is something about him that will always defy analysis."[4]

As the years went by, Brodie's feeling that some kind of psychological explanation was necessary grew. "Were I to write the book over," she told Morgan in 1950, "I should not hesitate to describe Joseph in 'clinical' terms. I think some knowledge of psychiatric literature can be enormously useful in explaining him. And though I wouldn't label him 'paranoiac,' I would certainly lay more stress on his neurotic tendencies."[5]

Brodie did not have to wait long before the literature of psychoanalysis and psychobiography provided a basis for a new look at Joseph Smith. The 1950s saw an explosion of studies in both fields.[6] Most important for her was a 1958 article by Phyllis Greenacre on a psychological type she called "the imposter," which seemed to fit Joseph Smith.[7] Brodie had already used the term to describe Smith—on the very first page of her biography in fact—and had compiled elaborate documentation of his consistent misrepresentation of reality.[8] It was not, however, until 1971 that Brodie made the difficult journey back into Mormon history to revise her biography to include, among other things, a supplement that offered Greenacre's theory as a possible explanation of Smith's motives.[9] Even then, Brodie was careful not to claim too much for her analysis. Greenacre's imposter diagnosis "is not necessarily the decisive key" to Smith's motives, she warned, and though her thesis fit the biographical data more aptly than any other psychological explanation, Brodie underlined "the difficulties of clinical diagnosis of a man long since dead, especially one who was supported by an audience with an insatiable appetite for the supernatural, an audience that included most importantly his own parents."[10]

As things turned out, Greenacre and Brodie were building better than they perhaps knew. Greenacre's "imposter" profile has been confirmed by subsequent psychoanalytical research, though it has been located as a form of narcissism, a neurosis that had not been adequately studied in 1958.[11] And Brodie's suggestion in her revised edition that "like a first novel, it [the *Book of Mormon*] can be read to a limited degree as autobiography" became the key to what is probably the definitive psychological study of Joseph Smith. *Inside the Mind of Joseph Smith: Psychobiography and the Book of Mormon*, by psychiatrist Robert D. Anderson, applies biographical data and the literature of narcissism to an analysis of the *Book of Mormon* as Smith's autobiography.[12]

The psychoanalysis in *No Man Knows My History*, then, was added after the field of psychoanalysis had provided Brodie with a terminology, backed up by clinical research, that she could use. She had already provided elaborate biographical information that enabled her to apply the psychoanalytic concepts to Joseph Smith without the need for further research. As noted above, the period between the first and second editions of her Joseph Smith biography was rich in psychoanalytical research and psychobiography, and the biographies she wrote during that time—of Thaddeus Stevens (1955) and Richard Burton (1967)—are Brodie's best books. In these two books, biographical research and psychoanalytical interpretation are integrated in an almost ideal partnership. They are models of psychobiography in which the psychoanalysis is, if not invisible, so logically linked with the external biographical narrative as to seem "dangerously like common sense."

Though Brodie had read widely in psychoanalytical literature, she had little if any formal training in psychology and felt more comfortable dealing with the external aspects of her subjects' lives than with the interior ones. So she used psychoanalysis sparingly and avoided clinical terminology as much as possible. Of her Thaddeus Stevens biography, for example, she said

> [T]his was really a piece of psychohistory; an important piece of psychohistory, even though there is no clinical language in it. But then I never use the clinical language, I don't believe in that for several reasons: (1) I am not comfortable with it; I think this is better left with the clinicians. (2) You alienate a large portion of the audience if you start using clinical language. I think the English language is very rich and the clinical language is not needed. You can be pretty exact using old-fashioned terms rather than the clinical language.

Advising the aspiring psychobiographer, she wrote, "Let him write like the poets with the insight of the good clinician."[13]

Brodie thus saw her approach to psychobiography as a middle ground between historical scholars such as Merrill D. Peterson or Dumas Malone, for example, who wrote monumental biographies of Thomas Jefferson but restricted their analysis to the external and rational aspects of their subject's life, and psychobiographers such as Erik Erikson, whose scholarly backgrounds were mostly in psychoanalysis or psychiatry, and whose biographies were closer to clinical diagnoses of historical figures than they were to conventional historical biographies. Brodie characterized Erikson, whom she knew personally and admired, as "a clinician who uses historical figures as case studies in order to understand the larger nature of Man." In contrast, she limited her application of psychoanalysis to being aware of childhood experiences that shaped the adult and to being aware of both the intimate life as well as the inner life of the subject. Going further than that was too risky for her; "it is easy to make an ass of yourself." In order to go further, one would need training in both history and psychoanalysis, as did her UCLA colleague Peter Loewenberg, whom she also admired.[14]

In her last two biographies, of Thomas Jefferson and Richard Nixon, Brodie's reach exceeded her grasp. She attempted a depth of psychoanalysis with Jefferson that many readers simply did not find convincing, and her psychoanalysis in the Nixon book was a poor cloak for her bias and attempts to denigrate her subject.

Brodie's Jefferson staggers under a burden of psychological problems that suggests a need for institutional confinement: his orderliness was "compulsive"; his farm books are "a record of extraordinary concealment"; his enthusiasm for the Revolution "was interrupted by periods of tormenting doubt"; and "he was in deep conflict." His rivalry with Alexander Hamilton can be reduced to "the special hatred of two sons jockeying for the favored position in the eyes of a powerful father [George Washington]." Jefferson's hostility to Marie Antoinette had more to do with his attitude toward his own parents than with the queen's politics, for "we know that expressions of intense feelings about reigning sovereigns—even elected ones—are sometimes clues to feelings about the sovereigns of one's childhood." How we know this is undocumented in either text or footnotes. Brodie even ventures into the occult art of handwriting analysis to diagnose the personality of Martha Jefferson, Thomas's wife. Her writing "is remarkable only for a tightness and rigidity of the calligraphy so extreme as to suggest a great tension in the writer." Finally, she puts words into Jefferson's mouth even while crediting him with such extreme precision of expression that one can read his meaning reliably even to the most minute nuance. Referring to the unreliability of the French postal system during his correspondence with Maria Cosway, for example, Jefferson complained that "so many infidelities in the post office are complained of since the rumors of war have arisen that I have awaited a safer opportunity of enclosing you a bill of exchange." Brodie claims, "Here, it would seem, he came very close to saying what was really bothering him—*So many complaints of our infidelities are coming through the post office*."[15]

The problem here is the amateurism of Brodie's cocktail-party psychoanalysis, in which the theory seems to be driving the facts. "Off the cuff psychoanalysis is good dinner table talk," she pointed out in a speech. "It can often be malicious and damaging as well as erroneous—but it does not belong in books." Yet that seems to be exactly what her psychoanalyzing of Jefferson was. Psychoanalytical methods in the hands of inadequately trained and insufficiently cautious biographers, Jefferson scholar Joseph J. Ellis observes, often depend upon a theory of "a hypothetical cause deep in the subconscious. . . . The adult behavior sanctions or confirms the theory, which then achieves the status of a 'fact,' and a circular process has begun that can generate some notorious conclusions." Such methods do not satisfy "the traditional canons of evidence employed by historians and biographers."[16]

Keeping in mind the concurrent developments in Brodie's own life during the writing of the Jefferson book, it is not difficult to see the inception of the theories that inform the book. Her struggle to come to grips with her husband's continuing middle-age sexuality leads her to assume that Jefferson's sexuality continued in a similar way, which becomes documentation for her conclusion that he had sexual liaisons with both Maria Cosway and Sally Hemings. Her observation of her son Richard's struggles to find himself in the rootless 1960s and her hopes that he would achieve his parents' strong career-mindedness leads her to conclude that Jane Jefferson had a profound influence on her son Thomas instead of being the "zero quantity" that Merrill Peterson saw in her. In short, as Ellis points out, Brodie's method was remarkable in "its capacity to 'create' its own evidence based on a purely hypothetical model."[17]

Brodie herself was well aware of the danger of the biographer's becoming too involved with the subject, of "the biographer in trying to throw light on the complexities of the loves and hates or the pathology of the loves and hates of his subject—mixes them up with his own complexities, and his own pathology." It was, she realized, an insidious danger, for the biographer naturally chooses subjects with whom he or she finds some kind of connection, some source of interest that can sustain the biographer throughout the arduous process of research and writing. "There is usually deep personal involvement between the biographer and his subject," she acknowledged, "esp. with a first biography. . . . The biographer cannot write about himself, but he seeks out someone who in some subtle fashion reminds him of himself, or shares the same problems, or reminds him of someone who has been psychologically of great consequence in his life, like a parent or parent substitute."[18] For the most part, Brodie was able to turn her involvement with her subjects into creative insight, but in the last two books she lost much of her objectivity and succumbed to the temptation to merge her life with the lives of her subjects.

Her method in the Nixon biography was grounded in a different motive, but was no less faulty. In that case, her goal was to exorcize the dark presence of Richard Nixon in American culture, which Brodie thought had poisoned the political process from the moment of his first appearance as a political power. Her colleague Peter Loewenberg had warned aspiring psychobiographers against the irresponsible use of "psychological categories as weapons with which to attack and discredit political figures, in expositions that make leaps directly from infantile traumata to public political conduct."[19] Brodie herself had identified the destructive use of psychological data as a serious transgression for a biographer. Such a biographer, she warned, cannot use "clinical material for destructive purposes. Sometimes, even if the intent, and I mean the unconscious intent, is not destructive, the end result is destructive."[20]

In examining the history of the Nixon biography, it is hard to escape the conclusion that Brodie was driven primarily by a political vendetta rather than an objective quest for truth. Both her husband and her editor discouraged the project, her husband feeling it was beneath her talents and her editor that it was not commercially promising. Brodie made few efforts to conceal her detestation for Nixon, referring to him as "an obscenity," as "a son-of-a-bitch," and in the book as a "shabby, pathetic felon." She made repeated attempts to discredit him by finding evidence of homosexual relations, particularly with Bebe Rebozo, but ultimately came up with nothing plausible.[21] As we have seen, the book was based on the tireless research that was the hallmark of all of Brodie's books, research that others continued to mine even while disagreeing with her conclusions. The book met with mixed reviews; even Peter Loewenberg was of mixed mind about it. He recognized its depth and narrative power, but pointed out that it fell short of the potential of psychobiography to reveal a dynamic development in the subject's personality, "stressing the longitudinal growth and adaptation of a person all his life." Instead, Brodie portrayed a Nixon that was "essentially static and while powerful is unbalanced in its neglect of Nixon's many ego strengths and adaptations in a long political career."[22]

Brodie's uneven success in applying psychoanalytical concepts to historical materials shows that historical interpretation, as any historian would agree, is a difficult proposition. Persuasive interpretation requires the scholar to weigh often contradictory facts against one another, to employ modern insights and interpretations while not holding the past to a modern standard, and to keep his own biases and values under leash. The use of methods imported from other disciplines like psychoanalysis presents additional perils along with enticing possibilities—perils that become all the more risky when the biographer lacks thorough training in those methods. Brodie, though she lacked training in both history and psychoanalysis, was mostly successful in using these methods. Her Thaddeus Stevens biography remains the standard work today, and her Burton biography is only slightly less universally accepted. Both books achieved the ideal blending of biography and psychoanalysis, of the humanistic and the scientific, the external and the internal, that Brodie sought, a blending that seemed "dangerously like common sense." Mormons and non-Mormons will always disagree over *No Man Knows My History*, but a better biography of Joseph Smith has not yet appeared. Even her last two less successful forays into psychobiography were far from failures. Brodie showed that a complete portrait of Thomas Jefferson would have to deal with his emotional and sexual sides, and her research on Richard Nixon delved deeper into that complex person than anyone had previously gone. At the same time Brodie was marking out the minefields through which psychobiographers must navigate, she was revealing the garden that lies beyond.

THE LEGACY

Utah Historians and the "New" Histories

There is a dialectic of historiography. A new interpretation, sometimes appearing audacious or even outrageous, arises to challenge an older orthodoxy. In time, what was once outrageous may become accepted and even conventional—a new orthodoxy. Eventually, yet another challenging new interpretation arises and the cycle begins again.[1] That dialectic delights historians, for it enables them to return to what was thought to be exhausted material and find new significance and meaning. At the same time, it frustrates some outside the historical profession, who wonder why the past keeps changing, or why historians keep changing their minds, and why it seems impossible to establish anything historical with any finality. So historians find that in addition to their daily work, they also must constantly explain themselves and their work to others.

Fortunately, most historians bear that additional burden gladly, embracing each opportunity to explain themselves as an opportunity to look inward as well, to make sure they have the larger purposes of their craft clearly in view. Why are historians held to a higher ideal of finality than other intellectual endeavors, including mathematics and the "hard sciences," whose frontiers are always being pushed back? Incontrovertible factual gains are constantly being made in history as in every other field. It is not the past that changes but our awareness of aspects of the past that previous historians had not thought to investigate. It is the issues of our own day that drive us back into the past to seek explanations of why our world has turned out to be what it is.

The historians who are the collective subject of this book all challenged the orthodoxies of their day, sometimes audaciously, and all lived to see their interpretations become accepted, in whole or in part, as a new orthodoxy. None lived to see their interpretations overturned in favor of another orthodoxy, but that has happened and is happening as new issues in the contemporary world drive us back into the past to seek new historical explanations. On the other hand, if any were alive today, they would be pleased that knowledge and interpretation of the past have continued to grow and that few interpretations are ever completely abandoned. They would be able to identify elements in our work as historians that they created and fashioned. (The combative Bernard DeVoto might not have acknowledged a lack of finality in his conclusions.)

In following their historiographical trail to the present, it is useful to examine their influence in two areas: Mormon history and western history at large. With Mormon history, it was the work of Brodie and Brooks, with Morgan encouraging and guiding them in the background, that led the way toward a new critical use of sources and a willingness to follow those sources to their most persuasive interpretation, regardless the consequences for orthodox church views (Juanita Brooks was the sole exception to this). Although Morgan worked on his projected multivolume history of the church during most of his active career, he published comparatively little explicitly "Mormon" history. Instead he acted as mentor to others and to broaden the scope of Utah history by writing about neglected Mormon themes like the ghost government of Deseret. He also wrote of non-Mormon aspects of Utah history like early explorers and emigrants whose stories showed that Utah history and Mormon history were not one and the same. The extant drafts of his unfinished history of Mormonism were not published until after his death and after the more startling aspects of his research had been absorbed into the literature. Stegner's work was much the same, calling attention to John Wesley Powell's influence on the Euro-American conquest of the arid West and giving equal space in his *Mormon Country* to Gentiles as well as Mormons. His *Gathering of*

Zion uncovered little if any new factual material, but it showed that Mormon history would lose none of its drama if written from a critical point of view rather than from a defensive, hagiographical one. Stegner also showed that the experience of Zion's humble foot soldiers, especially its women, was a story as valuable as the story of its well-known leaders. DeVoto had less influence on Mormon history than the others. The Menckenesque polemical tone of his early blasts against Utah and Mormon culture, for all the barbs that may have hit the bull's eye, were easily dismissible as the rantings of a smart-aleck disgruntled native son. His fair and judicious treatment of the Mormons in *The Year of Decision* was largely too little and too late to have had much influence on Mormon historians.

So it was Brodie and Brooks, then, who were the spearheads of a thrust toward a new Mormon historiography. Brodie, in the frontal assault of an exorcist on what she saw as the great lie of Mormonism's founder, Joseph Smith, and Brooks, in the villager's quiet relentlessness with which she pursued the darkest deed of Mormon history, the Mountain Meadows Massacre, applied the critical standards of the professional historian for the first time to two of Mormon history's most sensitive subjects. Each found herself strengthened in her own way by her commitment to truth. Brodie brandished truth like a weapon against what she considered the deception of Mormonism, and Brooks possessed an undying faith that her church had nothing to fear from truth. Although the Mormon community initially greeted Brodie's book with outrage and Brooks's with stunned silence, those two volumes opened a new window onto the Mormon past that could never be shut. Love them or hate them, the two women forced Mormon establishment to answer scholarship with scholarship. These works were not hotheaded polemics, but exhaustively researched and meticulously constructed narratives with which one might disagree, but which could not be ignored or shouted down.

Probably the greatest single forward leap in Mormon historiography came in 1958 with publication of Leonard J. Arrington's *Great Basin Kingdom: An Economic History of the Latter-day Saints, 1830–1900.*[2] Superlatives are difficult to avoid when describing this work. Its depth of research, clarity of writing, and judiciousness of interpretation made it an immediate classic and gave it an unimpeachable place on western history reading lists. It would be wrong to ascribe much direct influence on Arrington to Brodie and Brooks, for he was on a different intellectual and scholarly tack from them. Arrington was trained in economics at the University of North Carolina and was influenced more by economists like Richard T. Ely and rural sociologists than by any Mormon scholars, though he was a lifelong Mormon and of course intimately familiar with the literature of Mormon history. His personal and intellectual relationships with both Brodie and Brooks, moreover, were complicated. Although he maintained cordial personal relations with both, his opinion of *No Man Knows My History* was uncharacteristically caustic for Arrington, normally a kind and generous man. Surveying "Scholarly Studies of Mormonism" in the inaugural issue of *Dialogue: A Journal of Mormon Thought*, Arrington reserved his harshest judgments for Brodie's book, which he said minimized Joseph Smith's religious depth and misused its evidence to build a preconceived case of prevarication by the Mormon prophet.[3] At the same time, he praised Brooks's biography of John D. Lee as "the only Mormon biography which appears to have withstood historical criticism" from both pro- and anti-Mormon points of view.[4] On the other hand, he expressed dismay at Brooks's editing of both the Lee and Hosea Stout diaries, which he said overemphasized atypical elements of ugliness in the Mormon frontier experience.[5]

Nevertheless, it would be a mistake to miss the indirect influence Brodie and Brooks had on Arrington. The window they opened allowed critical light to fall on the dark recesses of Mormon history, which helped him to open a door through which most of modern critical Mormon scholarship has passed. Moreover, Arrington's method in dealing with Mormon materials may have owed more to Brodie and Brooks than he realized. Although he interpreted his material in a positive way, as Brooks did but Brodie did not, he characterized his method as "naturalistic"—a term employed by both Brodie and Morgan to characterize their own methods. In the preface to *Great Basin Kingdom*, Arrington spoke "a word to Mormon readers who will be troubled about my naturalistic treatment of certain historical themes sacred to the memories of the Latter-day Saints." Arrington urged that focusing on the secular consequences of ideas and institutions asserted to have been revealed by God neither confirmed nor refuted the authenticity of that revelation, and further that "in practice it is difficult, if not impossible, to distinguish what is objectively 'revealed' from what is subjectively 'contributed' by those receiving the revelation."[6] It was a brilliant methodological statement, a definition of a separate place for Mormon history, informed by Mormon theology but not affecting it. A faithful Mormon historian like Juanita Brooks could use Brodie's naturalistic method of studying secular influences on religious history without necessarily *reducing* religion to those influences.

Arrington's immense influence as a person and a scholar inspired other young Mormon historians to begin looking at their history with his naturalistic method, and their studies, while not uncritical of cherished Mormon myths, were largely accepted by the Mormon reading public. The Arrington approach became known as the New Mormon History, and from 1972 to 1982 when Arrington served as Church Historian, it was the official position of the Mormon Church. Handsomely funded and supported by the church leadership as a worthwhile experiment, the Church Historical Department during the Arrington decade attracted a cadre of talented young Mormon Ph.D.s and graduate students who mined the newly opened church archives to produce an outpouring of scholarly articles and books under Arrington's encouragement and assistance and sometimes with his coauthorship. It was a halcyon period of Mormon scholarship that Arrington's assistant, Davis Bitton, characterized as "Camelot."[7]

A cynic might say it was too good to last. A conservative backlash in the 1980s under the leadership of men like Elders Boyd K. Packer and Ezra Taft Benson of the church's Council of Twelve cost Arrington and his New Mormon Historians much of their official support. In 1982 they were transferred (not to say banished) to Brigham Young University, where they created what was eventually called the Joseph Fielding Smith Institute for LDS History. Reaction deepened as the decade progressed, and the conservatives attempted to suppress what Elder Packer cryptically referred to as "advanced history," which he thought might arouse doubts in the minds of the faithful. Some of Arrington's associates and others were persecuted. Linda King Newell, coauthor of a brilliant biography of Joseph Smith's wife Emma, was silenced, while D. Michael Quinn and Lavina Fielding Anderson were excommunicated.[8]

Through all the travails, however, the New Mormon History has continued to thrive. The critical spirit that Juanita Brooks brought to the writing of Mormon history has long been recognized as the fountainhead of the movement. Her editions of the journals of John D. Lee and Hosea Stout are classic bodies of source material, her biography of Lee has never been superseded, and her study of the Mountain Meadows Massacre was the classic account of that tragedy for more than a half century until the appearance of Will Bagley's new study.[9] When two of the leading practitioners of the New Mormon History, Davis Bitton and Maureen Ursenbach (later Beecher), published their interview with Brooks in *Dialogue* in 1974, it was an affirmation of their indebtedness to her and their solidarity with her goals and methods.[10]

Brodie's contribution to modern Mormon studies and the New Mormon History is more problematic. Mormon scholars recognize the bitterness of Brodie's bias and the shortcomings of her tendency to dismiss Joseph Smith's religious sincerity, but they are today much less inclined to demonize her than were their predecessors. Today they are more inclined to acknowledge the value of her attempts to probe into his psyche and his environment for explanations, unlike earlier biographers, who saw him as merely a saint or a demon. *No Man Knows My History* is now discussed critically but fairly in surveys of Mormon historical literature.[11] As Reorganized LDS scholar Roger Launius observes, "virtually everyone working in Mormon history must contend with it in some way in their own work."[12]

On the other hand, the book has been a straitjacket as well as a liberation. Launius contends that Brodie's tight focus on the truth or falsity of Smith's claims to revelation defined the issue in early Mormon studies for a generation, to the exclusion of other topics that might be more productively debated and definitively resolved. Furthermore, he contends, the debate imparted a defensive tone and an insular character to Mormon studies that repelled non-Mormon scholars. Mormon studies became isolated from interpretive and methodological innovations that were constantly renewing and invigorating other fields of study.[13]

Brodie, then, rolled a rock into the garden of Mormon historiography that scholars have not been able to dislodge or ignore, and her book has achieved the status of a dark classic. Although new research and new sources discovered since 1945 have rendered Brodie's work increasingly outdated, no subsequent Smith biographies have put forth a compelling alternative interpretation. Marvin Hill proposes that the reason for this curious state of affairs is that no non-Mormon scholars have been willing to master the materials and for the most part are unaware that they exist and are accessible to scholars. Mormon scholars, Hill suggests, are well aware of the fate of Newell, Quinn, and others who were rebuked by the Church and may be afraid to propose a bold interpretation that could challenge Brodie's.[14]

The work of Brooks and Brodie, then, perhaps has had a healthy effect on Mormon studies by pointing the way out of an earlier Mormon triumphalist theme and toward the more critical approach of by the New Mormon History. The effect their work and the work of DeVoto, Morgan, and Stegner on the larger field of western historiography is also complicated and ambiguous.

The death of Bernard DeVoto in 1955 and Wallace Stegner's abandonment of historical writing after 1964 marked the end of sweeping interpretive themes in western history until the advent of the so-called New Western History of the late 1980s. Few fields of American history have attracted scholars with the ability to think as largely about their materials and to write as powerfully as DeVoto and Stegner, and it is hardly surprising that no one immediately emerged to fill their shoes. Those of lesser ability found it easy to scoff at them (perhaps out of jealousy) as maverick novelists who had jumped the fence into the historians' pasture, arrogantly packing grandiose ideas that were not always supported by facts. Consequently, the only major thesis within which western historians were willing to work during the 1960s and 1970s was a refurbished Turnerism promoted by Ray Allen Billington.[15]

This is not to say that western historians produced no worthwhile scholarship during those years, nor that they were unwilling to pursue new historiographical directions. Literary historians, for example, followed the lead of Henry Nash Smith into studies of both elite and popular literature, Richard Wade and Robert R. Dykstra pointed the way to urban studies, and Gerald Nash and Neil Morgan pushed western scholarship beyond the end of the frontier and into the twentieth century.[16] Among our group of scholars, though, the work of Dale Morgan seemed to inspire western historians much more during the 1960s and 1970s than the work of DeVoto or Stegner, as scholars worked to establish carefully constructed factual narratives of limited scope and eschewed larger interpretations.

One must insist upon factual accuracy as a foundation of all historical scholarship, and scholars like Morgan deserve the admiration and gratitude of all western historians for seeking out and publishing new sources and for reconciling contradictions and exposing inaccuracies in them. But their work also had the effect, warned against by Joseph Ellis, of walling historians up into their exclusive playground of the past and cutting that past off from any vital connection to the present, a connection through which history achieves its highest significance. Not only were Morgan and his followers intellectually disconnected from the present, they were chronologically cut off as well in their unspoken belief that the nineteenth century was "real" history whereas the twentieth was current events. Morgan had made tentative ventures into twentieth-century history in the WPA *Guide* and in his books on the Humboldt River and the Great Salt Lake, but later in his career he burrowed deeply into the nineteenth century and subsequent western historians chose to follow that lead instead of the earlier one.

Fragmentation, Gerald Nash observes, was perhaps the most conspicuous characteristic of western history during the 1960s and 1970s. Scholars labored industriously and productively, but they were as isolated from each other and from the larger world as prairie dogs digging unconnected burrows. As late as 1989 Michael Malone could lament that "most of us who labor in western studies still bear the onus, as heavy as it was twenty-five years ago, of working in a field that is deemed by many to be intellectually barren and cluttered with trivia."[17] It was a telling indictment of a field that had achieved an immense virtuosity at the same time it lost its intellectual vitality and its larger audience, as Earl Pomeroy had warned was happening as early as 1962.[18]

As Malone was writing, a historiographical movement was already under way that would largely replace the orthodoxy of the Dale Morgan approach with a renewed vision of the significance of the West in American history, revitalizing the field and reconnecting it with a large national and even international audience. This movement, called the New Western History, was directly inspired by DeVoto and Stegner, but it rejected and modified some of their ideas.

The movement included many younger scholars, many trained in the Yale seminars of Howard R. Lamar, but it coalesced around the leadership of Richard White, Donald Worster, and especially the charismatic Patricia Nelson Limerick. She acknowledged what Charles S. Peterson called her "taste for the limelight" and called upon other historians to promote their profession through public involvement.[19] For the New Western Historians, western history was not primarily—or even at all—the Turnerian story of the development and spread of democracy throughout the continent along a frontier line, a process that had been completed by the end of the nineteenth century. For them, western history was a tragic story of racism, sexism, and environmental destruction that was neither unique to the West nor confined to the nineteenth century. Inspired by the civil rights, women's, and environmental movements of the sixties and seventies, they tried to find in the nineteenth century the roots of the abuses they were trying to eradicate in the twentieth.

The New Western Historians rejected DeVoto's and Stegner's almost exclusive focus on the nineteenth century, as well as DeVoto's triumphal vision of western history as the story of American democracy achieving a continental scope propelled by the *deus ex machina* of Manifest Destiny. Although DeVoto had seen the great exceptions to Turnerian triumphalism in the tragic end of the American Indian and environmental exploitation and waste, his close focus on the "winners" in the winning of the West was still too triumphalist for the New Western Historians, who wanted to concentrate instead on the "losers." What they found appealing about both DeVoto and Stegner was their commitment to conservation, which had by the 1980s expanded into environmentalism, and their determination to tell the story of women as well as men in the West. Though they did not say so explicitly, they may also have admired the older scholars' literary excellence, their boldness in advancing sweeping and controversial generalizations, and their involvement as "public intellectuals" in current issues where historical perspective can provide insights on policy and public opinion.

The dialectic of western historiography, then, has superseded much of the work of the group we have been examining, as their work had superseded much of the preceding generation's and had become an orthodoxy of its own. But as that dialectic cycle rolls forward, it never completely shakes off the work of past historians. Clearly, the accumulated wisdom that is the heritage of workers in the field today owes an enduring debt to a remarkable generation of earlier Utah scholars.

NOTES

INTRODUCTION

1. Pomeroy, "The Changing West," 64–81.

2. Ibid., 80.

3. In addition to the historians under consideration here, the postwar years saw the maturation of several other scholars both within and outside of academia whose careers would help reinvigorate western history. Ray Allen Billington, Henry Nash Smith, and Pomeroy himself are examples, in addition to popular writers like David Lavender, whose exhaustive research and lively prose closely resembled Morgan's and Stegner's.

4. It has become increasingly fashionable to lump some of these historians with a contemporary group of Utah writers whom Edward Geary calls the "lost generation" in Mormon letters. Although the term no doubt has some utility in other contexts, I do not find it useful here. Dale Morgan, who quietly apostasized from Mormonism, and Fawn Brodie, who was famously excommunicated, were certainly "lost" to the Mormon Church, but DeVoto and Stegner were never involved in it, and Brooks never left it. See, for example, Geary, "Mormondom's Lost Generation," 89–98; Bringhurst, "Fawn M. Brodie," 11–23; and Saunders, "A Social History of Dale L. Morgan," 39–58.

5. Anyone inclined to challenge Brooks's inclusion here on the grounds of the alleged provincialism of her work should first reflect upon the extent of "Mormon country," which was her field. From the polygamist colonies in Alberta to their counterparts in northern Mexico, from the Rockies to the Sierras, Mormon country includes much of northern and western Wyoming, Nevada, southern Idaho, and most of northern Arizona, in addition to the entire state of Utah. Brigham Young's geopolitical thinking was not lacking in ambition. In her work of editing the diaries of Hosea Stout and John D. Lee, Brooks had to become expert as well in the history of the Mormon Trail all the way across the Great Plains and the Mormon Battalion Trail through New Mexico and Arizona to California. Few definable cultural areas in

western history would include such a scope. One should also not forget that she was born and reared in Nevada, not in Utah.

6. Bringhurst, ed., *Reconsidering No Man Knows My History*. A similar symposium resulted in Charles E. Rankin, ed., *Wallace Stegner: Man and Writer*, but only two essays consider his historical works. An older collection, *Four Portraits and One Subject: Bernard DeVoto*, contains only one essay (by Catherine Drinker Bowen) on his histories, while Garrett Mattingly's *Bernard DeVoto: A Preliminary Appraisal* appeared before DeVoto's career as a historian had really begun.

7. Brodie's credentials as a western historian are admittedly open to challenge, as any claim to an influence of her psychobiographical techniques on western historiography would be. Brodie was such an integral part of the group I am defining here, however, and her reaction to her cultural background produced historiographical results so similar to the others, that it would seem indefensible not to include her. And even though Thaddeus Stevens and Thomas Jefferson can hardly be considered "western" subjects, her books dealt with western history more frequently than they might seem. Mormonism, already during the life of its founder, was a westward-migrating religion that sought its destiny on the Missouri and Illinois frontiers before its legendary westward hegira under Brigham Young. Richard Burton, an Englishman raised in France who made his fame as a soldier and explorer in India, Arabia, and Africa, visited Salt Lake City in 1860 and described his observations in one of the best books on nineteenth century Utah—a book Brodie edited in a modern edition, as she did for Frederick Hawkins Piercy's narrative of the Mormon Trail. Finally, Richard Nixon was a westerner, and Brodie maps much of the psychological profile that made him notorious in terms of influences and experiences during his Whittier, California, youth. Psychobiography otherwise has been slow to catch on in western historiography, one notable exception being Andrew Rolle's "relatively cautious psychiatric approach" in *John Charles Fremont: Character as Destiny*. Rolle acknowledges Brodie's assistance during his preparation of the manuscript (p. xvi).

8. Nash, *Creating the West*. Richard W. Etulain, a Stegner expert and probably the most knowledgeable student of western historiography, does discuss Stegner and DeVoto in his prize-winning *Re-imagining the Modern American West: A Century of Fiction, History, and Art*. See also his *Writing Western History: Essays on Major Western Historians*, which discusses none of my subjects, though of course his focus is on *major* historians of the caliber of Turner, Bolton, and Webb.

9. Ellis, *American Sphinx*, Prologue.

10. Hofstadter, *The Progressive Historians*, *xiv*; Bloch, *The Historian's Craft*, 19; Gilson, *The Unity of Philosophical Experience*, 7.

THE TRADITION: UTAH HISTORIOGRAPHY TO ABOUT 1940

1. Bitton and Arrington, *Mormons and Their Historians*, is still useful as a survey of Mormon historical writing, though largely superseded by Walker, Whittaker, and Allen, *Mormon History*. See also Adams and Larson, "A Study of the LDS Historian's Office," 370–89, and, to a lesser degree, Ellsworth, "Utah History: Retrospect and Prospect," 342–67.

2. Arrington, *Adventures of a Church Historian*, chapter 1. Chapter 5 discusses the

formation of the Historical Department and Arrington's appointment as Church Historian.

3. The bibliographies of two recent and particularly well-researched books, for example, John Alton Peterson's *Utah's Black Hawk War* and Ronald W. Walker's *Wayward Saints: The Godbeites and Brigham Young*, list the church compilations, but the chapter notes indicate virtually no use of them in Peterson's case and very little use in Walker's.

4. Bancroft, *History of Utah*.

5. Bancroft himself told the story best (and published and marketed it as well, of course) in his *Literary Industries*, but see also Caughey, *Hubert Howe Bancroft*; Clark, *A Venture In History*; Peterson, "Hubert Howe Bancroft," 43–70; and especially, for the background of the Utah volume, Ellsworth, "Hubert Howe Bancroft," 99–124. The story of the growth of the western history materials in the Bancroft Collection is told by Morgan, "Western Travels and Travelers," 100–111.

6. Ellsworth, "Hubert Howe Bancroft," 103–21.

7. Peterson, "Hubert Howe Bancroft," 48.

8. Ellsworth, "Hubert Howe Bancroft," 100.

9. Peterson, "Hubert Howe Bancroft," 50, 63.

10. Pomeroy, "Old Lamps for New," 110–11.

11. Bancroft, *History of Utah*, 202, 206.

12. Ibid., *vii*, *viii–ix*.

13. Ibid., *vi*.

14. The sincerity of Bancroft's neutrality, which was grounded in his own loss of religious faith, cannot be doubted. As Harry Clark points out, "After the death of his first wife, Bancroft had no strong religious feelings, and consequently, no interest in either advocacy or polemic." *A Venture in History*, 21.

15. Some of those to whom I am referring here include, chronologically, Andrew Love Neff (1918), LeRoy Hafen (1924), Leland Hargrave Creer (1926), and Milton R. Hunter (1936). After World War II, Berkeley continued to produce Utah Ph.D.s such as Brigham D. Madsen, Everett L. Cooley, S. George Ellsworth, Dello Dayton, and Richard Poll. Of these Berkeley Ph.D.s from Utah, only Hafen spent his career outside of Utah and mostly on non-Utah and non-Mormon subjects. Hafen became State Historian of Colorado and only returned to his home state to teach at Brigham Young University relatively late in his career.

16. Creer, "Introduction," *vii*. Although he does not discuss historical writing, Thomas G. Alexander's *Mormonism in Transition: A History of the Latter-day Saints, 1890–1930* is a thorough study of the cultural and institutional adaptations to which I refer.

17. Young, *The Founding of Utah*. The biographical data that follows is derived from Hinckley, "Register of the Papers" and "In Memoriam," 88.

18. Levi Edgar Young Diary, September 12, 1898, Utah State Historical Society.

19. Ibid., April 13, 1899.

20. Young, *The Founding of Utah*, 438.

21. Ibid., 23, 36.

22. Ibid., 292.

23. Unless otherwise indicated, biographical data on Neff is taken from Bitton

and Arrington, *Mormons and Their Historians*, 88–97, and the prefatory matter in his posthumous *History of Utah, 1847 to 1869* is contributed by its editor, Leland Hargrave Creer, and Adolph Ladru Jensen.

24. Bitton and Arrington, *Mormons and Their Historians*, 94. As Bitton and Arrington indicate, Neff's papers at the University of Utah's Marriott Library document discussions with publishers regarding ambitious writing projects like a history of the Pacific Northwest and a general history of the Trans-Mississippi West, none of which came to fruition.

25. A fuller version of this story is given in Topping, "One Hundred Years," 222–23.

26. Neff, *History of Utah*, vii–viii. Creer's books are *Utah and the Nation* and *The Founding of an Empire: The Exploration and Colonization of Utah, 1776–1856*. Comparison of Neff's manuscript with the published version of the book indicates that Creer's editorial hand was erratic. Chapter 9, for example, the first one edited by Creer, was expanded to almost three times the length of Neff's manuscript during the first three published pages (490 words to 1415 by my count, to the beginning of the last paragraph on p. 92). Neff changed his own chapter title from "The Mormon Migration to Utah," to "Founding a Colony by the Great Salt Lake." Creer changed it to "The Dawn of Civilization in the Great Basin." Other chapters, like "The Indian Problem" discussed below, were actually shorter in their published version through paring of what Creer regarded as nonessential clauses. On the whole, Creer's claim to have added research material of his own seems untrue, and his editorial work was mostly literary.

27. Neff, *History of Utah*, 351, 870–71.

28. To be fair to Neff, the title was Creer's, not his. Neff's title was the more prosaic—but nonracist—"Indian and White Relations in Utah." On the other hand, Creer blunted the racism in Neff's first subsection title, "The Red Man and His Problems," to "The Basin Indians." None of this title manipulation, unfortunately, mitigates the racist bias of the contents, for which both Neff and Creer bear responsibility.

29. Neff, *History of Utah*, 205–06, 364.

30. Ibid., 367.

31. Ibid., 368, 371.

32. Ibid., chapter 19.

33. Campbell, "Brigham Young's Outer Cordon," 220–53, examines Neff's development of the idea and its acceptance by Leland Creer, Milton R. Hunter, and later scholars, then demonstrates its shortcomings.

34. Nels Anderson to Leland H. Creer, February 14, 1941, copy in Morgan Papers. Anderson was the author of *Desert Saints: The Mormon Frontier in Utah*. Dale Morgan to Walter P. Cottam, May 15, 1947, in Morgan Papers.

35. Ibid.; Dwyer, *The Gentile Comes to Utah*, 253.

36. Sturges, "In Memoriam Leland H. Creer," 268–69.

37. Sturges, "In Memoriam Leland H. Creer," 196–97. Jennings (1909–97), who was known by such titles as "The Dark Lord" for his imperious manner in supervising archaeological excavations, tells the story of his career in *Accidental Archaeologist: Memoirs of Jesse D. Jennings*.

38. Creer, *Utah and the Nation; The Founding of an Empire*.

39. Dale Morgan to Fawn Brodie, April 20, 1948, Morgan Papers. Morgan's reference is to Harrison C. Dale, *The Ashley-Smith Explorations and the Discovery of a Central Route to the Pacific, 1822–1829.*

40. Hunter, *Brigham Young The Colonizer.*

41. Dale Morgan to Mary L. Ream, August 20, 1942, Morgan Papers. In his attack on Fawn Brodie's *No Man Knows My History* in *Pacific Historical Review* in June 1946, Hunter offers several trivial factual errors in rebuttal and writes Brodie's work off as "another of the numerous biographies of Joseph Smith." One of his criticisms, ironically, is that Brodie "breaks the rule of historical writing in taking misleading quotations from their texts"!

42. Madsen, *Against the Grain*, 193. The Hunter-Ferguson collaboration resulted in *Ancient America and the Book of Mormon.*

43. Wahlquist, "A Review of Mormon Settlement Literature," 6–7.

44. Hunter, *Utah in Her Western Setting* and *Utah–The Story of Her People.*

45. Hunter, *Utah in Her Western Setting*, 291, 313.

46. To be as fair as possible to Hunter, he did write a book of *Utah Indian Stories*, also in the centennial year, but the book is a compilation of supposed Indian religious stories and humorous anecdotes portraying them as buffoons, and does nothing to portray their vital role in Utah history.

47. Ely, "Economic Aspects of Mormonism," 667–78. On these pioneering social scientists who studied Mormon institutions, see Walker, Whittaker, and Allen, *Mormon History*, 39–42.

48. Ericksen, *The Psychological and Ethical Aspects*; Nelson, *The Mormon Village.*

49. Anderson, *Desert Saints.* My discussion is based on the 1966 revised edition by the same publisher.

50. Ibid., *xxi–xxii.*

51. DeVoto to Morgan, December 28, 1945, in Stegner, ed., *The Letters of Bernard DeVoto*, 277.

52. Bitton and Ursenbach, "Riding Herd," 22–23; Brooks, "A Close-up of Mormon Polygamy," 299–307.

53. Personal information on Dwyer in this section comes from Ms. Tomi Taniguchi and from the Dwyer papers in the archives of the diocese of Salt Lake City. See also Topping, *Robert J. Dwyer and the Writing of Utah History*, 4–19.

54. Dwyer, *The Gentile Comes to Utah*, 97.

55. Reinhold Neibuhr gives a more elaborate definition of irony in the preface to his *The Irony of American History*, *vii–viii.* For a definitive examination of the irony of Classical thought in the light of St. Augustine, see Cochrane, *Christianity and Classical Culture.*

THE PROPHET

1. DeVoto to "Art," January 24, 1929, DeVoto Papers. Like all recent students of DeVoto, I am deeply indebted to Wallace Stegner for one of the great biographies of twentieth-century American literature, *The Uneasy Chair: A Biography of Bernard DeVoto.* All biographical material given in this essay, unless otherwise attributed, is based on Stegner's book.

2. DeVoto to Kenneth P. Williams, November 14, 1949, DeVoto Papers.

3. Stegner, *The Uneasy Chair*, 107. See also Stegner's discussion of DeVoto's letter and the text of the letter itself in Stegner, *The Letters of Bernard DeVoto*, 121–23. DeVoto's skepticism of the kind of idealism beneath Brooks's conference is further elaborated in another letter declining another such invitation from the mystery writer Rex Stout, February 4, 1946, DeVoto Papers.

4. Stegner, *The Uneasy Chair*, 85. The story of DeVoto's involvement in the Hagler investigation appears on pp. 34–38.

5. DeVoto to Garrett Mattingly, July 4, 1946, DeVoto Papers.

6. DeVoto to Kate Sterne, January [?] 1935, DeVoto Papers. Because of its intensely personal nature, DeVoto's correspondence with tuberculosis patient Kate Sterne is not available to researchers at Stanford, and I of course have not seen it. My occasional citations of it are based on Wallace Stegner's archival calendar—an item-by-item summary of contents—of the DeVoto correspondence on index cards in the Stegner Papers, which sometimes contains direct quotations like the one used here. My citations of all other DeVoto letters come directly from the originals at Stanford, unless they have been published in Stegner's *Letters of Bernard DeVoto*, which I prefer to cite in the interest of accessibility to readers.

Oddly, the name of DeVoto's mother does not appear in Stegner's *The Uneasy Chair*, and I have gotten it from Sawey's *Bernard DeVoto*, 15. The full name of Msgr. Cushnahan, a locally legendary priest at St. Joseph's, is given in Mooney, *Salt of the Earth*, 73–75.

7. Stegner, *The Uneasy Chair*, 2, 45.

8. Stegner, "At Home in the Fields of the Lord," 159.

9. Chamberlin, *The University of Utah*, 328–37.

10. Mencken, *Prejudices*, 168.

11. DeVoto to "Art," May 10, 1928, DeVoto Papers.

12. DeVoto's review of Mencken's *Prejudices, Fourth Series* appeared in the *Evanston News-Index*, January 27, 1925; "Ogden: The Underwriters of Salvation," 27–60; "Utah," *American Mercury*, March 1926, 317–23; Stegner, *The Uneasy Chair*, 62, 64. My bibliographic discussion here and below is based on Barclay, "A Bibliography of the Writings of Bernard DeVoto," 109–206.

13. Stegner, *The Uneasy Chair*, 69; DeVoto, "The Centennial of Mormonism," 1–13; DeVoto to Robert C. Elliott, November 4, 1930, in Stegner, *The Letters of Bernard DeVoto*, 20.

14. Stegner, "The Personality," 82.

15. DeVoto, "Ogden: The Underwriters of Salvation," 27, 29–30, 32, 38–39, 57.

16. DeVoto, "Utah," 321–22.

17. DeVoto to "Warren," December 10, 1943, DeVoto Papers.

18. Stegner, *The Uneasy Chair*, 98–99, 106–10, explores the larger literary and cultural background and implications of DeVoto's attack on the Young Intellectuals much more extensively than I have either the ability or the space to attempt here. My concern is primarily with the shaping of his basic views about the West and its role in American history.

19. DeVoto, *Mark Twain's America*, 225, 190, 99, 101, 47, 50, 51.

20. Ibid., 28; DeVoto to Crane Brinton, May 17, 1937, DeVoto Papers.

21. Stegner, *The Uneasy Chair*, 106. DeVoto's work is so extensive and varied, and yet so integral an expression of a cultural point of view, that my focus on his histori-

cal thinking necessitates doing violence to the larger context in which his historical writings occur. Thus I have not discussed his novels nor most of his essays, even though they reinforce and elaborate some of the themes I discuss. By way of a feeble gesture toward reparation, I can only refer the reader to discussions of those works in the Stegner and Sawey volumes cited here, as well as, of course, to DeVoto's writings themselves.

22. Kazin, *New York Jew*, 36. The phrase was not always a sneer. Arthur M. Schlesinger, Jr., a DeVoto student and close friend, remembers DeVoto at Harvard as "a round-faced, generous-hearted, affectionate, testy, pugnacious, insecure, driven man, a failed novelist, an embryonic historian, a lusty polemicist and a professional westerner." *A Life in the Twentieth Century*, 168. Schlesinger observes, too, that DeVoto's "demolition of the Brooks thesis was total, as even Brooks himself tacitly conceded, but the abusive tone denied DeVoto the approval that his cogent argument should have won him." (p. 170)

23. Schlesinger, *A Life in the Twentieth Century*, 234.

24. DeVoto, *Across the Wide Missouri*, 180, 63–65.

25. Stegner, *The Uneasy Chair*, 239, 288; DeVoto to Stegner, July 7, 1952, in *Letters of Bernard DeVoto*, 323; DeVoto, *The Year of Decision 1846*, 447.

26. DeVoto was not subtle in presenting his thesis, which is manifest in some form on virtually every page in his trilogy. Perhaps his most extended development of it, however, occurs in chapter 10 of the final volume, *The Course of Empire*, especially pages 391–411 in which he examines the continental visions of Thomas Jefferson and Abraham Lincoln upon which his thesis mainly rests. His ideas on sectionalism, secession, and the Civil War are eloquently and elaborately developed in a letter to Clifford Dowdey, October 7, 1945, in the DeVoto Papers, and in two consecutive Easy Chair columns, February and March 1946, attacking the first two volumes of James G. Randall's *Lincoln the President*. DeVoto, *The Easy Chair*, 151–166. The basis, nature, and implications of DeVoto's alleged determinism are explored later in a supplementary essay.

27. Stegner, *The Uneasy Chair*, 239.

28. Ibid., 245, citing Morgan to Stegner, May 10, 1970.

29. Thomas, *A Country in the Mind*, 72.

30. DeVoto, *The Year of Decision 1846*, 33, 102–3.

31. Ibid., 79–80; 146.

32. Ibid., 204, 112, 172; Walker, "The Dogmas of DeVoto," 5.

33. DeVoto, *The Year of Decision 1846*, 38–39. DeVoto's caricature of Fremont, as I shall call it in a supplementary essay, is prominent in most readers' memories of the book, and has not always been sustained in recent literature, but one must not ignore the passages in which DeVoto gives him his due. "The myth of the Great American Desert went down before this literary man's examination. . . . [His report on his third expedition] was extraordinarily seeing and intuitive, remarkably accurate. In the book he wrote, Fremont deserves well of the Republic." Ibid., 46.

34. Ibid., 44.

35. Ibid., 499–501, note 1.

36. Ibid., 451–52.

37. Ibid., 289–90.

38. Stegner, *The Uneasy Chair*, 269–75; DeVoto's own summary of the negotiations

appears in DeVoto to Mae Reed Porter, May 24, 1948, in Stegner, *The Letters of Bernard DeVoto*, 295–301. In his introduction to that letter, Stegner calls *Across the Wide Missouri* "the most brilliant evocation of the mountain fur trade in historical literature." (p. 295) Stegner's high assessment is supported by the book's winning both the Pulitzer Prize and the Bancroft Prize in 1947.

39. This view puts me at a disagreement with John L. Thomas, who maintains that "DeVoto's own factual reach and personal interest did not extend to what a later age would call ethnic and gender pluralism or to issues concerning the cultural margins—of the whole West as a contested ground for Anglo-Saxons, Spanish, Mexicans, Native Americans, Asians, and women in all of these categories." *A Country in the Mind*, 81. In the pages that follow I attempt to show something of the breadth of DeVoto's reach on the issue of cultural diversity, which, to be sure, does not extend as far as modern scholars such as, to name two examples, Elliott West in *The Contested Plains: Indians, Goldseekers, and the Rush to Colorado* or Richard White's *"It's Your Misfortune and None of My Own": A New History of the American West*. But it seems to me nevertheless to be remarkably prescient for a man of his day and background.

40. DeVoto, *The Year of Decision 1846*, 337, 352; *Across the Wide Missouri*, 123, 148, 149, 232. DeVoto's ethnocentric denigration of the Shoshonean peoples of the Great Basin was already outdated by the work of Alfred A. Kroeber, Julian Steward, and others. See, for example, Steward's *Basin-Plateau Aboriginal Groups*.

41. DeVoto to Holger Cahill, June 24, 1949, in Stegner, *The Letters of Bernard DeVoto*, 148.

42. Ibid., 150; *Across the Wide Missouri*, 203, 355.

43. DeVoto, *The Year of Decision 1846*, 7–8; 52–56.

44. Bakeless, *Lewis and Clark*.

45. DeVoto to Mattingly, December 2, 1948, in Stegner, *The Letters of Bernard DeVoto*, 306.

46. Stegner, *The Uneasy Chair*, 335.

47. DeVoto, *The Course of Empire*, *xvi*.

48. Ibid., 232, 337.

49. Ibid., 239–42.

50. The much better maps by Peter H. Dana that illustrate Robert M. Utley's recent *A Life Wild and Perilous: Mountain Men and the Paths to the Pacific*, a book with a goal similar to DeVoto's, fulfill much the same collaborative role as Raisz's maps did in *The Course of Empire*.

51. DeVoto, ed., *The Journals of Lewis and Clark*.

52. DeVoto to Mattingly, December 2, 1948, in Stegner, *The Letters of Bernard DeVoto*, 305.

53. DeVoto, *The Course of Empire*, 436, 516.

54. Ibid., 436.

55. Whitman, "Starting From Paumanok," Section 12, line 1.

56. Whitman, "A Backward Glance O'er Travel'd Roads," 454.

ENVIRONMENT AS EXPLANATION

1. Etulain, ed., *Does the Frontier Experience Make America Exceptional?* reprints Turner's seminal essay of 1893, "The Significance of the Frontier in American His-

tory" and includes a superb collection of critical essays on Turner's importance. Webb's best work was *The Great Plains.* A handy summary of the careers, writings, and importance of these two historians and the other important theorist of western history, Herbert Eugene Bolton, is Jacobs, Caughey, and Frantz, *Turner, Bolton, and Webb: Three Historians of the American Frontier.*

2. See, for example, DeVoto to Henry Nash Smith, June 28, 1948, on Turner, and DeVoto to Kate Sterne, November 19, 1939, and to Kenneth P. Williams, November 14, 1949, on Webb, DeVoto Papers. (I have not seen the DeVoto-Sterne letters, which are closed to research, but I am aware of the contents of some, including this one, through Wallace Stegner's summaries of them on file cards in the Stegner Papers.) DeVoto, "Introduction" to *The Portable Mark Twain*, 1–34.

3. DeVoto, "Introduction" to *The Portable Mark Twain*, 5, 2.

4. Ibid., 6–7.

5. DeVoto did deal with the safety valve thesis in *The Year of Decision 1846* without specifically mentioning Turner. Making "the conventional genuflection" to the idea that the rejects of eastern industrialism found salvation in western land, DeVoto notes that "after due search, exceedingly few of them have been found in any of the events we deal with and none at all along the western trails." Later, he accepts a modification of the safety valve idea which counters the objection that only people of certain means could afford to emigrate, observing that their absence provided opportunity for those below them on the economic scale to move up. See pp. 47, 144, with note 8, p. 490.

6. DeVoto, *The Year of Decision 1846*, 62; *Across the Wide Missouri*, 371, 232.

7. DeVoto, *Mark Twain's America*, 29.

8. Ibid., 52.

9. DeVoto to Robert C. Elliott, November 4, 1930, in Stegner, *Letters of Bernard DeVoto*, 19–22. On the issue of DeVoto's attempts to make amends with the Mormons, see Fetzer, "Bernard DeVoto and the Mormon Tradition," 23–38. It seems to me that Fetzer sees more reconciliation than existed, explaining away such accusations of Mormon "smugness" as an outburst "of petulance and poor taste," in which DeVoto "succumbed . . . to the temptation to employ colorful phrases . . . which . . . are unfair and irritating to the reader." 35, 37. Such phrases strike me, by contrast, as deliberately chosen rather than succumbed to, and express a deep and lifelong scorn for Mormon theology and Mormon condescension toward outsiders. One wonders what euphemisms DeVoto might have chosen for terms like smugness and self-righteousness that would have expressed his scorn without offending Mormon readers. What one finds offensive, moreover, another finds delightfully pungent.

10. DeVoto to Jarvis Thurston, May 24, 1943, in Stegner, *Letters of Bernard DeVoto*, 23–27; DeVoto to Dale Morgan, March 12, 1941, DeVoto Papers.

11. DeVoto to Mr. Kostbar, December 26, 1951, DeVoto Papers.

12. Dale L. Morgan to DeVoto, October 26, 1941, Morgan Papers, and December 20, 1945, in Walker, *Dale Morgan on Early Mormonism*, 92–101.

13. DeVoto to Dale Morgan, December 28, 1945, in Stegner, *The Letters of Bernard DeVoto*, 277. On this point, however, see DeVoto to Mr. Chamberlain, April 18, 1935, DeVoto Papers: "I am probably the soundest authority on one small field of American history, the Mormon Church. I have studied it, quite literally, for twenty years." This, of course, was more than ten years before the debate with Morgan.

14. DeVoto to Morgan, December 28, 1945, in Stegner, *The Letters of Bernard DeVoto*, 277, 280. The metaphor of weight vs. musical pitch is interesting evidence that DeVoto was unaware of Morgan's deafness. DeVoto may never have learned of it, for the two never met.

15. DeVoto, *The Year of Decision 1846*, 77–78, 454.

16. DeVoto to "Haller," January 12, 1945; see also DeVoto to "Frank," July 16, 1941, where he hopes someone will undertake a psychological study of Mark Twain as well. Both letters in DeVoto Papers.

MANIFEST DETERMINISM

1. DeVoto, *The Year of Decision 1846*, 4.

2. Peter Skiles Pruessing explores this "paradox" in detail in his "Manifest Destiny and 'The Literary Fallacy': The Paradox in Bernard DeVoto's Treatment of Westward Expansion." DeVoto's biographer, Wallace Stegner, agreed that his historical works "are very much the product of the literary mind that he despised." Stegner notes on DeVoto, Stegner Papers.

3. Schlesinger, *A Life in the Twentieth Century*, 170. My sketchy description of Pareto's ideas is based on that of Stegner, *The Uneasy Chair*, 138–44.

4. Quoted in DeVoto, *The Course of Empire*, 392. Our focus here is on DeVoto's imperialism rather than Jefferson's, but it is worth noting that Jefferson was much less of an expansionist than DeVoto's interpretation of the Livingston letter makes him out to be. Jefferson saw the United States' acquisition of Louisiana as necessary in order to keep European nations out of the Mississippi Valley, but not necessarily as a building block of an American empire. Writing to Joseph Priestley on January 29, 1804, Jefferson speculated that Louisiana might eventually decide to go its own way outside the Union—an eventuality not to be feared, for it would remain a friendly republic. "Whether we remain in one confederacy, or form into Atlantic and Mississippi confederacies, I believe not very important to the happiness of either part. Those of the western confederacy will be as much our children and descendants as those of the eastern, and I feel myself as much identified with that country, in future time, as with this." Quoted in Ellis, *American Sphinx*, 253.

5. Quoted in ibid., 401–2.

6. DeVoto to Ted [Weeks], August 4, 1942, DeVoto Papers. We have previously examined DeVoto's complicated attitude toward the Indians. In that light, his statement here should not be construed as lack of sympathy for the loss of their land and independence, but rather as a statement of *realpolitik*, a recognition that the Indians were powerless to resist a force much larger than their rights of prior possession and self-determination.

7. DeVoto, *The Year of Decision 1846*, 182, 39; *Across the Wide Missouri*, 200–203, 371; *The Course of Empire*, 404.

8. DeVoto, *The Year of Decision 1846*, 291, 480; *The Course of Empire*, 236.

9. DeVoto, *The Year of Decision 1846*, 11; *The Course of Empire, xvi.*

10. DeVoto, *The Course of Empire, xiii.*

11. Limerick, "Mission to the Environmentalists," 176–77; Abbey, *Desert Solitaire*, 270, 273.

1846: YEAR OF CARICATURE

1. Hofstadter, *The Progressive Historians*, 17.

2. The following material on Hastings and DeVoto's interpretation of him is based on and employs some of the language of my "Overland Emigration, the California Trail, and the Hastings Cutoff" in Bruce R. Hawkins and David B. Madsen, *Excavation of the Donner-Reed Wagons: Historic Archaeology Along the Hastings Cutoff*, 9–30. My interpretation of Hastings is based in large part on the work of Thomas F. Andrews, whose "The Controversial Career of Lansford Warren Hastings: Pioneer California Promoter and Emigrant Guide" and "Lansford W. Hastings and the Promotion of the Salt Lake Desert Cutoff: A Reappraisal," 133–50, record significant details of Hastings's life and career ignored in DeVoto's negative appraisal.

3. Hastings, *The Emigrants' Guide*, 83, 87.

4. Ibid., 137–38.

5. The Donner story has been told many times, both before and after DeVoto. Two standard accounts are Stewart, *Ordeal By Hunger*, and McGlashan, *History of the Donner Party*.

6. DeVoto, *The Year of Decision 1846*, 44, 167.

7. Ibid., 114.

8. Nonspecialists in the literature of the California Trail need to know that my early views presented here on Lansford Hastings and the role of the Pioneer Palace wagon in the Donner tragedy have been subjected to criticism and modification by subsequent research. See, for example, Bagley, "Lansford Warren Hastings," 12–26; and Johnson, "The Pioneer Palace Car," 5–8. It is not necessary to go into the subtleties and complications either of my original thesis or of subsequent criticisms in order to make my basic point here that DeVoto's thesis was innocent of complications of any kind. He had his villain—Lansford Hastings—and that was enough for him.

9. DeVoto, *The Year of Decision 1846*, 64. The "bag of possibles" carried by mountain men fulfilled the function of pockets, which their simple, handmade leather clothes did not have. The contents of the sack were obviously highly individualized, but might have included things like needles or an extra flint for the rifle lock.

10. Ibid., 310.

11. Ibid., 112.

12. Ibid.

13. Walker, "The Dogmas of DeVoto," in *The Possible Sack*, July 1971, 5. (*The Possible Sack* was an in-house journal published intermittently during the 1970s by Don D. Walker through the English Department of the University of Utah. Files of the journal are available at the Marriott Library, University of Utah, and the Utah State Historical Society, among other places.)

14. DeVoto, "Introduction," *xxvii*; Walker, "The Dogmas of DeVoto," 7.

15. DeVoto, *The Year of Decision 1846*, 230, 218, 275, 355, 359, 456, 277.

THE MENTOR

1. There are, nevertheless, several brief biographical sketches as well as autobiographical passages in the Morgan papers at the Bancroft Library that I have consulted on microfilm at the Marriott Library at the University of Utah, upon which I

have based the following narrative. The only one that covers Morgan's entire life with any degree of comprehensiveness is Walker's introduction to his *Dale Morgan on Early Mormonism*. Also useful are Saunders, "'The Strange Mixture of Emotion and Intellect': A Social History of Dale L. Morgan, 1933-42"; and Foster, "Madeline McQuown, Dale Morgan, and the Great Unfinished Brigham Young Biography," 111–23.

2. Untitled autobiographical narrative, Reel 25, Morgan Papers.

3. Morgan to Marguerite Sinclair Reusser, May 22, 1951, Morgan Papers.

4. Ibid. The autobiographical narrative cited above contains a parallel account of this crisis.

5. Mulder, "Preface," 5; Roderick Korns to Charles Kelly, June 2, 1945, Kelly Papers; Saunders, "'The Strange Mixture of Emotion and Intellect,'" 51.

6. Foster, "Madeline McQuown," details this unsavory and ultimately, for Morgan, heartbreaking relationship.

7. Morgan to Jerry Bleak, August 13, 1938, Bleak Papers.

8. Morgan to Jack Thornley, May 23, 1947, Morgan Papers.

9. The name was changed in 1939 to the Work Projects Administration. One of the most concise descriptions and appraisals of the WPA programs is Leuchtenburg, *Franklin D. Roosevelt and the New Deal*, 124–30.

10. Ibid., 125.

11. See Peterson, "Introduction", *viii–ix*. Peterson's discussion is based on Mangione, *The Dream and the Deal.*

12. Texas, as Morgan pointed out, was an exception. As a result of the Texas Revolution of 1836, the Mexican province of Texas became an independent republic. As such, it was annexed by the United States as a state in 1845, the only such instance in American history.

13. Morgan, *The State of Deseret*, 8, 9, 34, 12–13.

14. There are two Morgan bibliographies: Walker, *Dale Morgan on Early Mormonism*, 401–14; and Saunders, *Eloquence from a Silent World*, which is oriented to the needs of Morgan collectors.

15. Quoted in Penkower, *The Federal Writers' Project*, 46.

16. Billington, "Introduction," *viii*. The only actual revision of the Utah guide was a massive (779 pages) literary nightmare by Ward Roylance, who interspersed large block quotations from the original edition with his own passages of revision. Many other travel guides have since appeared for the state or portions of it. The ones most obviously inspired by the WPA guide are Wharton and Wharton, *Utah*; and Powell, *The Utah Guide*. See also Saunders, "The Utah Writers' Project," 21–38.

17. Ibid., *x*.

18. *Utah: A Guide to the State*, 404, 317–21.

19. Ibid., 375, 42–44. Figures for Utah per capita income are found in U.S. Bureau of the Census, *Historical Statistics of the United States*, Table F-342.

20. Peterson, "Introduction," *x*.

21. Morgan to Ralph V. Chamberlin, March 17, 1951, Morgan Papers; Morgan to Charles Kelly, Kelly Papers; Morgan to Bernard DeVoto, February 6, 1958, Morgan Papers.

22. Morgan to DeVoto, March 23, 1941, Morgan Papers. "Kelly's bias destroys his objectivity to some degree, and his books have a name-calling air that is unfortu-

nate for the facts that he would develop." And, "My own research of the last two years has turned up a lot of stuff which discredits many of Kelly's sources and interpretations." On Stanley Vestal, see Morgan to Amy Loveman, September 13, 1946, where he indicates that Vestal's books, "unless he makes them worth while, . . . will just be cluttering up our literature," and Morgan to H. E. Tobie, January 3, 1950, where he refers to Vestal's book on Jim Bridger as "absolutely beneath contempt." On Alter, he wrote Marguerite Sinclair Reusser on September 2, 1964, that "his books comparatively speaking are second-rate." And on Paul Bailey's *Sam Brannan and the California Mormons*, Morgan told Juanita Brooks that it "gave me a more discouraged feeling about Mormon scholarship than I've had for a long time. . . . Bailey bowdlerized some original sources, misquoted others, badly misinterpreted others, didn't even trouble himself about others, and emerged with a pseudo-documented rehash that was a disgrace even to the pages of the Improvement Era, where the piece seems to have been originally serialized." He concludes by scorning "this Bailey bilge." Morgan to Juanita Brooks, December 9, 1943, Brooks Papers.

23. Morgan to Juanita Brooks, May 21, 1942, Brooks Papers.

24. Nels Anderson to Juanita Brooks, May 16, 1943, Brooks Papers; Morgan to Charles Kelly, March 11, 1943, Kelly Papers.

25. Copies of Morgan's newspaper transcriptions, "Mormons and the Far West," are available at the Yale, Huntington, and Utah State Historical Society libraries.

26. Bringhurst, *Fawn McKay Brodie*, 86–88; Walker, *Dale Morgan on Early Mormonism*, 10–11.

27. Morgan, *The Humboldt.* Quotations here are from the reprint edition, Lincoln: University of Nebraska Press, 1985.

28. Morgan to Juanita Brooks, June 27, 1942, Brooks Papers.

29. Peterson, "Introduction," *viii. West From Fort Bridger* was volume XIX of the *Utah Historical Quarterly* (1951), and *Jedediah Smith and the Opening of the West* was published in 1953 by Bobbs Merrill in New York.

30. A rare factual dispute is possible over Morgan's statement on p. 5 that the Humboldt was "the last-discovered of the American rivers." That distinction is ordinarily awarded to the Escalante, an intermittent tributary of the Colorado River in Glen Canyon, which was identified by the members of the *Canonita* survey under Maj. John Wesley Powell in 1872, almost a half century after Peter Skene Ogden's discovery of the Humboldt. Topping, *Glen Canyon and the San Juan Country*, 62.

31. Morgan, *The Humboldt*, 5, 8.

32. Ibid., 5, 331.

33. Billington, "Introduction," *xi–xvii.*

34. Ibid., *xxv.*

35. This was edited and published by George R. Brooks (with Morgan's assistance) as *The Southwest Expedition of Jedediah S. Smith: His Personal Account of the Journey to California, 1826–1827.*

36. Morgan to Harrison Platt [Bobbs Merrill publishers], June 13, 1953, Morgan Papers; *Jedediah Smith* , 10.

37. Morgan, *Jedediah Smith*, 10.

38. Ibid., 7.

39. Morgan, *Overland in 1846; Jedediah Smith and His Maps;* and *Mapping the Trans-Mississippi West*, the latter two with Carl I. Wheat.

40. Flake, *A Mormon Bibliography*.

41. Morgan to S. A. Burgess, April 26, 1943, in Walker, *Dale Morgan on Early Mormonism*, 43. Walker also uses this quotation as a statement of the book's theme, under a photograph of Morgan opposite the title page.

42. D. Michael Quinn, subsequent to Morgan's work, has delineated this climate of occult thinking and practice in the environment of Joseph Smith's youth much more elaborately in *Early Mormonism and the Magic World View*, rev. ed.

43. Walker, *Dale Morgan on Early Mormonism*, 310, 313, 317–18, 260.

44. Billington, "Introduction," *viii*; Peterson, "Introduction," *viii*; Bagley and Schindler, *West From Fort Bridger*, *viii*.

45. Walker, *Dale Morgan on Early Mormonism*, 43.

HISTORY WITHOUT HYPOTHESIS

1. Morgan to Juanita Brooks, December 15, 1945, Brooks Papers.

2. Bancroft, *History of Utah*, 40.

3. For background on the rise of the scientific school of historiography and the revolt against it by the "New History" and the relativists, see Higham, *History*, section II; and Hofstadter, *The Progressive Historians*, chapter 1.

4. Morgan to Todd I. Berens, December 10, 1965, Morgan Papers. See also Morgan to Ora Lee Parthesius, a reference librarian at the Salt Lake Public Library, who had asked him for a sketch of his life and philosophy as a historian. His reply contains only admonitions to skepticism and intellectual honesty and curiosity, with no apparent awareness of history as a search for answers to larger interpretive questions. Morgan to Parthesius, April 15, 1951, Morgan Papers.

5. Morgan to Bernard DeVoto, January 1946, in Walker, *Dale Morgan on Early Mormonism*, 110–11.

6. Hexter, "Carl Becker and Historical Relativism," 34.

7. Becker, "Everyman His Own Historian," 231–33. Becker was not alone in advocating what has come to be known as historical relativism. Charles A. Beard's AHA presidential address, "Written History as an Act of Faith," which also appeared during Morgan's formative years, reinforced Becker's insistence on the scientific method in establishing facts as well as his observation that each generation extracts different meaning from those facts in answering questions uppermost in its mind. Hexter's article on Becker cited above traces the lineage of historical relativism back to the late nineteenth century, so it was no novelty in Morgan's day. Although the implications of relativism and the limits of objectivity have been hotly debated since Becker and Beard gave the school its classic expressions, their basic idea that historical interpretations change as the questions historians ask of their sources change has become a foundation of modern historiography. On Becker and Beard, see Novick, *That Noble Dream*, chapter 9, especially 252–58.

8. The same can be said of Bancroft, whose book bristles with interpretive comments unacknowledged as such. Consider, for example, his assessment of Gov. Thomas Ford of Illinois, who negotiated the Mormon withdrawal from Nauvoo. "Not specially clear-headed, and having no brain power to spare, he was quite respectable and had some conscience, as is frequently the case with mediocre men. He had a good heart, too, was in no wise vindictive, and though he was in no sense a

strong man, his sense of right and equity could be quite stubborn upon occasion." To place this sketch of Ford's personal attributes into the realm of incontrovertible fact would require at least an IQ test, and one wonders how Bancroft would have scientifically substantiated his "good heart." Unintentionally exhibiting his lack of objective detachment, Bancroft even lapses into the first person. "Nevertheless, though bitterly censured by the Mormons, I do not think Ford intended to do them wrong." Bancroft, *History of Utah*, 172–73. This judgment contrary to the Mormons' assessment of one of their most proverbial enemies appears in Bancroft's text, rather than in a footnote as he initially promised anti-Mormon rebuttals would be, thus indicating a real passion behind his desire to vindicate Ford.

9. Morgan to Harrison Platt, June 13, 1953, Morgan Papers.

10. New York: Alfred A. Knopf, 1967.

11. Morgan, *Jedediah Smith and the Opening of the West*, 46, 115.

12. Ibid., 54. Ellipsis in original.

13. Walker, *Dale Morgan on Early Mormonism.*

THE ENIGMATIC TRAPPER

1. Sullivan, *Jedediah Smith: Trader and Trail Breaker*, 1–3; 198–200.

2. The text of these letters is conveniently available in Appendix B of Morgan, *Jedediah Smith and the Opening of the West*, 350–60.

3. Ibid., 350–53. In his first commercially published book, *The Humboldt: Highroad of the West*, 25, Morgan quoted the passage given here in the letter to Smith's brother, but only to speculate that it refers to his near-fatal crossing of the Great Salt Lake Desert, rather than to explore what it might indicate about Smith's personality.

4. Morgan, *Jedediah Smith and the Opening of the West*, 312–13. The appearance of George R. Brooks's edition of Smith's 1826–27 diary forced Morgan to reconsider his statement that Smith was humorless. "In my biography I called into question whether Jedediah had a sense of humor, saying that in all his writings there were only two remarks that had the ghost of a smile in them, and in those there was as much of wryness as of humor. There is another such case after he reached San Bernardino Valley in the fall of 1826. The commandant, or corporal, he said, presented him a note from Father Sanchez 'written in Latin and as I could not read his Latin nor he my english [sic] it seemed that we were not likely to become general correspondents.'" Morgan to Charles Camp, October 10, 1969, Morgan Papers.

5. Neihardt, "The Song of Jed Smith," 31.

6. Sullivan, *Jedediah Smith: Trader and Trail Breaker*, 200–202.

7. Dale, *The Ashley-Smith Explorations*, 300. Novelist Don Berry, in his popular history of the fur trade, stated but did not develop the thesis of Smith's religion as a torment instead of a comfort. "Smith was a haunted man; his letters to his family constantly reiterate his tremendous feelings of guilt in religious matters." *A Majority of Scoundrels*, 74.

8. Walker, "The Mountain Man as Literary Hero," 23–25.

9. Brooks, *The Southwest Expedition of Jedediah S. Smith* 36–37.

10. Morgan to LeRoy Hafen, September 28, 1952, Morgan Papers; *Jedediah Smith and the Opening of the West*, 431, n. 5.

CLASS CONFLICT WITHOUT MARX

1. DeVoto, *Across the Wide Missouri*, 30–33. Russell's comment is in Haines, *Osborne Russell's Journal of a Trapper*, 60.

2. Wishart, *The Fur Trade*.

3. Ibid., 1.

4. See also Clokey, *William H. Ashley*, particularly chapter 8, "Rationalizing the Mountain Fur Industry, 1825–1827," which deals with Ashley's role as a fur entrepreneur using primarily the same statistics as Morgan and Wishart.

5. Hine and Faragher, *The American West*, 146, 149, 150, 154.

6. Ibid., 154.

7. Morgan to Harrison Platt [Bobbs Merrill publishers], June 13, 1953, Morgan Papers.

8. Morgan, *Jedediah Smith and the Opening of the West*, 8–9.

9. Clokey, *William H. Ashley*, 159.

10. Ibid., 232.

11. Berry, *A Majority of Scoundrels*, 122. Those risks, as Clokey points out, convinced the shrewd Ashley to reduce his relationship with Smith, Jackson & Sublette to that of banker and supplier, where the likelihood of profits was more consistent. Clokey, *William H. Ashley*, 171–72.

12. Woodward, *Origins of the New South*, 180

13. Utley, *A Life Wild and Perilous*, 85, 87–88.

14. Even David Wishart, whose sophisticated economic analysis calls the rendezvous system "a kind of sharecropping arrangement," fails to point out the brutality and cynicism inherent in its exploitation of the trappers. Wishart, *The Fur Trade*, 125.

15. DeVoto, *The Year of Decision 1846*, 62, 64.

THE VILLAGER: JUANITA BROOKS

1. Dale Morgan to Juanita Brooks, December 28, 1943, Brooks Papers.

2. Arrington, Fox, and May, *Building the City of God*, chapter 7.

3. Larson, "*I Was Called to Dixie*," *vii*.

4. Ibid., 168.

5. Brooks, *On the Ragged Edge*, 130–31.

6. Brooks, *Quicksand and Cactus*.

7. Larson, "*I Was Called to Dixie*," 168, 172.

8. Brooks, *Quicksand and Cactus*, 64–66, 162.

9. Larson, "*I Was Called to Dixie*," 176; Brooks, *On the Ragged Edge*, 134–6.

10. Charles S. Peterson, "Life in a Village Society," 78–96. See also Peterson's introduction to the Utah State University reprint of *Quicksand and Cactus*, *xix–xxxvi*. Peterson's brother, Levi S. Peterson, is the author of the prize-winning biography, *Juanita Brooks: Mormon Woman Historian*, the basis of much of the biographical data presented here.

11. Brooks, *Quicksand and Cactus*, 278–9.

12. Peterson, "Introduction," *xxi*; Brooks to Dale Morgan, February 11, 1943, quoted in Peterson, *Juanita Brooks*, 134.

13. Brooks, *Quicksand and Cactus*, 60–61, 76–80.

14. Ibid., 112.

15. Peterson, *Juanita Brooks*, 102, 111.

16. Ibid., 229.

17. Juanita Brooks diary, July 19, 1933, Brooks Papers, Utah State Historical Society. In *Quicksand and Cactus* she remembers the instrument as an organ.

18. Brooks, *Quicksand and Cactus*, 194–208; 301.

19. Bitton and Ursenbach, "Riding Herd," 22. Anderson "was baptized, I think more as a matter of ceremony; it didn't change him," Brooks adds to her characterization of him as "unconventional." Anderson himself claimed only "a nominal affiliation with the Latter-Day Saints [*sic*]." *Desert Saints, xxxiii.* Anderson's autobiography is on pp. *xxi–xxiii.*

20. Brooks, "Jest a Copyin'–Word f'r Word," 375–95.

21. Brooks, "A Close-up of Polygamy," 299–307.

22. Bitton and Ursenbach, "Riding Herd," 23–24, tells the story of the stolen story.

23. Brooks, *Dudley Leavitt.* The book was reprinted in 1955 and 1969 before being reissued in a revised form in 1973 by the Utah State Historical Society under the title *On the Ragged Edge: The Life and Times of Dudley Leavitt.* Citations here are to the revised edition.

24. Peterson, *Juanita Brooks*, 123, 127.

25. Morgan to Brooks, April 26, 1945, quoted in Peterson, *Juanita Brooks*, 163.

26. Brooks, *On the Ragged Edge*, 3, 22.

27. Peterson, *Juanita Brooks*, 127.

28. Brooks, *The Mountain Meadows Massacre*, *xx*.

29. This is the title of chapter six of Peterson, *Juanita Brooks.*

30. Peterson, *Juanita Brooks*, 38.

31. Brooks, *Quicksand and Cactus*, 229.

32. Brooks to Myron F. Higbee, September 7, 1937, Brooks Papers.

33. Peterson, *Juanita Brooks*, 158–76, passim.

34. Brooks, *Quicksand and Cactus*, 229.

35. This summary is extracted from various places in Brooks's writings. The "Nuremburg defense" doctrine in Mormon justice is given in Brooks, *The Mountain Meadows Massacre*, 40.

36. Ibid., 59.

37. Ibid., 43–46. Recent research in the National Archives and in California records has added greatly to our knowledge of the so-called Fancher party. See, for example, Lee and Loving, "The Fancher Train of 1857," and Logan, Jr., "New Light on the Mountain Meadows Caravan," 224–37. Wise, *Massacre at Mountain Meadows*, offers a new interpretation that blames Brigham Young for creating the climate of vindictiveness that led to the massacre and even for planning it to take place in the remoteness of southern Utah. Wise largely exonerates the emigrants of provocation and sees the role of the Indians as minimal. A forensic report on the skeletal remains of eighteen victims accidentally excavated in 1999 established bullet wounds or blunt instrument traumas as the cause of death in all but one case, in which the cause could not be determined. This evidence might exonerate the Indians, who the Mormons

claimed used knives and hatchets on the women and children. *Salt Lake Tribune*, January 21, 2001.

38. Brooks to J. S. Foster, January 6, 1951, Brooks Papers.

39. She may have feared more serious reprisals. I spent perhaps an hour visiting with Juanita Brooks at her home in St. George one afternoon in 1979, with my supervisor at the Utah State Historical Society, Jay Haymond. As we were leaving, she showed me the place beside the door where she said she had kept a gun for a time after *The Mountain Meadows Massacre* appeared. Fixing those piercing dark eyes upon me, she said meaningfully, "And it wasn't to protect me from the Gentiles." I've never known what to make of that statement, whether she had been truly afraid of her zealous neighbors, or was just seizing an opportunity to wow a wide-eyed newcomer to Utah history. If it was the latter, she succeeded.

40. Peterson, *Juanita Brooks*, 284.

41. Ibid., 479–80.

42. Brooks and Cleland, *A Mormon Chronicle*; Brooks, *On the Mormon Frontier*.

43. Quoted in Peterson, *Juanita Brooks*, 312.

44. Quoted in Peterson, *Juanita Brooks*, 320, 357, 364–65. Brooks detailed her testy relationship with Zucker and some of her other frustrations in writing Jewish history in a letter to Dale Morgan, December 15, 1966, Brooks Papers.

45. Ibid., 385–87.

46. The creation of the book and its frustrating publishing history is expertly told by Charles S. Peterson in the introduction to the Utah State University reprint edition of 1992.

47. Peterson, *Juanita Brooks*, 423.

ORIGINAL SIN ON THE CALIFORNIA TRAIL

1. McMurrin, *Theological Foundations*, 57–68.

2. Brown, *Augustine of Hippo*, discusses the Pelagian controversy extensively in chapter 29.

3. Brooks to Pamela Faust, November 1, 1949, quoted in Peterson, *Juanita Brooks*, 203.

4. Brooks to J. S. Foster, January 6, 1951, Brooks Papers.

5. Brooks, *The Mountain Meadows Massacre*, 32–33; 61.

6. Ibid., 48. Brooks gives the name as "Robinson" in the revised edition, misspelling the name given her by Albert R. Lyman, who was Robison's nephew (Robison was Lyman's middle name). Lyman implausibly ascribes the poisoning to Robison's having merely scratched his itching face, rather than rubbing his eyes. Lyman to Brooks, February 16, 1951, Brooks Papers.

7. Brooks, *The Mountain Meadows Massacre*, 48.

8. Peterson, "The Mormon Reformation of 1856-1857," 61.

9. Ibid., 66.

10. Bigler, *The Forgotten Kingdom*, chapter 6. The Hurt quotation is on pp. 130–31. A specimen of the catechism is on p. 127. A more elaborate version of the catechism which apparently represents Grant's final revised version, printed for distribution to the home missionaries who preached the Reformation, is given in Peterson, "The Mormon Reformation of 1856–1857," 70.

11. Even Bigler, in *The Forgotten Kingdom*, presents no evidence of the Reformation having spread further south than Nephi except through secondary reports, before George A. Smith's brief journey through the southern settlements in August 1857. See pp. 129–30. In fact, the Reformation was preached in the south, most notably by one who would become a major player in the Mountain Meadows Massacre—Isaac Haight. Brooks would have been aware of this if, as she told J. S. Foster in a previously cited reference, she had made a detailed study of the Haight and Higbee families. If she wanted to establish a direct connection between the Reformation and the massacre, she should have sought it in Haight, not in George A. Smith. See Peterson, "The Mormon Reformation," chapter 7.

12. Bigler, *Forgotten Kingdom*, 167.

13. Brooks, *The Mountain Meadows Massacre*, 35, 31.

14. Ibid., 35–39.

15. Ibid., 53, 31. "Recreation" here refers to a popular play about the murder of Joseph Smith written by James H. Martineau.

16. Ibid., 33. Lewis's bitterness was due to his being one of the few survivors of the Haun's Mill massacre. The dubious sweetness of revenge was not to be his, however, for he died in 1855 before he had a chance to exact an eye for an eye at Mountain Meadows. Brooks, *John D. Lee*, 36, gives a synopsis of Lewis's life.

17. If the Mormons held a long-term desire for revenge, it would be understandable, for the record is clear that they had suffered severely and unjustly on many occasions. On the other hand, they had not always been innocent victims either, for their arrogance, chauvinistic rhetoric, and political power had sometimes provoked retaliation. Nor were the Mormons always inclined to turn the other cheek when words turned to blows. Modern Mormon scholars, far removed from the rawness of life on the Utah frontier and having presumably gotten over the anti-Gentile passions of their ancestors, have a tendency to explain away the blood atonement doctrine as merely a rhetorical device used to impress those whose faith had grown lukewarm with the gravity of their sins. Peterson's "The Mormon Reformation of 1856-1857," for example, points out that "The Mormon prophet [Brigham Young] was not above using hyperbole or incendiary talk to bring about desired results. If biting invective would improve the people, Brigham would use it." (p. 67) Davis Bitton observes that "Mormons have insisted that blood atonement, by necessity a voluntary action, was never carried out in practice." "'I'd Rather Have Some Roasting Ears,'" 210. In direct refutation of this idea, D. Michael Quinn offers documentation for some two dozen murders or mutilations carried out under orders from the Mormon hierarchy in obedience to the doctrine before, during, and after the Mormon Reformation. See Quinn, *The Mormon Hierarchy*, 242–99. Quinn's research suggests a long-standing, deep-seated tradition of Mormon violence of which the Mountain Meadows Massacre was a part rather than an aberration caused by momentary hysteria. Although Brooks of course did not have the advantage of Quinn's research, she was more instinctively aware of and willing to acknowledge Mormonism's violent tradition than were most Mormon scholars, even though she shrank from a full acknowledgement of it in her interpretation of the Mountain Meadows Massacre.

18. Brooks to Morgan, December 9, 1945, Brooks Papers.

19. Brooks, *The Mountain Meadows Massacre*, 44–47.

20. Ibid., 46.

21. Brooks, *John D. Lee*, 372.

22. The identity of the "Missouri Wildcats" and their ultimate fate—if indeed there was such a group—continues to elude scholarship. Brooks, whose focus was on the Mormon side of the incident, made little effort to study the emigrant party at all, and seems to accept the Mormon descriptions of them and their actions at face value. As I indicate in the text, the Wildcats' provocative acts as reported by the Mormons seem suicidal and their motivation hard to explain. Recent scholarship has disclosed that the party was both an emigrant group and a speculative venture in cattle of which they were driving a large herd—perhaps 300 to 1,000—to California's gold country to sell to hungry miners. Accordingly, some members of the party would have been drovers, a usually unruly group of cowboys who may indeed have been hired from Missouri and unwilling to suffer the Mormon embargo gladly. It would not have taken many of them or many unwise acts, perhaps against the wishes and orders of the family contingent, to provoke a fatal conflict. See Bigler, *Forgotten Kingdom*, 160. This speculation—and it is only that—was not available to Brooks because of her limited research on the emigrants. Will Bagley's forthcoming book on the massacre promises better answers to this and other questions than we now have.

23. Bigler, *Forgotten Kingdom*, 175, n. 50. Bigler neglects to mention that Forney's report says the emigrants were accused of having used both arsenic and strychnine—the former to poison the water and the latter somehow to "impregnate" the carcasses of the dead cattle. 36th Congress, 1st Session, *Senate Executive Document 42*, 75. This elaborateness of the emigrants' alleged poison inventory and the delay and effort it would have cost them to wait for the animals to die, then further doctor the carcasses with poison, would seem to add to the implausibility of the story. Of course, as Brooks points out, the cow may have died from a natural poison like the *datura* plant, and the emigrants might have been blamed for it.

24. Brooks, *The Mountain Meadows Massacre*, 59.

25. Ibid., *xix–xx*.

26. Peterson, "Juanita Brooks as a Mormon Dissenter, 221–22. This essay first appeared in the *John Whitmer Historical Association Journal*, 13–29.

27. Peterson, *Juanita Brooks*, 179.

THE CONVERSION OF A ZEALOT

1. Brooks, *John Doyle Lee*, 17–18.

2. Lee, *Mormonism Unveiled*, 37. Brooks of course was intimately familiar with *Mormonism Unveiled*, as she was with every other source for Lee's life. She cites the book in an unpublished manuscript, "John Doyle," a study of his family background, in her papers at the Utah State Historical Society. She noted that Lee wrote it "while he was in prison and without his journals," and yet noting that "the surprising thing is that Lee is as accurate as he is. His account of his birth date and christening, of William Morrison standing as his god-father, are all verified by records of the Catholic Church." (p. 2) Yet she failed to use that information and to follow up on its significance in her Lee biography, I suggest, because it did not fit the pattern for his conversion that she had already determined to build.

3. Ibid., 38–39.

4. Ibid., 51.

5. Ibid.
6. Ibid., 54.
7. Ibid., 52.
8. Ibid.
9. Ibid.
10. Peterson, *Juanita Brooks*, 282, 284; Juanita Brooks, notes for a speech at Utah State University summer school, Brooks Papers.
11. Merton, "A Devout Meditation," 45–52.
12. Brooks, *John Doyle Lee*, 210–11.

THE NOVELIST: WALLACE STEGNER

1. *Collected Stories of Wallace Stegner*, *ix*.
2. Stegner and Etulain, *Conversations*, 17. Other warnings appear on pp. 77 and 80–81.
3. Benson, *Wallace Stegner*. Benson of course does not ignore Stegner's autobiographical writings and the many interviews he gave about his life and work, and I draw upon them as well. Colberg, *Wallace Stegner: A Descriptive Bibliography*, is a reasonably complete survey of Stegner's prolific output, while Etulain and Howard, "Wallace Stegner," 380–84, lists the secondary literature.
4. Stegner, *The Big Rock Candy Mountain*.
5. Stegner, "At Home in the Fields of the Lord," 157–58.
6. Stegner, "Chip Off the Old Block," 205–19.
7. Stegner, *Crossing to Safety*.
8. Stegner, *Angle of Repose*; *Beyond the Hundredth Meridian*; *The Uneasy Chair*.
9. Stegner, *Wolf Willow*.
10. Etulain, *Conversations*, 62.
11. Ibid., 23.
12. Stegner, *Mormon Country*.
13. Benson, *Wallace Stegner*, 44.
14. Quoted in Benson, *Wallace Stegner*, 44.
15. Stegner, "It is the Love of Books I Owe Them," 114.
16. Stegner, *The Preacher and the Slave*; *The Big Rock Candy Mountain* and *Recapitulation* also draw upon his Salt Lake City years.
17. Benson, *Wallace Stegner*, 382.
18. This is one fictional departure from Stegner's real life. As he told Richard Etulain, he never did put a headstone on his father's grave. Etulain, *Conversations*, 8.
19. Stegner, *Clarence Edward Dutton*, 13–14. The quotations given here are taken directly from the dissertation, but I chose for the reader's convenience to cite them in this twenty-three-page pamphlet issued by the university while Stegner was an instructor there.
20. Stegner, "Clarence Edward Dutton," 42; Stegner, *Clarence Edward Dutton*, 14.
21. Stegner, *Crossing to Safety*.
22. Stegner had learned from bitter experience, with the Mary Hallock Foote family's objections to the literary license he had taken in dealing with Foote's papers in *Angle of Repose*, not to risk similar objections to *Crossing to Safety* from the Gray family.

23. Although Stegner's *Clarence Edward Dutton: An Appraisal* was published in 1936, it was only a pamphlet-sized synopsis of his dissertation.

24. Etulain, *Conversations*, 116–17. In a letter asking Dale Morgan to read the galleys to see if he could catch any major errors, Stegner admits that "I started out with no particular interest and no particular respect for Mormon history, intending to use the book only as a stopgap between novels and not caring much if I made a thousand boners. By the time I got finished I was wishing I had had time to do a reputable job." Stegner to Morgan, June 8, 1942, Morgan Papers.

25. Benson, *Wallace Stegner*, 123.

26. Stegner, *One Nation.*

27. Stegner, *Beyond the Hundredth Meridian.*

28. Stegner, *This Is Dinosaur.*

29. Stegner, *The Gathering of Zion*; with Page Stegner, *American Places.*

30. Topping, "Wallace Stegner and the Mormons," 25–41, explores this theme further.

31. Benson, *Wallace Stegner*, 122.

32. Stegner, *Mormon Country*, 189.

33. Stegner, "Living Dry," 70.

34. See, for example, May, *Utah: A People's History*; Alexander, *Utah, The Right Place.*

35. Utah Work Projects Administration, *Utah: A Guide to the State.*

36. Powell, *Report on the Lands of the Arid Region.*

37. Darrah, *Powell of the Colorado*; Worster, *A River Running West.*

38. Stegner, notes on biography and fiction, Stegner Papers.

39. Benson, *Wallace Stegner*, 216.

40. See, however, Slaughter and Landon, *Trail of Hope*, which is based upon full access to the Library-Archives of the Church of Jesus Christ of Latter-day Saints into which Stegner was not allowed, and which includes in addition a dazzling collection of illustrations in the form of rarely seen photographs and paintings, artifacts, and copies of manuscripts.

41. Benson, *Wallace Stegner*, 292.

42. Stegner, *The Gathering of Zion*, 313.

43. Ibid., 314, 12–13. A group of unlabeled notes on unruled sheets of yellow paper in the Stegner collection at the University of Utah appears to be Stegner's side of a conversation with Dale Morgan as he was planning the Mormon Trail book. "Except for Benny DeVoto's 1846 [*The Year of Decision*], I've got almost a mandate to take the faith promotion out *of the whole migration* which will not get me loved," he wrote.

44. "Once the 1847 trip has been handled, the later years will have to be syncopated," he wrote in a conversation note to Dale Morgan, Stegner Papers. Thus the emigration of the first year stood as a sort of synecdoche for the entire movement.

45. Benson, *Wallace Stegner*, 298–99.

46. Stegner, *The Gathering of Zion*, 13.

47. Stegner, "Born a Square," 170–85.

48. Benson, *Wallace Stegner*, 4. This is a paraphrase, Benson says, of something in a novel by Robert Stone.

49. Etulain, *Conversations*, 15.

50. Benson, *Wallace Stegner*, 321; Stegner notes on Bernard DeVoto, Stegner Papers.

51. Stegner, "Field Guide to the Western Birds," 126–94; *All the Little Live Things*; *The Spectator Bird*.

52. Stegner, *All the Little Live Things*, 86.

53. Ibid., 195.

54. Etulain, *Conversations*, 83–84, discusses the inception of the project. Stegner's notes for the project defend his bending of historical figures to fictional purposes. "As to using historical people for a fictional purpose, so did Hawthorne, & for the same reason: the search for a usable past." Notes on *Angle of Repose*, Stegner Papers.

55. Stegner, notes on *Angle of Repose*, Stegner Papers.

56. Stegner, *The Letters of Bernard DeVoto*.

57. The DeVoto Papers at Stanford include materials closed to research at this writing, including most notably the correspondence with Katherine Grant Sterne, a tuberculosis patient with whom he corresponded from 1933 until her early death in 1944. Partly out of consideration for DeVoto's widow and also out of Stegner's own sense of decency, he refrained from dealing with whatever skeletons lurk in that closet.

58. Stegner, notes on biography and fiction, Stegner Papers.

59. The Stegner Papers at the University of Utah contain, in his notes on DeVoto, a list of criteria for selection of letters for the *Letters* volume:

> Any letter which reveals BDV as thinker, as friend, as champion of a cause, as teacher, as antagonist, as submerged artist; omit those letters, especially in conservation controversies, where general principles are buried under many transient facts; omit those letters where the personal attacks or opinions are violent to the point of libel.
>
> Any letter in which he expresses himself fully about the West, conservation principles, writing, the teaching of writing, Harvard, Breadloaf, psycho-analysis and the psychoanalytic underpinning of literature, history.
>
> Any letter which reveals his relationships to certain people, places, and institutions, as above: Utah, the West, Breadloaf, Harvard, Northwestern, Saturday Review, Harper's and its editors.
>
> Certain letters written for publication, with polemic intent.

60. Stegner, *Marking the Sparrow's Fall*.

61. Doig, "Thoughts on Wallace Stegner," 35.

THE GOD THAT FAILED

1. Stegner, *Beyond the Hundredth Meridian*, 50, 201.

2. Ibid., 6.

3. Ibid., 316.

4. Ibid., 219, 365, 337.

5. Ibid., 350, 342, 299, 313.

6. Ibid., *viii*.

7. Ibid., 123–25.

8. Etulain, *Conversations*, 170.

9. Stegner, *Beyond the Hundredth Meridian*, 361; Aton, *Inventing John Wesley Powell*, 15.

10. Worster, *A River Running West*, 362. To be fair to Worster, he does conclude that in his advocacy of "a more thoughtful, scientifically informed ethic of conservation . . . conservationists and environmentalists would rightly look back on him as one of their founding giants" (p. 573). It takes a subtler portrayal of a more complex Powell than Stegner's, however, to sustain such a view.

STATE MANAGING A MIGRATION

1. Thomas, *A Country in the Mind*, 182.

2. Stegner, *The Gathering of Zion*, 181–82.

3. Ibid., 114, 120, 176, 191.

4. Ibid., 224.

5. Ibid., 174.

6. Ibid., 184.

7. Unruh, *The Plains Across*, especially chapter 4, "Emigrant Interaction," describes the various organizational and cooperative practices among non-Mormon emigrants on the Oregon Trail.

8. Stegner, *The Gathering of Zion*, 144. Peterson, "Beyond the Problems of Exceptionalist History," 133–51, explores the problem of Mormon exceptionalism and mentions Stegner among the Gentile historians who began placing Mormon history in its regional context, but it says nothing of the residual exceptionalism in Stegner's interpretation.

9. Etulain, *Conversations*, 160–61.

10. Stegner, *The Gathering of Zion*, 46–47.

11. Ibid., 47–48.

12. Ibid., 107.

13. Ibid., 297.

14. Ibid., 311. Stegner is perhaps inadvertently echoing the thesis of Pomeroy in "Toward a Reorientation of Western History," 579–600, that western emigrants tended to replicate eastern institutions and cultural values more than they abandoned them in response to the experience of the frontier.

15. The Frost quotation appears in Stegner, *The Uneasy Chair*, 241.

16. Bloch, *The Historian's Craft*, 140.

THE EXORCIST

1. Brodie, *No Man Knows My History*, 1.

2. Merton, *The Waters of Siloe*, 242–49.

3. Alexander, *Mormonism in Transition*, is a masterful narrative of these and other dimensions of this cultural revolution.

4. Stephenson, "Fawn McKay Brodie," 99–102. Brodie's biography has been expertly written by Bringhurst, *Fawn McKay Brodie*.

5. Brodie to Dale Morgan, June 15, 1943, Morgan Papers. She introduces herself and invites him to dinner to discuss her Joseph Smith research, indicating that she

had been prompted to do this by their mutual friends Jarvis Thurston and Nels Anderson.

6. Bringhurst, "A Biography of the Biography," 7–38, tells this story much more elaborately than I can here. Biographical detail throughout this section is derived mostly from Bringhurst's *Fawn McKay Brodie*.

7. See, for example, DeVoto's use of the term in his review, "The Case of the Prophet, Joseph Smith."

8. Brodie, *No Man Knows My History*, 1.

9. Ibid., 16, 18.

10. Ibid., 31, 33, 159–60.

11. Ibid., 62–63, 69.

12. Ibid., 421.

13. Ibid., 403, *viii*, 93. Some of these ideas, to be sure, come from Brodie's later reflections as included in the 1971 second edition, but the ideas are integral, nevertheless, to her original thesis.

14. Bringhurst, "Applause, Attack, and Ambivalence," 39–59.

15. Dale L. Morgan to Fawn Brodie, June 1946, in Walker, *Dale Morgan on Early Mormonism*, 125–26; Brodie to Morgan, May 27, 1946, Morgan Papers; Launius, "From Old to New in Mormon History," 211.

16. Bringhurst, "Applause, Attack, and Ambivalence," 57, n. 29.

17. Morgan, "A Prophet and His Legend," 7–8.

18. Fisher, *Children of God*; "Mormonism and Its Yankee Prophet," 1.

19. Brodie, *No Man Knows My History*, 4.

20. Fisher, "Mormonism and Its Yankee Prophet," 1.

21. DeVoto, "The Case of the Prophet, Joseph Smith."

22. Both sides of the exchange are fortunately in print, Morgan's in Walker, *Dale Morgan on Early Mormonism*, 92–101; 106–15, which also includes his letters to Brodie on the same issue; DeVoto's in Stegner, *The Letters of Bernard DeVoto*, 274–82.

23. Stegner, *The Letters of Bernard DeVoto*, 277.

24. Brodie to Dale Morgan, December 18, 1945, Morgan Papers; DeVoto to Brodie, December 28, 1945, Brodie Papers; Brodie to Morgan, December 30, 1945, July 25, 1946, Morgan Papers.

25. Brodie to Dale Morgan, December 30, 1945, Morgan Papers.

26. In Bringhurst, *Reconsidering*, 60–63, 219.

27. Brodie, *Thaddeus Stevens*. Citations here are to the 1966 paperback edition. Bringhurst, *Fawn McKay Brodie*, chapter 4, gives the biographical context.

28. Brodie to Dale Morgan, November 22, 1954, quoted in Bringhurst, *Fawn McKay Brodie*, 137.

29. Korngold, *Thaddeus Stevens*.

30. Current, *Old Thad Stevens*.

31. Brodie became embittered by Knopf's lack of faith in her *Thaddeus Stevens*. She did one more book for him, her edition of Burton's *City of the Saints*, but otherwise stayed with Norton for the rest of her career. She did negotiate with Knopf briefly regarding the Nixon biography, but Bringhurst thinks it was a flirtation designed only to generate competition with Norton and enable her to command a larger advance. If so, the strategy worked, for Norton gave her $75,000. Bringhurst, *Fawn McKay Brodie*, 234.

32. Bringhurst, *Fawn McKay Brodie*, 140.
33. Brodie, *Thaddeus Stevens*, 10.
34. Bringhurst, *Fawn McKay Brodie*, 138.
35. Brodie, *Thaddeus Stevens*, 10, 373.
36. Ibid., 236.
37. Ibid., 161–63; 305; 371.
38. *Ex parte Milligan* (1866) ruled that military courts have no jurisdiction outside a theater of war. This threatened the authority of the governors in the five military districts in the South during Reconstruction, an authority upon which the entire success of Stevens's program depended. *Ex part McCardle* (1867) threatened to extend the rights guaranteed to blacks under the Reconstruction Acts of 1867 to whites who were attempting to subvert those very rights and resubjugate the Freedmen.
39. Brodie, *Thaddeus Stevens*, 321–23.
40. Ibid., 292–93.
41. Ibid., 188.
42. Ibid., 363, 370–71.
43. Brodie, *The Devil Drives*. Citations here are to the 1984 Norton paperback reprint.
44. Burton, *The City of the Saints*.
45. Shirley E. Stephenson, interview with Fawn Brodie, November 30, 1975, p. 16; Bruce Brodie, "Monologue on Fawn M. Brodie," p. 12, both in Brodie Papers.
46. Brodie was both flattered and irritated that the BBC used her biography without payment or acknowledgment as the basis of its Nile series, but told Shirley Stephenson that she "loved what the British did with it. It was a beautiful series."
47. Bringhurst, *Fawn McKay Brodie*, 156–57.
48. Rice, *Captain Sir Richard Francis Burton*, *xv*.
49. Brodie, *The Devil Drives*, 74.
50. Ibid., 16, 75.
51. She does call Burton an imposter, with a small "i," in the same place she describes his recognition of the same thing in Smith, during his studies of Mormonism in connection with his journey to Salt Lake City. Brodie, *The Devil Drives*, 187.
52. Ibid., 25, 74.
53. Ibid., 77, 105.
54. Ibid., 150–53.
55. Ibid., 335.
56. Ibid., 331.
57. Ibid., 335.
58. Brodie, *Thomas Jefferson*.
59. Malone, *Jefferson and His Time*, eventually a six-volume work, was only complete through the fourth volume, covering Jefferson's first presidential term, when Brodie's book appeared; the standard single-volume biography in modern times is Peterson, *Thomas Jefferson and the New Nation*.
60. Brodie, *Thomas Jefferson*, 15.
61. Bringhurst, *Fawn McKay Brodie*, 213–19, discusses the reception of the book, and describes the Wills debate on 227–28. Brodie's extensive notes in preparation for her debate with Wills are in the Brodie Papers.

62. Ibid., 229. Foster, "Jefferson Fathered Slave's Last Child," 27–28, presents the DNA evidence supporting the Jefferson-Hemings relationship.

63. Gordon-Reed, *Thomas Jefferson and Sally Hemings*, 225.

64. Brodie, lecture notes on "The Biographer in Today's World: The Artist Under Oath," Brodie Papers.

65. Bringhurst, *Fawn McKay Brodie*, 184, 205, 238–39; Brodie, *Thomas Jefferson*, 43.

66. Bringhurst, *Fawn McKay Brodie*, 207–08, 238.

67. Ibid., 187. Bringhurst finds other personal and psychological roots for Brodie's interest in Jefferson as well, including her memories of her own Monticello—the family home in Huntsville—and her relations with what she remembered as her despotic father. See also his "Fawn M. Brodie—Her Biographies," 203–29.

68. Brodie, *Thomas Jefferson*, 15–16, 32.

69. Ibid., 40–42.

70. Brodie, *Richard Nixon*.

71. Quoted in Bringhurst, *Fawn McKay Brodie*, 263.

72. Brodie, *Richard Nixon*, 9–10. Unfortunately for Nixon's reputation, the larger body of tapes, ably excerpted and interpreted in Kutler, *Abuse of Power*, only adds further weight to the "shabby, pathetic felon" image rather than the "responsible decision-maker."

73. Quoted in Bringhurst, *Fawn McKay Brodie*, 265.

74. Ibid., 27. Brodie repeats her assertion that Nixon majored in history on p. 117. The college transcript is given on p. 107.

75. Ibid., 117–18.

76. Ibid., 154–55; chapter one, "Man of Paradox" and chapter nineteen, "Checkers," focus on the issues discussed here. Beschloss, *Taking Charge*, 553. Beschloss quotes biographer William Manchester in the same place as saying "that for Johnson the shortest distance between two points was a tunnel."

77. Brodie, *Richard Nixon*, 445.

78. Ibid., 233–34.

79. Ibid., 108, 130.

"DANGEROUSLY LIKE COMMON SENSE"

1. Erikson, *Young Man Luther*, 14.

2. For further comparison, see Bringhurst, "Juanita Brooks and Fawn Brodie," 105–27.

3. "Leonardo da Vinci and a Memory of His Childhood," a paper Freud wrote in 1909, was, in his biographer's words, "a scouting expedition for the massive invasion of cultural subjects he planned to undertake, weapons of psychoanalysis in hand." In the same year, Freud wrote to Carl Jung that "[t]he domain of biography, too, must become ours." Gay, *Freud: A Life For Our Time*, 268.

4. Brodie to Dale Morgan, December 18, 1945; January 19, 1946, Morgan Papers.

5. Brodie to Dale Morgan, April 11, 1950, Morgan Papers.

6. Examples of pioneering psychobiographies include Phyllis Greenacre, *Swift and Carroll: A Psychoanalytic Study of Their Lives*; E. Sterba and R. Sterba, *Beethoven*

and His Nephew: A Psychoanalytic Study of Their Relationship; and Erik Erikson, *Young Man Luther*.

7. Greenacre, "The Imposter," 359–82.

8. There were, of course, those during Smith's lifetime who called him an imposter, and Brodie, in *No Man Knows My History*, 1, was only quoting the use of the term in a nineteenth-century gazetteer. But see also p. 31, for example, where she refers to him as "the deliberate imposter."

9. "It was a *terrible* ordeal to just go back into the literature and write the supplement," she told Shirley Stephenson. "Mormon historiography is a swamp. You get up to your neck right away, it is so complicated. What is a fact? That is a big question. No devout Mormon and non-Mormon can agree on what is a fact. So it is terribly hard." Stephenson, "Fawn McKay Brodie," 111.

10. Brodie, *No Man Knows My History*, 2d ed., 419.

11. Narcissism was first adequately described in the 1970s in the work of Heinz Kohut, *The Analysis of the Self*, and Otto Kernberg, *Borderline Conditions and Pathological Narcissism*.

12. Brodie, *No Man Knows My History*, 2d ed., 413; Anderson, *Inside the Mind of Joseph Smith*. "I think the *Book of Mormon* is absolutely vital to an understanding of Smith's inner conflicts," Brodie wrote to a clinical psychologist who proposed to study Joseph Smith, "I didn't use it enough." Brodie to J. B. Molineaux, October 14, 1964, Brodie Papers.

13. Shirley Stephenson, interview with Fawn Brodie, Brodie Papers; Brodie, lecture on "Psychoanalysis in Biography," at Pitzer College, December 11, 1968, p. 12, Brodie Papers.

14. Shirley Stephenson, interview with Fawn Brodie, Brodie Papers.

15. Brodie, *Thomas Jefferson*, 22, 23, 26, 27–28, 45, 222.

16. Ellis, *American Sphinx*, 396.

17. Ibid. Brodie has sometimes been credited with the last laugh on the Sally Hemings liaison after DNA research in 1998 suggested that Hemings' descendants were indeed Jefferson's progeny. See Foster, et al., "Jefferson Fathered Slave's Last Child," 27–28. But Brodie's conclusion was based entirely on circumstantial evidence that proved no more than that one could not rule out the possibility of such a liaison. Brodie made a lucky guess.

18. Brodie, lecture on "Psychoanalysis in Biography," 12–13; lecture notes on "The Biographer in Today's World: The Artist Under Oath," both in Brodie Papers.

19. Loewenberg, "Psychohistory," 414.

20. Brodie, lecture on "Psychoanalysis in Biography," 13.

21. Bringhurst, *Fawn McKay Brodie*, 224–26; 229–34; 244–49. Brodie, *Richard Nixon*, 10.

22. Loewenberg, "Psychohistory," 409; review quoted in Bringhurst, *Fawn McKay Brodie*, 263.

THE LEGACY: UTAH HISTORIANS AND THE "NEW" HISTORIES

1. See Kuhn, *The Structure of Scientific Revolutions*, for a description of a similar dialectic in the evolution of scientific theories.

2. Arrington, *Great Basin Kingdom.*

3. Arrington, "Scholarly Studies of Mormonism in the Twentieth Century," 24–25.

4. Ibid., 25.

5. Peterson, *Juanita Brooks*, 242, 312. Despite these criticisms, Arrington was an admirer of Brooks, telling her on the occasion of his support for her Distinguished Service Award in Letters from the Utah Academy of Sciences, Arts, and Letters that "we have, in the truest sense, honored the Academy by honoring you." Ibid., 256.

6. Arrington, *Great Basin Kingdom*, ix.

7. Bitton, "Ten Years in Camelot," 9–33. Other studies of the Arrington years and the New Mormon History include Arrington, *Adventures of a Church Historian*; Quinn, *The New Mormon History*; Bitton and Ursenbach Beecher, *New Views of Mormon History*; Walker, Whittaker, and Allen, *Mormon History*, 60–112; and Alexander, "Historiography and the New Mormon History," 25–49.

8. Arrington, *Adventures of a Church Historian*, soft-pedals but nevertheless discusses his increasing frustration with trying to write history on the one hand and defend it to skeptical church leaders on the other, and chapter 14 describes the transfer to BYU. Smith, *Faithful History*, explores the degree to which Mormon history should be "faith-promoting" (Elder Packer's term "advanced history" is reported by D. Michael Quinn on p. 71). See also Walker, Whittaker, and Allen, *Mormon History*, chapter 3, and Lavina Fielding Anderson's narrative of the events leading to Quinn's (and her own) excommunication in "DNA Mormon: D. Michael Quinn," 329–63.

9. Bagley, *Blood of the Prophets.*

10. Bitton and Ursenbach Beecher, "Riding Herd," 11–33.

11. Walker, Whittaker, and Allen, *Mormon History*, 46–47; Bitton and Arrington, *Mormons and Their Historians*, 111–18; Bringhurst, *Reconsidering* No Man Knows My History.

12. Launius, "From Old to New Mormon History," in Bringhurst, *Reconsidering* No Man Knows My History, 220.

13. Ibid., 219. There has been a trickle of non-Mormon scholars working in Mormon history, from Thomas O'Dea and Mario DePillis to Jan Shipps and Polly Aird.

14. Hill, "Secular or Sectarian History," in Bringhurst, *Reconsidering* No Man Knows My History, 62.

15. Billington, *America's Frontier Heritage*; and *Frederick Jackson Turner.*

16. Etulain, "The American Literary West," 311–48; Wade, *The Urban Frontier*; Dykstra, *The Cattle Towns*; Morgan, *Westward Tilt*; Nash, *The American West in the Twentieth Century.*

17. Nash, *Creating the West*, 264–65 (the prairie dog metaphor is mine, not Nash's); Malone, "Beyond the Last Frontier," 409.

18. Pomeroy, "The Changing West," 80. Pomeroy himself labored to pull the field of western history out of its mire of Turnerism and trivia through several notable articles and books, but the influence of his powerful mind was felt more strongly in his seminar room at the University of Oregon than through his relatively meager list of publications. See Malone, "Earl Pomeroy and the Reorientation of Western History," 311–34.

19. It was Charles S. Peterson who jestingly referred to Limerick's "taste for the

limelight" in "Speaking for the Past," in Milner, O'Connor, and Sandweiss, *The Oxford History of the American West*, 767. Limerick defends and advocates her promotional orientation in, among other places, "A How-to Guide for the Academic Going Public," 323–32. An early manifesto and collection of critical essays on the New Western History is Limerick, Milner, and Rankin, *Trails: Toward a New Western History*. See also Limerick, *Legacy of Conquest*; Worster, *Rivers of Empire*; and White, *"It's Your Misfortune and None of My Own."*

BIBLIOGRAPHY

MANUSCRIPT COLLECTIONS

Archives of the Catholic Diocese of Salt Lake City

Robert J. Dwyer Papers

Marriott Library, University of Utah

Dean Brimhall Papers
Fawn Brodie Papers
Leland H. Creer Papers
Madeline McQuown Papers
Dale L. Morgan Papers
Andrew Love Neff Papers
Wallace Stegner Papers

Green Library, Stanford University

Bernard DeVoto Papers

Utah State Historical Society

Juanita Brooks Papers
Stanley S. Ivins Papers
Charles Kelly Papers
Roderick Korns Papers
Dale L. Morgan Papers
Levi Edgar Young Papers

GOVERNMENT DOCUMENTS

Forney, J. Superintendent of Indian Affairs, Utah Territory, to A. B. Greenwood, Commissioner of Indian Affairs, Washington, D.C., September 29, 1859, in *Report of the Secretary of the Interior for 1859* (December 1, 1859), 36th Congress,

1st Session, Senate Executive Document No. 2. Washington, D.C.: George W. Bowman, 1860: 730–41.

Forney, J. Superintendent of Indian Affairs, Utah Territory, to A. B. Greenwood, Commissioner of Indian Affairs, Washington, D.C., August 1859, in *Message of the President of the United States, Communicating in Compliance with a Resolution of the Senate, Information in Relation to the Massacre at Mountain Meadows, and Other Massacres in Utah Territory*, 36th Congress, 1st Session, Senate Executive Document No. 42. Washington, D.C.: George W. Bowman, 1860: 75–80.

Powell, John Wesley. *Report on the Lands of the Arid Region of the United States*. Washington, D. C.: Government Printing Office, 1879.

ARTICLES

Adams, Charles P. and Gustive O. Larson, "A Study of the LDS Historian's Office," *Utah Historical Quarterly* 40 (Fall 1972): 370–89.

Alexander, Thomas G. "Historiography and the New Mormon History: A Historian's Perspective," *Dialogue: A Journal of Mormon Thought* 19 (Fall 1986): 25–49.

Andrews, Thomas F. "Lansford W. Hastings and the Promotion of the Salt Lake Desert Cutoff: A Reappraisal," *Western Historical Quarterly* 4 (April 1973): 133–50.

Arrington, Leonard J. "Scholarly Studies of Mormonism in the Twentieth Century," *Dialogue: A Journal of Mormon Thought* 1 (Spring 1966): 15–28.

Bagley, Will. "Lansford Warren Hastings: Scoundrel or Visionary?" *Overland Journal* 12 (Spring 1994): 12–26.

Barclay, Julius. "A Bibliography of the Writings of Bernard DeVoto," in Catherine Drinker Bowen, et al. *Four Portraits and One Subject: Bernard DeVoto*. Boston: Houghton Mifflin, 1963.

Beard, Charles A. "Written History as an Act of Faith," *American Historical Review* 39 (January 1934): 219–29.

Becker, Carl. "Everyman His Own Historian," *American Historical Review* 37 (January 1932): 221–36.

Billington, Ray Allen. "Introduction" to Dale L. Morgan, *The Great Salt Lake*. Albuquerque: University of New Mexico Press, 1973: *vii–xxviii*.

Bitton, Davis. "'I'd Rather Have Some Roasting Ears': The Peregrinations of George Armstrong Hicks," *Utah Historical Quarterly* 68 (Summer 2000): 196–222.

_______. "Ten Years in Camelot: A Personal Memoir," *Dialogue: A Journal of Mormon Thought* 16 (Autumn 1983): 9–33.

Bitton, Davis and Maureen Ursenbach, "Riding Herd: A Conversation With Juanita Brooks," *Dialogue: A Journal of Mormon Thought* 9 (Spring 1974): 11–33.

Bringhurst, Newell G. "Fawn M. Brodie—Her Biographies as Autobiography," *Pacific Historical Review* 49 (May 1990): 203–29.

_______. "Fawn M. Brodie, 'Mormondom's Lost Generation,' and *No Man Knows My History*," *Journal of Mormon History* 16 (1990): 11–23.

_______. "Fawn McKay Brodie and Her Quest for Independence," *Dialogue: A Journal of Mormon Thought* 22 (Summer 1989): 79–95.

_______. "Juanita Brooks and Fawn Brodie—Sisters in Mormon Dissent," *Dialogue: A Journal of Mormon Thought* 27 (Summer 1994): 105–27.

Brooks, Juanita. "A Close-up of Mormon Polygamy," *Harper's* 168 (February 1934): 299–307.

_______. "Jest a Copyin'–Word f'r Word," *Utah Historical Quarterly* 37 (Fall 1969): 375–95.

Campbell, Eugene E. "Brigham Young's Outer Cordon—A Reappraisal," *Utah Historical Quarterly* 41 (Summer 1973): 220–53.

DeVoto, Bernard. "The Case of the Prophet, Joseph Smith. First Dependable History of Mormonism Written From the Inside," *New York Herald Tribune Weekly Book Review*, December 16, 1945.

_______. "The Centennial of Mormonism," *American Mercury* (January 1930): 1–13.

_______. "Introduction" to *The Life and Adventures of James P. Beckwourth*. New York: Alfred A. Knopf, 1931.

_______. "Ogden: The Underwriters of Salvation," in Duncan Aikman, ed., *The Taming of the Frontier*. New York: Minton, Balch & Co., 1925: 27–60.

_______. [Review of H. L. Mencken's *Prejudices: Fourth Series*] *Evanston* [Illinois] *News-Index*, January 27, 1925.

Ellsworth, S. George. "Hubert Howe Bancroft and the History of Utah," *Utah Historical Quarterly* 22 (April 1954): 99–124.

_______. "Utah History: Retrospect and Prospect," *Utah Historical Quarterly* 40 (Fall 1972): 342–67.

Ely, Richart T., "Economic Aspects of Mormonism," *Harper's Monthly* 106 (April 1903): 667–78.

Etulain, Richard W. "The American Literary West and Its Interpreters: The Rise of a New Historiography," *Pacific Historical Review* 46 (August 1976): 311–48.

Fetzer, Leland A. "Bernard DeVoto and the Mormon Tradition," *Dialogue: A Journal of Mormon Thought* 6 (1971): 23–38.

Fisher, Vardis. "Mormonism and Its Yankee Prophet," *New York Times Book Review*, November 25, 1945: 1.

Foster, Craig L. "Madeline McQuown, Dale Morgan, and the Great Unfinished Brigham Young Biography," *Dialogue: A Journal of Mormon Thought* 31 (Summer 1998): 111–23.

Foster, Eugene A. "Jefferson Fathered Slave's Last Child," *Nature* 396 (1998): 27–28.

Geary, Edward. "Mormondom's Lost Generation: The Novelists of the 1940s," *BYU Studies* 18 (Fall 1977): 89–98.

Greenacre, Phyllis. "The Imposter," *Psychoanalytic Quarterly* 27 (1958): 359–82.

Hunter, Milton R. [Review of Fawn M. Brodie, *No Man Knows My History*] *Pacific Historical Review* 15 (June 1946): 226–28.

"In Memoriam [Levi Edgar Young]," *Utah Historical Quarterly* 32 (Winter 1964): 88.

Johnson, Kristin. "The Pioneer Palace Car: Adventures in Western Mythmaking," *Crossroads Newsletter* (Summer 1994): 5–8.

Logan, Roger B. "New Light on the Mountain Meadows Caravan," *Utah Historical Quarterly* 60 (Summer 1992): 224–37.

Loewenberg, Peter. "Psychohistory," in Michael Kammen, ed., *The Past Before Us: Contemporary Historical Writing in the United States*. Ithaca, New York: Cornell University Press, 1980.

Malone, Michael P. "Beyond the Last Frontier: Toward a New Approach to Western American History," *Western Historical Quarterly* 20 (November 1989): 409–28.

______. "Earl Pomeroy and the Reorientation of Western History," in Richard W. Etulain, ed., *Writing Western History: Essays on Major Western Historians*. Albuquerque: University of New Mexico Press, 1991: 311–34.

Morgan, Dale L. "A Prophet and His Legend," *Saturday Review of Literature*, November 24, 1945: 7–8.

______. "The State of Deseret," *Utah Historical Quarterly* 8 (April, July, and October 1940).

______, ed. "West From Fort Bridger," *Utah Historical Quarterly* 19 (1951): 1–328.

______. "Western Travels and Travelers in the Bancroft Library," in John Francis McDermott, ed., *Travelers on the Western Frontier*. Urbana: University of Illinois Press, 1970.

Peterson, Charles S. "Beyond the Problems of Exceptionalist History," in Thomas G. Alexander, ed., *Great Basin Kingdom Revisited: Contemporary Perspectives*. Logan: Utah State University Press, 1991: 133–51.

______. "Introduction" to Dale L. Morgan, *The State of Deseret*. Logan: Utah State University Press, 1987: *vii–xiv*.

______. "Introduction," to Juanita Brooks, *Quicksand and Cactus: A Memoir of the Southern Mormon Frontier*. Logan: Utah State University Press, 1992: *xix–xxxvi*.

______. "Life in a Village Society, 1877-1920," *Utah Historical Quarterly* 49 (Winter 1981): 78–96.

______. "Speaking For the Past," in Clyde A. Milner II, et al., *The Oxford History of the American West*. New York: Oxford University Press, 1994: 743–70.

Peterson, Levi S. "Juanita Brooks as a Mormon Dissenter," *John Whitmer Historical Association Journal* 8 (1988): 13–29.

Peterson, Paul H. "The Mormon Reformation of 1856–1857: The Rhetoric and the Reality," *Journal of Mormon History* 15 (1989): 59–87.

Pomeroy, Earl. "The Changing West," in John Higham, ed., *The Reconstruction of American History*. New York: Harper & Brothers, 1962: 64–81.

______. "Toward a Reorientation of Western History: Continuity and Environment," *Mississippi Valley Historical Review* 41 (March 1955): 579–600.

Saunders, Richard L. "'The Strange Mixture of Emotion and Intellect': A Social History of Dale L. Morgan, 1933-42," *Dialogue: A Journal of Mormon Thought* 28 (Winter 1995): 39–58.

______. "The Utah Writers' Project and Writing of *Utah: A Guide to the State*," *Utah Historical Quarterly* 70 (Winter 2002): 21–38.

Stegner, Wallace. "It is the Love of Books I Owe Them," in Elizabeth Haglund, ed., *Remembering the University of Utah*. Salt Lake City: University of Utah Press, 1981: 111–22.

______. "The Personality," in Catherine Drinker Bowen, et al., *Four Portraits and One Subject: Bernard DeVoto*. Boston: Houghton Mifflin, 1963: 79–108.

Stephenson, Shirley E. "Fawn McKay Brodie: An Oral History Interview," *Dialogue: A Journal of Mormon Thought* 14 (Summer 1981): 99–102.

Sturges, Philip C., "In Memoriam Leland H. Creer," *Utah Historical Quarterly* 36 (Summer 1969): 195–97.

Topping, Gary. "One Hundred Years at the Utah State Historical Society," *Utah Historical Quarterly* 65 (Summer 1997): 200–302.

______. "Overland Emigration, the California Trail, and the Hastings Cutoff," in

Bruce R. Hawkins and David B. Madsen, eds., *Excavation of the Donner-Reed Wagons: Historic Archaeology Along the Hastings Cutoff.* Salt Lake City: University of Utah Press, 1990.

_______. "Robert J. Dwyer and the Writing of Utah History," *Utah Historical Quarterly* 71 (Winter 2003): 4–19.

_______. "Wallace Stegner and the Mormons," *South Dakota Review* 23 (Winter 1985): 25–41.

Wahlquist, Wayne. "A Review of Mormon Settlement Literature," *Utah Historical Quarterly* 45 (Winter 1977): 4–21.

Walker, Don D. "The Dogmas of DeVoto," *The Possible Sack* (July 1971): 5.

_______. "The Mountain Man as Literary Hero," *Western American Literature* 1 (Spring 1966): 15–25.

BOOKS AND DISSERTATIONS

Abbey, Edward. *Desert Solitaire: A Season in the Wilderness.* New York: McGraw Hill, 1968.

Alexander, Thomas G. *Mormonism in Transition: A History of the Latter-day Saints, 1890-1930.* Urbana: University of Illinois Press, 1986.

_______. *Utah, The Right Place: The Official Centennial History.* Salt Lake City: Gibbs Smith, 1995.

Anderson, Robert D. *Inside the Mind of Joseph Smith: Psychobiography and the Book of Mormon.* Salt Lake City: Signature Books, 1999.

Anderson, Nels. *Desert Saints: The Mormon Frontier in Utah.* Chicago: University of Chicago Press, 1942.

Andrews, Thomas F. "The Controversial Career of Lansford Warren Hastings: Pioneer California Promoter and Emigrant Guide." Ph.D. dissertation, University of Southern California, 1970.

Arrington, Leonard J. *Adventures of a Church Historian.* Urbana: University of Illinois Press, 1998.

_______. *Great Basin Kingdom: An Economic History of the Latter-day Saints, 1830-1900.* Cambridge, Mass.: Harvard University Press, 1958.

Arrington, Leonard J., Feramorz Y. Fox, and Dean L. May. *Building the City of God: Community & Cooperation Among the Mormons.* Salt Lake City: Deseret Book Co., 1976.

Aton, James M. *Inventing John Wesley Powell: The Major, His Admirers and Cash-Register Dams in the Colorado River Basin.* Cedar City, Utah: Southern Utah State College, 1988.

Bagley, Will. *Blood of the Prophets: Brigham Young and the Massacre at Mountain Meadows.* Norman: University of Oklahoma Press, 2002.

Bagley, Will, and Harold Schindler, eds., *West From Fort Bridger.* Logan: Utah State University Press, 1994.

Bakeless, John. *Lewis and Clark: Partners in Discovery.* New York: William Morrow, 1947.

Bancroft, Hubert Howe. *History of Utah, 1540 to 1886.* San Francisco: The History Company, 1889.

_______. *Literary Industries.* San Francisco: The History Company, 1890.

Benson, Jackson J. *Wallace Stegner: His Life and Work*. New York: Viking, 1996.
Berry, Don. *A Majority of Scoundrels*. New York: Ballantine Books, 1971.
Beschloss, Michael R. *Taking Charge: The Johnson White House Tapes, 1963–1964*. New York: Simon & Schuster, 1997.
Bigler, David L. *The Forgotten Kingdom: The Mormon Theocracy in the American West, 1847–1896*. Spokane: Arthur H. Clark, 1998.
Billington, Ray Allen. *America's Frontier Heritage*. New York: Holt, Rinehart and Winston, 1966.
_______. *Frederick Jackson Turner: Historian, Scholar, Teacher*. New York: Oxford University Press, 1973.
Bitton, Davis, and Leonard J. Arrington. *Mormons and Their Historians*. Salt Lake City: University of Utah Press, 1988.
Bitton, Davis, and Maureen Ursenbach Beecher, eds. *New Views of Mormon History: A Collection of Essays in Honor of Leonard J. Arrington*. Salt Lake City: University of Utah Press, 1987.
Bloch, Marc. *The Historian's Craft*. New York: Vintage Books, 1953.
Bowen, Catherine Drinker, et al. *Four Portraits and One Subject: Bernard DeVoto*. Boston: Houghton Mifflin, 1963.
Bringhurst, Newell G. *Fawn McKay Brodie: A Biographer's Life*. Norman: University of Oklahoma Press, 1999.
_______, ed. *Reconsidering* No Man Knows My History: *Fawn M. Brodie and Joseph Smith in Retrospect*. Logan: Utah State University Press, 1996.
Brodie, Fawn M. *The Devil Drives: A Life of Sir Richard Burton*. New York: W. W. Norton, 1967.
_______. *"No Man Knows My History": The Life of Joseph Smith, the Mormon Prophet*. New York: Alfred A. Knopf, 1945.
_______. *Richard Nixon: The Shaping of His Character*. New York: W. W. Norton, 1981.
_______. *Thaddeus Stevens: Scourge of the South*. New York: W. W. Norton, 1959.
_______. *Thomas Jefferson: An Intimate History*. New York: W. W. Norton, 1974.
_______, ed. Richard Burton, *The City of the Saints and Across the Rocky Mountains to California*. New York: Alfred A. Knopf, 1963.
Brooks, George R., ed. *The Southwest Expeditions of Jedediah S. Smith: His Personal Account of the Journey to California, 1826–1827*. Glendale, California: Arthur H. Clark Co., 1977.
Brooks, Juanita. *Dudley Leavitt: Pioneer to Southern Utah*. St. George, Utah: The author, 1942.
_______. *The History of the Jews in Utah & Idaho*. Salt Lake City: Western Epics, 1973.
_______. *John D. Lee: Zealot-Pioneer Builder-Scapegoat*. Glendale, California: Arthur H. Clark, 1961.
_______. *The Mountain Meadows Massacre*. Norman: University of Oklahoma Press, 1962.
_______. *On the Ragged Edge: The Life and Times of Dudley Leavitt*. Salt Lake City: Utah State Historical Society, 1973.
_______. *Quicksand and Cactus: A Memoir of the Southern Mormon Frontier*. Logan: Utah State University Press, 1992.

_______, ed. *On the Mormon Frontier: The Diary of Hosea Stout, 1848–1861*. Salt Lake City: University of Utah Press and Utah State Historical Society, 1964.

Brooks, Juanita, and Robert Glass Cleland. *A Mormon Chronicle: The Diaries of John D. Lee, 1848–1876*. San Marino, Calif.: The Huntington Library, 1955.

Brown, Peter. *Augustine of Hippo: A Biography*. Berkeley and Los Angeles: University of California Press, 1969.

Caughey, John Walton. *Hubert Howe Bancroft: Historian of the West*. Berkeley: University of California Press, 1946.

Chamberlin, Ralph Vary. *The University of Utah: A History of Its First Hundred Years, 1850 to 1950*. Salt Lake City: University of Utah Press, 1960.

Clark, Harry. *A Venture in History: The Production, Publication, and Sale of the Works of Hubert Howe Bancroft*. Berkeley: University of California Press, 1973.

Clokey, Richard M. *William H. Ashley: Enterprise and Politics in the Trans-Mississippi West*. Norman: University of Oklahoma Press, 1980.

Cochrane, Charles Norris. *Christianity and Classical Culture*. Oxford: The Clarendon Press, 1940.

Colberg, Nancy. *Wallace Stegner: A Descriptive Bibliography*. Lewiston, Idaho: Confluence Press, 1990.

Creer, Leland H. *The Founding of an Empire: The Exploration and Colonization of Utah, 1776–1856*. Sale Lake City: Bookcraft, 1947.

_______. *Utah and the Nation*. Seattle: University of Washington Press, 1929.

Current, Richard N. *Old Thad Stevens, A Story of Ambition*. Madison: University of Wisconsin Press, 1942.

Dale, Harrison C. *The Ashley-Smith Explorations and the Discovery of a Central Route to the Pacific, 1822–1829*. Glendale, California: Arthur H. Clarke, 1941.

Darrah, William Culp. *Powell of the Colorado*. Princeton, N.J.: Princeton University Press, 1951.

DeVoto, Bernard. *Across the Wide Missouri*. Boston: Houghton Mifflin, 1947.

_______. *The Course of Empire*. Boston: Houghton Mifflin, 1952.

_______. *The Journals of Lewis and Clark*. Boston: Houghton Mifflin, 1953.

_______. *Mark Twain's America*. Boston: Little, Brown, 1932.

_______. *The Year of Decision 1846*. Boston: Little, Brown, 1943.

_______, ed. *The Portable Mark Twain*. New York: The Viking Press, 1946.

Dwyer, Robert Joseph. *The Gentile Comes to Utah: A Study in Religious and Social Conflict (1862-1890)*. Washington, D.C.: The Catholic University of America Press, 1941.

Dykstra, Robert R. *The Cattle Towns: A Social History of the Kansas Cattle Trading Centers Abilene, Ellsworth, Wichita, Dodge City and Caldwell, 1867 to 1885*. New York: Atheneum, 1968.

Ellis, Joseph J. *American Sphinx: The Character of Thomas Jefferson*. New York: Alfred A. Knopf, 1997.

Ericksen, Ephraim Edward, *The Psychological and Ethical Aspects of Mormon Group Life*. Chicago: University of Chicago, 1922.

Erikson, Erik H. *Young Man Luther: A Study in Psychoanalysis and History*. New York: W. W. Norton, 1958.

Etulain, Richard W. *Re-imagining the Modern American West: A Century of Fiction, History, and Art*. Tucson: University of Arizona Press, 1996.

_______, ed. *Does the Frontier Experience Make America Exceptional?* Boston: Bedford/St. Martin's, 1999.

_______, ed. *Writing Western History: Essays on Major Western Historians.* Albuquerque: University of New Mexico Press, 1991.

Etulain, Richard W., and N. Jill Howard. *A Bibliographical Guide to the Study of Western American Literature.* Albuquerque: University of New Mexico Press, 1995.

Fisher, Vardis. *Children of God: An American Epic.* New York: Harper & Bros., 1939.

Flake, Chad J. *A Mormon Bibliography, 1830–1930.* Salt Lake City: University of Utah Press, 1978.

Gay, Peter. *Freud: A Life For Our Time.* New York: W. W. Norton, 1988.

Gilson, Etienne. *The Unity of Philosophical Experience.* New York: Charles Scribner's Sons, 1937.

Gordon-Reed, Annette. *Thomas Jefferson and Sally Hemings: An American Controversy.* Charlottesville: University Press of Virginia, 1997.

Greenacre, Phyllis. *Swift and Carroll: A Psychoanalytic Study of Their Lives.* New York: International Universities Press, 1955.

Haines, Aubrey, ed. *Osborne Russell's Journal of a Trapper.* Portland: Oregon Historical Society, 1955.

Hastings, Lansford W. *The Emigrants' Guide to Oregon and California.* Cincinnati: George Conclin, 1845.

Hexter, J. H. *On Historians.* Cambridge, Mass.: Harvard University Press, 1979.

Higham, John. *History: The Development of Historical Studies in the United States.* Englewood Cliffs, N.J.: Prentice-Hall, 1965.

Hine, Robert V., and John Mack Faragher. *The American West: A New Interpretive History.* New Haven, Conn.: Yale University Press, 2000.

Hofstadter, Richard. *The Progressive Historians: Turner, Beard, Parrington.* New York: Alfred A. Knopf, 1953.

Hunter, Milton R. *Brigham Young the Colonizer.* Salt Lake City: Deseret News Press, 1940.

_______. *Utah Indian Stories.* Springville: Art City Publishing Co., 1946.

_______. *Utah in Her Western Setting.* Salt Lake City: Deseret News Press, 1943.

_______. *Utah–The Story of Her People.* Salt Lake City: Deseret News Press, 1946.

Hunter, Milton R., and Thomas Stuart Ferguson. *Ancient America and the Book of Mormon.* Oakland, Calif.: Kolob Book Co., 1950.

Jacobs, Wilbur, John W. Caughey, and Joe B. Frantz. *Turner, Bolton, and Webb: Three Historians of the American Frontier.* Seattle: University of Washington Press, 1965.

Jennings, Jesse D. *Accidental Archaeologist: Memoirs of Jesse D. Jennings.* Salt Lake City: University of Utah Press, 1994.

Kernberg, Otto. *Borderline Conditions and Pathological Narcissism.* New York: Jason Aronson, 1975.

Kohut, Heinz. *The Analysis of the Self.* New York: International Universities Press, 1971.

Korngold, Ralph. *Thaddeus Stevens: A Being Darkly Wise and Rudely Great.* New York: Harcourt Brace, 1955.

Kuhn, Thomas. *The Structure of Scientific Revolutions.* Chicago: University of Chicago Press, 1962.

Kutler, Stanley I. *Abuse of Power: The New Nixon Tapes*. New York: The Free Press, 1997.

Larson, Andrew Karl. *"I Was Called to Dixie": The Virgin River Basin: Unique Experiences in Mormon Pioneering*. St. George, Utah: The Dixie College Foundation, 1992.

Lee, John D. *Mormonism Unveiled*. St. Louis: M. E. Mason, 1891.

Leuchtenburg, William E. *Franklin D. Roosevelt and the New Deal*. New York: Harper & Row, 1963.

Limerick, Patricia Nelson. *The Legacy of Conquest*. New York: W. W. Norton, 1987.

_______. *Something in the Soil: Legacies and Reckonings in the New West*. New York: W. W. Norton, 2000.

Limerick, Patricia Nelson, Clyde A. Milner II, and Charles E. Rankin, eds., *Trails: Toward a New Western History*. Topeka: University Press of Kansas, 1991.

McGlashan, Charles F. *History of the Donner Party: A Tragedy of the Sierra*. Sacramento, Calif.: H. H. Crocker, 1880.

McMurrin, Sterling M. *The Theological Foundations of the Mormon Religion*. Salt Lake City: University of Utah Press, 1965.

Madsen, Brigham D. *Against the Grain: Memoirs of a Western Historian*. Salt Lake City: Signature Books, 1998.

Mangione, Jerre. *The Dream and the Deal: The Federal Writer's Project, 1935–1943*. Philadelphia: University of Pennsylvania Press, 1983.

Mattingly, Garrett. *Bernard DeVoto: A Preliminary Appraisal*. Boston: Little, Brown, 1938.

May, Dean L. *Utah: A People's History*. Salt Lake City: University of Utah Press, 1987.

Mencken, H. L. *Prejudices: A Selection*. New York: Vintage Books, [1955].

Merton, Thomas. *Raids on the Unspeakable*. New York: New Directions, 1966.

_______. *The Waters of Siloe*. New York: Harcourt Brace, 1949.

Miller, James E. *Complete Poetry and Selected Prose By Walt Whitman*. Boston: Houghton Mifflin, 1959.

Mooney, Bernice Maher. *Salt of the Earth: The History of the Catholic Diocese of Salt Lake City, 1776–1987*. Salt Lake City: Catholic Diocese of Salt Lake City, 1987.

Morgan, Dale L. *The Great Salt Lake*. Indianapolis, Ind.: Bobbs Merrill, 1947.

_______. *The Humboldt: Highroad of the West*. New York: Farrar & Rinehart, 1943.

_______. *Jedediah Smith and the Opening of the West*. Indianapolis, Ind.: Bobbs Merrill, 1953.

_______, ed. *Overland in 1846: Diaries and Letters of the California-Oregon Trail*. Georgetown, Calif.: Talisman Press, 1963.

Morgan, Dale L., and Carl I. Wheat. *Jedediah Smith and His Maps of the American West*. San Francisco: California Historical Society, 1954.

_______. *Mapping the Trans-Mississippi West, 1540–1861*. San Francisco: Institute of Historical Cartography, 1957–63.

Morgan, Neil. *Westward Tilt: The American West Today*. New York: Random House, 1963.

Nash, Gerald D. *The American West in the Twentieth Century: A Short History of an Urban Oasis*. Englewood Cliffs, N.J.: Prentice Hall, 1973.

_______. *Creating the West: Historical Interpretations, 1890–1990*. Albuquerque: University of New Mexico Press, 1991.

Neff, Andrew Love. *History of Utah, 1847 to 1869*. Salt Lake City: Deseret News Press, 1940.

Neibuhr, Reinhold. *The Irony of American History*. New York: Charles Scribner's Sons, 1962.

Neihardt, John G. *The Mountain Men*. New York: Macmillan Co., 1961.

Nelson, Lowry. *The Mormon Village: A Pattern and Technique of Land Settlement*. Salt Lake City: University of Utah Press, 1952.

Novick, Peter. *That Noble Dream: The "Objectivity Question" and the American Historical Profession*. Cambridge: Cambridge University Press, 1988.

Penkower, Monty Noam. *The Federal Writers' Project: A Study in Government Patronage of the Arts*. Urbana: University of Illinois Press, 1977.

Peterson, John Alton. *Utah's Black Hawk War*. Salt Lake City: University of Utah Press, 1998.

Peterson, Levi S. *Juanita Brooks: Mormon Woman Historian*. Salt Lake City: University of Utah Press, 1988.

Peterson, Paul H. "The Mormon Reformation." Ph.D. dissertation, Brigham Young University, 1981.

Powell, Allan Kent. *The Utah Guide*. Golden, Colo.: Fulcrum Publishing, 1995.

Preussing, Peter Skiles. "Manifest Destiny and 'The Literary Fallacy': The Paradox in Bernard DeVoto's *Treatment of Westward Expansion*." Master's thesis, Iowa State University, 1968.

Quinn, D. Michael. *Early Mormonism and the Magic World View*. Salt Lake City: Signature Books, 1998.

———. *The Mormon Hierarchy: Extensions of Power*. Salt Lake City: Signature Books, 1997.

———, ed. *The New Mormon History: Revisionist Essays on the Past*. Salt Lake City: Signature Books, 1992.

Rankin, Charles E., ed. *Wallace Stegner: Man and Writer*. Albuquerque: University of New Mexico Press, 1996.

Rice, Edward. *Captain Sir Richard Francis Burton*. New York: Charles Scribner's Sons, 1990.

Rolle, Andrew. *John Charles Fremont: Character As Destiny*. Norman: University of Oklahoma Press, 1991.

Roylance, Ward. *Utah: A Guide to the State*. Salt Lake City: Utah Arts Council, 1982.

Saunders, Richard L. *Eloquence From a Silent World: A Bibliography of the Published Writings of Dale L. Morgan*. Salt Lake City: Caramon Press, 1990.

Sawey, Orlan. *Bernard DeVoto*. New York: Twayne Publishers, 1969.

Sillito, John, and Susan Staker, eds., *Mormon Mavericks: Essays on Dissenters*. Salt Lake City: Signature Books, 2002.

Slaughter, William, and Michael Landon. *Trail of Hope: The Story of the Mormon Trail*. Salt Lake City: Shadow Mountain, 1997.

Smith, George D., ed. *Faithful History: Essays on Writing Mormon History*. Salt Lake City: Signature Books, 1992.

Stegner, Page, ed. *Marking the Sparrow's Fall: The Making of the American West*. New York: Henry Holt, 1998.

Stegner, Wallace. *All the Little Live Things*. New York: The Viking Press, 1967.

———. Angle of Repose. Garden City, N.Y.: Doubleday and Co., 1971.

_______. *Beyond the Hundredth Meridian: John Wesley Powell and the Second Opening of the West*. Boston: Houghton Mifflin, 1954.

_______. *The Big Rock Candy Mountain*. New York: Duell, Sloan and Pearce, 1943.

_______. *The City of the Living, and Other Stories*. Boston: Houghton Mifflin, 1956.

_______. *Clarence Edward Dutton: An Appraisal*. Salt Lake City: University of Utah Press, 1936.

_______. "Clarence Edward Dutton, Geologist and Man of Letters." Ph.D. dissertation, University of Iowa, 1935.

_______. *Collected Stories of Wallace Stegner*. New York: Wings Books, 1994.

_______. *Crossing to Safety*. New York: Random House, 1987.

_______. *The Gathering of Zion: The Story of the Mormon Trail*. New York: McGraw Hill, 1964.

_______. *Mormon Country*. New York: Duell, Sloan and Pearce, 1942.

_______. *On a Darkling Plain*. New York: Harcourt, 1940.

_______. *One Nation*. Boston: Houghton Mifflin, 1945.

_______. *The Preacher and the Slave*. Boston: Houghton Mifflin, 1950.

_______. *Recapitulation*. Garden City, N.Y.: Doubleday and Co, 1979.

_______. *Remembering Laughter*. Boston: Little, Brown, 1937.

_______. *The Sound of Mountain Water*. Garden City, N.Y.: Doubleday, 1969.

_______. *This Is Dinosaur: Echo Park and Its Magic Rivers*. New York: Alfred A Knopf, 1955.

_______. *The Uneasy Chair: A Biography of Bernard DeVoto*. Garden City, N.Y.: Doubleday, 1974.

_______. *Where the Bluebird Sings to the Lemonade Springs*. New York: Random House, 1992.

_______. *Wolf Willow: A History, a Story, and a Memory of the Last Plains Frontier*. New York: Compass Books, 1962.

_______, ed. *The Letters of Bernard DeVoto*. Garden City, N.Y.: Doubleday, 1975.

Stegner, Wallace, and Richard W. Etulain. *Conversations on History and Literature*. Salt Lake City: University of Utah Press, 1983.

Stegner, Wallace, and Page Stegner. *American Places*. New York: E. P. Dutton, 1981.

Steiss, Albert J. *Ecclesiastes: The Book of Archbishop Robert J. Dwyer*. Los Angeles: National Catholic Register, 1982.

Sterba, E., and R. Sterba. *Beethoven and His Nephew: A Psychoanalytic Study of Their Relationship*. New York: Pantheon, 1954.

Steward, Julian. *Basin-Plateau Aboriginal Groups*. Washington, D.C.: Smithsonian Institution Bureau of American Ethnology Bulletin 120, 1938.

Stewart, George R. *Ordeal By Hunger*. New York: Henry Holt & Co., 1936.

Sullivan, Maurice S. *Jedediah Smith: Trader and Trail Blazer*. New York: Press of the Pioneers, 1936.

Thomas, John L. *A Country in the Mind: Wallace Stegner, Bernard DeVoto, History, and the American Land*. New York: Routledge, 2000.

Topping, Gary. *Glen Canyon and the San Juan Country*. Moscow: University of Idaho Press, 1997.

United States Bureau of the Census. *Historical Statistics of the United States*. New York: Basic Books, 1976.

Unruh, John D. *The Plains Across: The Overland Emigrants and the Trans-Mississippi West, 1840–60*. Urbana: University of Illinois Press, 1979.

Utah Writers Project. *Utah: A Guide to the State*. New York: Hastings House, 1941.

Utley, Robert M. *A Life Wild and Perilous: Mountain Men and the Paths to the Pacific*. New York: Henry Holt, 1997.

Wade, Richard C. *The Urban Frontier: Pioneer Life in Early Pittsburgh, Cincinnati, Lexington, Louisville, and St. Louis*. Cambridge: Harvard University Press, 1959.

Walker, John Phillip, ed. *Dale Morgan on Early Mormonism: Correspondence & a New History*. Salt Lake City: Signature Books, 1986.

Walker, Ronald W. *Wayward Saints: The Godbeites and Brigham Young*. Urbana: University of Illinois Press, 1998.

Walker, Ronald M., David J. Whittaker, and James B. Allen. *Mormon History*. Urbana: University of Illinois Press, 2001.

Webb, Walter Prescott. *The Great Plains*. Boston: Ginn & Co., 1931.

Wharton, Tom, and Gayen Wharton. *Utah*. Oakland, Calif.: Compass American Guides, Inc., 1991.

White, Richard. *"It's Your Misfortune and None of My Own": A New History of the American West*. Norman: University of Oklahoma Press, 1991.

Wise, William. *Massacre at Mountain Meadows: An American Legend and a Monumental Crime*. New York: Thomas Y. Crowell, 1976.

Wishart, David J. *The Fur Trade of the American West, 1807–1840: A Geographical Synthesis*. Lincoln: University of Nebraska Press, 1979.

Woodward, C. Vann. *Origins of the New South, 1877–1913*. Baton Rouge: Louisiana State University Press, 1951.

Worster, Donald. *A River Running West: The Life of John Wesley Powell*. New York: Oxford University Press, 2001.

_______. *Rivers of Empire: Water, Aridity, and the Growth of the American West*. New York: Pantheon Press, 1985.

Young, Levi Edgar. *The Founding of Utah*. New York: Charles Scribner's Sons, 1923.

INDEX